FROM MIMESIS
TO
INTERCULTURALISM

EXETER PERFORMANCE STUDIES

Exeter Performance Studies aims to publish the best new scholarship from a variety of sources, presenting established authors alongside innovative work from new scholars. The list explores critically the relationship between theatre and history, relating performance studies to broader political, social and cultural contexts. It also includes titles which offer access to previously unavailable material.

FROM MIMESIS
TO
INTERCULTURALISM

Readings of theatrical theory before
and after 'modernism'

Graham Ley

UNIVERSITY
of
EXETER
PRESS

First published in 1999 by
University of Exeter Press
Reed Hall, Streatham Drive,
Exeter, Devon EX4 4QR
UK
www.exeterpress.co.uk

© Graham Ley 1999

This paperback edition published 2021

The right of Graham Ley to be identified as author of this
work has been asserted by him in accordance with the
Copyright, Designs and Patents Act 1988.

British Library Cataloguing in Publication Data
A catalogue record of this book is available from the British Library

ISBN 978-1-905816-17-0

Designed and typeset in Caslon 11/12.5
by Mike Dobson, Pallas (Humanities Computing),
University of Exeter

Contents

Preface   ix

Part One: Before...

1: The Idea of Sight: Plato and Aristotle

1.1	– Plato	3
1.1.1	– Plato and the narration of dialogue	3
1.1.2	– *Phaedo* and the prison-house of the body	4
1.1.3	– *Republic* (a): narration and imitation in the education of 'guardians'	10
1.1.4	– Excursus on the meaning of *mimesis* and cognate terms	17
1.1.5	– *Republic* (b): *mimesis* and the corrupting pleasure of sympathy	21
1.2	– Aristotle	27
1.2.1	– Platonic invitation and the Aristotelian treatise	27
1.2.2	– *Poetics* (a): an anatomy of method	28
1.2.3	– *Poetics* (b): towards a theory of the emotions	35
1.3	– Between Academy and Lyceum: the idea of sight	44

2: Performances of the Mind: Rousseau and Diderot

2.1	– Rousseau	52
2.1.1	– The degenerative arts in Rousseau's academic *Discourses*	54
2.1.2	– The *Letter to d'Alembert*	65
2.2	– Diderot	74
2.2.1	– The dissatisfactions of Dorval: the *Conversations* on *The Natural Son*	75
2.2.2	– The question of a third genre in the third *Conversation*	79

2.2.3 –	The *Discourse on Dramatic Poetry*	84
2.2.4 –	The *Paradox on the Actor*	91

Part Two: ...and After

3: Brook and the Rhetoric of Theory

3.1 –	Metaphor and dismissal in *The Empty Space*	111
3.2 –	The genesis of theory: the 'Theatre of Cruelty' season in 1964	122
3.3 –	Intertextuality: *The Empty Space* and *Orghast at Persepolis*	125
3.4 –	Theoretical 'failure' and *Conference of the Birds*	130
3.5 –	A metaphoric formula	134
3.6 –	Mystery, but no secrets	137

4: Theatre Anthropology

4.1 –	VICTOR TURNER	141
4.1.1 –	Symbolism and social process: ritual theory and the drama analogy	142
4.1.2 –	Further components of a performance theory: 'liminality', communitas' and the 'social drama'	146
4.1.3 –	From 'liminal' to 'liminoid'	153
4.1.4 –	Some case studies from an anthropology of performance	166
4.2 –	RICHARD SCHECHNER	175
4.2.1 –	The eye of theory in *Public Domain* and *Environmental Theater*	175
4.2.2 –	The discursive figures of performance theory	181
4.2.3 –	Cultures and theories transported and transformed	192
4.3 –	EUGENIO BARBA	210
4.3.1 –	Barba and Grotowski: theatre in the laboratory	210
4.3.2 –	Isolation and the "social cell": the Third Theatre	216

4.3.3	– Going beyond technique: the discourse of a theatre anthropology	229
4.3.4	– Revising the anatomy of theory: later essays	240

Part Three

5: Some Observations on Stanislavski and Brecht

5.1	– STANISLAVSKI	251
5.2	– BRECHT	261

6: The Significance of Theory

6.1	– Disposing of interculturalism: Bharucha, Schechner and Pavis	275
6.2	– A modest look at the discourse of semiology and semiotics: Pavis and de Marinis	287
6.3	– The significance of theory	292

Notes and References 303

Bibliography 329

Index 341

Preface

This book is concerned with propositions that have been made about the theatre, and it was written as a result of two coincident perceptions.

The first was that a canon of modern theatrical theory from Stanislavski through Brecht and Artaud to Grotowski had received repeated scholarly attention, but had received it more or less—and perhaps increasingly—in isolation. The second perception was that the study of theoretical texts on the theatre, whether inside or outside that canon, seemed to have remained relatively unaffected by contemporary developments in textual and literary criticism. These two perceptions could then be summarized in the conclusion that our reading of theatrical theory was naive, if not exactly credulous, in the case of many dominant propositions and arguments, from those originally made by Plato to those now current.

As a consequence of those perceptions, and of that conclusion, this book offers close readings of the language and arguments of selected writers both 'before' and 'after' that canon of theorists. It also includes some observations on two writers from the canon, although these are far more restricted. It seemed to me imperative that the readings were detailed, and followed the chosen texts closely, since criticism of summaries could hardly be satisfactory. My selection of Plato and Aristotle accepted their remarkable influence; that of Rousseau and Diderot acknowledged a different principle, which was that despite their significance their propositions on the theatre and on performance were less familiar to English-language readers than they might be. In making this decision I was hoping to take advantage of what seemed to be a shift of critical attention in recent years to the Enlightenment. Further reasons for the selection may become apparent as the book is read.

For the selection of writers 'after' Grotowski I relied on my impressions of those who had been most read, or most influential, with the proviso that their propositional writings should be substantially 'completed', if not exactly finished. My selection then closed on Brook, Turner in association with Schechner, and on Barba. If, as a consequence, this means that I am paying close attention to what has been termed, diversely, as the 'anthropology of theatre' or 'theatre anthropology', then this may be considered to be a particular feature of the book. I would rather understand it to be a feature of recent and contemporary writing on the theatre and on performance.

My methods of criticism are completely open to scrutiny in what is by most standards a long book, and criticism should invite almost any reservations or qualifications about its value, or its validity. I have attempted to notice what it seemed most important to notice, and I have been influenced eclectically as a critic by what I found most effective as a reader of criticism myself. I should perhaps note that this book is not a thesis and has no thesis. Since this is becoming a rarity in publications on the arts in general, I might state that I reasonably regard a thesis as the demonstration of a single proposition over a moderate length suitable for academic examination. I have no single proposition to make about propositions on the theatre, nor would I, as might be guessed, be particularly sympathetic to one.

The exclusions in any selection rightly prompt speculations about an ideological or cultural bias. My own attitude was that I should write from my own situation, which was in England at the present time, acknowledging and attempting to cater for a readership that found itself subject primarily to a similar cultural inheritance. As one consequence, the book does not attempt to include in Part One an assessment of work by notable writers from South or East Asia. I have also felt it would be presumptuous to offer a critique of feminist theory on the theatre and on performance, which is highly self-critical as a discursive practice and by no means 'completed' as a set of propositions. I have concluded the book with a review of the introduction of the term 'interculturalism' to theatrical theory, because I feel that the presentations on that subject permit a critical discussion. My attitude to semiotics has been that, although the presentations are certainly unfinished, they do permit some commentary; my own, accordingly, is very brief.

Discussions of 'postmodernism', 'postmodernity' and 'the postmodern' abound. Although I was tempted to review the usage of these terms, and of 'modernism' and its cognates, as they impinge on our largest assumptions about the theatre and its associated writings, it was eventually clear to me that the terminological debate would add little except unacceptable length to the book. There are remarkably few presentations on the theatre that use these terms as anything more than plausible or (at times) meretricious assumptions, and my concern in this book is with presentations, not with terms as such. One other conspicuous term which does not receive discussion in this book is that of the avant-garde, and here I defer to the work of Poggioli and Burger, which has been followed recently by the provocative study by Mann.[1] According to Mann, the avant-garde exists almost exclusively as discourse, and so the appearance of the term in discursive formulations should not be a particular cause for critical commentary. I may be accused here of being too lax; but I rarely found that appearance of the 'avant-garde' in writings gave me pause for thought.

As to discourse itself, this book intermittently takes advantage of that term, which I have adopted because of its amplitude and uncertainty. I am by no means convinced that everything written can helpfully be called a 'discourse', but this book contains considerations of lectures, dialogues, manifestos, treatises, autobiography, letters, documentation and diverse forms of writing that advance propositions about the theatre. The simplest formula I can offer, in this context, is that I understand by discourse an address to an audience or readership with a view to persuasion.[2]

Further comments are technical. I have found it necessary to use two slightly different forms of reference or citation, one in the endnotes to the text, and a second in the bibliography; my aim is to help the reader. The bibliography is restricted to those works to which I directly refer by abbreviation in the main text; contrastingly, some few editions and translations are cited in full in the endnotes, and do not appear in the bibliography. In a work which quotes repeatedly, the use of double quotation marks indicates direct quotation, while the use of single quotation marks indicates either a term in question, or a word subsequently adopted into my own main text in a grammatically different form from that in which it appears in an original quotation. These are authorial conventions that I hope will offer reasonably comfortable reading, rather than cause confusion. For works that I discuss at length, I have given an initial and full reference in the endnotes, and from that point forwards have given a page number to that edition or publication at the end of each quotation in my main text.

This book has been difficult to write, because many of the arguments and presentations on the theatre are difficult. I have not attempted to simplify arguments, nor to complicate them, although I may mistakenly have done so on occasion. The design of the book corresponds to my initial perception that the canon of modern theorists is by now relatively familiar. So the early writings in Part One are followed immediately, in Part Two, by the contemporary writings, before I offer some observations on two of the 'canonic' writers that are hopefully consistent with the critique I have established. The extent of each critique is not intended as an indication of my view of the relative importance of any writer within the selection: it has been judged on the principle of what I feel needs attention at the present time.

I am particularly grateful to the friendly staff at Ryde Library on the Isle of Wight. My thanks are also due to the University Library, Cambridge; the library of the School of Oriental and African Studies, London; the Bodleian Library, Oxford; the library at Senate House, London; and colleagues in the University Library at Exeter. Simon Trussler and Clive Barker, as editors of *New Theatre Quarterly*, allowed the book to develop by publishing several articles related to it; I am consequently grateful to Cambridge University Press for permission to reincorporate my study of Peter Brook's *The Empty Space* (1993) in the chapter for which it was intended.

Other individuals to whom I should like to record a sincere debt of gratitude are Peter Holland; Philip Hardie; John and Marion Rodrigues, kind and supportive hosts; Richard Willis and Anna Henderson, editors for the Press; Peter Thomson, Steve Nicholson, and anonymous readers for the Press; and my colleagues at Exeter.

GRAHAM LEY
Department of Drama
School of Drama and Music
University of Exeter

PART ONE: BEFORE...

1

The Idea of Sight

Plato and Aristotle

1.1 PLATO[1]

By the age of thirty, Plato had seen the collapse of Athenian imperial power at the close of the fifth century BC, and the imposition of the death penalty on Socrates by an Athenian court in 399 BC. As a wealthy citizen, he might have chosen to involve himself in the political life of his city; but, instead, he devoted his life to teaching and to writing. His school of philosophy, the Academy, was established outside the city walls of Athens by 385 BC.

Plato's dialogues contain the exposition of his philosophy, and are critically and philosophically remarkable for their persistent 'impersonation' of Socrates. The biographical tradition on Plato, which is likely to be accurate in its principal outlines, attests that he spent a considerable time in Sicily, and this might support the proposition that he was also interested in mime.[2] The leading practitioner of this Greek-Sicilian performance art was Sophron, whose name, with that of his son Xenarchus, is linked to Socratic dialogue by Aristotle in the *Poetics*.[3] This curious association introduces the question of what might be called the 'performing' or 'reading' voice in the dialogues. On this large topic I shall simply make some preliminary observations.

1.1.1 Plato and the narration of dialogue

The work of Havelock, supported by the studies of Ong and others, has made it unavoidable that we should accept that the culture of

Athens, traditionally perceived through its written literature, was caught in a balance between orality and writing.[4] The practice of the law-courts, the persistent originality demanded in theatrical and other poetic-musical festivals, and the self-promotion of visiting teachers certainly provided an increasingly elaborate substance to the context of writing and record established by the administration of empire. But it was, in fact, a distinctive cultural capacity for 'listening' which was the silent middle-term between speech and writing. The Athenians were habituated to listening, and probably, in addition, to the art of recalling speech or argument.

'Recall' is probably the most elusive term in this now extremely alien cultural context; but much of what was written depended on it, on an acceptance of a capacity for it, and on an understanding of the difference between recall and the record presented by a prepared script, or transcript. With a tolerance and an expectation of this kind the Platonic dialogues can be presented, their introductions suggesting at times a complexity of recall which might otherwise appear flatly ridiculous. The most extreme example of narrative recall occurs in the introduction to Plato's *Symposium*. The text opens as a reply by Apollodorus to an unnamed enquirer (A); the reply refers to an occasion, "the day before yesterday", when Apollodorus was asked by another man (B) to recall the speeches and conversation at a symposium, a celebratory drinking-party, held by the tragic poet Agathon. Yet Apollodorus himself had not been at the party; he had heard of what had been said from one Aristodemus. And the party had occurred many years ago. Admittedly, the *Symposium* is substantially an account of speeches, rather than of dialogue. But the composition presumably encourages tolerable conviction by virtue of the fact that it *is* so circumstantial; and this prompts the thought that dialogues that might otherwise be called 'dramatic' (a direct exchange, without narrator) might rather be considered as a form of cancelled 'recall', a narrative that suspends the circumstantial requirement for a narrator.

1.1.2 *Phaedo* and the prison-house of the body

Phaedo is one of a number of dialogues which have Socrates in prison, surrounded by friends and awaiting the hour of his execution, and it culminates in his death.[5] The dialogue has a narrative introduction, which is a 'recall' by Phaedo. Socrates has no regrets in dying, because death is, by common understanding, a separation of soul from body, and philosophers are indifferent to the body. The opening arguments are important for their clarity in the distinction between thought and the body and its senses. In this section, the first speaker is Socrates, the respondent Simmias the Theban, a friend and admirer:

> What, then, of the actual acquisition of thought? Is the body an obstruction or not, if someone takes it along with him as a companion in the search? What I am saying is something like this: do sight and hearing provide human beings with truth of any kind, or, as the poets repeat to us, is it the case that we neither hear nor see anything accurately? But if even these of the bodily sensations are neither accurate nor clear, the rest will hardly be so. For they are all inferior to these two, are they not?
> They certainly are, he said.
> So when, Socrates continued, does the soul grasp the truth? For whenever the soul attempts to contemplate something in conjunction with the body, then it is clear that the body deceives the soul.
> True.
> Then most surely it must be in reasoning, if anywhere, that any of the things that really are become accessible to the soul?
> Yes. (65a–c)

The first line of argument is quickly followed by a second:

> But what about this, Simmias: do we say that there actually is something which is in itself 'just', or do we not?
> We certainly do.
> And something in itself beautiful, and something good?
> Of course.
> Now did you ever see any of these things with your eyes?
> No, never, he said.
> Or did you ever grasp them with any other of the bodily senses? I am speaking here of everything, of greatness, health, strength, in sum of everything that forms a part of what really is. Is the greatest truth about them seen by means of the body? Or is it, rather, like this: that the man who has prepared himself to think most thoroughly and accurately about each object of the enquiry will come closest to understanding each one?
> Most assuredly.
> And the man who would do this most purely would be he who approaches each with thought alone, not adding the evidence of sight to thought, nor dragging in any other of the senses to join with reasoning; but who, in deploying pure thought, makes his attempt to track down each part—also pure—of what really is, separating himself to the greatest possible extent from his eyes and ears and, so to speak,

> from his body as a whole, in the conviction that whenever it participates the body disturbs and inhibits the acquisition of truth and thought by the soul. Would not this be the man, if anyone ever might be, Simmias, to encounter what really is? Who, if not he, is likely to attain to the knowledge of true being?
>
> You have spoken the truth wonderfully, Socrates, said Simmias. (65d–66a)

The conclusion then follows, without qualification:

> But in fact experience has shown to us that if we ever wish to have pure knowledge of something we must be separated from the body. The soul by itself must look at things in themselves. And then, it seems, we shall have that which we desire and of which we claim to be lovers: thought. Not while we are living but, as the argument indicates, when we are dead. For if it is impossible to know anything purely in conjunction with the body, one of two things follows: the acquisition of knowledge either never happens, or it happens after death.
>
> (66d–e)

It is debatable, in regard to this remarkably swift succession, whether death is used as an allegory for the separation of mind from body presented as necessary to the acquisition of true knowledge.

But if it is evident from these exchanges that death is a necessary condition for an understanding of the soul, then it becomes apparent that the doctrine of the perception of the forms or ideas—as true knowledge—is a necessary condition for the soul's existence. The soul must have a function, and this is 'recollection' or *anamnesis*, which is given a playful and highly figurative exposition in another dialogue, *Phaedrus*. Socrates' contention in *Phaedrus* is that the soul, or *psyche*, may have a recollection (*anamnesis* 249c) of what it has seen in its journey to the upper heavens, of "knowledge that really is" and "being that really is", which is "colourless and shapeless and intangible, visible only to mind as the steersman of the soul" (247c). To express this, he draws on comparison, on the associations of a metaphoric image extended into a simile. The soul is compared to "the united power of a winged pair of horses and a charioteer". This equipage follows the chariots of the gods towards the "region beyond the heavens" in an attempt to look upon true knowledge in the "plain of truth", which furnishes the pasturage by which the soul's wings are nourished. The difficulty is that only the horses of the gods are thoroughbred; the souls make do with a mixed pair, one of which is of poor stock, and tends to pull outwards, and downwards.

Initially, all souls pass into human beings, in classes that accord with how much of the truth each soul has seen. The first class is that of philosophers, of lovers of beauty, of those inspired by the muses and passion; the second, of constitutional kings and war-leaders; the third, of those who manage public affairs, or their own estates, or make money in trade; the fourth, of gymnasts or physicians; the fifth, of prophets or those involved with the mysteries; the sixth, of poets and imitative artists; the seventh, of craftsmen and farmers; the eighth, of sophists and populist politicians; the ninth, and last, of tyrants (248d–e).

The less flighty argument for recollection in *Phaedo* is engaged by the variability of sense impressions, judged by our understanding of an absolute 'equality':

> There again it is from the senses that we must conceive that all perceived equality aims for that equality that really is, and yet falls short of it. Or am I wrong?
> You are right.
> So before we began to see or to hear or to perceive in the other ways, we must have somehow gained the knowledge of what equality by itself is, if we were to refer perceived equality to it. For all these kinds of perceived equality desire to be actual equality, and yet fall short of it.   (75b)

The dialectic concludes in a direct choice: this kind of knowledge is either present at birth, or is gathered as learning through a process of recollection. But not all men can give an account of how they have reached the state of knowledge; so knowledge must be a function of the soul, acquired before the union of the soul with the body (76c).

The Platonic doctrine of the Forms is an argument from the visible to the invisible, and, as presented, it may strike the modern reader as fundamentally a linguistic argument. Socrates' respondent is now Cebes:

> Then what do you say of the many beautiful—whether these are men or horses or garments or anything else—or of the many equal, or of everything that bears the same name as what really is? Do these remain the same, or is their state the opposite to what really is, in that they are never, so to speak, the same at all, in themselves or in relation to each other?
> I am in agreement again, Cebes replied; they are never the same.
> And these you may touch, or see, or perceive through the other senses. But no one may grasp what remains constantly the same by

> any other means than by the reasoning of thought; these things are invisible, and cannot be seen.
> What you are saying is very true, he said.   (78e–79a)

The doctrine is achieved, dialectically, by a passage from attribute to essence, and from comparison to absolute. The major examples occur at 100–101, where "nothing makes a thing beautiful but the presence or participation of beauty", and "the greater is greater by reason of greatness". Understood in this way, the Forms are a guarantee of the validity of language, as the participants in the dialogue are said to have agreed, in admitting "that the Forms exist individually, and that other things participate in them and derive their names from them" (102b).

The doctrine of the Forms is the most influential, but by no means the first, of the attempts in antiquity to escape from the play of language and the relativity of sense impressions. By means of the enduring presence of dialectic, and the vocation of philosophy, Plato is able to condemn the body as a prison:

> The lovers of learning know that when philosophy took on their soul it was simply bound and glued to the body... Philosophy saw the ingenuity of the prison, that it comes into being through desire, so that the prisoner is himself a principal accomplice in his own imprisonment. As I was saying, the lovers of learning know that philosophy, in taking on their souls in this state, encourages them gently and tries to free them, with a demonstration that visual enquiry is full of deceit, as is aural enquiry, and enquiry by the other senses. Philosophy persuades the soul to withdraw from the senses, in so far as reliance is unnecessary, urging it to gather up itself into itself and be collected, and to trust in nothing other than itself, in what it by itself thinks of what really is; and not to consider truthful whatever it investigates through other means, which will be variable. For things of this kind are perceptible and visible, but what the soul sees is conceptual and invisible.   (82e–83b)

It is the intensity of sense experience that prompts this release. The passage continues directly:

> The soul of the truly philosophical man thinks it should not oppose this release, and so it abstains from pleasures and desires and pains and fears as much as it can. Its reasoning is that, whenever someone experiences intense pleasures, pains, fears, or desires, he suffers not just the evils of which one might think, such as illness or expenditure

on his desires, but the greatest and most extreme of evils, of which he takes no account although he is suffering from it.

What is that, Socrates? said Cebes.

That the soul of every man is compelled, in intense pleasure or pain, to consider the particular object of this feeling to be clearest and truest, when this is not the case. These objects are, above all, things which are visible. Or are they not?

Most certainly.   (83b–c)

In his overt rejection of sense experience in favour of knowledge, Plato is fulfilling a complicated inheritance from his predecessors. Of these, the most significant is undoubtedly Parmenides, whose thoughts were developed and sustained by his companion and follower Zeno. Parmenides wrote a hexameter poem, of which substantial fragments exist, and in which he is carried in a chariot to the gates of the goddess Justice, in an image which may well be the model for the revelation in *Phaedrus*.[6] There he is shown two paths of enquiry, the one of Persuasion, the other of Truth, which are presented as mutually exclusive alternatives.[7] Parmenides' central conception is that the objects of thought and thought itself are the same, and that this is what is, and is immortal and unchangeable. This entails that the visible, perceptible or sensible world of change and dissolution is merely "what seems to be", the subject of impermanent human "opinion".

Despite the challenge posed by Parmenides' insistent logic, there was a firm inclination amongst later pre-Socratic thinkers to keep open the correspondence between understanding and the senses. Perhaps the most impressive attempt to reconcile the testimonies of the senses with their obvious limitations (variability, relativity, uncertainty) came from the atomists, Leucippus and Democritus. The following summary is from Aristotle, who concentrates on Leucippus:

> Leucippus thought he had arguments that would assert what is consistent with sense perception, and not do away with coming-into-being or dissolution or motion, or the plurality of existents... He claimed that being is not a unity, but is limitless in number, and invisible through the smallness of the particles. These are carried about in the void... and when they come together they effect coming-into-being, and when they separate they effect dissolution.[8]

But an intuitive theory of invisible particles was bound to leave sense perception in a partly dubious position, which gravitates in the fragments of Democritus towards scepticism. His central position is succinctly expressed:

> By convention sweet, by convention bitter, by convention hot, by convention cold, but in reality atoms and void.[9]

Yet although he apparently distinguished between a legitimate (through *dianoia*, 'thought') and an illegitimate or obscure (through sense perception) knowledge, he clearly allows for some collusion between the two. Here the senses are speaking in protest, apparently at the pretensions of understanding:

> "Wretched understanding, would you take your assurances from us and then overthrow us? Our overthrow is your downfall."[10]

Of particular interest in the discussion by Democritus is the occurrence of the word *ideai*, for the two 'forms' of knowledge. This is one of the alternative terms used by Plato for his category of what can be truly known; the second is *eidos*, and both are cognates of a verbal root for vision (*idein*). The extent to which Plato is dependent, far beyond the amplifications of metaphor, on the suppression of vision in his formulation of conceptual thought will emerge more strongly from a discussion of the *Republic*.

1.1.3 *Republic* (a): narration and imitation in the education of 'guardians' [11]

The formal title of the *Republic*, *Politeia*, is more simply translated as *Constitution* or *Government*. An enquiry into justice is the overt topic of the narrative fiction, but the dialogue rapidly becomes, after its opening book, an extended consideration of an exemplary or 'just' constitution for a city-state. This constitution is only utopian in the sense that it appeals to Plato, in the person of Socrates, as a 'paradigm' (*paradeigma*). Questioned by an interlocutor Glaucon on the possibility of the constitution he is outlining, Socrates replies with a comparison:

> Would you consider a painter to be less good because, after drawing a paradigm of the most beautiful man, and putting everything he could into his drawing, he was then unable to demonstrate that such a man could possibly have existed?
>
> Certainly not, he said.
>
> Well, then. Were we not creating a paradigm of a good city, in argument?

> Assuredly.
> And is our argument any the worse because we are unable to demonstrate the possibility of a city being founded according to our argument?
> Surely not, he replied.   (472d–e)

The comparison is repeated a little later in the context of a debate over the most appropriate rulers for the city-state. Socrates' favoured candidates as rulers are the philosophers, and he denigrates the second-class "lovers of appearance" for their lack of true vision:

> What of those who are deprived of the knowledge of the real being of each thing, and have in their souls no clear paradigm; who are unable, as a painter can, to look at the absolute truth and to refer to it repeatedly, looking as sharply as possible at it; and who are unable to establish laws in this world about beauty, justice, and goodness, if that is required, or to guard them if established? Do not men of this sort seem little short of blind to us?   (484c–d)

By this means the 'paradigm' that is the *Republic* is associated with the vision of absolute truth by the soul and with the process of the recollection of the Forms, or *anamnesis*, that were presented in *Phaedrus* and *Phaedo*.

The city-state is taken to be constituted from the needs of its inhabitants, and in its original construction by Socrates the emphasis falls on practical and specialized craftsmen. But this utopian simplicity is almost immediately transformed by the desire all will feel to have the addition of minor comforts, in cooking, furniture and decoration. A cereal diet gives way to one mixed with meat, engaging a class of hunters; and the call for luxury, beyond the original sufficiency of the healthy city, also introduces the class of imitators (*mimetai*), "many of them concerned with forms and colours, many with the arts of the muses, poets and their subordinates, rhapsodes, actors, chorus-members, contractors, craftsmen for all kinds of outfits, including the adornment of women" (373b). Furthermore, these demands will create the need for the addition of territory, and so for war.

It is, in fact, war which first introduces the class of 'guards' (*phylakes*), on the grounds of specialism and of the impossibility, acknowledged in principle, that "one man can practise more than one skill successfully" (374a). And the 'guard' rapidly assumes the attention given to the state as a whole, because the guard needs to exercise discrimination between friend and enemy, by knowing.

> So he who is to be a fine and good guardian of the city-state for us must be philosophical, hearty, swift and strong.   (376c)

The comparison has been with a house-dog, so we should not be surprised by the language: in his discriminating between friend and enemy, even the dog is "philosophical" (376b). But the crucial transition here is between guards, soldiers for the city-state, and guardians of the city-state. The education of this civic parallel to the house-dog has two parts, "gymnastic for the body, and the arts of the muses for the soul". The "arts of the muses" include the verbal arts, which take two forms, "the one true, the other false" (376e). Children are told stories from a very early age, and they must not be allowed to hear just anything, and "take it into their souls" (377b).

> There must be, then, as it seems, a superintendence of the composers of stories, and any good story they compose should be approved, but any that is not good rejected. And we shall persuade the nurses and the mothers to tell the approved stories to their children, and to mould their souls far more than they mould their bodies with their hands. But the majority of those stories that are now told to children must be discarded.   (376b–c)

In this context Plato introduces, as a comparison to his true and false myths and stories, the notion of an inaccurate likeness in painting, in the answer that Socrates makes to the question of when exactly poets are blameworthy:

> Whenever one makes a bad likeness in his story, about the nature of the gods or heroes, just as a painter paints something which has no similarity to what he wishes to paint.   (377e)

The list of condemned—blameworthy, and so condemned—subjects starts with euphemistic references to the castration of Uranus by Cronus, of father by son, and to the binding of Cronus by Zeus, again of father by son. Even if these tales were true, "they should not be told to the mindless and the young". Instead, the kinds of story that poets will compose, and mothers and nurses tell, must not infringe the paradigmatic conditions of a good and perfect god, of filial obligation, and of the supposition of perfectly amicable relations between citizens. It is this "theology", as Adeimantus terms it, which the women of the exemplary city are to tell to their sons. The proscriptions and prescriptions are exact. Stories of the grimness of the underworld "make all listeners shudder", and the guardians "may become more excitable and softer than they should be as a result of this shuddering" (387c). If death is not to be feared, it should not be feared for a comrade, and so laments by famous men must also be rejected from poetic compositions, and given only to women, "that is those women who are not serious, and to cowardly men" (387e–388a). If a guardian listened to a story of lamentation, such as Achilles mourning for Patroclus in Homer, he would have no shame in repeating this behaviour. Laughter is also to be forbidden, because it produces a "strong change" in a person. So poems must not be composed about gods or men who are "worthy of mention" overcome with laughter. Self-indulgence, in food, drink and sex, is an enemy to self-command and to obedience, and must be forbidden, as must all stories that in any way suggest that "the gods engender evil, and that heroes are no better than men" (391d).

If there is an aesthetic conception behind this initial survey of compositions on the subjects of "gods, spirits, and heroes" (392a), it is that listeners will accept what they hear as a ratification of similar behaviour on their own part. This is, in effect, a subjection of any examination of the processes of reception to a cultural assumption about learning. The suggestion that "shuddering" may make young men "more excitable and softer" is a relatively crude reference to the possibility that their behaviour may approximate to that of women in the society, and is a companion to the assumption that young men will repeat the behaviour of the male role models presented to them. But there is, as yet, no specific term to describe this repetition of behaviour, and this is eventually introduced in a turn of the dialogue away from subjects to modes of composition. Socrates is still talking to Adeimantus:

> You accept that everything which is said by storytellers or poets is a narration of what has happened, of what is, or of what will come to be?
> What else could it be? he said.
> And so the poets accomplish their task either with simple narration, or by means of imitation, or by means of both?   (392d)

The Greek word translated by "narration" is *diegesis*, and that by "imitation" is *mimesis*. *Mimesis* is a cognate of *mimetai*, which was the term earlier applied to those who were "concerned with forms and colours", and to "poets and their subordinates", in the preliminary depiction of a taste for luxury afflicting an originally healthy city.

Socrates's respondent, Adeimantus, does not understand the distinction drawn between the subjects ("what should be told") and the modes ("how it should be told") of composition; and, in addition, he fails to understand the division of the universal category of narration into what might appear to be itself ("simple narration") and also something else ("imitation"). The explanation of the distinctions given by Socrates is meant to be plain, and at a primary level. Narration (*diegesis*) is the mode found in the Homeric epics, the *Iliad* and the *Odyssey*, and the word describes the full content of the poems:

> So narration it is, both when the poet recounts speeches as the occasion offers itself, and when he recounts what comes between the speeches? (393b)

This is the general category of narration (sense 1); but the term is, according to Socrates, also susceptible of a more precise definition (sense 2), which leaves room for the addition of a contrasting term (*mimesis*). This 'is' and 'is not' had confused Adeimantus, but it is dependent on an acceptance of the poet (or his substitute the professional reciter, the rhapsode) as a performer. All speeches in the epic narrative are contained within the narration, generically with formulaic introductions and/or conclusions, identifying the speaker: "this/that is what Achilles/Odysseus/Helen said". In this sense, they are clearly retained as part of the total narration (*diegesis* in sense 1). But Socrates maintains, by fusing the figure of the poet-as-composer with that of the reciter-as-performer, that the epic speeches may be understood in another way:

> But when the poet recounts a speech as if he were another person, shall we not then say that he is assimilating his speech as closely as possible to the person who, as the poet tells you in advance, is going to speak?
> We shall. What would prevent us?
> So, to assimilate himself to another, in either voice or gesture, is to imitate that person to whom he assimilates himself?
> Certainly.
> Then in such cases, as it seems, this poet [Homer] and all others compose their narration by means of imitation.
> Absolutely.
> But if the poet did not conceal himself at any point in his poem, his composition would be without imitation, and so would his narration. (393c–d)

"Simple narration" in epic poetry would have no direct speeches. A mixed narration contains narrative and direct speeches, which are understood to be imitation "in voice or gesture" by the poet as potential performer. The contrasting pole is represented by tragedy, which is (direct) speech without narration:

> So you must understand, I said, that the opposite occurs when someone removes what the poet recounts between the speeches and leaves behind the spoken exchanges.
>
> I understand that too, he said; that such a thing occurs in relation to tragedy.   (394b)

As Plato narrates at this point, he also alludes to tragedy as a reduction of epic, in a manner that assumes that poetic composition is essentially one art. But the problem posed by impersonation might similarly leave the Platonic dialogue, which engages this discussion, as a close approximation to, or reduction of, the primary art of epic.

The general problem is taken to be "whether our guardians should be imitative or not" (394e), and this entails an examination of whether poets should be allowed to imitate, and so of whether tragedy and comedy should be admitted into the constitution of the city. Specialization determines that each individual practises one art or vocation best, and the same argument must apply to imitation. This is a matter of capacities: as things stand, tragic and comic writers are generic specialists, rhapsodes and actors do not double for each other, nor do comic and tragic actors (395a). Tragic and comic compositions, and the arts of the reciter and the specialist actors, are all classed together as "imitative works" or "practices" (*mimemata*). The question concerns the education and leisure of the guardians, and is closed before it is open: as specialists, the guardians should not exercise any vocation other than their own.

> ...they must be craftsmen of the freedom of the city, strictly confined to the exercise of that concern and no other which has no bearing on it, and really they should engage in nothing else, and should not imitate.   (395b–c)

Yet absolute exclusion is unlikely, because imitation has a natural potency and appeal, which must accordingly be regulated:

> Have you not observed that imitations, if they extend from childhood into greater age, settle into an individual's character and nature, physically, in the voice, and in thought?   (395d)

As the child may follow the example expressed to him in a story, so the activity of imitation may affect the developing body and mind. Strictly speaking, guardians should not imitate; but if the attractions or potency of imitation are accepted, then the guardians should only imitate "brave, moderate, holy, free men" (395c). The list of explicit exclusions runs through many of the categories of dramatic character: women of all ages, in conflict with husband or gods, and overwhelmed by sorrow or passion; slaves; bad, cowardly, comically abusive, drunken, or insane men; artisans or seamen (395d–396a). As men, and good men, the guardians must not mimic the sounds of animals, or of natural forces, a prohibition which indicates a curious repertory of performance available in Plato's time, either in public or private. The role left to them might seem to coincide with the mature and supposedly responsible male in tragedy; but these figures, or, indeed, comparable models in epic, rarely appear without agitation and disturbance. So this potentially acceptable role must itself be strictly regulated. The "measured man", when he comes in his narration to a speech or an action of a good man,

> will be willing to speak as that person, and not to be ashamed of an imitation of that kind. This will particularly apply when he is imitating a good man acting securely and intelligently, less so when that man is overcome by disease, love, or drink, or any other disaster. But when he comes to someone unworthy of him, he will not be willing seriously to liken himself to an inferior man, unless it is briefly, when the man is doing something good..., thinking it to be dishonourable to him, unless it is done for the sake of amusement.   (396c–e)

The mention of amusement (*paidia*), and the ensuing contrast with the kind of man who will imitate anything "in front of a large audience", confirms that Plato has personal education and exclusive performance firmly in mind for his guardians. Of the four qualities attached to the exemplary men (in 395c)—namely bravery, self-control (*sophrosyne*), piety (and therefore purity) and freedom of spirit—the first two and the last, if not all four, may be readily considered as having ideal Forms. So the missing argument in favour of the controlled acceptance of *mimesis* in education, and against its total exclusion, may be supplied from our understanding of *anamnesis*. The guardians, like Socrates and Adeimantus themselves, and all who make a conscious exercise of *anamnesis*, must also know "the Forms of self-control, bravery, and freedom of spirit", and be able to "recognize both the Forms and images of them" (402c).

The recommendation at this point is for a poet who will compose in the manner of Homer, but according to restrictions: "His style will share both in imitation and in narration, but there will be a small part of imitation in a long story" (396e). An absolute ban is placed on "unmixed" imitation, which "finds most favour with children and their attendants, and the masses" (397d). Yet the preferred composer is himself also described as "the imitator of the reasonable man" (397d) in the conclusion, and as one who "will imitate the style of the reasonable man" (398b). Imitation is repeatedly intrusive because it permits the composition of the Platonic dialogue and of the exemplary words of that eminently reasonable man, Socrates, regularly held in the narrative frame of recall.

1.1.4 Excursus on the meaning of *mimesis* and cognate terms

It is possible to read the *Republic*, and all subsequent and dependent theory, without questioning the suggestion of *mimesis* as a theoretical term. I have tried, in the analysis above of the introduction to the argument in the *Republic*, to give some indications of the value of the term to Plato, in its relatively unexplored connections with cultural assumptions about (childhood and adolescent) behaviour, and with the practice of *anamnesis*. Plato is manifestly concerned with poetry as performance, and with composition as the production of a determining script for performance. The performances he has in mind are closely limited to the personal and the exclusive, with public performance—in the formal conventions of theatre—apparently a convenient victim of the exclusion of unmixed imitation from the paradigmatic city-state. Nonetheless, the prominence given by Plato to a series of cognates on the root *mim-* contains some problems, which prompt attention to what might be called a 'proper' meaning for the group.

In Plato's argument, *mimesis* is initially an intrusion into *diegesis*, or narration, and appears as an activity of composition which has also strong performative implications. Yet the same word can be applied, by Plato, to the act of composition as a generic distinction (in the case of comedy and tragedy), and to an act of representation achieved and fulfilled by a casual performer (such as a guardian), who may well be adversely affected by it, if it is repeated from youth forwards (395d). Poets and painters are classed together with rhapsodes, actors, and chorus-members as *mimetai* (373b). The poem, or play, becomes an imitative work (*mimema*, 395a–b), and the collusion of all implications of the term occurs in the verb, which demands a specific object, readily supplied by Plato in the human form of the good or reasonable man, of the inferior man doing something good, or of the (spoken) style of the reasonable man.

For Plato, the argument at this point of the dialogue confines the object and activity of *mimesis* to human speech. There is a passing reference to *mimesis* in both voice and gesture at 393c, and the brief conjunction of poets with those "concerned with forms and colours" at 373b suggests that this confinement has been carefully imposed. The immediate objectives of dialectic exercise a marginal and temporary control which will be released later, in the tenth book, as the argument is adapted into a wider and more captious theory. But before that point is reached, the standard translation itself—*of mimesis* as 'imitation'— demands examination, and usage offers some interesting definitions which alert us to the fragility of theoretical language.[12]

The early use of any of the *mim-* words is post-Homeric, and occurs in the *Hymn to Delian Apollo*, which may date from as early as the seventh century BC. The Delian choruses are praised towards the close of the hymn, and their vocal skills are identified: "they know how to mimic the voices of all men; and each would say that he himself was singing, so finely put together is their song" (162–65).[13] This vocal mimicry recurs in Aeschylus' *Oresteia*, when Orestes returns from exile and adopts a foreign accent familiar to him to deceive his mother and her lover (*Libation Bearers* 563–64). Instruments may also mimic, producing sounds reminiscent of the cries of humans or animals.[14] A fragment from the tragedian Aeschylus, which must date from before 456 BC when he died, provides the earliest reference to *mimoi*: "fearful *mimoi*, bull-voiced, bellow from the unseen ...", in a context of Dionysiac worship, which suggest loud instruments (the bull-roarer?) rather than human agents, or anything like the Sicilian performance art.[15]

By far the greatest number of examples drawn from fifth-century and pre-Platonic usage refer to matching an example, or emulating an achievement. In Euripides' *Electra*, Clytemnestra argues that a wife will follow the example of an unfaithful husband (*Electra* 1035–38), and the historian Thucydides has Pericles summarize Athens in an interesting passage:

> We have a constitution in which we do not seek to emulate the laws of others, we ourselves providing a model for others to follow, rather than imitating them.[16]

The word for model is, in fact, *paradeigma*; but the passage also introduces a pejorative connotation to the term 'imitating', which is not severe, but which seems to accept the failure or weakness of repetition. This sense comes out most strongly in usage which relates to vision, or resemblance. Two particularly striking examples occur in the account of Egypt by the historian Herodotus, referring to the wooden images of corpses, carved and painted, where conviction is impossible, and this quality is emphasized in drama.[17] In Euripides' *Helen*, the Greek Teucer, who has come to Egypt to seek prophetic advice, is appalled to see a woman who is a *mimema* of Helen. He knows that this cannot be Helen herself, because the capture of Troy had released or returned her to her husband Menelaus. This must be merely a likeness (*eikos*; *Helen* 71–77); the irony of the play is that his conviction of a misleading resemblance is actually misplaced.[18] The potential value of a misleading, or debased, resemblance is actively exploited by comedy. In Aristophanes' *Frogs*, Dionysus dresses as Heracles, carrying his club, and then calls in this weak disguise on Heracles himself. The disguise is a mockery of a resemblance, and so deserves the term *mimesis* (*Frogs* 109).

It is noticeable in this last case that theatrical presentation is able to draw a ready distinction between its own impersonations, and an act of mimicry it may contain within that presentation. This distinction occurs in an earlier comedy by Aristophanes, when the tragic playwright Agathon is visited by Euripides and a relative of his. Agathon appears partly clothed as a woman, and explains that this adaptation is necessary for a tragedian writing a play about women:

> When you are dealing with masculine affairs, your own bodily experience is sufficient. But as for what we men do not have, imitation hunts it out with us.[19]

In both cases, of Dionysus in the *Frogs* and of Agathon in *Women at the Thesmophoria*, the sense of falsity, and, indeed, of pretension, is paramount. The other, negative connotation is of inadequacy, and all of these are implied in the comparison involved in the term. In particular, there is an explicit confidence in these comic scenes that the inferior qualities of *mimesis* can be distinguished from the supposed stature of theatrical comedy. That this awareness is not only comic is apparent from Euripides' tragedy *The Madness of Heracles*, when, in utter dejection at his insane slaughter of his wife and children, Heracles sees himself debased to the point of legendary criminality:

> I can see the depths of disaster that wait for me. The earth will take voice and cry "Do not touch me!", and the sea and rivers will forbid me passage on them. I shall provide an imitation of Ixion in chains, bound to his wheel. Best of all that no Greek sees me in that state, who knew me when I was blessed with good fortune.[20]

This same word, the verb *ekmimeisthai*, recurs in Aristophanes' *Birds* after the foundation of the city of the birds, when human beings are reported as "mimicking everything that birds do", instead of adopting the manners and appearance of Spartans. This behaviour is flattering to the chorus, but futile, and as such is ironically distinguished from the comic presentation, throughout which theatrical performers appear as birds.[21]

The connotations of *mimesis* and its cognates are, to my mind, culturally specific, and the pattern of usage in late fifth-century theatre securely confirms this conclusion: *mimesis* is used of something that is known and/or acknowledged not to be what it shows itself to be, what it cannot possibly be, like the images of corpses. So Heracles, earlier in Euripides' tragedy, in a fit smashes the skull of his own son with a wooden club, in an horrific parody of a blacksmith beating iron—"an iron-beating imitation" or "mimicry" (*mudroktupon mimema*) is the phrase.[22] Each element in the reported tableau is not, and cannot be, what it perversely may seem like. In a different, but related sense, this is also true of the parody of Euripides' *Helen* announced and achieved by Euripides' relative in Aristophanes' comedy, *Women at the Thesmophoria*.[23] But to this certainty of definition should be added the important attraction of the mime (*mimos*) as performance art. It is relatively clear that by the later fifth century the Sicilian mime had made an impact in Athens, and in Xenophon's *Symposium* a Sicilian mime-master displays his performers. This is a sophisticated performance for a private party, and the theme for music, dance and dialogue is an erotic scene between Dionysus and Ariadne. But the subjects undoubtedly varied, and perhaps included animals: the oblique reference in Aristophanes' *Birds*, cited above, may connect with another in his *Clouds*, where roosters are the suggested objects of mimicry.[24] A scene from Aristophanes' latest surviving comedy, *Wealth*, of 388 BC, which may be closely contemporary with Xenophon's *Symposium*, has the leading slave Carion inviting the chorus to join with him in song and dance. Carion first mimics the Cyclops with his dance, and the chorus are to be the sheep and goats following him. The chorus then insist that they are the companions of Odysseus, coming to blind the Cyclops. Carion then turns the tables on them by mimicking the sorceress Circe, who changed Odysseus' companions into swine, and the chorus threatens revenge (*Wealth* 290–315). Forms of the verb *mimeisthai* occur three times throughout the whole dance, and the conclusion that this is comedy parodying mime is hard to avoid.[25]

The application of *mimesis* to direct speech in epic narration or recitation, or, by extension, to theatrical presentation in general is a radical linguistic decision by Plato which carries unequivocal connotations of debasement.[26] As for the arts themselves, of composition or of acting, in either tragedy or comedy, there is no evidence that even the broadest assumptions of theatrical audiences, in an extended period from the late fifth century to the early fourth, would have included *mimesis* as an appropriate term for these forms of representation or impersonation.[27] Yet the connotations of debasement, of approximation to a performance art with which Plato was supposed to have been fascinated, are by no means invalid for the paradigm that Plato presents in the *Republic*. His guardians are, even at the stage of the argument reached in the third book which was discussed above in section 1.1.3, quite clearly defined as 'men apart': for this exceptional and unprecedented class, who are detached from standard cultural assumptions, the act of impersonation is attended by constant risks of debasement. To be other than themselves is strictly unnecessary, were they not caught, as their composer is himself, in an extended—and insistently invasive—concept of 'imitation', composition and presentation, as one of very few paths to the unavoidable act of 'recollection' (*anamnesis*).

1.1.5 *Republic* (b): *mimesis* and the corrupting pleasure of sympathy

The central propositions of the *Republic* are both tripartite and closely related in scheme. One of the first objectives is the formation of classes in the constitution, and this is achieved by way of a binary division of those originally regarded as guardians into rulers and auxiliaries (414b). The final class added is that of traders and business-men, whose concern is money (434b–c). The motivation for this classification is initially obscure, but is clarified by analogy. An individual should be like his city, and if the city is tripartite in its classes, then this automatically engages an enquiry into the possibility of a tripartite division of the soul (435).

The three divisions, or 'forms' of the soul are presented as that part (a) which is susceptible to *logos*, or reasoned argument; that part (b) which has the form of the 'temper' (*thumos*), and is auxiliary to the first; and that part (c) which is likely to be in conflict with both, the appetitive, which is highly susceptible to desires or pleasures (439–

41).[28] The auxiliary role ascribed to the 'temper' is the result of observation: a man's desires (c) may at times struggle with his reason (a), and his anger (b) at this conflict is the sign of an intervention between the two. This intervention is understood to be structurally related to his impassioned resentment at any injustice that is inflicted on him (440a–d). However unsatisfactory this analysis may be, it provides an escape from an absolute polarity, with the advantages of a suitable predisposition of the soul to justice. Without this structural bias of the soul towards its reasoning function, the elaborate imagery of aspiration in *Phaedrus* of the charioteer and his two horses of radically different stock would be impossible, and all mediation between mind and body would be precluded. The problem of pleasure, hesitatingly introduced by Adeimantus in connection with the ascetic lives of the guardians (419), is first considered as a simple division of power, in which "the desires of the many and the worse are ruled by the desires and intelligence of the few and reasonable" (431c). But with the tripartite division of the soul comes the careful assignment to each part of its respective form of pleasure: the reason cares to know the truth, the temper is engaged with power, victory and fame, while the appetitive part of the soul is dominated by sensual appetites, and a love of money (580d–581b).

If the soul is construed to correspond by analogy to the class divisions of the constitution, the individual must then be a microcosm of the city.[29] As control should be exercised in the soul by the reasoning part, so in the constitution the guardian-ruler should be a philosopher. These philosophical guardian-rulers will need to have "a clear paradigm in their souls" (484c), and this will result from the vision of "an unchanging order", such as is available to the charioteer in *Phaedrus*:

> A philosopher who keeps company with the divine order becomes as divine and orderly as it is possible for a human being to be. (500c–d)

As microcosms of the political order the guardians will implement the constitution to a design drawn from the divine paradigm, which is the cosmos itself. The correspondence, between social class and part of the soul, is supposed to be exact. But the only person who can judge between the merits of the satisfactions offered by the disparate pleasures is the philosopher, the man of judgement, who alone has ascended to a knowledge of all three kinds (582). His decision will, predictably, be in favour of reason. So it is only when the entire soul follows the philosophical inclinations of reason that each part may do its own work, and reap its own pleasures in the best and truest realization of them possible (586e).

These are the specific conclusions which prompt a reconsideration in the tenth book of composition (*poiesis*) and of *mimesis*, eventually summarized in three separate charges against *mimesis*: that imitative composition/creation is "poor in relation to the truth", that it is not associated with "the best part of the soul", and that it is "sufficient to ruin even the reasonable", which is "a terrible thing" (605a–b, and 605c). The word "ruin" announces the argument: tragic poetry and other imitative practices all "seem to be a ruin of the understanding of those who listen, unless those that do have a remedy [*pharmakon*] in the knowledge of their actual nature" (595b).

To achieve the argument, *mimesis* must be closely defined by means of division, and to do this Plato has Socrates re-introduce the denominative and generic quality of the Forms:

> We are accustomed to attribute a single Form to any multiplicity of objects which bear the same name. (596a)

Although the Forms, or 'ideas', that have been repeatedly discussed in the *Republic* have been ethical qualities—bravery, moderation—Plato chooses for his example the 'idea' of a material object, of a couch or a table (596b). This choice is convenient and apposite, because it entails the activity of creating or making, which is dependent on the same verb as that used for composition in words (*poiein*, and so *poiesis*). With the emphasis placed on *poiesis*, a division can follow, and an ascending scale in creation can be adduced and agreed: god is the "craftsman" of all objects and living beings in creation, in their true existence as 'ideas'; the human craftsman "looks to the idea", and creates a material couch; while the painter, as a representative of mimetic skills, will create what appears to be a couch. The painter falls into a third and remote category, because he is neither a creator nor a craftsman, but an imitator (*mimetes*) of what god and the craftsman create. One initial conclusion is that "if the tragedian is an imitator" he is likewise at the second remove from truth, from the ideas or Forms which are held to be created by god (596c–597e).

The painter is designated as a "painter of/from life" (*zographos*), of objects or of living things, and as such his confinement to the two-dimensional plane contrasts unfavourably with the spatial depth available to the craftsman. This contrast would obviously be removed were the artist chosen a sculptor, or a bronze-caster, who might cast and create a bronze chariot, alike in every detail to an actual chariot, but unable to be used. The division of one kind of craftsman from another would then come down to the question of functionality, and would permit a widely divergent definition of *mimesis*. But the painter, confined to his two dimensions, is subject to a further debasement, on a charge which condemns the mobility of vision:

> If he sees the couch from the side, or from in front, or from any particular direction, is the couch actually different in each case? Or is it not different at all, but merely seems to be other than it was? (598a)

It follows that the images of the painter are of appearance only, not of objects (598b).[30]

From this problematic prelude, which explicitly redefines *mimesis* in the images reproduced from specific visual appearances, the argument turns to tragedy by way of "its leader", Homer. The complaint lies initially against the pretence that these poets "know all the skills, everything in human life that relates to excellence and evil, and everything divine" (598d–e). These cultural pretensions are wide, and are dismissed through the diverse denotations of the word *poiesis*: if the same person could "create" both the real thing and its image, he would hardly be satisfied with creating its image (599a). Incapable of creating excellence in city or individual, "all poets, beginning from Homer, are imitators of the image of human excellence and the other matters about which they compose, but do not touch the truth" (600e). But apart from the comparison of the poet's use of words to the painter's use of colours, there is nothing to link this assertion to the explicitly visual definition of *mimesis* achieved in the example of the contrast between the painter and the craftsman. If a narrated or performed poem, as an entity or unity, is an image of the work of the appropriate craftsman, namely the legislator or teacher, then it should be an image of the political constitution of a city, or of the ethical constitution of an individual. The *Republic* itself certainly aims to be a paradigm of both; it is not made clear how this is true of poetry.[31]

The second charge against imitative composition proceeds from a remarkably concise definition of imitative poetry:

> We say that imitative composition imitates men carrying out actions, under constraint or voluntarily, from which, as they think, a good or bad result has been obtained; and in all of this they either feel pain or are happy. Is there anything else contained in it?
> Nothing. (603c)

There is, in fact, more, because it is also agreed that "in all of this a man's mind is not composed", but in the same way as sight may produce conflicting opinions in the soul through visual distortion or illusion, "in all his actions a man is in conflict and at war with himself" (603c–d). In public, in front of "his equals", the reasoning part of his soul will restrain his distress; in private, and alone, "he will dare to give voice to many things he would be ashamed to be heard saying, and he will do many things he would not allow anyone to see him doing" (604a).

The second charge against *mimesis* can now be clearly stated:

> So that part of us which is given to complaint offers much to imitation, and a great deal of variety; but the intelligent and quiet disposition, which is nearly always at one with itself, is not easy to imitate, nor easy to appreciate when imitated, especially in a large gathering when men of all kinds have collected in theatres. For the feelings imitated are alien to them.   (604e)

Since the theatrical audience, as a mass, does not consist of individuals or "equals" of the necessary kind, it cannot and will not perform the appropriate function of providing support for the reasoning part of the soul. The social conclusion follows:

> Then it is evident that the imitative poet is not by nature inclined to that part of the soul, nor is his expertise fixed on pleasing it, if he intends to win a good reputation with the masses, but is instead inclined to the mobile and complaining part of the soul, because that is most easily imitated.   (605a)

Both painter and imitative poet create works which are poor in relation to the truth, and associate with a part of the soul that is not the best.

The imposition of censorship, earlier in the *Republic*, is translated into a general ban on the imitative composer. In this, the analogy between the individual and the constitution, between microcosm and macrocosm, is decisive:

> And so now we should be justified in not receiving him into a city which is going to be well-regulated, because he awakes and nourishes and gives strength to that part of the soul, and destroys the reasoning part. Just as when someone hands over power in a city to the worst people, and breaks down the best, so, we shall say, does the imitative poet create a bad constitution in the soul of each individual, gratifying the thoughtless part of it...   (605b)

But the greatest charge remains to be stated: this is that imitative poetry "is sufficient to ruin even the reasonable, apart from a very few of them, which is a terrible thing." (605c).

Despite the grand opening to the final count, there is only one conspicuous innovation in the details of the charge. An imitative performance of a hero in grief, speaking or singing, has an effect on even "the best of us" (605c–d). This is the familiar appeal of *mimesis* to that part of the soul that is not reasoning; but the explanation for its effect on those who pride themselves on their control of psychic disturbance is the instrumental role of "sympathy" (605d). Because these are the sufferings of another, the spectator or auditor thinks there can be nothing shameful in his praise of, and pity for, another good man in distress, and believes that he gains by the pleasure he feels. He fails to calculate that the influence will pass into his own life:

> For if he nourishes his pity to strength on the sufferings of others, it is not easy for him to repress it in his own sufferings.   (606b)

The same is true of laughter. Jokes that you would be ashamed to make yourself, you laugh at in comic imitations in the theatre, and do not despise. The restraint imposed by reason is released, and what is let out in the theatre follows you into domestic life.

> And the same may be said of sexual desire, anger, and all desires and pains and pleasures in the soul, which we say follow on every action of ours: imitative poetry works on us in these respects as well. For it waters them and feeds them, instead of drying them up, and puts them in control, when they should be controlled, if we are to be better and happier men, and not worse and more miserable.   (606d)

In this adaptation and extension of the argument against composition-as-performance Plato returns, in his use of the term sympathy (*sympaschein*, "to experience fellow-feeling"), to the process he had first attempted to describe by his appropriation of the term *mimesis*. Both individual and city are subject, in Plato's impersonating dialogue, to a constitution designed and articulated by the written word as argument, and it is this *logos* which compels the exclusion of imitative poetry (607b). Ironically, the ban is provisional. It may be lifted, if "poetry which is directed to pleasure and imitation have an argument to make" in their defence, in verse; or, alternatively, if their "representatives", not poets themselves, can produce one in prose that demonstrates that this practice "is not only sweet, but useful to constitutions and to human life" (607c–d).³² But if the defence proves invalid, Socrates and Glaucon have a charm, which they can sing to themselves while they listen: that charm (*pharmakon*, 595b) is the transcendental argument of the *Republic*.

1.2 ARISTOTLE ³³

Aristotle was a pupil of Plato, tutor to Alexander the Great, and the son of a doctor. His father, Nicomachus, had been a physician at the court of Macedon, and in his youth Aristotle came to study under Plato at the Academy in Athens, where he stayed for twenty years until Plato's death in 347 BC. It is possible that he was involved with teaching in the Academy, but he only founded his own philosophical school at Athens, the Lyceum, after some years of absence abroad. Both periods of teaching may well have left their mark on the final versions of the *Poetics*, the *Rhetoric* and the Nicomachean *Ethics*.³⁴ The *Politics*, to which I shall also refer, was left unfinished, and seems to have been compiled from sections written at various stages in Aristotle's life.

1.2.1 Platonic invitation and the Aristotelian treatise

It is relatively clear, from one or two references in the *Rhetoric*, that the full text of the *Poetics* included a substantial discussion of laughter and the ridiculous, and so almost certainly of comedy.³⁵ The allusions to this second part of the *Poetics* confirm that the emphasis of the complete work lay firmly on dramatic composition, which in the case of tragedy is linked to epic. Yet there is no obvious or given reason for the selection of drama from the many established forms of composition-for-performance.

In his final books (VII and VIII) of the *Politics* Aristotle pays serious attention to the role of *mousike* (the performance of poetry to musical accompaniment) in his assessment of the best education for the best constitution.³⁶ The rhetorical works were completed by a survey of earlier treatises on the subject. But there is, despite this accumulation, a vast gap between these kinds of study and Aristotle's work in natural and physical science and, most notably, in logic and metaphysics. One solution to this problem of orientation is to accept a broader grouping, which would allow a set of general interests to substitute for the bare subject-categories. In the *Poetics*, Aristotle is concerned to relate tragedy closely to pleasure. In the *Ethics*, pleasure enters easily into a consideration of human conduct.³⁷ The *Politics*, *Ethics* and the *Rhetoric* are all alike in accepting human social practice as an appropriate object for study, and so as susceptible to systematic investigation.³⁸

Aristotle's existing works are generally taken to be 'esoteric', that is produced for use or circulation in teaching, notably at the Lyceum. The possibility then arises that they are lectures, or lecture notes, or perhaps works written to summarize a course of teaching. The *Politics*, *Ethics*, *Rhetoric* and *Poetics* all deal with subjects that were treated in dialogue by Plato, in the fictional narrative of 'recall'. Philosophical writing, in the hands of Aristotle, discards the attractions of impersonation and transforms itself into an annotation which records the speaking voice of the lecturer, who is a practitioner of no skill other than his own.³⁹ The acceptance of existent patterns of human social practice which is so much a characteristic of these works by Aristotle is conspicuously absent from Plato, whose dialectic is reductive and transcending. One consequence of this is that the evocative and apparently prescriptive paradigm yields place to the systematic study.

Aristotle's theoretical studies of politics were supported by a series of largely historical monographs produced by his school on the constitutions of specific states. Perhaps similarly, the theoretical examination of tragedy (and comedy) in the *Poetics* was accompanied by compilations of historical lists of victorious dramatists at the festivals of Dionysus at Athens, and of the plays that were produced. But the emphasis on tragedy, in close relation to epic, is hard to divorce from the explicit invitation issued by Plato in the closing book of the *Republic*. Plato may have been thinking of a public-speaker, one who could compose a speech to defend the indefensible. Theatrical history has been distinctly affected by the fact that his challenge was taken up by an academic.

1.2.2 *Poetics* (a): an anatomy of method ⁴⁰

> What I wish to discuss is poetry itself and its forms, the capacity each of them has, how plots should be constructed if the composition is to be successful, the number and qualities of its component parts, and similarly any other things which belong to the same systematic enquiry, beginning in the natural order, and taking the first thing first. The composition of epic and of tragedy, also of comedy, of the dithyramb, and most compositions for the pipes or for the lyre can all collectively be taken to be imitations.   (*Poetics* ch. 1)⁴¹

Since the imitators imitate people in action, these people must be either serious or inferior types (for character nearly always follows this division: all people differ in character in respect of virtue and vice), either better or worse than us, or like us, just as the painters show them to be...It is clear that each of the imitations mentioned will admit these differences, and will be distinguished by their imitation of different objects in this way.   (ch. 2)

For it is possible to imitate the same objects using the same medium at times through narrative report, either by becoming someone else as Homer does in his poems, or by maintaining the same personality and not changing, or with all the people in action and enacting.   (ch. 3)

The creation of poetry seems as a whole to be attributable to two particular causes, and both of these are natural. For imitation is a part of human nature from childhood, and human beings differ from the other animals in this, that they are most imitative and learn their first lessons by means of imitation; it is also natural for all human beings to delight in imitative works. What happens in practical experience bears this out: for we delight in viewing the most accurate images of things which we find painful to look at, such as the forms of the lowest animals, or corpses. The cause of this is that not only philosophers, but all other men alike find pleasure in learning, although their acquaintance with it may be limited. For that reason, they delight in looking at images, because the result of looking at them is learning, and inferring what each thing is, for example that 'this' is 'that'.   (ch. 4)

Comedy is, as I said, an imitation of inferior people, not worse in the sense of every kind of evil, but in the sense that the ridiculous is part of what is ugly. For what provokes laughter is an error of some sort, or a form of ugliness that is not painful or destructive: for example, a mask that is ridiculous is ugly and distorted, but not painful.   (ch. 5)

So tragedy is an imitation of a serious action brought to its end, one of some magnitude, in discourse which is pleasantly seasoned...with people acting, not a narrative report, accomplishing by means of pity and fear the purgation of the emotions of this kind.   (ch. 6)

Most modern readers with an interest in theatrical or critical theory will probably first encounter the concept of *mimesis* in the *Poetics*, although the term is quite clearly derivative. What is evident from the *Poetics* is that Aristotle had no difficulty in accepting a conceptual validity for *mimesis*, and one that was unproblematic and unitary, with all poetic composition effectively gathered under the one term. His opening theoretical statements from the first six chapters of the treatise reveal the traces of a detailed obligation to Plato in the *Republic*, and the treatise sustains the attention given to drama in comparison to epic, and to poetry above the visual or plastic arts.[42] Central to this acceptance is the facility which the term *mimesis* affords to the relationship between a composition and its apparent subject. Aristotle's emphasis on action, which gains some support in his treatise from etymology,[43] is a direct inheritance from a key definition of imitative composition in the *Republic*:

> We say that imitative composition imitates men carrying out actions, under constraint or voluntarily, from which, as they think, a good or bad result has been obtained; and in all of this they either feel pain or are happy.   (*Republic* 603c)[44]

This formulation of *mimesis* is repeated by Aristotle in chapters 2, 3, 4, and 6 of the *Poetics*. Much of his remaining argument is devoted to a reexamination of the appropriate kind of 'result' and how it is best achieved; while his suggestion of the role of *hamartia* aims to provide a more accurate analysis of the kind of action featured in tragedy, resolving the rather sterile polarity contained in "under constraint or voluntarily".[45]

What is important about this academic inheritance is that it proves impossible to question Aristotle, in the *Poetics* and his other written works, about his own definition of the term. Aristotle provides no analysis of *mimesis* in the *Poetics*, apart from its presence in a series of formulations; and the most plausible explanation for this is that his attention was fixed on providing a justification for what he accepted as a recognizable group of human activities.[46] Acceptance is not an incidental or submissive gesture in Aristotle's stature as a philosopher, but a substantial diversion from the dismissal of normative human practice in Plato's transcendental idealism. If the *Rhetoric* is, most obviously, a restoration of the status of public-speaking from its scornful condemnation in Plato's *Gorgias* and *Phaedrus*, then the *Ethics* and *Politics* also offer a more tolerant review of normal, socialized human behaviour than emerges from the convicting tenor of the dialectic. Aristotle has no reason to subject the concept of *mimesis* to a critical examination or analysis if an acceptance of it as an inclusive category of human activity can allow him to provide a generic justification for that activity.

His means to that end are complex, and embrace most of the innovative formulas for which the *Poetics* is now famous. The vigour, repetition and sustained invective of the Platonic condemnation demand perhaps the most capacious term in the Greek philosophical vocabulary, which is 'nature'.[47] The initiative for the definition of *mimesis* as natural comes from the Platonic connection of *mimesis* with human actions (*Republic* 603c). This provides Aristotle with the opportunity to insist (chapter 4) on two "natural causes" for *mimesis*: the proposition that human beings are categorically distinct from other animals by their extreme propensity to *mimesis* from childhood forwards and to learning by means of *mimesis*, and the assertion that human beings enjoy mimetic works (*mimemata*). The first proposition readily recalls Plato's understanding of *mimesis* in education, which was the initial motive for the stringent regulation of compositions-for-performance in the *Republic*. This subject forms a major part of Aristotle's consideration of the best constitution in the *Politics*, where a diffuse and reiterated examination reveals a profound concern about the presence of *mousike* in education (*Politics* VIII.2.3–6, and 4.3 to the close of the treatise at 7.11). In this discussion, whose irresolution may have required the composition of the *Poetics*, musical compositions are readily subsumed under the term *mimesis*, in the need to describe the function of performance as educative role-playing. By contrast to the objects of the senses of touch and taste, and even to the objects of vision, "in the songs themselves there are imitations of character types" (*Politics* VIII.5.8). It seems to be understood here that character can only be presented through a realization of human beings in action, which is difficult for painting, and that action is at least readily expressed by words. But in principle, and throughout the discussion, Aristotle accepts that *mousike* is justified by its traditional contribution to the pleasures of relaxation, which can be reasonably reconciled with a role in education.

The introduction of pleasure into his account of music as a form of *mimesis* parallels the second of Aristotle's "natural causes" in *Poetics* 4, and constitutes a major part of his defence of poetry. The anxiety caused by pleasure was a significant feature of Plato's condemnation, but for Aristotle pleasure can be integrated without undue anxiety into an understanding of the human condition. The concluding Book X of the *Ethics* contains a refutation of the arguments against hedonism advanced by Plato (notably in the *Philebus*) and the Academy, and Aristotle's position there is that pleasure is vital, and a natural accompaniment to the proper exercise of the human senses. Pleasure, in the *Ethics*, is also related to "contentment" (*eudaimonia*), which is found in the contemplative exercises of the philosopher. In the *Rhetoric*, he provides a careful gradation of the relationship between pleasure and learning, which leads directly into a consideration of learning from imitations. Pleasure is initially defined as "a kind of movement of the soul, a sudden and perceptible settling-down into its natural state, and pain is the opposite" (*Rhetoric* I.11.1). The contemplative bias of his interest then locates learning easily in this framework:

> And learning and wondering are pleasant for the most part; for in wondering lies the desire to learn, so that what excites wonder is desired, while learning is a settling-down into the natural state.
> (*Rhetoric* I.11.21)

The argument continues into a terminology that is closely related, if not exactly parallel, to that advanced in the *Poetics*:

> And since learning and wondering are pleasant, all things of that kind are also pleasant, such as a work of imitation, like painting, sculpture, and poetry, and everything which is imitated well, even if the object imitated is not pleasant. For it is not this which delights, but the inference that 'this is that', with the result that we learn something. The same is true of reversals of fortune and narrow escapes from danger; for all these things excite wonder. (I.11.23–4)

The choice of the paradoxical example (pleasure in the imitation of an unpleasant object) is common to both the *Poetics* (chapter 4) and the *Rhetoric*, and not only adds strength to the insistence that pleasure accompanies *mimesis*, but also acutely identifies a serious—and thoroughly respectable—kind of pleasure in the activity of learning. This identification is instrumental in a defence of *mimesis* on some of the pictorial grounds which Plato adduced, largely by way of a preliminary analogy, in the *Republic*. As Plato removed pictorial representation (taken to be that of living creatures or of material objects) twice over from the truth which alone was susceptible of knowledge, Aristotle deftly returns the assessment of painting to the realm of logical inference. This paradox may well have played a significant role in the discussion of comedy in *Poetics* II, because the objects of comedy are the "worse" kinds of men: if this assumption is correct, then the pleasure of laughing may have been partly justified through its role in learning, in a development from the formal simplicity of inference.

There is no particular connection between this cognitive pleasure, which would seem to relate only to the objective accuracy of the *mimesis* ('this is that'), and the subjective cultural practice—*mimesis* as imitative performance—apart from the inclusion of both under the term 'nature'. But the identification of both of these human activities, contemplative and performative, as "natural causes", carries strong connotations of a scientific treatment, which is prepared to accept phenomena in whatever form they appear as appropriate objects of knowledge, provided that they can be subjected to systematic study. In his works on natural and physical science, and in his general scheme for knowledge outlined in the *Metaphysics*, Aristotle recognized principles or "causes" that should be the objects of a full enquiry. In the philosophical dictionary of *Metaphysics* IV and the methodological chapters of *Metaphysics* I, these are detailed as the formal, the material, the motive and the final causes, following a presentation in the *Physics*.[48] The language may seem obstructive; but the formal cause relates to what constitutes the form of an object, the material to its essential matter, the motive to what sets it in motion or brings it into being, and the final to its overall function, or 'end'. In the biological works in particular, an additional emphasis is placed on the analysis of the whole into its parts, and the relationship of the parts to the whole.

It is relatively clear that in the *Poetics* pleasure, specifically the proper pleasure of each form, is for Aristotle the final cause, the aim and objective of *mimesis*. This is not simply a matter of inference from the argument in the *Rhetoric*, but is implied in chapter 14 of the *Poetics*, where "not every pleasure should be sought from tragedy, but only its proper one", and "the poet should by means of imitation prepare the pleasure that results from fear and pity". The first of these formulas is repeated in the concluding comparison between epic and tragedy in chapter 26 of the *Poetics*, where both arts "should create not any kind of pleasure but the one we have stated", in what is most easily understood as a summary of the treatise as a whole.[49] A basic outline of the scheme of enquiry in the *Poetics* might then have the poet as the motive cause; the parts of tragedy (detailed in chapter 6) as providing the form, which includes the relationship of parts to the whole; and human discourse (*logos*), identified in the concise definition in chapter 6, as the material or essential cause. In the philosophical dictionary contained in *Metaphysics* IV, with 'causes' the subject of chapter 2, the sculptor is identified as the motive cause of the statue, as, in general, "the maker is the cause of the thing made". Some commentators would prefer to contain all four causes in the concise definition of tragedy in *Poetics* chapter 6, finding the motive cause (for example) in the "people acting";

but this seems to me to conflict, in the one specific instance, with the obvious analogy between sculptor and poet. Yet the possibility of divergent readings should at least confirm that an enquiry into poetics was not easily integrated with Aristotle's established analytic methods, although its outline may show traces of their systematic influence.

The six parts of tragedy detailed in chapter 6 of the *Poetics* are story (*muthos*), character (*ethos*), linguistic style (*lexis*), thought (*dianoia*), visual effect (*opsis*) and the composition of songs (*melopoia*). Since tragedy is a *mimesis* of human action (*praxis*), of men doing things, it is perhaps inevitable that Aristotle considers *muthos* as the most dominant and decisive of the formal elements. Because *muthos* is "the putting-together (*synthesis*) of the things done (*pragmata*)" and so is what we might reasonably call plot, it may also be considered indistinguishable from the "end" of tragedy, and "the end is the greatest of all things" (*Poetics* chapter 6).[50] As a 'formal' cause, *muthos* is considered to participate in the final cause, and so is closely connected with the generation of tragic pleasure. This justifies the important role that Aristotle, with acute critical perceptions, assigns to reversal of fortune (*peripeteia*) and to recognition (*anagnorisis*), which are "parts of *muthos*, and the greatest means by which tragedy entrances us". The ineradicable participation of *muthos* in the end of tragedy also entails the firm subordination of character (*ethos*) to plot, on which Aristotle is repeatedly insistent: "Tragedy is not a *mimesis* of human beings, but of actions and life." In Aristotle's teleological enquiry, the end or the 'final' cause is bound to subject all others to a subservient role: "Without action there would be no tragedy, without character there would be one."

Of the six parts of tragedy, Aristotle manifestly passes little comment on thought, music or visual effect. Linguistic style is given an extended treatment towards the end of the treatise (chapter 22), where the emphasis lies on metaphor. The unique role of metaphor in a poetic *mimesis* is perhaps established by its function in evoking resemblances: "For to use metaphor well is to watch for what is similar." Since an adroit use of metaphor cannot be learnt, it is "a mark of a natural talent", yet by this joint definition it cannot effectively be the subject of a treatise. The lack of extended commentary on music may indicate that Aristotle felt that he had treated, or was intending to treat, the full range of this subject in another work, the lost *On Music*. It is also plausible that a similar explanation (relating in this case to the *Ethics*) underlies the limited space he allows for his eventual observations on *ethos* (chapter 15). The principle of avoiding unnecessary duplication finds a direct expression in reference to thought (*dianoia*), of which he comments (chapter 19): "As for what concerns thought, let that be covered by the *Rhetoric*, for it belongs more properly to that systematic enquiry."[51] Yet music is, for Aristotle, "the greatest of the pleasant seasonings" of tragedy, and since "people acting create the imitation, it necessarily follows firstly that the ordered arrangement of visual effect should be a part of tragedy" (chapter 6). This logical priority confirms visual effect as the single mode of presentation, in contrast to the dual media or means (linguistic style and song) and to the three objects of *mimesis* (*muthos*, character and thought); but the potential for close attention to the presentation of a *mimesis* as theatrical practice is negated by the close of chapter 6. In the concluding summary there, "visual effect is entrancing, but has least to do with artistic method, and is least germane to the art of poetic composition."

I shall return to the question of the suppression of *opsis* in the final section of this chapter (1.3). For the time being, it is sufficient to note the theoretical tension that exists between the possible, schematic scope of the treatise and a preponderant bias to that constituent part of tragedy that is most intimately related to its proposed 'end'. This bias is intricately involved with, and almost certainly entailed by, a theory of the specific emotions which are engaged in theatrical reception, and which dictate its peculiar pleasures.

1.2.3 *Poetics* (b): towards a theory of the emotions

So tragedy is an imitation of a serious action brought to its end, one of some magnitude, in discourse which is pleasantly seasoned...with people acting, not a narrative report, accomplishing by means of pity and fear the purgation of the emotions of this kind.   (ch. 6)

However, tragedy is an imitation not only of a complete action, but also of things that are frightening and pitiful, and these arise most of all when things happen unexpectedly but through the course of events; for in that case they will arouse more wonder than if they arise spontaneously and by chance.   (ch. 9)

The finest kind of recognition occurs with a reversal of fortune, like the one in *Oedipus*...A recognition of this kind in conjunction with a reversal of fortune will contain either pity or fear—tragedy has been defined as an imitation of actions like this—since good or bad fortune are their result.   (ch. 11)

> So the construction of the best tragedy should not be simple but complex, and one that is an imitation of things that are pitiful and frightening (for this is a property of this kind of imitation). Firstly, then, it is clear that good men should not be shown passing from good to bad fortune, for this is not frightening or pitiful but repulsive. Nor should bad men be shown passing from bad to good fortune, for this is the most untragic of all possibilities: it has nothing of what it should have, and it is neither humane, pitiful, nor frightening. Nor, again, should a worthless man fall from good to bad fortune. For this arrangement would be humane, but would not contain either pity or fear. This is because the former is felt for someone suffering undeservedly, and the latter for someone like us—pity for the undeserving, and fear for the person who is like us; so that the resulting situation will be neither frightening nor pitiful. What is left is the mean between these. This is the kind of man who is not distinguished by his personal excellence or sense of justice, and who passes into bad fortune not through vice or depravity, but on account of some error: one of those who are famous and have good fortune, such as Oedipus... (ch. 13)[52]
>
> Things that are frightening and pitiful can be created by visual effect, but they can also be created out of the arrangement of the actions, and this comes first, and is the mark of a better poet. For the plot should be put together in such a way that, even without looking, someone who is listening to the actions as they are happening, will shudder with fear and feel pity at what is going on. Those would be the emotions of anyone listening to the story of Oedipus...Since the poet should by means of imitation prepare the pleasure that results from fear and pity, it is obvious that this must be produced in the actions [of the plot]. (ch. 14)

It seems fair to say that these repeated statements of the same formulaic pairing of pity and fear, which appears to be closely related to the generation of the pleasure which is proper to tragedy, would remain enigmatic and unexplained if deprived of the broader context of Aristotle's other works on social practice. This is perhaps particularly true of their conjunction with the puzzling term *katharsis* ("purgation", "purification", or literally, "cleansing") in chapter 6, a word which appears just once more in the *Poetics*, but in relation to a purification of an image of Artemis in Euripides' *Iphigenia in Tauris* (chapter 19), and so without theoretical value.

Aristotle's theoretical silence on *katharsis* would be inexplicable were it not for an explicit statement made in the *Politics*, towards the close of the discussion of music. He concludes with the compromise that music has several benefits, which include education, relaxation and purification, which is *katharsis*:

> But what it is I mean by purgation, which I use here without explanation, I shall discuss more clearly in my treatise on poetry.
> (*Politics* VIII.7.4)

If this is, as it seems, a reference to the *Poetics*, it does not seem satisfied by the existing book of the treatise, and a possible argument is that the promised discussion must have been located in the lost second book on comedy. Reassuring as this might be, and just plausible, it is hardly revealing as things stand.[53] Fortunately, at this point in the *Politics* Aristotle is unable to resist a slight digression on purification. He sees a distinction, in music, between the ethical harmonies which should be used for education,

> and the active and enthusiastic ones for listening to others as practitioners: for any emotion which occurs strongly in one soul exists in all, and differs only in degree—such as pity and fear, and, again, religious excitement. For some are prone to this emotion, and in the case of sacred music we see these people, when they use songs which are orgiastic for the soul, in a state as if they were taking medical treatment and undergoing purgation. So the same must necessarily be true of the emotions of those who are pitying and fearful, and in general of those who are emotional in the degree to which each is affected: all must experience a purgation and a lightening in conjunction with pleasure. Similarly, the purgative melodies provide harmless delight to people. (*Politics* VIII.7.5–6)

It would be difficult, if not perverse, to divorce this set of propositions from the deployment of *katharsis* in the *Poetics*. The direct reference to performance by practitioners for an audience is accompanied by a division between "active and enthusiastic" harmonies, and between "pity and fear" and "religious excitement". *Katharsis* applies to both groups of people, but it is only in the context of religious excitement that it is given its unequivocally medical interpretation; the statement is that the use of songs which are orgiastic for the soul is the equivalent to the "medical treatment", and so consists, metaphorically, of a "purge" (presumably a drug) which leads to purification of the body. The language of what follows is explicit—"the same must necessarily be true of the emotions of those who are pitying and fearful"—and in this equation by Aristotle tragic performance must take the place of orgiastic songs. The passage, unless it was contradicted or drastically adapted in *Poetics* II, provides an explanation for the deployment of the metaphor of *katharsis* in the discussion of tragedy. The role of the metaphor in both cases is also quite apparent from this passage: what is believed to be happening to the soul is expressed in terms of what is believed to happen, in medical practice, to the body.

The link between purification and philosophy is not original to Aristotle, and as a consequence should not be seen as surprising. The popular appeal of purification undoubtedly gained its strength from a juxtaposition of religious or mystical beliefs to the provision of relief from physical ailments. The early doctors encountered awkward competition from those they described as "purifiers", amongst many others, and the collusion of religious feeling with physical remedy remained the cultural environment in which the systematic claims both of medical practitioners and of philosophers were advanced.[54] Plato acknowledges this symbiosis of religion and medicine in his dialogue *Cratylus*, in which the god Apollo is identified as "the purifier, and the washer, and the absolver from all impurities", as his son Asclepius was the patron of physical healing:

> In the first place, the purgations and purifications which doctors and diviners use, and their fumigations with drugs magical or medicinal, as well as their washings and lustral sprinklings, have all one and the same object, which is to make a man pure in both body and soul.[55]

In *Phaedrus*, Socrates' sense of the offence given to Eros, the god of love, by speeches praising the non-lover prompts him to compose a recantation, which will be his purification of a religious error (243a). But the attractions of a division of responsibilities, for the health of the body and of the soul, between medicine and philosophy account for the recurrence of the medical analogy in a variety of forms throughout his dialogues. Perhaps the most facetious of all these comparisons is that near the opening of the *Charmides*, where Socrates claims that he has been instructed by a physician from the far north not to attempt to cure the body without also curing the soul: the subject is a beautiful young boy, in a gymnasium at Athens, who has a headache.

For Plato, ultimate purification is achieved by the release of the soul from the prison-house of the body, either in philosophical self-discipline or in death, as is argued in *Phaedo* (67c–d; section 1.1.2 above); and in relation to the constitution, the macrocosm of the microcosm that is the individual human being, the close regulation and partial expulsion of some kinds of imitative composition and musical forms from the state is understood to be a purgation (*Republic* 399e). The metaphorical range of *katharsis* and its cognates, which, strictly speaking, includes its application to the effect of medicine on the body, can only be a result of an intense religious and cultural insistence on the vital distinction between pure and impure. The choice of *katharsis*, or 'cleansing', as a metaphor entails an object, something which contains the impurity, and it is clear from the digression in the *Politics* that this is considered by Aristotle, in general terms, to be the soul. The rule of the metaphor designates pity and fear as the impurities, but nothing written of these two emotions in the *Poetics* clarifies why they should have this status.

The absence of any further explanation for the selection of the emotions of fear and pity can almost certainly be ascribed to the existence of a review of the emotions addressed by public-speaking in the *Rhetoric*.[56] Aristotle introduces this review with the general proposition that public-speaking is concerned with judgement, and that the speaker should display "intelligence, personal excellence and goodwill" (*Rhetoric* II.1.8 and 15). He should also be able to "prepare the disposition" of those who are judging. A general definition introduces the argument:

> The emotions are the means by which men change their judgements, and which are accompanied by pain and pleasure: such as anger, pity, fear, and all other similar states, and their contraries.
>
> (*Rhetoric* II.1.8)

In the discussions of the paired contraries, anger and mildness, love and hate, Aristotle admits varying admixtures of pleasure and pain, and of self-interest and concern for others. The presentation of the review is methodical, and its relationship to a broader theoretical framework, in which the object of study is human social practice, is apparent. The analysis of fear is detailed (II.5.1–15), and proceeds from an opening definition:

> Let fear be a pain or disturbance arising from the imagined appearance of an impending evil, which is either destructive or painful.
>
> (II.5.1)

Magnitude and proximity are major stimuli, and fear, as an apprehension, is particularly responsive to "signs" of threat (II.5.1–3). A marked characteristic is its reflexive relationship to pity:

> To put it simply, all things are to be feared which, when they are happening to others or are about to, are pitiable. (II.5.12)

Aristotle also emphasizes, in some contrast to his opening remarks, that fear has a special relevance to political debate, the category of public-speaking which he calls 'deliberative', because the presence of fear reveals some hope:

> Fear makes men deliberate, whereas no-one deliberates about things that are hopeless. So that when it is better for the audience to feel fear, they must be brought to realize that they are the kind of people who may suffer, that others greater than they are have suffered, and they must be shown that those who are like them are suffering or have done so, and at the hands of those whom they did not suspect, and in ways and at times they did not expect. (II.5.15)

The contrary of fear is confidence.

If there is a sharp distinction, between self and others, in the reflexive relationship between fear and pity (II.5.1), this is nonetheless mediated by the central term of "those who are like them" (*homoioi*), a term which also denotes social equality. There is, in addition, a temporal element, which may be expressed in terms of distance: fear is distinctly a species of apprehension, whereas pity operates in the present, or the near-present. It is not difficult to see how these emotions might be related to dramatic performance, considered as a "synthesis" of connected incidents extending over a controlled period of time in what Aristotle terms a *muthos*, or plot. Anticipation (diachronic) and immediacy (synchronic) are two concurrent aspects of theatrical presentation, and "reversals of fortune" (*peripeteiai*) and "recognitions" (*anagnoriseis*) can act in both the diachronic and the synchronic planes, on both emotions, with drastic efficacy (*Poetics* chapters 9, 11 and 13). The theoretical importance assigned in *Poetics* chapter 13 to "someone who is like us", to the *homoios*, is also clarified by the unique and powerful mediation that the term exercises in the relationship determined between pity and fear, and between the self and others.

The discussion of pity in the *Rhetoric* provides further clarification, and proceeds in the same manner, from an initial definition:

> Let pity be a kind of pain occurring at the imagined appearance of a destructive or painful evil affecting one who does not deserve it: an evil which the subject might expect to suffer himself, or one of those close to him to suffer, and an evil that seems close. (II.8.1–2)

Immediacy for the person suffering, and close anticipation for the audience. The reflexive qualities of fear and pity in II.5.12 appear to be expressed again here in the second clause of the definition, which might readily be summarized as 'fear'. Similarly, those who believe themselves fortunate, or who are completely ruined, do not pity; the old and experienced, the weak, the educated, and those who have a dependent family are prone to it (II.8.3–6). Events or states evoking pity are death, ill-treatment, isolation, and "when an evil result comes from a direction from which a good one was to be expected" (II.8.10). The dramatic capacities and aspects of pity are gradually made explicit, firstly in a description of the persons people pity:

> They pity those similar to them in age, character, habits, and family background; for in all of these qualities it becomes more apparent that the same thing may also happen to themselves. For the general conclusion must be that what people fear in relation to themselves they pity when they see the same things happening to others.
> (II.8.13)

The mediation of the *homoioi*, "those who are like themselves", between the self and others is again apparent, and the relationship with fear is established on this basis. Because the emotion of pity is stimulated by immediacy,

> it is inevitable that those who elaborate with gestures, voice, dress and with their general performance are more pitiable; for they make the evil appear in front of our eyes, either as future or as past.
> (II.8.14)

This is dramatic, because the immediacy of a theatrical presentation of suffering (if not, here, of a performance in the theatre itself) can unite the past or the future with the present. Aristotle is undoubtedly thinking of the potential theatricality of public address, most pertinently of the kind of appeals that might be made in the political assembly (for support or asylum, for example) or in the law courts, in a demonstrative or evocative display. In such evocations, the value of quotation, a rhetorical form of impersonation with obvious theatrical connotations, is immediate and emphatic. Words spoken, for instance at the point of death, contribute to the arousal of pity, and this may well include those who are themselves directly threatened in the courts by a death penalty:

> And when people show themselves to be worthy of serious respect at such critical times, this is particularly pitiable...both because the

> sufferer does not deserve his suffering, and because it takes place in front of our eyes.   (II.8.16)

"Worthy of serious respect" is my expanded translation here of *spoudaioi*, which with its implications of social and probably ethical stature is the word used in *Poetics* chapter 2 to indicate the likely subjects of tragedy, who are contrasted to the "inferior" people later defined (chapter 5) as the subjects of comedy.[57]

Although Aristotle is prepared to accept, following Plato's generic definition of imitative poetry in the *Republic* (603c), a general distinction between serious and inferior people as the objects of dramatic *mimesis*, his theoretical position in *Poetics* chapter 13 is made more complicated by the subtlety of his emotional theory. The contraries to fear and pity in the *Rhetoric* are respectively confidence and indignation (or envy), emotions which are insulated from the disturbing self-referentiality and reflexivity which unite and bind their opposites. Confidence is a feeling of superiority, which excludes emotive consideration of others, and indignation and envy firmly relate to someone other than the self, or else they would change into fear (II.9.3). Fear and pity fluctuate through an identification of the self with the other, and this determines that the object most suited to their arousal is the *homoios*. But the transition from this theoretical requirement to the identity and pre-eminence of leading figures in actual tragedies, specifically Oedipus (in *Poetics* chapter 11, chapter 13 and chapter 14), remains extremely awkward, and seems to be the direct result of the translation of a rhetorical scheme to the theatre. The phrasing in chapter 13 insists firstly on a kind of mediocrity perhaps appropriate to an *homoios* as the mean-figure between the good and bad man ("not distinguished by his personal excellence or sense of justice"), and then passes to "those who are famous and have good fortune", namely the socially prominent heroes of traditional myth who form the accepted subjects of tragedy. In order to explain this final formulation, it would be possible to introduce a distinction between a predominantly *ethical* mediocrity on the one hand and social prominence on the other. But this interpretation would run directly counter to the force of "not distinguished by his personal excellence", which deploys the term used to designate the pre-eminence of the Homeric and other heroes, who form the regular subjects of tragedy. One might represent Aristotle's dilemma best by saying that he found his position theoretically convincing, but critically extremely hard to express.[58]

There is also little, or nothing, in the discussions of the emotions of fear and pity in the *Rhetoric* which can add to the substantiation of *katharsis* in the *Politics*. It is certainly true that, as a metaphor, *katharsis* can escape strictly denotative characteristics in favour of what I have indicated is a pervasive range of cultural connotations. It is also true that the *Rhetoric* provides clear evidence that Aristotle determined the theoretical importance of fear and pity, and their inter-relationship, in connection with their status as emotions of audience reception. This in itself should resolve a continuing argument about whether pity and fear are understood as objective or subjective emotions in the *Poetics*, as belonging to the actions of the play itself, or to the audience. This is a difficulty that, ideally, should not exist, but which does, because Aristotle writes regularly in the *Poetics* of what is "frightening" or "pitiful".[59] These apparently objective terms, however, could hardly be divorced from the receptive emotions of fear and pity in the audience, with or without the additional weight of evidence from the discussion in the *Rhetoric*. A *katharsis*, a "cleansing", "clarification", or "purification" of what is frightening and pitiful in the actions of the play cannot be satisfactorily understood without some corresponding event in the audience: the fact of the matter is that neither possibility is exposed in the argument of the *Poetics*, which is undeniably content with the resonance of metaphor.

Nonetheless, Aristotle's far more expansive interest in fear and pity themselves is comprehensible, and it accounts, through the implication of these two interrelated emotions in the incidents of the plot, for most other aspects of the theory. So amplitude of plot (chapter 7) is subject to the requirement that a satisfactory *muthos* should contain a change of fortune, itself a likely instrument of pity and fear. Probability, which distinguishes drama from the particularity of history in chapter 9, induces conviction, and operates through the actions presented as a mediating term between the watching and listening subject and the 'other' of dramatic presentation: what is generally the case will have a wide application, and a similar function to that contained in the dramatic character "who is like" the audience.[60] The desire for unity in the plot (chapter 8) exists between these two criteria, as a selection of those incidents which are conducive to the 'end' of tragedy.[61] The integration of *hamartia*, the "error" which precipitates the drastic "reversal of fortune" in chapter 13, into this scheme is not immediately obvious. But the suggestion of "error" permits a theoretical dissolution of Plato's unyielding and critically sterile distinction between those who act "under constraint or voluntarily" (*Republic* 603c). The theoretical function of *hamartia* as a mediating term is extremely close to that exercised in the concept of the *homoios*, and its relationship to fear and pity, and to probability, is secured by the consistency of the general scheme.

If there is to be a final and convincing interpretation of the metaphor of *katharsis* in the *Poetics*, it must presumably be found in the attempt to resolve an apparent conflict between pleasure and pain. The end of tragedy is a pleasure, yet it is achieved "by means of" two emotions which are categorically identified as "pains" in the *Rhetoric* (II.5.1 and 8.1–2). An admixture of pleasure and pain had been ascribed to the emotions by Plato in his dialogue *Philebus*, in a list which seems to anticipate the review in the *Rhetoric*. The first speaker is Socrates, his interlocutor Protarchus:

> Do we not speak of anger, fear, desire, sorrow, love, emulation, envy and the like as pains which belong to the soul only?
> Yes.
> And shall we not find them also full of the most wonderful pleasures?   (*Philebus* 47e)

The argument continues with reference to the mixture of pleasure and pain experienced at performances of tragedy, and, perversely, at performances of comedy. Mixed pleasures are inferior to pure pleasures, but pleasure is subject to human knowledge for its perfect fulfilment: the purest form of knowledge is philosophy. A harsher view is presented in *Phaedo*, where abstinence from pleasure and pain is the release which is the objective and the achievement of philosophy (*Phaedo* 82–4). The most plausible, interpretation of *katharsis* in the *Poetics* must be that it provides a release from (a burden of) pain into a residual pleasure, the "lightening in conjunction with pleasure" of the *Politics*. There is, in this formulation, an absolution for the corrupting role of "sympathy" in the Platonic conception of the effect of the emotions, including pity, on the appetitive and sensual part of the soul (*Republic* 606 b and d: section 1.1.5 above).[62] But the absolution can only be granted by metaphor, within the system of academic theory.

1.3 BETWEEN ACADEMY AND LYCEUM: THE IDEA OF SIGHT

Towards the close of the sixth book of the *Republic* Plato has Socrates compelled by his interlocutor Glaucon to direct the argument into a consideration of 'the good', since the guardians must have a philosophical knowledge of the good. Socrates introduces the familiar distinction between the many and the one, and the resolution of that distinction into the "single idea":

> And we say that the many are seen, but not thought, and that the Ideas are thought, but not seen.   (507b)

This leads to the relationship of sight (*opsis*), and the eye, to the light of the sun, and to the suggestion that "the good" has engendered the sun as an analogue to itself:

> What the good is in the realm of thought in relation to thinking and to what is thought, so the sun is in the visible realm in relation to sight and what is seen.   (508b–c)

The soul is like the eye; in dim light, the eye sees badly, and when the truth, the Idea of good, shines out then the soul has knowledge, but when turned to the shadows and images of truth has only opinion. This analogy transpires to be the preamble to an exceptional image, which takes the analogy and transforms it at the beginning of the eighth book into what we should call an allegory. Socrates asks Glaucon to see, in this image, human beings in a cave who have been chained by the neck and legs from childhood, and behind whom a fire burns casting shadows on the end-wall of the cave. A raised path with a low parapet wall runs between the fire and the prisoners, and people pass along the path carrying images and artefacts: the wall is like the screening used by puppeteers, and the prisoners see only shadows, and hear only echoes coming from those shadows.[63] To people of this kind, chained in the prison, the truth would be nothing other than the shadows of artefacts (514a–515c).

The power and the pathos of this image are inescapable for the reader of Plato's *Phaedo*: the designation of the cave as a prison evokes the material condition of Socrates in that dialogue, and the release promised by philosophy from the prison-house of the body. The allegory begins to move with the release of a prisoner, who, once he turns around, finds the light from the fire glaring, the actual objects discordant with their shadows. As he is dragged up towards the open entrance to the cave, the light from the sun itself is painful, and blinding, and even in the open he finds it easier to see the shadows of objects first. Glaucon must interpret the image,

> comparing the living-space of the prison to the realm of sight, the light from the fire in it to the power of the sun. And if you construe

> the progress of the prisoner upwards, and his sight of the world above, to the ascent of the soul to the realm of thought, you will come close to my conviction, since this is what you are keen to hear. (517b)

Dialectic will be the systematic practice by which "the eye of the soul" can be turned upwards to true knowledge, "to see the good and make that ascent" (518–19). In any rhetorical study of writing it would be tempting to advance the word metaphor to account for the play of words in Plato's initial analogy and in his allegory. But in Plato's central doctrines the play of metaphor rounds on itself: without the visual metaphor there is no abstraction. Yet the metaphor of sight insistently accomplishes its own impossible cancellation in the "idea", the "visible form" of the invisible realm of knowledge. The diatribe against *mimesis* is subsumed in a larger play, in which knowledge becomes the idea of sight.

At the beginning of *Metaphysics* I, Aristotle privileges the faculty of sight:

> All human beings naturally desire knowledge. This is clear from the pleasure we have in sense perception, for its own sake, and not just for its usefulness. Most of all we value sight; without regard to its uses, I believe that we prefer it to all other senses, even when we have no objective. This is because sight is the major sense of knowledge and reveals many differences between one object and another.[64]

Aristotle is probably thinking here of the predominant role of sight in observation, and of its detection of colour, movement, and form, which are its proper objects as a sense. But in his treatise *On Perception*, he offers a different assessment:

> Of the faculties for the necessities of life, and in itself, sight is predominant; but for the mind, and indirectly, hearing is the most important... Indirectly, hearing makes the greatest contribution to intelligence. For reasoning speech is the cause of learning because it is audible, but it is audible not through itself, but indirectly, since speech is composed of words, and each word is a symbol.[65]

In Plato's allegory of the cave, Glaucon is at first invited to "see" the human beings chained in their prison (514a); at its conclusion, Socrates believes that it, and its interpretation, are what Glaucon is "keen to hear" (517b).

In his treatment of *opsis* in the *Poetics*, Aristotle is concerned with the objective sense(s) of the word, rather than with the faculty of sight.

Opsis, as the "visual effect" of theatrical production, is first introduced as a "part" of tragedy in chapter 6, but as one which commands a significant logical priority, as I have noted in the previous section:

> Since people acting create the imitation, it necessarily follows that the ordered arrangement of visual effect should be a part of tragedy; then the composition of songs and linguistic style, because it is in these media that they create the imitation.

This initial distinction corresponds to the division, later in chapter 6, between the single 'mode' (or "how they imitate") of *mimesis*, which is visual effect, and the two media (or "means by which they imitate"), which are the composition of songs and linguistic style. But despite this apparent priority, 'means' and 'mode' are subjected throughout the argument of the treatise to the three objects of *mimesis*: plot, character, and thought ("what they imitate"). These take precedence because they participate directly in the 'end' of tragedy, and because they also distinguish tragedy from other forms of *mimesis*, which might use visual effect (the "shapes and colours" of painting, for example: chapter 1, and chapter 6), or song and speech, as their mode or media. The result of this subordination is that language and song are reduced to the "pleasant seasonings" of what is determined, from chapter 6 forwards, to be an essential triad. The full definition of tragedy, which I abbreviated for the purposes of the earlier discussions (in sections 1.2.2 and 1.2.3 above), already includes this 'meat and sauce' metaphor:

> So tragedy is an imitation of a serious action brought to its end, one of some magnitude, in discourse which is pleasantly seasoned, with each kind of seasoning occurring in separate sections, with people acting, not a narrative report, accomplishing by means of pity and fear the purgation of the emotions of this kind.[66]

This rather allusive reference, which apparently relates to the language of spoken verse and song in their alternation throughout the play,[67] prepares for the later description of the composition of songs as the "greatest of the pleasant seasonings" of tragedy, at the close of chapter 6. Visual effect, for its part, is similarly complimented, but also dismissed:

> Visual effect is entrancing, but has least to do with artistic method, and is least germane to the art of poetic composition. For the power of tragedy exists without a production and without actors, and in addition

the art of the property-maker has greater influence over the elaboration of visual effect than the art of the poets.

The progress of the argument in chapter 6 marks a theoretical reduction of *opsis* from the primary visual mode of production to the construction of properties, a diminution which effectively excludes the term from serious consideration in the body of the treatise. Yet, initially, the "ordered arrangement of visual effect" (*opseos kosmos*) seems to refer to all that a spectator may see at any moment, while the primacy of *opsis* as the single mode of tragic *mimesis* points to the succession of specific moments throughout the duration of the performance. *Kosmos*, however, can carry both the solemn sense of a total and subsuming order, which might be implicit in a primary 'mode', and also the theoretically more trivial sense of decoration and embellishment. It is conceivable that this ambivalence permits the slide to the quality (and perhaps the range) of material and scenic objects (large and smaller properties, masks, and possibly the magnificence of costume) in the practical skills of the property-maker, or *skeuopoios*. But the full implications of *opsis* would refer to the art of the playwright and the producer, and of the actors themselves, in the disposition and movement of performers in the playing-spaces appropriate to tragedy. The closing formulation of chapter 6 is, in this respect, an abrupt dismissal, which permits theoretical attention to remain fixed on the imitated actions composed in the plot, and on their emotional effect on the audience.

Yet there are echoes of the wider implications of *opsis* later in the treatise. In the following discussion of an appropriate extent for the plot (chapter 7), the close relationship of questions of scale to the capacities of the human eye is carefully expressed in terms of a synchronic order: an object which can be assessed as beautiful must be neither too large nor too small for viewing. The term used for 'viewing' here is *theoria*, which is, in one of several applications, an appropriate term for the activity of *theatai* ('spectators') in the *theatron*, but which is also used, metaphorically, for the 'viewing' that constitutes theoretical comprehension. The discussion itself, in chapter 7, parallels this shift from the act of vision to the act of theory.[68] As the object is to the eye, so the plot is to the memory. Perception may be alluded to in relation to a synchronic disposition which forms a "visual effect", but theory, with the collusion of memory, is required for a diachronic succession such as a plot. Plot is by definition a theoretical object for Aristotle, which precludes any theoretical consideration of a succession of visual effects which might be implied in an "ordered arrangement".

Visual effect makes intermittent appearances in the main body of the treatise, but is generally subject to this suppression. There is an acknowledgement, in chapter 11, that recognitions may well be achieved by means of physical objects, and later (chapter 16) these include physical marks, but Aristotle is contemptuous of these material aids, which do not develop from the incidents themselves. This is also the tenor of the remarks on *opsis* and the emotions of fear and pity (chapter 14), which I abbreviated slightly in the opening of the previous section (1.2.3). The full text is as follows:

> Things that are frightening and pitiful can be created by visual effect, but they can also be created out of the arrangement of the actions, and this comes first, and is the mark of a better poet. For the plot should be put together in such a way that, even without looking, someone who is listening to the actions as they are happening will shudder with fear and feel pity at what is going on. Those would be the emotions of anyone listening to the story of Oedipus. To prepare this by means of visual effect is less artistically methodical, and requires the expense of production. Those who do not prepare what is frightening by means of visual effect, but merely what is monstrous, have no share in tragedy. For not every pleasure should be sought from tragedy, but only its proper one. Since the poet should by means of imitation prepare the pleasure that results from fear and pity, it is obvious that this must be produced in the actions [of the plot].

The suppression of visual effect in favour of the *muthos*, that which can be heard, amplifies the preference expressed in the relegation of *opsis* in chapter 6. Yet the visual aspect of action cannot satisfactorily be dismissed from the performance, or from the composition of tragedy:

> In composing the plots and working them out in conjunction with a linguistic style the tragedian must place everything in front of his eyes as much as he can. For in this way, seeing things as clearly as possible, as if he were himself present as the actions are occurring, he will find what looks and fits best, and avoid the opposite.   (ch. 17)

Aristotle chooses for his example here an appearance of a character from the scene-building which was misjudged by a tragic playwright, and found illogical or implausible by the audience. The disposal of characters in the playing-space intrudes into the successful composition of the succession of incidents, and physical expression and gesture are similarly invasive when it comes to the successful portrayal of emotion:

> As far as possible, the tragedian should work through his script using gestures. For of playwrights with the same natural ability, those who enter into the emotions are the most convincing: the man who is distressed creates distress most truthfully, and an angry man rages most truthfully.   (ch. 17)

To some extent, the dramatic script is understood to entail physical expression, as it evidently should direct and control the larger scale of movement in and out of the playing-space. The theoretical problem contained in the suppression of *opsis* is persistent, but it is never resolved.

For Plato, the *logos*—that reasoning speech which finds its perfected form in dialectic—has a unique access to the recall of the truth by the soul, but one which can only be adequately expressed through the self-negating metaphor of vision. For Aristotle, "reasoning speech is the cause of learning because it is audible" (*On Perception* 437a), and this formula confirms the priority afforded to the *muthos* in attaining the proper end of tragedy. Yet even in his discussions of fear and pity in the *Rhetoric*, Aristotle had admitted the role played in their constitution as emotions by *phantasia*, an "imagined appearance" of an impending evil (*Rhetoric* II.5.1 and 8.1). In *Theaetetus*, Plato had accepted that the soul uses the senses as channels through which it perceives, but he had, consistently, equated *phantasia* with appearance and so with opinion.[69] This acknowledgement, with its accompanying low estimate, was paralleled in *Philebus*, where the images and questions that accrue from observation are written down as propositions, like words on the book of the soul, and also drawn or painted, by a combination of memory and perception.[70]

By contrast Aristotle, in his treatise *On the Soul*, was inclined by the etymological links between *phantasia*, *phainesthai* (to 'appear'), and *phaos* ('light') to favour the predominance of sight as a faculty, in his persistent theoretical hesitation over the intellectual senses, and to conclude that thinking was dependent on these "imagined appearances" (*phantasmata*).[71] His general discussion in this treatise (*On the Soul* III.427–29) was exposed to further refinement in the later, and shorter treatise *On Memory and Recollection*, of which the second term in the title had fulfilled a crucial if unexamined role in Platonic philosophy. In an allusion to his general theory, Aristotle re-affirms "that it is impossible to think without a *phantasma*" (449), and on this basis asserts that memory "belongs to that part of the soul to which *phantasia* belongs" (450): if thinking was compared to "drawing a diagram" (449), then memory is a kind of "drawing from life", a *zographema* (450). Furthermore, the activity of recollection "is the search for a *phantasma* achieved in sensation"; and the annoyance people show when they fail confirms that recollection is, in some part, a physical activity (453).[72]

If Aristotle's partial emancipation of drama from its condemnation by Plato failed to question the inadequacy of *mimesis*, this is a particular failure engendered by a grander, and more imposing, academic inheritance. Sight is the metaphorical victim of the ascent to a transcendent vision of the truth in the impersonating dialogues of the founder of the Academy. The discursive *logos* of his meticulous student apparently had the means, but could not command the resolution, to dislodge the memory of the master. One result is the metaphysical tradition in European philosophy; a second, minor result is a restrictive theory of theatrical performance, constrained between a denial of its participation in truth, and a socially medicinal function in the translation of pains into pleasure. It is, according to your viewpoint, either an oppressive or an exhilarating legacy.

2

Performances of the Mind

Rousseau and Diderot

2.1 ROUSSEAU (1712–78)

Jean-Jacques Rousseau was born in Geneva in 1712, the son of a watchmaker and his wife Susanne. His mother died at his birth. Rousseau was brought up by his father and an aunt, and left Geneva as an adolescent, converting to Catholicism. He spent his life partly supported by a succession of patrons, earning his living from copying music, while he wrote extensively. His early interests lay in music, but an association with writers such as Diderot encouraged a series of speculative works, culminating in the educational and political treatises, *Émile* and *On the Social Contract*.[1]

The youthful conversion to Catholicism is directly associated in the *Confessions* with the sensuality and instabilities of freedom in his adolescent 'escape' to France from Geneva.[2] But in later life, the question of religious creed became secondary to the problems of identity and citizenship, and Rousseau renounced Catholicism in favour of Geneva in 1754, although he failed to take up residence in the city. This contrast between the home he had left and the uncertain tracts of the cultural landscape into which his ambition had drawn him haunted him as he composed the *Confessions* in the 1760s. In the conclusion to the first book there is an almost Platonic insistence on the virtue of a single skill, and its capacity to locate the subject in a series of firm, patriarchal identities:

> Nothing was more suited to my temperament, nor more likely to make me happy, than the peaceful and obscure state of a craftsman, above all in certain classes, like that of the engravers at Geneva. This state... would have confined me to my sphere without offering me any means of leaving it ... I should have passed a sweet and peaceful life in the bosom of my religion, my country, my family and my friends, of the kind required by my character, in the uniformity of work that was to my taste and a society after my own heart. I should have been a good Christian, a good citizen, a good father, a good friend, a good tradesman, a good man in everything...
> But instead of that, what a picture I have to paint! [VO 46–7][3]

At the opening of the second part of the *Confessions*, Rousseau returns to this idea of the *tableau*, the picture. He fears that his grief will oppress him and the reader, and make him unable to "make pleasing pictures and give them an attractive colouring" [VO 324]. But if the *tableaux* cannot be "pleasing" or "attractive", they must be animated by another means, and both parts of the *Confessions* declare unequivocally that this is *sentiment*. "Feeling" has the capacity to construct a narrative and to act as a substitute for the factual record in composing a life. The *Confessions* are a species of recall, and at the beginning of the seventh book Rousseau regrets the loss of all the relevant documents, relying instead on his "one faithful guide", which is "the chain of feelings which have marked the succession of my being" [VO 322]. This priority of *sentiment* has an almost theoretical value in relation to the *Confessions*, and provides an authoritative assurance of truth. In the first book, the pivotal statement is "I feel my own heart, and I know human beings", which offers a definitive interpretation of the opening declaration that "I want to show to my equals a man in all the truth of nature..." [VO 3]. The priority of feeling is also established in terms of personal growth: "I felt before I thought...", and "I had no idea of things, at a time when all feelings were already known to me. I had conceived of nothing, I had felt everything." [VO 7–8]. The advertisement stands as a contradiction of the traditional Cartesian emphasis on thought, and is offered to the reader as an enticement to the emotive scenes of Rousseau's narrative.

One incident in particular seems definitive, for the child whose maturity can be so insistent on feeling, in providing an indication of the Geneva to which Rousseau chose to address several of his major discourses. His closest childhood friendship was with his cousin Bernard, and this kept him for the most part "highly occupied at home, and not tempted even to go out into the road...". There was, however, one colourful exception:

> An Italian showman came to Geneva, called Gamba-Corta; we went to see him, and then had no wish to go again; but he had puppets, and we set ourselves to make puppets. His puppets played a kind of comedy, and we created comedies for ours. Lacking any skill, we mimicked from deep in our throats the voice of Pulcinella, in performances of these charming comedies which our poor, good parents had the patience to listen to and watch. But one day my uncle Bernard read to the family a fine sermon in his style; we left off writing comedies, and set ourselves to compose sermons. These details are not very interesting, I admit; but they show the degree to which our first education must have been well directed... [VO 26–7]

There is something disingenuously programmatic in this mature recollection, with its solemn memory—the boys "had no wish to go again"—of an infectious enthusiasm. Well before starting on the *Confessions*, and after a successful involvement with the comic opera in Paris, Rousseau had defended his native Geneva from the corrupting influence of foreign theatre in his *Letter to d'Alembert on Public Performances*. I shall discuss this *Letter* in detail in section 2.1.2 below; but before that I should like to consider briefly the temptations that the French academies offered to this supposedly precocious, sermonizing tendency.

2.1.1 The degenerative arts in Rousseau's academic *Discourses*[4]

As a young man attempting to impress others with standard social skills, Rousseau was embarrassed by his inability to read music at sight:

> Fundamentally, I had a strong knowledge of music; I only lacked that liveliness in reading at sight which I have never had in anything and which can only be acquired in music by continual practice.
> [VO 244]

The problem seems to have haunted him, and in his first serious venture at a sustained residence in Paris in 1741–2 he attempted to remove this symbolic obstacle to social integration with a paper on musical notation, which he presented to the Academy of Sciences. The subsequent publishing project was not a success, and in 1743 Rousseau left Paris in what proved to be an untenable position as secretary to the French ambassador in Venice.

As an act of social and intellectual integration, the initiative resulting in the *Project Concerning New Symbols for Music* was of limited value, but it did bring Rousseau to the attention of Denis Diderot.[5] The nascent friendship was confirmed on Rousseau's return to Paris in 1744, and Diderot later engaged Rousseau to write on musical subjects for the *Encyclopédie*, of which he had become joint editor with the mathematician d'Alembert in 1747.[6] As editor, Diderot was to encounter recurrent hostility from influential sources, to an extent that was rarely personally threatening. But his brief, if relatively civilized, confinement in the Donjon de Vincennes outside Paris in 1749 upset both Rousseau and Diderot profoundly, and also served as a decisive stimulus to Rousseau's ambitions as a controversialist. Rousseau's visits to the Chateau de Vincennes became a repeated pilgrimage, and in the course of one of them, resting briefly from the excessive summer heat, Rousseau read in the periodical *Mercure de France* of the subject proposed by the Academy of Dijon for its prize essay of the following year. The title for the essay took the form of an evenly balanced question of suitable sobriety: "Has the Restoration of the Arts and Sciences Contributed More to the Corruption or the Purification of Morals?"[7] Yet Rousseau's claim, in the *Confessions*, was that he was in a state of extreme excitement and agitation when he reached Vincennes, and that his inclination to write on the subject was fatefully encouraged and confirmed by Diderot. The *Discourse on the Sciences and the Arts*, to give the work its abbreviated title, was submitted, and won the prize in 1750; when printed, it seems to have satisfied every possible requirement on the part of its author for reputation.

A learned argument in favour of ignorance was the paradox favoured by Rousseau, sustained by the assertion that the arts and sciences help civilized peoples to "the appearance of all the virtues, without being in possession of one of them".

> Rich clothes may indicate a wealthy man, and elegance a man of taste; the man who is healthy and robust may be recognized by different marks. It is under the rustic smock of the labourer, not the gilt of the courtier, that we shall find physical strength and vigour.
>
> [G/R 8][8]

Drawn from this apparently social antithesis, the body can then be made to serve as a metaphor for the moral condition:

> The good man is an athlete, who delights in fighting naked; he despises all those worthless ornaments, which inhibit the full use of his strength,

> and most of which were invented only to hide some deformity. [ibid.]

The logical inference from the position expressed in this imagery is that a lack of covering must precede artifice, and that in the absence of the "worthless ornaments" of culture human nature and human morals were revealed without distortion to the eye.

> Before art had shaped our manners, and taught our passions to speak an affected language, our morals were rustic but natural; and the difference in conduct indicated at the first glance the difference of character. Human nature was not at bottom better then, but men found their security in the ease with which they could see through each other, and this advantage, of which we no longer sense the value, spared them many vices. [ibid.]

The sophistication of society is identified with dissemblance, and this degeneration is attributed to the advance of the arts and sciences. The logic is curious: Egypt, Greece, Rome, and Byzantium are judged by their indulgence of the arts and sciences and by their ultimate collapse, and submission to slavery, rather than by their long survival. The arts and sciences provide a degenerate scheme of cultural history whose authenticity can be judged by its results. The origin of the sciences lies in the vices:

> Astronomy was born of superstition, eloquence of ambition, hatred, flattery, and mendacity; geometry of avarice; physics of an idle curiosity; all of them, even moral science, of human pride. The arts and sciences owe their birth to our vices; we should be less in doubt about their advantages, if they had owed their birth to our virtues. [G/R 17]

There is little directly on the arts in the *Discourse on the Sciences and the Arts*, but what little there is is distinctive. If learning is opposed to virtue, as "worthless ornaments" are opposed to the virile body of the athlete, it follows that those artists who create "when learning is in fashion" may be readily accused on the same line of argument of catering to a cultural effeminacy. This rhetorical figure is transferred by Rousseau into a social critique of his own times. What will the young artist do, if he is born into an age

> when men have sacrificed their taste to tyrants of their liberty, and one sex dares to approve only of what is proportionate to the pusillanimity of the other; when masterpieces of dramatic poetry are disregarded, and wonders of harmony are scorned? [G/R 21]

The offence to women is meant to be withdrawn in an accompanying footnote:

> I am far from thinking that this ascendancy of women is an evil in itself. It is a gift which nature has provided for the happiness of humankind. If better directed, it might produce as much good as it now does evil. We are insufficiently aware of what advantage would arise in society from a better education for that half of humankind which governs the other. Men will always be what pleases women. So if you want them to be great and virtuous, teach women what greatness of soul and virtue are.   [ibid.]

Rousseau's degenerative historical scheme suggests the possibility of a theoretical regression to a state of simplicity and transparent morality. But it is also allied, quite evidently, to the tradition of comparisons between European explorers and colonists and the peoples encountered by them. Relying on this source, the proposition of simplicity can dissolve from an evocative image to a resumption of an invigorated, primitivist argument:

> We cannot reflect on morals without recalling with pleasure the image of the simplicity of the earliest times. This is like a beautiful shoreline, dressed only by the hands of nature; to which our eyes are constantly turned, and which we see receding with regret.   [G/R 22]

The conclusion of the *Discourse* is the resolution of its initial problem, a rhetorical solution entailed by the academic argument in favour of ignorance, and the method chosen is the reliable rhetorical resource of sustained and appropriate flattery of the Academy.

The controversial success of this prize essay was followed by a period of considerable involvement with the theatre, which was terminated by another controversy. Rousseau had been greatly impressed, while in Italy, by the light comedy of the *opera buffa*, and was encouraged by the enthusiasm of a friend to consider "how one might proceed to give an idea of a drama of this kind in France" [VO 443–44]. The resultant *Devin du village* was quickly composed, and in 1752 was taken up for performance at Court in the palace of Fontainebleau. It was staged again, in the following year, in Paris, when Rousseau also presented his comedy *Narcisse*, written many years earlier, at the Comédie Française. *Narcisse* failed in the theatre, but Rousseau countered this rejection by publication, with the addition of a preface defending himself from criticism, and attempting to reconcile his position as a theatrical author with the critique of the arts advanced in his prize-winning essay.[9] Here Rousseau suggests that the purpose of theatrical writing is to provide a distraction from worse activities, an objective which the theatre could share with the Academies, colleges, universities and libraries:

> It is not a matter of inducing people to be good, one need only distract them from being bad; they must be preoccupied with trifles if they are to be turned from bad actions; they must be amused, not given a sermon.[10]

According to the *Préface*, in a state of corruption music and theatrical performances may at least act to defend a range of threatened moral values, which are apparently collapsing through the degeneracy of men:

> I should think myself happy to have a play to hiss at every day, if I could at this price contain during two hours the evil designs of one single spectator, and save the honour of the daughter or of the wife of his friend, the secret of his confidant, or the fortune of his creditor. Since there are no longer any morals, one must think only of refinement; and we know well enough that music and theatrical performances are two of its most important instruments.[11]

The *Discourse on the Origin of Inequality* is the second of the major academic treatises, or the third if the proposal on musical notation is included. In composing it, Rousseau responded to the question set by the Academy of Dijon for its prize essay for 1754: "What Is the Origin of Inequality Among Men, and Is It Authorized by Natural Law?". Unsuccessful in the competition, it was later published in Holland in 1755, with a dedication to the Republic of Geneva. From the beginning, Rousseau maintains a critical and problematic approach, which casts doubt on the concept, advanced in theories of natural law, of "the state of nature".

> The philosophers, who have examined the foundations of society, have all felt the need to go back as far as a state of nature; but not one of them has got there.   [G/R 132]

This critical rigour insists on the replacement of a theoretical history by more appropriate hypotheses:

> Let us start by discarding all facts, because they do not affect the question. One must not take the researches which must be entered into on this subject for historical truths, but only as hypothetical and

conditional arguments: more suited to clarifying the nature of things than to showing an actual origin, and similar to those which our physicists make every day on the formation of the world.
[G/R 132–33]

By this insistence, "natural man" becomes far more readily a term in a non-historical theoretical discourse, whose only certainty of reference can be to the state of human beings in contemporary society. The *Discourse* will, almost inevitably, be a critique, rather than a validating document:

> It is, so to speak, the life of your species which I am going to describe to you according to the qualities you have been granted, which your education and your habits may have depraved, but have not entirely destroyed.   [ibid.]

This merely theoretical hypothesis of natural man can draw with conviction on analogies with tribes and societies discovered in the movement of colonialism, and Rousseau's 'wild man' participates in an extensive history of speculation and critique that stretches from Herodotus and Tacitus in antiquity through to Montaigne and Hobbes.[12] For Rousseau, the hypothetical image is of a solitary and dispersed creature, who would satisfy rather than gratify appetites. Wild animals are more vigorous than the domestic:

> So it is with man as well; in becoming sociable and a slave, he becomes weak, frightened, and servile; and his soft and effeminate way of life manages to weaken at one and the same time his strength and courage.   [G/R 139]

Self-preservation is "almost his sole care", and "seeing and feeling will be his first state":

> The only goods he recognizes in the universe are food, a female, and sleep: the only evils he fears are pain and hunger.   [G/R 143]

The reflections on the eventual origins of languages in the *Discourse* are, by Rousseau's determination, also reflections on the origins of thought:

> Let us pass over for the moment the immense distance which must exist between the pure state of nature and the need for languages; and, supposing languages to be necessary, let us look and see how they could begin to be established. A new difficulty, worse than the last; for

> if humans need speech in order to learn how to think, they must have been in greater need of knowing how to think in order to be able to discover the art of speech. [G/R 147][13]

With this formulation Rousseau, consistently with his general scheme, accepts the inscrutability of the historical origins of communication, and substitutes a series of hypotheses. "The first language of humanity ... is the cry of nature", which was gradually varied by inflexion, and by the addition of gesture. The development of language beyond that point and its infinite complexities belie close description or investigation.

In principle, Rousseau is insistent that his theoretical natural state of dispersion, and instinctive reversion to solitude, was self-sufficient:

> In fact, it is impossible to imagine why, in this primitive state, one man should be more in need of another man, than a monkey or wolf of another of its species: or, supposing that need did exist, what motive could induce that other to attend to him; or, even then, in this last case, how could they agree the conditions between themselves.
> [G/R 151]

This insistence is partly intended as a refutation of the negative view of the state of nature advanced by Thomas Hobbes in *The Leviathan*.[14] But Rousseau also affirms the existence of an internal control:

> There is in addition another principle which Hobbes has not perceived; which, having been granted to humanity to mitigate, on certain occasions, the ferocity of self-love, or, before its birth, the desire of self-preservation, tempers the ardour which he has for his own well-being by an innate repugnance at seeing a fellow-creature suffer. I think I need not fear contradiction in according to human beings the only natural virtue which even the most extreme detractor of human virtues was forced to recognize. I am speaking of pity... [G/R 154]

Pity "precedes the use of all reflection", and Rousseau's most vivid example is of a *tableau* which he draws from a contemporary satirical fable:[15]

> the pathetic image of a man who sees outside his place of confinement a ferocious animal snatching a child from its mother's breast, breaking its feeble limbs between its teeth, and ripping with its claws at the child's palpitating entrails. What frightful agitation must this witness of the scene experience, although he himself has no stake in it

personally! What anxieties must he suffer at this sight, in his inability to bring help to the fainting mother, and the dying infant!

The pure movement of nature, which is prior to all reflection, is like that; the force of natural pity, which the most depraved morals have still to destroy, is like that. For one sees every day at our theatrical performances the kind of man who, while softening and crying at the sufferings of some unfortunate, would redouble the torments imposed on his enemy were he himself in the position of the tyrant.

[G/R 154–55]

The theatrical qualities of Rousseau's illustrations hardly need emphasizing, but it is noticeable that his 'ideal' spectator in the first instance is, categorically, removed from the possibility of action and intervention. This contrasts forcibly with the two classical examples with which Rousseau immediately follows his reference to the theatre, and which are both drawn from the classical author, Plutarch. The Roman general and dictator, Sulla, who sacked the Greek city of Corinth and led his army against the Roman senate, was preposterously "sensitive to evils he had not caused", and the tyrant Alexander of Pheros

> did not dare to take his seat at the performance of any tragedy, for fear of being seen to grieve with Andromache and Priam, while he could listen without emotion to the cries of so many citizens butchered daily on his orders. [G/R 155] [16]

The degeneration expressed in the description of theatrical performances (*spectacles*) is located in the person of the spectator, who is assumed to be inclined to depraved action, although the quality of pity itself has not suffered corruption. By this problematic and complex juxtaposition of illustrations Rousseau asserts the continuity of the natural impulse, without exposing to analysis the process of degeneration. The effectiveness of the social critique lies in the careful preselection of a "ferocious animal" rather than a human being as the dramatic 'beast' in the primary *tableau*.

Rousseau equates pity (*pitié*) with compassion (*commisération*), and from this one emotion he derives "generosity, clemency, humanity", and "benevolence and friendship". A feeling which "puts us in the place of the person who is suffering" may well dispense with reason, by identifying subject and object:

> In fact, compassion will be that much more energetic the more intimately the animal spectator identifies himself with the animal

> sufferer. Now it is evident that this identification must be infinitely more tight in the state of nature than in the state of reasoning. [ibid.]

From this point, Rousseau directs an attack upon reason:

> It is reason which engenders self-love, and it is reflection which strengthens it; it is reason which divides man from everything which upsets or afflicts him. [G/R 156]

In a lengthy footnote which accompanied his first introduction of the terms "self-love" (*amour propre*) and pity, Rousseau had effectively defined self-love by the contrast drawn between it and self-interest (*amour de soi*), which is the motive force in self-preservation:

> Self-love must not be confused with self-interest, two very different passions in their nature and in their effects. Self-interest is a natural feeling which leads every animal to be alert to self-preservation, and which, directed in man by reason and modified by pity, creates humanity and virtue. Self-love is a purely relative and factitious feeling, one born in society, which leads each individual to make more of himself than of any one else, which is the cause in men of all the harm they inflict on each other, and is the true source of the 'sense of honour'. This being understood, I say that in our primitive state, in the true state of nature, self-love did not exist; for as each man regarded himself as the only spectator watching his actions, as the only being in the universe who took any interest in him, and as the only judge of his actual merits, no feeling which had its origin in comparisons he had not been led to make could germinate in his soul... [G/R 219]

If natural pity accomplishes the *identification* of subject with object, then, as an emotion, it is the counterpart to the civilized *comparison* of subject with subject. Pity is also theoretically engaged in the series of unique subjects that constitutes observation in the state of nature. What these subjects observe are their own objective actions, or the objective world of 'otherness'; in the socialized world of "self-love", the subject reflects uncomfortably on the condition of being an object for others.

The first part of the *Discourse on the Origin of Inequality* is devoted to the definition of a hypothetical state of nature which contrasts with the contemporary, civilized state. So in the conclusion to the argument Rousseau confronts the problem of sexual passion, *amour*, which might seem in its violence to escape the constraints imposed by self-interest, and pity or compassion. Rousseau's solution is to pose a division between what he terms "the moral and the physical in the feeling of love": the physical urges sexual union, while "the moral part is that which determines and fixes this desire exclusively on a single object" [G/R 157–58]. As in the first *Discourse*, Rousseau's negative and passive view of women ascribes subject-status to the male in composing the required theoretical formula:

> Now it is easy to see that the moral part of love is a factitious feeling, born of social usage, and solemnized by women with much ingenuity and care to establish their empire, and give dominion to the sex that ought to obey. [G/R 158]

Sexual discrimination is associated with the mechanism of comparison, which is the major component of *amour-propre*. Natural man, in Rousseau's theory of contradiction, finds every woman equal to his purpose:

> The imagination, which causes such ravages among us, never speaks to the heart of savages; each waits quietly for the impulse of nature, yields to it involuntarily with more pleasure than frenzy, and with the satisfaction of the need the desire is extinguished. So it is incontestable that even love, just like all the other passions, acquired in society that impetuous intensity which makes it so often disastrous to human beings. [ibid.]

Even the most powerful of the passions does not entail the formation of society.

The impulse to social formation, which Rousseau has already briefly introduced under the term *perfectibilité*, is the subject of the second part of the *Discourse*. Although Rousseau polemically identifies the claim to property as the foundation of civil society, and consequently as the source of inequality, the general context for the process of socialization is clearly an expansion of the human population:

> In proportion to the spread of the human race, difficulties multiplied for human beings. [G/R 165]

The erosion of the solitary life of the theoretical and individual natural subject of the first part of the *Discourse* brings with it physical juxtaposition, and stimulates the faculty of comparison. Both language and 'comparison' suffered stimulation from the nuclear social life of the family, and social life found its expression in idle congregations:

> They accustomed themselves to assemble before their huts or around a large tree; singing and dancing, the true children of love and leisure, became the amusement or rather the occupation of a crowd of idle men and women.   [G/R 169]

Dance and song are the 'occupations of idleness', "the true children of love and leisure", and assemblies of this kind enhanced and complicated individual comparison by creating the conventions of public opinion:

> Whoever sang or danced best, whoever was the most handsome, the strongest, the most dexterous, or the most eloquent, became the most respected; and this was the first step towards inequality, and at the same time towards vice. From these first preferences arose on the one side vanity and contempt and on the other shame and envy: and the fermentation caused by these new leavens finally produced compounds that were disastrous for innocence and happiness.   [G/R 169–70]

The conclusion to the *Discourse*, which follows an extended discussion of the effects of property, inheritance, law and government, returns with the benefits of detailed argument to the theoretical division between civilized and hypothetical, 'natural' man. The careful and curious reader must be struck by "the immense distance which separates the two states", and he will find himself able to solve "a vast number of problems of morals and politics":

> In a word, he will explain how the soul and the human passions gradually alter, changing, so to speak, their nature; why our needs and our pleasures in the long run rely on changed objects; and why, the original man having vanished by degrees, society now only offers to the wise man's eyes an assembly of artificial men and factitious passions, which are the work of all these new relations, and which have no true foundation in nature.   [G/R 192]

The "assembly of artificial men and factitious passions" is the product of "all these new relations", and together they constitute society".

> This is, in fact, the true cause of all these differences: the savage lives within himself, the social man is permanently outside himself, and only knows how to live in the opinion of others, and it is, so to speak, solely from their judgement that he derives the feeling of his own existence.   [G/R 193]

The final assertion is placed here in "permanently", "only" and "solely", because Rousseau—although he declines to do so—professes to be able to show that there is no moral interior to this constant and unbroken social exterior.

2.1.2 The *Letter to d'Alembert* [17]

If the academic essay proved the most effective means to intellectual integration for Rousseau, then it was the intellectual ambition represented by the *Encyclopédie* that provoked him to gather his thoughts into a specific critique of the theatre as a cultural institution. In 1755 Voltaire had moved to an estate at Les Délices, outside Geneva, and d'Alembert as co-editor of the *Encyclopédie* had gone to Geneva to research an article on the city he was preparing to write for the seventh volume. When he received his copy late in 1757, Rousseau was disturbed by d'Alembert's advocacy of Voltaire's scheme for the establishment of a theatre in the Republic, an institution banned from Geneva by statutes dating from 1617.[18] Rousseau's acute sense of national identity, and his increasing estrangement from Diderot, made a public response to d'Alembert virtually inevitable.[19] The apparently relaxed scheme of an open letter does permit a considerable degree of influence from rhetorical models of defence and accusation in argument. In an ideal sense, Rousseau is defending his city, and his discussion of the proposal is, from its beginning, an accusation of the moral and social institution of theatre. In the first section of the *Letter* Rousseau defines the nature of theatre, then subjects it to an examination, and concludes this discussion with a refutation of the claims made on its behalf as a beneficial institution. But although the *Letter to d'Alembert* maintains some characteristics of an academic discourse, strongly influenced by an assumed and idealized rhetorical debate (on the welfare and moral continuity of an independent, republican city), it is liberally disordered by a variety of acknowledged digressions, and extended by considerations of practical and monetary issues, and by a set of alternative proposals.

Rousseau's first step is to define a *spectacle* as an entertainment, an *amusement*, and to suggest that amusements are only welcomed or permitted if they are necessary. "A father, a son, a husband, a citizen" has his duties, with little time for boredom, and "a good conscience extinguishes the taste for frivolous pleasures" [L 65; F 20].

> But it is self-dissatisfaction, the weight of inactivity, the neglect of simple and natural tastes which makes an alien amusement so necessary. I do not accept that one has any need to attach one's heart incessantly to the stage, as if it were ill at ease inside us.
> [L 66; F 21]

The use of the word *étranger*, which I have translated as "alien", allows Rousseau to associate the external, spectatorial amusement of theatre with the impact of an institution that is foreign to the native culture of Geneva. The determination of what is necessary for a people will be achieved by a consideration of social effects: public performances abound in variety, and so do the moral constitutions of 'peoples'. By implication, no one institution is universally appropriate for all, and, against the monocultural imperatives assumed by Voltaire and d'Alembert, Rousseau advances an assertion of cultural relativity and pluralism.

In the historical context of an elaborate but by now rather exhausted debate between pleasure or moral instruction as the justifying objective of theatre, Rousseau has no hesitation in associating the broader category of *spectacles* with entertainment:

> As to the species 'public performances', it is necessarily the pleasure that they give, and not their usefulness, which defines it. If usefulness can be found in them, so well and good; but the principal object is to please, and, so long as the people is amused by them, this objective has been sufficiently achieved. [L 68; F 23]

But what follows from this is ominous. Nations vary in their tastes; in order to please them, the kinds of public performances required will be those that favour their inclinations, rather than those which might moderate them. The theatre is, in general, "a picture of the human passions", and the "painter" is bound to "flatter these passions", to show them in a good light, and in this to "follow the feeling of the public" [L 68–9; F 23–4]. The conclusion to this initial argument has its origins with Plato, and is meant to be damning in its cynicism:

> Reason alone is good for nothing on the stage. A man without passions, or one who constantly dominates them, would not know how to interest anyone; and it has already been remarked that a Stoic in tragedy would be an unbearable character; in comedy, he would make people laugh, all the more. [L 69; F 24]

The overtly Platonic allusions of this section of the argument are undoubtedly the results of the time Rousseau devoted to composing a narrative résumé of the arguments of *Republic* 10, which he entitled *On Theatrical Imitation: An Essay Drawn from the Dialogues of Plato*.[20] In the 'advertisement' to this short and unassuming work, which was published at a later date than the *Letter*, Rousseau dates its execution to the time of the composition of the *Letter*:

> The occasion of this work was the letter to M. d'Alembert on public performances: but finding myself unable to include it there with ease, I put it aside to be employed elsewhere, or to be completely discarded.[21]

In the *Letter*, Rousseau proceeds with relative ease from his general thesis that the theatre must follow public taste to a derisive contradiction of the Aristotelian doctrine of *katharsis*:

> I know that the poetics of theatre pretends to achieve the contrary, and to purge the passions in exciting them; but I have difficulty in conceiving this rule. Would the argument be that, in order to become temperate and wise, one must begin by being furious and mad?
> [L 71–2; F 26]

Similarly, what is, in an Aristotelian poetics, described as "pity" bears little relation to the "natural feeling" described so vividly in the *Discourse*:

> I hear it said that tragedy leads to pity by terror; perhaps, but what is this pity? An emotion that is fleeting and useless, which lasts no longer than the illusion which has produced it; the remainder of a natural feeling which is soon extinguished by the passion; a sterile pity which feeds on a few tears, and has never produced the least act of humanity. [L 78; F 32]

This is, marginally, a more pessimistic view of the contemporary theatrical emotion than was presented in the *Discourse*, where the instinct of pity was still active even in the spectator who, in reality, "would redouble the torments imposed on his enemy" by the dramatic tyrant. But the theatrical spectator is, in both arguments, representative of the depravity or degeneration of morals and of the "natural feeling" of pity, and the compatibility of the *Discourse* and the *Letter* is confirmed by the repetition of the two classical examples of ruthless hypocrisy drawn from Plutarch, Sulla and Alexander of Pheros.[22] The tears of the theatrical spectator cost him nothing, because in his reception of "beautiful actions in fables" no action is demanded of him. The theatre deals in distance, which is apparent in its conventions and material form as well as in its subject-matter:

> The theatre has its rules, its maxims, its separate morals, as well as its own language and clothing. It is well observed that nothing of all that is suitable for us, and one would believe oneself to be as ridiculous in adopting the virtues of its heroes as in speaking in verse, and in putting on a Roman costume.   [L 80; F 34]

Rousseau's specific dramatic criticism is strongly affected by his sense of the failure of both dominant forms of drama to achieve an appropriate perfection which would be consonant with "public utility". In reviews of tragedies by Crébillon (*Atrée* and *Thyeste*) and Voltaire (*Mahomet*), he emphasizes the distance between tragic elevation with its remote heroes and the humanity of the contemporary audience, and in his extended critical appreciation of Molière's comedy *The Misanthrope* he expresses a profound indignation that a figure of high moral quality should be subject to ridicule. The consistency of moral portrayal demanded by Alceste's "ardent love of virtue" is defeated by the need "to make the pit laugh", and so *The Misanthrope* is flawed by the "alien ridicule" which the author has given to its leading character [L 106; F 57]. The unavoidable conclusion to this train of argument is that even this most admirable comedy, "which contains the best and most healthy moral values", is controlled by the author's intention "to please corrupt spirits" [L 109–10; F 59]. These "corrupt spirits" are readily identified as "a debauched youth and women without morals" [L 110; F 60], and the moral lack and degradation implanted in this definition lead without difficulty to the idea of decadence. For Rousseau, this is the best way to understand the introduction of love-interest into both tragedy and comedy, and "since Molière and Corneille one sees nothing succeed in the theatre except romances, which pass under the name of plays" [L 113; F 63].

The critique of *amour* in French drama is almost as old as the establishment of the *Académie Française*, whose first official publication in 1637 was prompted by concern over the supposed indecency and classical impropriety of Corneille's *Le Cid*. For Rousseau, "love is the reign of women", who are its legislators, and a theatre conceived to include a love-interest will extend "the empire of the female sex, and make women and young girls the preceptors of the public" [L 113; F

63].²³ The high moral tone that Rousseau adopts after this opening is matched, predictably enough, by vituperation and further misogyny:

> The most charming object of nature, the most capable of moving a feeling heart and of turning it towards goodness is, I avow, a woman who is lovable and virtuous; but where does this heavenly object hide itself? Is it not cruel to contemplate it with pleasure in the theatre, yet to find such different objects in society? [L 113; F 63]

Antiquity praised the anonymity and obscurity of women:

> With us, to the contrary, the woman who has the highest reputation is she who makes the most noise; she whom people most discuss; she whom one sees most often in the world; at whose residence one dines most often; who passes judgement, settles matters, decides, pronounces, assigns to talents, to merit, to the virtues their degrees and order; whose favour men of learning, in humility, most abjectly implore.
> [L 115; F 65]

In the opinion of Rousseau, this is the result of a theatrical emphasis on *amour*, which reverses the "natural relations" between the sexes, giving "the ascendant to women over men" [L 116; F 66]. Similarly, an insistent love-interest leads to the subordination of the old, who in the theatre may only be hateful through their opposition to a love-intrigue, or become amorous themselves, and so ridiculous [L 117; F 66]. The proposition that the theatre may "cure us of love by painting its weaknesses" is preposterous: love "seduces, or it is not itself" [L 125; F 74]. The diatribe against *amour* concludes Rousseau's disabling of the conventional forms of French drama, which he regards as being "without any sort of real utility". As a public amusement, the theatre is driven by its need to favour the inclinations of its audience:

> The continual emotions which we feel there enervate us, enfeeble us, make us incapable of resisting our passions; and the sterile interest that we take in virtue serves only to satisfy our self-love, without constraining us to put virtue into practice. [L 128; F 76]

The second part of the *Letter* is dominated by a discursive move from what Rousseau regards as the "necessary" effects of theatre as drama to a consideration of the effects of its institution at Geneva. The definition of public performances as "amusements" encourages a consideration of their value in relation to "the nature of the occupations which they interrupt" [L 129; F 77]:

> Reason demands that one favours the amusements of people whose occupations are harmful, and that one turns away from the same amusements those whose whose occupations are useful.
> [L 130; F 77]

In a large city, the depravity of many in the population might recommend "two hours a day stolen from the activity of vice", but in small towns the case is different. In a small town there is greater industry stemming from "more original spirits", because in that setting each is "less of an imitator, having fewer models, draws more on himself, and puts more of himself into everything he does" [L133; F 80]. It is at this point that Rousseau begins to reveal the ambiguity he means to exploit in the word *spectacle*, and to substitute the personal vision of the theorist for the collective attention of the theatrical audience. A direct derivative of the Latin, *spectacle* like *spectaculum* is what is open to the sight of the *spectateur*, notably as an organized 'show' or theatrical production. But the presentation of the 'sight' may not be institutional, and may be organized through discourse:

> I remember having seen in my youth in the neighbourhood of Neuchâtel a sight that was particularly pleasing and perhaps unique on the earth. A mountain entirely covered with dwellings of which each was the centre of the land which depended on it; the effect was that these houses, at distances from each other which were as equal as the fortunes of their proprietors, offered at one and the same time to the numerous inhabitants of this mountain the calm of seclusion, and the charm of society.   [L 133; F 80–81]

This ideal community exists without recourse to the individual skills of artisans, in the curious assertion that "all are everything to themselves, none is anything for another", and as they build their own houses so these artisans also create their own relaxing activities. Recreations include inventing and designing, playing the flute and singing: "one of their most frequent amusements is singing psalms in four parts with their wives and children" [L 135; F 82]. The vision encompasses an interior, and a timescale of seasons in succession, and provides the evocative ground for a contrast in *spectacles*:

> After this light idea, let us suppose that on the summit of the mountain of which I have just spoken, in the centre of the dwellings, one were to establish a fixed and inexpensive public performance... and let us find out what would result from its establishment.   [L 136; F 83]

The conclusions are decisive: there would be, as results, less work, more expense, a gradual exodus from an increasingly expensive region, the imposition of taxes to create suitable access (new roads), and emulation between the inhabitants in dress, notably women's dress. For Rousseau, the contrast in *spectacles* confirms a theoretical paradox: for corrupt people, an institutional *spectacle* may be good, but for a morally sound people it is demonstrably the reverse.

It is hardly surprising, in this general context of disapproval, that Rousseau draws on the standard topic of the immorality and corrupting influence of the players themselves.[24] There is a passing reference to "this scandalous mixing of men and women" in contemporary performance, which was avoided by the Greeks, and the moral objection is given a theoretical dimension:

> What is the talent of the actor? The art of disguising himself, of assuming a character other than his own, of appearing different from oneself, of becoming impassioned in cold blood, of saying something other than one thinks as naturally as if one were really thinking it, and ultimately of forgetting one's own place from continually taking that of another.   [L 163; F 106]

The contrast between this definition of the actor and the portrayal of the inhabitants of Neuchâtel is absolute: the member of the Neuchâtel community is himself, the actor is not. The diatribe against the acting profession gains particular force in the discussion of the role of actresses, an institution which Rousseau is convinced contradicts a list of distinctions between the sexes, which his rhetorical fervour hastens to ascribe to 'nature'. For the theorist, "there are no good morals for women outside of a life of retirement and domesticity" [L 168; F 110], and the concept of the non-theatrical *spectacle* is deployed for a second time to reinforce this assertion:

> Is there in the world a sight as touching, as respectable as that of a mother of the family surrounded by her children, regulating the work of her servants, procuring for her husband a happy life, and governing the household wisely? It is there that she shows herself in all the dignity of an honest woman...   [L 175–76; F 117]

The expansive rhetoric that follows is automatic and trite enough, and it leads forward to a final description of actresses in terms which are intended to suggest that their profession is an absolute alternative to the continued existence of domestic virtue:

> Returning now to our actresses, I ask how a status whose unique object is to show oneself in public and, what is worse, to show oneself for money could be suitable for honest women, and could be compatible in them with modesty and good morals? [L 179; F 120]

If the attack on the morals and moral influence of performers totally lacks any redeeming features of originality, then the concluding section of the *Letter* is remarkable for its practical sociology of the theatre and public gatherings. The fundamental contrast between the resources and requirements of the large city and the small community is re-established with specific comparisons and calculations, and subsequently given the detail that only a local knowledge could supply. Initially, Rousseau is insistent on numbers and scale: Geneva has a population of only 24,000, and is expected to be able to support a theatre. Yet Lyons, some five or six times the size of Geneva, is host to only one theatre, and Paris with its 600,000 inhabitants supports just three. Precise calculations on the size of the audience, and the list of unavoidable expenses, render a self-supporting institution out of the question, and an effective subsidy would have to come either from the wealthy, or from the state. Rousseau's doubts ironically shape the financial questions that would attend the imposition of a national theatre:

> But how will the State support it? Will this be by retrenching on necessary expenses, for which its modest revenue is hardly sufficient, in order to provide for it? Or will the State instead designate for this important purpose sums which the economies and integrity of the administration permit, from time to time, to be put in reserve for the most urgent needs? [L 190–91; F 130]

The price of a theatre must be weighed against other financial commitments, and a specific theatre-tax on all citizens is a gross improbability.

But this negative assessment of the effects of the imposition of a theatre on Geneva is disturbed by the logic which has exploited an alternative significance in the term *spectacle*. Rousseau's declared preference is for pleasures drawn "from our own state and ourselves", but he concedes that republics are traditionally the birthplaces of festivals, and so Geneva may readily add to its own stock of *spectacles* of this kind. In what seems to be a remarkable adaptation to the theatre of Plato's imagery of the cave, Rousseau insists on the priority of active, communal celebration over the passivity of theatrical reception:

> We already have several of these public festivals. By all means let us have more: I should only be the more charmed. But let us not adopt those exclusive public performances which drearily enclose a small number of people in a gloomy cavern; which hold them fearful and motionless in silence and inaction; which offer nothing to the eyes but partitions, steel points, soldiers, and distressing images of servitude and inequality. No, happy peoples, these are not the festivals for you! You must assemble in the open air, under the sky, and give yourselves over to the sweet feeling of your own happiness.   [L 233; F 168]

These, however, are summer activities, and to create year-round diversions calls for a further expedient, which Rousseau finds in closely administered social dancing for the marriageable young. Like Plato in the *Laws*, whose legislation for culture and leisure Rousseau seems to follow, Rousseau approves of physical exercise and what we might call subjective, or participating performances. On such occasions, the behaviour of the young will be under public scrutiny: a magistrate should preside, and mothers and fathers should attend, to approve and to enjoy "the sweetest *spectacle* which can touch a father's heart" [L 239; F 173]. The old, understood earlier to be victims of the prejudices encouraged by drama, are to have their own special enclosure, which must be saluted by all who enter or leave the ballroom. As a prelude to marriage, the competition should result in the choice of a 'queen', who will receive a gift from the Senate if she marries within the year. This carefully controlled institution, as Rousseau designs it, should "satisfy self-love, without offending virtue" [L 240; F 175].

What emerges from this relatively radical set of legislative proposals is a graduated definition of the public vision. Advanced initially as the absolute alternative to the theatre of objects, participating performance reveals itself as subject for approval to the eye of the state, and, in this last instance, particularly to the eye of the father and the mother. As Rousseau concludes,

> these balls, organized in this way, will resemble less a public performance than the assembly of a large family.   [L 242; F 176]

But although there are sound rhetorical reasons for the social respectability of this interpretation, it conceals the true eye of theory. The *Letter to d'Alembert* is a profoundly theoretical work, because it discloses the ultimate and logically complete ambition of *theoria*, which must always be to transcend vision with a unique understanding. Rousseau's extensive critique of drama and theatrical performers is an elaborate feint which draws attention away from his fundamental hostility to the act of theatrical reception. The community must be organized away from the passivity and 'servitude' of reception into the closure of subjective performance. Once positioned and organized there, the *spectateurs* become the *spectacle*, and legislative theory may order its own view. A gesture towards social hierarchy, in a presiding magistrate and a rewarding Senate, may be readily allied to parental vision, and the "father's heart" of patriarchy. But the ultimate *spectacle* of the *Letter* re-orders the theoretical vision decisively, in an idyllic description of a dance that followed the military exercise performed by the residents of Saint-Gervais in the lower city of Geneva, where Jean-Jacques was born. The men, reunited after their supper, gather in the square to form a dancing chain; the women watch from their windows, *spectatrices* of *acteurs*, and when they descend into the square with their children the dance is suspended. This *spectacle* was watched by Jean-Jacques and his father, and the young boy was implored to love his country [L 248-49; F 181-82]. Through recall, it furnishes the final example of his discourse, with the eye of the father subsumed in the theory—and the unique and prescriptive understanding—of his son.

Throughout the *Letter*, the notion of what is 'outside' and 'alien', conveyed in the adjective *étranger*, is consistently deployed to restrict the definition of an appropriate subject. This is the dominating concept: d'Alembert has no intimate knowledge of Geneva, French drama is alien, its heroes are alien, actors are other than themselves. But the supposed subjectivity of the festival as opposed to the theatre, and of the community as opposed to the audience, is belied by the objectivity that the eye of theory brings to the communal participants. The *Letter* is profoundly indebted to and involved with Rousseau's vehemence in the earlier *Discourses*, and clarifies above all his intense hostility to *amour-propre*. Self-love arises from comparison; but its gross misdemeanour for the social theorist, the incipient anthropologist, is that it removes and insulates a person from external judgement: *amour-propre* might effectively be translated as 'self-regard'. Sophistication, and a plurality of *spectateurs* must be cancelled, at least in writing, since innocence and immanence alone are fully exposed to the unifying gaze of theory.

2.2 DIDEROT (1713–1784) [25]

Denis Diderot, the son of a provincial cutler, completed his education in Paris, and became a tutor and translator. From 1746 he combined original speculation as a philosopher with his editorship, with d'Alembert, of the *Encyclopédie*, a compendium of technical and theoretical knowledge which gave expression to the rationalism of the Enlightenment, and was completed in 1765. A prolific writer, he is best known theatrically for his *Paradoxe sur le comédien*, a provocative consideration of the qualities required of an actor composed in the form of a dialogue. The *Paradox* was written towards the end of Diderot's life, starting as a set of observations prompted by a pamphlet on the English actor, David Garrick, but only published in 1830, long after Diderot had died.

Two earlier works, by contrast, in their close association with plays intended for presentation, stand forward as engagements with the continuities of theatre practice, and as calls for reform. The three *Conversations*, of 1757, that followed the edition of Diderot's play *The Natural Son*, constitute an energetic manifesto in favour of theatrical reform and a defence of the dramaturgy employed in *The Natural Son*, although the play itself was not performed until 1771. The *Discourse on Dramatic Poetry*, a more general work of dramatic theory, was published in 1758 with an edition of a second play by Diderot, *The Father of the Family*; the play was performed in Marseilles in 1760. Outstanding in the *Conversations* is Diderot's advocacy of a third genre of drama to be placed between tragedy and comedy, *le genre sérieux*, which many have identified as the theoretical genesis of bourgeois realism.[26]

2.2.1 The dissatisfactions of Dorval: the *Conversations* on *The Natural Son* [27]

The three *Conversations* appended to the published text of *The Natural Son* are intimately involved with the play through the figure of Dorval, who is both the hero of Diderot's drama, the 'natural son' of the title, and the leading speaker in the sequence of dialogues that follows.[28] Diderot introduces this device in a non-dramatic prologue to the complete publication, in which he supposes that he has met Dorval on a recent countryside vacation away from his duties on the *Encyclopédie* in Paris. The fiction of the prologue extends to identify Dorval as the author of what we would otherwise understand to be Diderot's play. In both the first and the second *Conversations*, he is subjected to a cross-examination as a playwright by Diderot, in an anticipation of the kinds of criticism which might be directed at the text of the play.

The first *Conversation* is brief, and suggestive rather than illustrative of more profound convictions about theatre practice. A supposed contrast between the events that provided the material for the play and the theatrical form of Dorval's script provides a starting-point for the discussion, and prompts a rather conservative *apologia* from Dorval for the formal and traditional dramatic unities of place, time and action. Further criticisms of aspects of dramaturgy are also little more than pedestrian, and acknowledge conventional assumptions about *décence*: there is some doubt over the importance assigned to a valet, and over the open declaration of love by one of the female characters. But the dramaturgy of the play suddenly comes into sharper focus with the theoretical dismissal of contrived and trite *coups de théâtre*, such as unexpected entrances, in favour of what are termed *tableaux*, and definitions follow.[29] The speaker is Diderot, signified simply by 'I' in the dialogue:

> A *coup de théâtre* is an unforeseen incident which passes into action, and which suddenly changes the state of the characters. A *tableau* is a disposition of the characters on the stage, one so natural and true that if it were rendered faithfully by a painter would please me on canvas.
> [VE 88][30]

Verisimilitude is again at stake here, but Dorval's firmly stated preference is for the pictorial over action, in a critical allusion to the notion that the French theatre had achieved perfection:

> Theatrical action must as yet be distinctly imperfect, since one sees on stage hardly any situation of which one could make a tolerable composition in painting. But why is this? Is truth less essential on stage than on canvas?... For my part, I think that if a dramatic work had been well executed and well performed, the stage would offer the spectator as many realistic *tableaux* as there would be, in the action, moments favourable to the painter.   [VE 89–90]

A rendezvous is fixed to continue the dialogue, and 'events' are allowed to conspire to reintroduce the question of *tableaux* at the beginning of the second *Conversation*. Dorval has been to visit a local village, where a man has been killed accidentally by his brother-in-law, and has there seen a *tableau*: the wife of the dead man collapsed in grief on the ground at the feet of the corpse. But what struck him forcefully was the conjunction of speech to picture. The wife was responsible for sending her husband away to the village, and her cry as reported by Dorval forms an inscription to the pictorial image:

> "Alas, when I sent you here, I had no thought that your steps were leading you to your death."   [VE 99]

Dorval believes that the *tableau* has the strength of universality, that passes across the ranks of society. The same situation would always inspire the same words,

> and what the artist must find is what the whole world would say in the same case; what no-one could hear, without at the same time recognizing it in himself.   [ibid.]

In returning abruptly to the play, Dorval alludes to the role of what he terms *pantomime*, the physical expression of feeling and emotion on the stage in mime:

> We talk too much in our plays; and, as a consequence, our actors do not act enough in them. We have lost an art, whose resources were well known to antiquity.   [VE 100]

Gesture responds to speech at every moment, and in writing the script Dorval found himself obliged at times to record detailed movements, as stage directions, under the name of a character.

> What is it that affects us at the sight of a man moved by some great passion? His speech? Sometimes. But what always move us are cries, inarticulate words, a voice that breaks, monosyllables that escape at intervals, indefinable murmurs in the throat, between the teeth... Voice, tone, gesture, action, these are what belong to the actor.
> [VE 101–102]

Intonation and gesture are crucial in performance, but intonation poses problems for annotation. This difficulty is apparent in one scene of the play, which seemed on reading the script to be excessively long. The reason, Dorval insists, is that he did not write down the *pantomime*:

> We do not as yet know how far pantomime can influence the composition of a dramatic work, and its performance.   [VE 111–12]

The impersonation of Dorval has gradually been moved, in a portrayal of growing confidence and enthusiasm, to a point of advocating theatrical reform. Initially the suggestion, building on earlier thoughts, is for multiple staging:

> I only ask, in order to change the face of the dramatic genre, for a theatre of greater extent, where one might show, when the subject of a play demanded it, a large square with adjacent buildings, such as the colonnade of a palace, the entrance to a temple, different places distributed in manner that allowed the spectator to see the whole action. [VE 114]

This proposal is mitigated at first by a reference to antiquity, in a vision of the multiple settings required for Aeschylus' *Eumenides* in the *Oresteia* trilogy, but the full possibilities are explored in an imagined example, which is both "domestic and common". In this proposed sequence of scenes and *tableaux*, speech alternates with silence, and with *pantomime*. A servant reports, with understandable reluctance, the death of a son to his father in a room on one side of the stage. The servant then runs to a second room, to break the tragic news to the mother, who clasps a crucifix to her breast. In the meantime, the corpse of the son is introduced into the father's room. The climax of the sequence comes with the advance of the mother towards the body of her son [VE 115–17].

This evocation is undoubtedly tragic, and it prompts a reflection by Diderot that the occasion of writing a script has led Dorval to establish "some precepts common to all the dramatic genres" [VE 118]. Despite his general cynicism about the likelihood of reform, Dorval is drawn into an appeal to Voltaire as a "man of genius" who might introduce into the theatre a new genre incorporating scenes of a similar power.[31] A definition for this new genre is not hard to find: "domestic and bourgeois tragedy", for which the precedents exist in the English plays by Lillo, *The London Merchant*, and by Moore, *The Gamester*, both of which Diderot was later to translate, in 1760 [VE 119–20]. The use of prose is essential for the reform, but the difficulty is that the French theatre is dominated by "decency" and verse. As a consequence, the only effective solution will be to restore one of the prime characteristics of the ancient theatre, that of a mass audience:

> We no longer have, properly speaking, any public performances. What connection is there between our theatre audiences on their most numerous days, and those of the people of Athens or of Rome? The ancient theatres had a capacity of up to twenty-four thousand citizens... [VE 121]

The mass assault on decency prompts a sympathetic expansion in the estimate of numbers:

> Judge the force of a great gathering of spectators by what you yourself know of the effect of men on each other, of the communication of feelings in popular gatherings. Forty to fifty thousand people do not restrain themselves through decency. [VE 122]

The effects of the mass audience are felt by actors and writers, in addition to spectators:

> But if the gathering of a great number of people should add to the emotion of the spectator, what influence should it have on the authors, and the actors? What a difference there is between several hundred people entertaining themselves on one day, between fixed hours, in a small, dark place, and the concentration of a whole nation on its solemn holidays, the occupation of the most sumptuous buildings, surrounded and filled with an immeasurable multitude, whose entertainment or boredom depends on our talents. [VE 122–23]

The image of the theatre as a gloomy space, perhaps a prison, is confirmed by an anecdote from Diderot himself, about a friend on the run from the provinces whom he took to the theatre. The iron grid of the box-office, and the oppressive feel of the foyer were enough to make him feel that he was in a house of correction. After its publication, Diderot sent a copy of *The Natural Son* and the *Conversations* to Rousseau,[32] and the influence of the idea of a mass spectacle in direct contrast to theatrical confinement became combined with Platonic imagery in the related critique advanced one year later in the *Letter to d'Alembert on Public Performances*.

2.2.2 The question of a third genre in the third *Conversation*

At the close of the second *Conversation*, Dorval is faced by the demand from Diderot for a more precise definition for his own work, which is clearly not the type of the "domestic and bourgeois tragedy" he has suggested:

> I have only one more question to put to you: it is on the genre of your work. It is not a tragedy; it is not a comedy. So what is it, then, and what name should we give to it? [VE 133]

The answer is postponed to the following day, since the continuing virtues of Dorval require his financial intercession in a local *amour* of the children of parents unmatched in income.

Thunder and high winds form the brief narrative introduction to Dorval's arrival at the rendezvous for the third *Conversation*, but the starting-point of the discussion is, more tamely, the definition of a midpoint between two extremes. In the case of drama, two extremes already exist in tragedy and comedy, and the illustration of the middle point is drawn academically by Dorval from antiquity, in a description of *The Mother-in-Law* (*Hecyra*) by the Roman playwright Terence.

> Terence composed a play, and this is its subject. A young man marries. He has only just got married, when business draws him away...
>
> My question is: to which genre does this play belong? To the comic genre? There is not a word in it to make you laugh. To the tragic genre? Terror, pity, and the other grand passions are not excited by it. Yet it holds the interest; and that will always be the case—leaving aside the caricatures that make you laugh, the dangers that make you shudder—in every dramatic composition where the subject is important, where the poet takes up the tone that we have in serious matters, and where the action advances through perplexity and difficulties. Now it seems to me that since these actions are the most common in life, the genre that has them for its object should be the most useful and the most extensive. I shall call this the serious genre. Once this genre has been established, there will be no condition of society, no important actions in life, that we cannot refer to some part of the dramatic system.   [VE 136]

The basic scheme of dramatic genres is supplemented by two further extremes, burlesque and *le merveilleux*, which are seen to exist beyond comedy and tragedy respectively, but which are also "outside nature", and so cannot be allowed to influence the central triad.

Their places at the extremes of the triadic scheme make both comedy and tragedy extremely difficult to compose, whereas *le genre sérieux* can offer an excellent model for the trials and fundamental techniques of composition. The comparison that Dorval draws is with the use of the nude in the instruction of a student of painting. The nude 'underlies' all clothed figures, and so once practised in life-drawing the student is free to choose a subject, from either an elevated or a commonplace level. Similarly, one who "has made a lengthy study of humanity in exercising the serious genre" will then choose to write either tragedy or comedy [VE 137–38]. There are further advantages, of a universal appeal:

> If the serious genre is the easiest of all, it is by way of compensation the least subject to the vicissitudes of time and place. Carry a nude

into any place on the earth that you like; it will command attention, if
it is well designed. If you excel in the serious genre, you will please at
all times and amongst all peoples. [VE 138]

By contrast, the existing tragicomedy is a confusion of two genres which are naturally separated, and farce and parody do not deserve the title of 'genre', since they are merely species of comedy or burlesque.

Dorval's conception of the 'mean' and the 'universal' dramatic genre constitutes a proposition which is in total accord with *raison*, *humanité* and educational progress, and he confirms it with a brief 'poetic'.

The subject should be important; and the plot simple, domestic, and close to real life. [VE 139]

Servants are to play no part, since they should not be involved in the affairs of their masters. There should be no pronounced attempt to make the audience laugh or cry, but the genre should contain monologues, and the moral of the play should be "general and strong". *Pantomime* should be included, *coups de théâtre* excluded, and *tableaux* substituted for them, as in the prescriptions of the second *Conversation*. But despite these guidelines, Dorval draws back from allowing his formative proposals to contribute to the rigidity of classification:

And above all remember that there is no general principle: I cannot think of any of those [principles] that I have just indicated which a man of genius might not infringe with success. [VE 140]

The Natural Son offers an excellent example of a work composed for the central, serious genre because it is susceptible of transposition into both tragedy and comedy. Dorval mentions a comic parody of an act of the play composed by one of the 'characters', and hands a tragic version, which culminates in his own suicide, over to Diderot. The effects of this lachrymose version allow Dorval to reconcile his central genre with the radical proposal for a domestic and bourgeois tragedy advanced in the second *Conversation*:

If you are convinced... that what you have just read is tragedy, and that there exists between tragedy and comedy an intermediate genre, then you have two branches of the dramatic genre which are yet uncultivated, and only await men to attend to them. Make comedies in the serious genre, make domestic tragedies, and rest assured that applause and immortality are reserved for you. Above all, neglect *coups de théâtre*, search out *tableaux*, bring yourself close to real life, and have

> besides a performance space which allows for the exercise of *pantomime* to its full extent. People say that there are no longer any grand tragic passions to stir us; that it is impossible to present elevated feelings in a new and striking way. That may be the case with tragedy, as the Greeks, the Romans, the French, the Italians, the English, and all the peoples of the earth have composed it. But domestic tragedy will have a different action, a different tone, and a sublimity which will be its own... [VE 148]

Dorval's suggested subject lies in the relationship between father and son, but when pressed by Diderot, he provides a more detailed analysis of the resources of this kind of tragedy:

> Can you not conceive the effect that would be produced on you by a realistic setting, by contemporary dress, by language proportionate to actions, by simple actions, by dangers which you yourself must have known, and which made you tremble for your parents, for your friends, for yourself? A reversal of fortune, fear of ignominy, the consequences of poverty, a passion which leads a man to his ruin, from his ruin to despair, from despair to a violent death, are not rare events; and you believe they would not affect you as much as the mythical death of a tyrant, or the sacrifice of a child on the altars of the gods of Athens or of Rome? [VE 149]

The recommendations for a revision of comedy—"comedies in the serious genre"—follow those for domestic tragedy, and are no less precise. The key to the reformation lies in the substitution of an attention to conditions for that traditionally granted to characters:

> Up to the present day, in comedy, character has been the principal object, and condition of life has been only secondary; today the condition of life must become the principal object, and character must be secondary. It was from character that writers drew the whole of their plot. They looked for the circumstances that would bring it out, and then would link these circumstances together. But it is the condition of life, its duties, its advantages, its difficulties, which should serve as the basis for the work. It seems to me that this source is more abundant, more extensive, and more useful than that of characters. However little the character may be caricatured, a spectator may say to himself "I am not like that". But he cannot hide from himself the fact that the condition that is represented in front of him is his own; he cannot fail to recognize his duties. He will be bound to apply what he hears. [VE 153]

Beyond a list of established designations—"man of letters, *philosophe*, business-man, judge, lawyer, politician, citizen, magistrate, financier, magnate, steward"—and the close family relationships, Dorval considers the "new conditions of life that come into being all the time":

> The conditions of life! How many important details, public and domestic actions, unknown truths, new situations to draw from this source! And do not the conditions of life have the same contrasts between themselves as characters? And cannot the playwright place them in opposition to each other? [VE 154]

If there is an Aristotelian influence in the concept of a 'likeness' between spectator and character, it has been drastically adapted to accommodate the importance granted to conditions. But in a subsequent reference to the depiction of a diversity of characters in epic poetry, the Aristotelian division between high and low genres of composition is flatly dismissed:

> It seems to me that there is a great advantage in portraying men as they are. What they ought to be is something too systematic and too vague to serve as the basis for an art of imitation. There is nothing so rare as a man who is completely evil, unless, perhaps, it is a man who is completely good. [VE 160]

The conclusion to the third *Conversation* is expressed in what amounts to an agenda, a set of reformist theses:

> To create domestic and bourgeois tragedy. To perfect the serious genre. To substitute the conditions of man for characters, perhaps in all the genres. To tie *pantomime* tightly to dramatic action. To change the arrangement of the stage, to substitute *tableaux* for *coups de théâtre*, a new source of invention for the poet and of study for the actor. What use is it for the poet to imagine *tableaux*, if the actor remains attached to his taste for symmetry and his circumscribed actions? To introduce the tragedy of real life into the lyric theatre. Finally to subject dance to the form of a true poem, one which can be written, and which would be distinct from every other art of imitation. [VE 167]

Dorval had been insistent that *la danse* should be a poem, a form of "rhythmical *pantomime*", and before listing his final theses he provided a draft of three scenes of a ballet. Both dance and "lyric theatre" were to find their reformers: in Noverre and the *ballet d'action*, advocated in the *Lettres sur la danse* of 1760, and in Gluck, who was first influenced by Noverre in his ballet *Don Juan* of 1761, and who then realized his own dramatic objectives in *Orfeo* (1762) and the operas of that same decade.[33]

2.2.3 The *Discourse on Dramatic Poetry*

Towards the close of his extended impersonation in the *Conversations*, Diderot had—with consistency, if not with great conviction—attributed his own current work on a second play, *The Father of the Family*, to 'Dorval', while the 'I' of the dialogues was to be satisfied with the publication of the seventh volume of the *Encyclopédie*. This pretence has faded by the time of the publication of the *Discourse on Dramatic Poetry* in the following year, which accompanied the text of *The Father of the Family*.

The *Discourse* is, at least overtly, a more plainly academic work than the *Conversations*, and perhaps its most obvious predecessor in the varieties of French theatrical poetics was *La Pratique du théâtre* of d'Aubignac, which was first published in 1657. Indeed, Diderot's recurrent use of painting as an analogue to the visual and physical 'representation' of theatre was indebted to the comparisons established for French classicizing theory by d'Aubignac, although Diderot himself was perhaps more directly affected by the *Critical Reflections on Poetry and Painting* of du Bos (published 1719), who had insisted on the pictorial quality of poetic imagery at work in the imagination.[34] What distinguishes the *Discourse*, however, is its combination of a mild apologetic with the formal progress of a practical manual, which moves, at times laboriously, from dramatic composition through to theatrical presentation.

Although it may seem just to note that the dialogue form, so essential to the declamatory mode of the *Conversations*, has been suppressed in favour of a treatise in the *Discourse*, it is at least as important to accept that the reciprocation of question and answer is also a feature of the later work. The text of the *Discourse* is, at times, punctuated by unattributed questions which seem tolerant and supportive of the progress of the argument. The technique is comparable to that of Rousseau in the *Letter*, although Rousseau is far more inclined to contain predictable or supposed objections, born of prevalent assumptions or platitudes drawn from a tradition of theory, within the firmly rhetorical scheme of exposition. "You will say that...", "I hear it said that...", "It will be said to me that..." are relatively mechanical forms of timely, and suitably contained, rhetorical (self-)interrogation, although

Rousseau is also prepared to put words into the mouths of "the partisans of the theatre", for example.[35] For Diderot, it seems that the interrogation which intermittently sustains the argument in the *Discourse* derives in the first instance from his self-examination as a theatrical writer, which he is keen to publicize.

In the preface to his friend Melchior Grimm and the introductory chapter to the *Discourse*, Diderot returns to his proposals for an intermediate genre and for an emphasis on the 'conditions of men'. Yet the general substance of the first part of the *Discourse* fails either to examine or to amplify the propositions advanced in the *Conversations*, as Diderot gradually adopts a scheme which records his contemplation of the progress of composition, passing from plot through character to action. There is little of any theoretical significance in these observations, and similarly little that would prove exceptionable, although the cynical assertion that the theatre flourishes "more securely amongst a corrupt people than elsewhere" [VE 192] seems potentially indebted to Rousseau, as perhaps is Diderot's expressed distaste for ridicule [VE 194]. In so far as the *Discourse* is a *Poetics*, Diderot is prepared to acknowledge the authority of Aristotle, Horace, and Boileau [VE 206], and there are recurrent and respectable references from this dramatist of eighteen months' standing to the achievements of the Roman comedian Terence, and allusions to the stature of Aristophanes, Sophocles, Molière, and Voltaire.

But the particular fascination of the *Discourse* lies in its unexpected, and almost certainly unprogrammatic, shift of attention away from composition towards a problematic of performance and production. A disciplined practice of composition, such as the treatise envisages, entails some pre-consideration of performance, and one of Diderot's most insistent prescriptions is that the playwright and the actor should be absorbed in the action and characters of the play to the exclusion of the unseen spectator:

> So whether you are composing or you are acting give no more thought to the spectator than if he did not exist. Imagine, at the edge of the theatre, a great wall that separates you from the pit; act as if the curtain had not been raised. [VE 231]

Similarly, the act of composition may easily be defined, following the precedent set by Aristotle, as an act of imaginative embodiment:

> For my own part, I cannot conceive how the poet can begin a scene if he does not imagine the action and the movements of the character

> he is introducing; if his bearing and his mask are not in front of him. It is this image [*simulacre*] which inspires the first word, and the first word provides the remainder. [VE 249]

This is Diderot's version of Aristotle's advice in *Poetics* chapter 17:

> In composing plots and working them out in conjunction with a linguistic style, the tragedian must place everything in front of his eyes as much as he can. For in this way, seeing things as clearly as possible, as if he himself were present as the actions were occurring, he will find what looks and fits best, and avoid the opposite.

Scene-composition also involves the consideration of movement, and following the precepts of the *Conversations* Diderot is prepared to classify:

> I call 'composite' scenes those where several characters are occupied with something, while other characters are engaged with something different, or with the same thing, but separately.
> In a 'simple' scene, the dialogue goes forward without interruption. Composite scenes are either spoken, or *pantomime* with speech, or completely *pantomime*.
> When they are *pantomimes* with speech, the spoken parts should be placed in the intervals between *pantomime*, and everything will happen without confusion. But one needs skill to manage the gaps. [VE 250]

In addition to this classification, Diderot is also prepared to admit the kind of scene which contains two simultaneous *tableaux*. In the case of a conjunction of this kind he considers the possibility of a text printed in two columns, which would convey the interrelationship of speech with *pantomime*.

Yet, as they stand, these are passing references to production and to the imaginative embodiment or execution of performance, and the motive for reform has yet to confront Rousseau's elaborate critique of the degeneracy of a society totally subsumed under the rule of *amour-propre*. This dilemma ultimately confirms the role of reform, because neither the present nor the past can muster the arguments that would now be required for an acceptable defence of the theatre.

> Every people has prejudices to destroy, vices to prosecute, ridiculous behaviour to discredit, and has need of public performances, but ones which are appropriate to it...
> To attack public performances through the abuse of them is to make

a stand against every form of public instruction; and what has been said up to the present on this subject—applied to how things are, or have been, and not to how they could be—is without either justice or truth. [VE 259]

Nonetheless, the argument for a reformed future is muted, in the accumulation of successive charges against the state of society:

Amongst an enslaved people, everything is degraded. Debasement is necessary, in tone and gesture, to strip from the truth its weight and offence. Then poets are like fools at the court of kings...

In general, the more a people is civilized, cultured, the less its morals are poetic; everything becomes enfeebled as it becomes softer. When is it that nature prepares models for art? At the time when children tear their hair at the bedside of a dying father... [VE 259-60]

The last sentence could be decisive in moderating Rousseau's stringency, because it determines the possibility of a contemporary dramatic subject, which accords completely with Diderot's theoretical emphasis on the paternal bond. But in the long list that immediately follows it, it is quite evident that Diderot is alluding to the mythography of antiquity—Clytemnestra baring her breasts to her son Orestes, Bacchants ranging in the mountains—as a site of morals that are poetic, even if they are not good. His diversion of Rousseau's argument is even more pronounced in a decisive definition of the nature of the poet, and of poetry:

What is it that a poet needs? Is it a brute or a cultured nature, peaceful or troubled? Will he prefer the beauty of a pure and serene day to the horror of the darkness of night? Poetry demands something huge, barbarous, and savage. [VE 261]

This conclusion is the antithesis to Rousseau's self-performative moral order in the *Letter*, although it appropriates against the models of classicism what might easily be considered a facile misreading of the supposed primitivism of Rousseau's *Discourses*. Civil war, fanaticism and bloodshed are, according to Diderot, the stimuli to poetry, which "withers in times of peace and leisure" [ibid.]:

So what will be the resource of a poet amongst a people whose morals are feeble, petty, and mannered; where the rigorous imitation of conversations forms only a tissue of false expressions, senseless and base; where there is no longer any sincerity, or fellow-feeling; where a father calls his son 'monsieur', and where a mother calls her daughter

> 'mademoiselle'; where the public ceremonies have nothing awe-inspiring in them, domestic conduct nothing touching or honourable, solemn acts nothing true? He will try to embellish them... [VE 262]

The larger confrontation with Rousseau is only partly achieved, and it is this apparently trivial susceptibility to decoration which directs Diderot's principle of reform towards the failings and excesses of scenic design, and of theatrical *représentation* in general.

> But what shows above all how far we still are from good taste and from truth is the poverty and falsity of [scenic] decoration, and the luxury of the costumes.
>
> You demand of your poet that he subjects himself to the unity of place; and you abandon the stage to the ignorance of a bad decorator.
>
> Do you want to bring your poets closer to truth, both in the conduct of their plays, and in their dialogue, and your actors closer to natural playing and realistic declamation? Raise your voice, just insist that the setting is shown to you as it should be.

The reformist tone is marked by the address to what appears to be a general, and probably a national public, which replaces the dramatic poet as the subject of initiative in the matter of taste. The mandate issuing from the public can also be taken to instruct the dramatic poet in what is taken to be a reformation of theatrical practice:

> Your poet, when you have judged his work worthy of being performed for you, should send for the decorator. He should read to him his play. Once the setting is well known to him, he should execute it as it is, and should be concerned above all that theatrical painting should be more rigorous and truthful than any other genre of painting. [ibid.]

Accidental distraction is the enemy of illusion in the theatre, and this ensures that "the most beautiful theatrical decoration will never be other than a picture of the second rank". What is particularly remarkable in this discussion is the realignment of theoretical vision in a changing structure of discourse. In the earlier parts of the treatise, the explicit addressee of the preface (Melchior Grimm) is relatively easily replaced by any reader moderately willing to be interested in the process of dramatic composition, as this is mediated through Diderot's own experience. But the attribution to a general public of the imperative to reform, which is in Diderot's terms to progress further towards "good taste" and "truth", liberates Diderot from his authorial role as dramatist, and permits his visual concentration to act decisively as a theoretical principle. The theorist assumes control, through the general public, of the scenic decorator and of the liaison of the dramatic poet with the apparatus of theatre. It is an ambitious model for the activity of theory, and markedly contrasts with Aristotle's cancellation of a consideration of visual effect in the *Poetics*.

The principle applied to costume is consistent, although the preference for simplicity and severity as opposed to ostentation more explicitly demands the kind of play that Diderot had himself written. Comedy should be played in informal dress, and costume related to the action and the status of the characters in the play, not to ostentation directed to the audience: "The more serious the genres, the more severity is needed in costume" [VE 266]. To show "nature" and "truth" is the duty of the performer, and it is the predisposition or inclination of the actors to "leave the action" and "speak to the pit" which makes them "become awkward and false" in Diderot's firm conviction about the need for an unseen fourth wall in the theatre [VE 268–69]. This excess of performer over character might be controlled by some kind of external authority:

> One observation that I have made is that our insipid subordinate characters remain more commonly in their humble role than the principal characters. The reason, it seems to me, is that they are constrained by the presence of an other who commands them: it is to this other person that they address themselves; it is in that direction that all their actions are turned. And everything would proceed very well, if there was as great an imposition on the leading roles as that which dependence imposes on the subordinate. [VE 269]

The argument from truth also engages a full theatrical statement of the place to be reserved in dramaturgy and performance for *pantomime*:

> I have said that *pantomime* is a part of the drama; that the author should occupy himself with it seriously; that if it is not familiar and vivid to him he will not know how to begin, nor to carry on, nor to finish his scene with truth; and that gesture should often be written in place of speech.
>
> I add that there are some entire scenes where it is infinitely more natural to characters to move rather than speak; and I am going to prove it. [ibid.]

What is "natural", in a typical scene or situation from everyday life, requires *pantomime* to achieve "truth" in performance. Both Terence and Molière are cited as authorities for its use, and in relation to Act V, scene 2 of *The Miser* Diderot even goes so far as to state that "the dialogue is established between speech and gesture" [VE 270]. According to this thesis, *pantomime* becomes a requirement, not merely a resource:

> One must write *pantomime* on every occasion when it affords a *tableau*; when it gives energy or clarity to speech; when it binds dialogue; when it characterizes; when it consists of a delicate game which remains undeclared; when it occupies the place of a reply, and nearly always at the beginning of scenes... [ibid.]

Diderot's interest in *pantomime* as a means of theatrical expression goes back to an essay of 1751, the *Letter on the Deaf and Dumb*, when he was profoundly involved with the philosophical implications of the *Encyclopédie* project.[36] From the arguments advanced in the *Letter on the Deaf and Dumb*, it seems clear that Diderot did not regard physical expression in the theatre as a systematic alternative to language, but as a resource which might either transcend or illustrate the range of the spoken word.[37] Gestures and words are not equivalent, but, as in his cited example of Lady Macbeth, gestures may act as the most expressive image of a discursive idea, in this case of remorse:

> I know of nothing so pathetic in speech as the silence and the hand-movements of this woman. What an image of remorse! [38]

The insistence in the *Conversations* and the *Discourse* that *pantomime* should contribute to *tableaux* leaves the theoretical onus on the term *tableau*. In the first *Conversation*, Dorval had envisaged a play with "as many realistic *tableaux* as there would be in the action moments favourable to the painter".[39] In the narrative *tableau* of the corpse and the grieving wife at the opening of the second *Conversation*, the universality of the image is accompanied by a text in the remorseful words of the wife, which are "what all the world would say in the same case". As in the example of Lady Macbeth from the *Letter on the Deaf and Dumb*, for Diderot the image is held in a discursive framework, either as an illustration of a specific script, or as an emblematic image of a conceptual moment. If the *tableau*, supported by language or inscription, refers to an emotion such as 'remorse', it will communicate to the general experience of the spectators without, supposedly, any further complication. In this respect, the role of the dramatist should be decisive:

> *Pantomime* is the *tableau* which existed in the imagination of the poet when he was writing, and which he wanted the stage to show at each instant the actors are playing.   [VE 278]

The art of writing *pantomime* is also one of the disposition of the performers, which may prove to be a substantial alternative to the indulged art of declamation:

> If that is the case, what kind of art is declamation? When everyone is master of his role, it has virtually nothing to do. What is required is to fit the figures together, bring them close to each other or disperse them, isolate them or group them, and to draw from them a succession of *tableaux*, all of which are composed in a grand and truthful manner.   [VE 277]

The control exercised by the dramatist through incorporating physical action and the disposition of performers in a series of *tableaux* is the equivalent of 'directorial' instruction in the limitations it places on the performer's autonomy. The art of speaking, of projection and delivery to the audience will be subject to a composition in which the 'point of view' of the directorial playwright coincides with that of the spectator.

There is, however, an implicit contradiction in this argument, which reveals how far Diderot is prepared to rely upon an appeal to concepts like 'truth' and 'nature' to achieve theoretical conviction. If the *tableaux* are characterized by their "grand and truthful manner", they are, nonetheless, acknowledged to exist in "an artificial state" in composition, which is a reduction from the "natural state" [VE 277]. The relationships between *le vrai* and *vraisemblance*, between a 'real action' and a *tableau*, and between a "grand and truthful manner" and artifice are unresolved. Within limits, the reforms may be proposed on the basis of a common conviction about taste and verisimilitude, subject to only minor modifications. But the theoretical problems remain, and it was eventually those involved in the art of performance itself that attracted Diderot's ironic attention in the *Paradox on the Actor*.

2.2.4   The *Paradox on the Actor*[40]

The evolution of Diderot's most discussed study of the theatre is complicated, but relatively well documented. In 1747 Rémond de Ste Albine published *The Actor*, some unremarkable observations on the temperamental requirements of a successful performer. The treatise was translated into English, and then, ironically, retranslated in 1769 into French by an Italian actor resident in Paris, Antonio Sticotti, with the title *Garrick, or English Actors*. The choice of title was almost certainly influenced not just by the examples taken from leading English performers that characterized the English version, but by the vogue for Garrick in particular, which followed his travels in Europe between 1763 and 1765, and his presence in Paris in 1764–5.

From 1759 Diderot had been contributing reviews of the biennial Paris *Salons* to the privately circulated *Correspondence littéraire* of Melchior Grimm, and a copy of Sticotti's pamphlet seems to have been passed to him by Grimm in the course of editorial exchanges. The pamphlet provoked Diderot almost immediately into contradiction, in a short rejoinder to the work which he already describes in a letter to Grimm of November 1769 as "a fine paradox". Diderot chose to contrast a "capacity for feeling" (*sensibilité*) in the actor with what he describes in the letter as a "cool sense and mind" (*le sens froid et la tête*), but he was content to confine his arguments in favour of *la tête* to the small circle of foreign subscribers to the *Correspondence littéraire*. The first version of his argument appeared in the *Correspondence littéraire* of October 1770 as a short essay, and from that point forwards the text appears to have been expanded and reworked at repeated intervals, remaining unpublished at his death. A full version became known only through the edition of 1830, under the title of *Paradox on the Actor*, and its thesis has intermittently been the focus of debate in both the nineteenth and the twentieth centuries.[41] The *Paradox*, in its final version, is cast in the form of dialogue, with the First speaker assuming the discursive argument of the original essay. The Second speaker is apparently a friend of Sticotti, and approximately one-third of the way through the *Paradox* the First speaker confirms his own identity as 'Diderot'.

The opening gambit of the *Paradox* is an attack on the commonplace quality of a pamphlet that can offer nothing to the improvement of the art of acting, and it asserts a dichotomy between nature and artifice:

> At the end of reading it, a great actor will be no better, and a poor actor will be no less bad. It is nature that gives qualities to an individual: appearance, voice, judgement, wit. It is the study of great models, knowledge of the human heart, exposure to the ways of the world, repeated work, experience, and the practice of theatre which perfect the gift of nature.   [VE 303]

From the beginning, Diderot seems prepared to face the problem which he had repeatedly avoided in both the *Conversations* and the *Discourse*:

> And how would nature without art form a great actor, when nothing happens exactly on the stage as in nature, and when dramatic poems are all composed according to a fixed system of principles? [VE 304]

No two actors will perform the same script in the same way, no matter how 'precise' its author has been, because

> words are and can only be signs approximating to a thought, a feeling, an idea: signs whose value is completed by movement, gesture, tone, facial expression, eyes, and given circumstances. [ibid.]

Theatrical writing requires the presence of the actor, and a full technique of performance to achieve its meaning, which, as in the *Discourse*, is a 'representation' securely placed within the discursive capabilities of the spectator: "a thought, a feeling, an idea". The art of the performer is supplementary to language conceived as a sign system of this quality, and by implication it must itself be systematic.

Sticotti has served his purpose by the end of the preamble, and he remains in the dialogue as little more than the inverse of the First speaker. The resulting form of the paradox is given its *précis*, directed by the First to the Second speaker:

> *First*: ...But the important point, on which we have completely opposed opinions, your author and I, is that of the primary qualities of a great actor. For my part, I want him to have a great deal of judgement; for me, there must be in this man a cold and calm observer; as a consequence, I demand from him penetration and no sensibility, the art of imitating everything, or, what amounts to the same thing, an equal aptitude for all sorts of characters and roles.
> *Second*: No sensibility!
> *First*: None. [VE 306]

The removal of *sensibilité* from the actor forms the core of the paradox, and immediately shocks the Second speaker. There is no positive definition of this key term; but its qualities may be determined from the contrasting adjectives "cold and calm", and from the description of the actor as an "observer" (*spectateur*) who has the intellectual qualities of "judgement" and "penetration".[42] Fundamentally, the actor is aligned with the totalizing eye ("all sorts of characters and roles") of theoretical vision, which had previously been used in the *Discourse* to readjust theatrical practice to the view of the 'beholder'-theorist. *Sensibilité*, which is by inference 'warm' and 'troubled', unintellectual and non-theoretical, cannot be the basis of the "art" of the performer, which according to these precepts has all the characteristics of a science.

The separation of the actor from the cultural embrace of sensibility is a drastic act, which effectively sunders the performer from full participation in his society. The elevated cultural role assigned to *sensibilité* is eloquently expressed in the extended explanation, which follows its short definition, in the *Encyclopédie*:

> *Sensibility*—tender and delicate disposition of the soul which makes it prone to being moved, to being touched.
>
> Sensibility of soul provides a kind of wisdom in relation to matters of appropriate conduct, and goes further than penetration of mind by itself. Souls that feel can, through vivacity, fall into faults that would not be committed by men of controlled behaviour, but they have a far greater advantage in the number of benefits they can produce. Souls that feel exist to greater extent than others: so the benefits and the disadvantages multiply on that account. Reflection can make a man honest; but sensibility makes a man virtuous. Sensibility is the mother of humanity, of generosity; sensibility is at the service of merit, brings assistance to the mind, and carries persuasion along behind it.[43]

A profession with the cultural eminence of the theatre will need a formidable and equally prestigious 'art' if it is to be excluded from this aspirational definition. *Humanité* is, of course, a central term of the Enlightenment, and as a child of *sensibilité* it might be expected to betray some tokens of its parentage. A convincing inclination of editors is to assign the responsibility for its definition in the *Encyclopédie* to Diderot himself:

> *Humanity (in morals)*—a feeling of goodwill for all human beings, which hardly ever ignites except in a great and feeling soul. This noble and sublime enthusiasm is tormented by the pains of others and the need to assuage them; it would like to run through the universe to abolish slavery, superstition, vice and unhappiness. It hides from us the faults of those like us or inhibits us from feeling them; but it makes us severe on crimes... I have seen this virtue, source of so many others, in a large number of heads and in very few hearts.[44]

In this crusading definition, 'humanity' is a fiery feeling of the soul of some complexity, although the objects of its abolitionist fervour are explicitly programmatic. It is not, however, a comprehensive term except in its altruism; it is, in fact, relatively exclusive ("very few hearts"), which it might not be in the explanation given of *sensibilité*.

But despite potential divergences, both definitions are uniform in marking an emphatic distinction of feeling from the capacities and achievements of mind (*esprit*). In asserting an objective art for the actor, Diderot has to reverse this immensely confident—and more than mildly self-righteous—emotional priority.

The First speaker has his "reasons" for the paradoxical thesis which he has expressed in the form of a wilful prescription. If the actor depended on *sensibilité*, was himself *sensible*, a consistent repetition in successive performances of his portrayal of a character would be impossible: "Very warm on the first performance, he would be exhausted and cold as marble by the third" [VE 306]. But as an "attentive imitator and reflective disciple of nature", and "a rigorous copyist of himself or of his studies and a continuous observer of our feelings" his playing would gradually be strengthened by new reflections, and the satisfaction of the audience would increase. The standard perception that the actor is in some sense 'other' than himself, an alienation which was deeply suspicious to Rousseau, is used by the First speaker to confirm his insistence on an essential artifice in performance:

> If he is himself when he plays, how will he stop being himself? If he wants to stop being himself, how will he seize on the exact point at which he must situate himself and come to a halt? [128]

If nature is subject to altered states, art should be subject only to improvement.

At this point, the argument of the First speaker apparently demands the resources of rhetoric:

> What confirms me in my opinion is the inequality [in their performances] of those actors who play from the soul. Do not expect any unity from them; their playing is alternately strong and weak, warm and cold, flat and sublime. They will, tomorrow, miss the spot where they excelled today; to make up for that, they will excel in something that they missed the day before. On the other hand, the actor who plays from reflection, from the study of human nature, from constant imitation of some ideal model, from imagination, from memory, will be one and the same at all performances, always equally perfect. All has been measured, combined, learnt, ordered in his head; there is neither monotony nor dissonance in his declamation. His warmth has its progression, its outbursts and its appeasement, its beginning, its middle, its end. These are the same accents, the same positions, the same movements; if there is any difference between one performance

> and another, it is ordinarily to the advantage of the latter. He is not variable: but a mirror, always placed to show objects, and to show them with the same precision, the same force, and the same truth.   [ibid.]

In this extended flourish the balance of the writing, almost mocking in its own artifice, emphasizes the disappointment consequent on inconsistency, even though the disappointment could only be felt by a recurrent observer, critic or theorist. The paradoxical performer gathers his existence in this passage from an overwhelming accumulation of flattering repetitions, and the monosyllables here do emphatic work: the preposition "from", the ordering simplicity of the possessive, and the unfailing consistency resolutely expressed in the triumphant reiteration of "the same...". Pervading the ease of this rhetorical exhibition is the persuasive concept of unity, which is, with some reservations that allow for a process of improvement, made synonymous with perfection. The classicizing concepts (unity, imitation, perfection, the 'beginning, middle and end') and conviction are unremarkable in themselves. But unity here takes account not only of the full extent of the actor's role, which might be considered comparable to the extent of dramatic composition, but of its repetition over successive performances. This peculiar characteristic of acting threatens to divorce the paradoxical thesis from the familiar precept of classical poetics, and to render the paradox into a theory of practice almost before it has fully emerged from the rhetorical strategies of contradiction.

The paradoxical actor is complimented with a virtual barrage of allusions to his use of mental capacities, but the indications of his method are slight. Rhetorical assertion has carried the paradox into two points of extreme difficulty: the first is the unresolved relationship between nature and art, and the second is the artistic anomaly of the actor's fundamental need to repeat. Diderot's solution of these problems is expressed concisely in the theoretical formula of the "constant imitation of an ideal model", and he attempts to provide it with validity by means of an example, the method of the distinguished actress Mlle Clairon. Exemplary though Clairon may be—"What playing is more perfect than that of Clairon?"—it is ultimately her diminutive stature which provides Diderot with substance for the image he requires:

> Without doubt she has made a model for herself to which she has then tried to conform; without doubt this model is the highest, the greatest, and the most perfect that she could conceive; but the model she has borrowed from history, or that her imagination has created like a great

phantom, is not herself. If this model had only her own height, how feeble and small her playing would be! When, as the result of hard work, she has approached as near as she can to this idea, all is done; to keep herself firmly in that position is purely a matter of exercise and memory.   [VE 307–8]

The tendency of the *paradox* is one of continual contrast. The progress of the argument is irregular, succumbing to a principle of variety that is willing to leave suggestion as the prime component of a controversial thesis. The *fantome* said to be conceived and conjured into existence by Clairon provides an evocative entity which establishes the separation of the role from the performer; but the process of its formation, and its relationship to the theatrical stability of an "ideal model", remain unexplained. The image seems designed at this moment almost to belittle the activity of theatre, by exaggerating the distance between the monstrous grandeur of a role and the minimal stature of its performer. This mode of disdain and dissatisfaction recurs throughout the dialogue, as if the impulse to reform of the earlier writings has only reluctantly submitted to a constrained consideration of the actualities of contemporary performance. The Second speaker gives voice to this impression:

To listen to you, nothing would seem to resemble an actor on the stage or at study so much as those children who at night play at ghosts in the graveyards, lifting over their heads a great white sheet on the end of a stick, and emitting from under this cover a lugubrious voice to frighten the passers-by.   [VE 309]

The First speaker seems willing to accept this image, but hurries to a comparison of a second actress, Mlle. Dumesnil, with Clairon. Dumesnil may reach "one sublime moment", but in general she is unprepared, and "half of the time she does not know what she is saying" [ibid.].

The new order of 'feeling' that the paradox proposes dissociates actors from the audience, and aligns them with the artistic discipline of the dramatic poet. This movement of thought also engages a complementary theatrical metaphor, which has the poet as the observer or 'spectator' of life, and relocates those with powerful feelings "on the stage" of actual human conduct.

The great dramatic poets are above all assiduous spectators of what is going on around them in the physical and the moral world...
 The great poets, the great actors, and perhaps in general all the great imitators of nature, whoever they may be, endowed with a fine

imagination, with great judgement, with a precise touch, with sure taste, are the least feeling of creatures.   [VE 309–310]

The great actors have also been observers, and only mediocrities have rejected observation in the belief that they 'feel'. The illustration offered is of a disciplined art of the voice:

> "But what", someone may say, "of those plaintive and sorrowful sounds that are drawn from the entrails of the mother in front of me, and which so violently disturb my own? Is it not actual feeling which produces these? Is it not despair which inspires them?" Not at all; and the proof is that they are measured, that they form part of a system of declamation; that lowered or raised by the twentieth part of a quarter of a tone, they are false; that they are submitted to a law of unity; that they are, as in harmony, arranged in chords and discords; that they can only be brought to satisfy all the required conditions through extended study; that they fit the solution of a given problem; that to be uttered correctly, they have been repeated a hundred times, and that despite these frequent repetitions, they may still not be right...   [VE 312]

The accumulated detail once again supports the paradox, but here for the first time it constitutes the art rather than the artist. Declamation is systematic, in analogy with music, although how far it is simply dependent on a tonal 'ear' is not examined. But the language itself is that of a science, which proposes a problem and then solves it, and the issue of repetition (in performance) is successfully addressed through the integration of repetitive rehearsal into the system. The paradoxical performer offers an imitation controlled not merely through discipline and observation, but by a constant attention which takes the place of feeling:

> The cries of his sorrow are noted by his ear. The gestures of his despair come from memory, and have been prepared in front of a mirror. He knows the exact moment when he will pull out his handkerchief and when the tears will fall; expect them with this word, this syllable, neither sooner nor later. This trembling of the voice, these halting words, these stifled or drawn-out sounds, these shaking limbs, these quaking knees, these faintings, these rages—pure imitation, a lesson recorded in advance, a grimace arousing pathos, a sublime aping which the actor retains in his memory long after he has studied it, of which he was acutely aware at the moment he was executing it, which leaves him—fortunately for the poet, for the spectator, and for himself—all

the freedom of his mind, and which takes from him, just like other exercises, only his physical strength. [VE 312–313]

When he has finished his performance, he is tired but not upset: he will change his clothes, and perhaps go to bed. The paradoxical moral is plain:

> The actor is weary, you are sad; that is because he has worked hard without feeling a thing, and you have been feeling without doing any work. If it were otherwise, acting would be the most miserable of all professions; but he is not the character, he plays the character, and he plays it so well that you take him for the character. The illusion is yours alone; he knows full well that he is not what he plays.
> [VE 313]

The paradox has now been firmly established, and the First speaker is at the height of his confidence, which leads him from the formal presentation of a set of theses to a satirical extension of the art of performance into society at large:

> So I am insistent, and I say this: an extreme sensibility makes actors mediocre; a mediocre sensibility creates the multitude of bad actors; but it is the absolute absence of sensibility which engenders sublime actors. The tears of an actor fall from his brain; those of a man of feeling rise up from his heart. The entrails immeasurably trouble the head of a man of feeling; but it is an actor's head which from time to time, and momentarily, carries trouble down to his entrails. He weeps like an unbelieving priest who preaches on the Passion; like a seducer at the feet of a woman whom he does not love, but whom he wants to deceive; like a beggar in the street or at the door of a church, who insults you when he despairs of touching your heart; or like a courtesan who feels nothing, but who faints in your arms. [ibid.]

The satirical tone would seem to be a consequence of a sense of completion, as the paradox, in an act of reversion, turns against the absence of feeling it has determined for the act of performance. This mode of revulsion, or of dissatisfaction and disappointment as I earlier termed it, finds its fullest expression in *Rameau's Nephew*, Diderot's grand satire of the conditions and professions of life in contemporary Paris. In this dialogue, which was first drafted in the early 1760s and also remained unpublished during Diderot's lifetime, the mimicry performed by the dissolute nephew of the composer Rameau displays extravagant vocal and physical skills in a heartless *pantomime* of the conditions of life, which leaves Diderot caught between admiration and disgust. Rameau's nephew is a man without position or security, a pathetic and appalling imitator of anything, from the sounds of musical instruments to the walk of his dead wife. His satirical role in the dialogue is to play a set of variations on the theme of instability and uncertainty, from which Diderot takes refuge through assertions of the equanimity of philosophy. The objective quality of performance skills renders them excessively mobile, and it is this that can provoke adulation or dismay.[45] Without the reform of the dramatic genres proposed in the *Conversations* and the *Discourse*, the theatre remains for the satirist an irritant and a source of anxiety, the performer everything and nothing.

The impetus to express and advocate reform may have failed in the *Paradox*, but it remains as a source of Diderot's evident dissatisfaction. One potential corollary of the divorce between feeling and its imitation is that what wins acclaim in the conventional theatre may have no relationship to natural feeling. According to the First speaker, the characters of classical French tragedy are, as in the example of the acting method of Clairon, no more than "imaginary phantoms of poetry" or, less still, "the spectres of the particular manner of this or that poet" [VE 315]. The same figures presented in society would occasion a burst of laughter; no one speaks in verse except the characters of Corneille and Racine, who speak poetically in a "pompous language" sustained by convention, against which no one revolts. This diatribe has one inevitable consequence, and that is to bring Diderot back up against the contrast between artifice and truth:

> Reflect for a moment on what one calls in the theatre *being true*. Is this to show things there as they are in nature? Not at all. Truth in this sense would be nothing more than commonplace. So what is the truth of the stage? It is the conformity of actions, of speech, of facial expression, of voice, of movement, of gesture with an ideal model imagined by the poet, and often exaggerated by the actor. This is what is marvellous. This model does not just influence the tone; it modifies the actor's walk, the way he holds himself. From that comes the fact that the actor in the street and the actor on the stage are two such different people that you would have difficulty identifying them.
> [VE 317]

Diderot's general disinclination to explain in the *Paradox* what exactly he means by an "ideal model" is almost certainly attributable to the fact that he considered he had already expressed his ideas most clearly in the *Salons*. The announcement of this conviction is carelessly postponed to a later moment in the *Paradox*, when the Second speaker attempts to force the First to a satisfactory definition:

> *Second*: But would not this ideal model be a chimaera?
> *First*: No.
> *Second*: But since it is ideal, it does not exist; and there is nothing in the understanding which has not existed in sensation.
> *First*: That is true. But let us take an art in its origins, sculpture, for example. It copied the first model which presented itself. It then saw that there were models which were less imperfect which it preferred. It corrected their obvious faults, and their less obvious faults, to the point at which, after a great deal of work, it attained a figure which no longer existed in nature.
> *Second*: Why?
> *First*: Because the development of a machine as complicated as an animal body cannot be regular. Go to the Tuileries or to the Champs-Elysées on a fine holiday; look at all the women who fill the pathways, and you will not find one who has the two corners of her mouth perfectly matched... But if you would like to know more on these speculative principles of art, I will show you a copy of my *Salons*. [VE 338–40]

Art criticism had occupied Diderot almost continuously since his considerable initiatives in dramatic theory and practice in the late 1750s. In the *Essays on Painting* of 1766 addressed to Grimm he had made clear his belief in the mutual influence of poetry and the fine arts, in his insistence on

> the action and reaction of the poet on the sculptor or the painter, of the sculptor on the poet, of one and of the other on the animate or inanimate beings of nature.[46]

This insistence was first expressed, with little explicit relation to the specifics of the preceding argument, in a coda to the *Discourse* on criticism and the discipline of authorship. In considering the temperament and natural gifts appropriate to a writer, Diderot cited the example of one Ariste, a man of forty, who passed under the title of a *philosophe*. Ariste is concerned that although he has the reputation for philosophy, he cannot claim to know the identity or the nature of the (Platonic) triad of "the true, the good, and the beautiful" [VE 283]. In a self-interrogation, he submits that the variability of human beings, between each other and in themselves, provides no basis for certain knowledge. What he requires is "a measure, an external model", and his starting-point is afforded by "the ancient sculptors", who determined "the proportions which seemed to them the most beautiful" [VE 284–85]. Yet progress from this point forwards, from the physical and external into the moral qualities, would seem to require a formidable course of study. His solution is that the writer and critic should propose to himself an ideal model of "the most accomplished man of letters", with the result that it will be "by the mouth of this man that he will judge the works of others and himself" [VE 285]; the same procedure might be adopted by the philosopher.

> But what use shall I make of this ideal model when I have it—one which is appropriate to my state as a philosopher, since people wish to call me one? The same as painters and sculptors have made of the model they have. I shall modify it according to circumstances.
> [VE 286]

As the artist observes and records physical variations which go with the conditions of life, so he himself will study "the passions, morals, characters, and habits" of human beings. The observed variety will then permit the composition of all kinds of poetry, from hymn to satire.

The portrait of Ariste may readily be suspected to be a self-portrait by Diderot, and it combines the means of critical judgement with those of poetic execution, although it contains virtually no reference to dramaturgy as such. The indications are, in fact, much more of the kind of preparation suited to the satire of *Rameau's Nephew*, and there is no reason to suppose that by this time Diderot's inclinations had not turned in that direction. The obvious precedent for the ideal model in classical sculpture was the *Canon* of Polyclitus, the Greek sculptor of the fifth century BC who had written a treatise on proportion to accompany the statue known as the *Spear-Carrier* (*Doryphorus*). The second precedent which is apparent is in philosophy, most conspicuously in the idealism of the triad "the true, the good, and the beautiful", and in the notion of an ideal figure through whom judgements might be made, which strongly recalls the Platonic Socrates.

An explicit relationship between the notion of the ideal model and Plato is presented assertively in Diderot's critical review of the *Salon of 1767*, which was completed in 1768 for Grimm's *Correspondence littéraire*.[47] In the preliminary address to Grimm, Diderot expresses his profound dissatisfaction with the commonplace assumptions and jargon of mediocre artists, who rely on Greek and Roman subjects, but talk no less about the "imitation of nature":

> ...and these people who talk incessantly of the imitation of beautiful nature believe in all faith that there is a beautiful nature that exists, that it is there, that one sees it when one wants, and that all one has to do is to copy it. If you said to them that it was a totally ideal entity, they would open their eyes wide, or laugh in your face.[48]

Even the most beautiful living model, if copied, would produce no more than a portrait. What is required to pass beyond particular traits to the general is an awareness of the three stages outlined in the tenth book of Plato's *Republic*. Alluding to Plato's use of the word *phantasma* (*Republic* Bk 10, 598b) to describe the aspect of objects, Diderot lists "the truth", "the existing phantom" and the painting itself as his version of the Platonic scale descending from truth through object to image. Truth is "the type, the general ideal of beauty" which does not exist in nature, and the activity of antiquity was one of alteration and refinement in the achievement of "a true, ideal model of beauty", which exists in the head. To confirm this assertion, Diderot 'quotes' the views of Garrick on acting:

> However much nature has made you someone of feeling, if you play according to yourself, or to the most perfect existing nature that you know, you will only be mediocre. When I tear out my entrails, when I utter inhuman cries, these are not my entrails, nor my cries, but those of another being whom I have conceived, and who does not exist...[49]

The concept of the ideal model is clearly meant to apply across the arts, from the fine arts themselves—with the paradigm in figurative sculpture—to the many varieties of poetry and to acting; it is even applied, in the *Discourse*, to the act of criticism and to philosophy. But although the term is constant, and the relatively unmistakeable Platonic allusion parades a guarantee of rigour, the concept is imprecise, and its application difficult. According to the statements attributed to Garrick, the "ideal model" is the agent of performance, to which the actor Garrick lends his body. What 'Garrick' describes in the *Salon* is very close to what Diderot attributes to Clairon in the *Paradox*, when she creates a model for herself which is the "highest, the greatest, and the most perfect that she could conceive". But Diderot then calls this model a "phantom", which is the term he uses for the observable world of aspects in his version of the Platonic triad, and which cannot afford to be confused with the artistic product itself. The attractions of the Platonic scheme are clearly very strong, but Diderot's distortion of it to a figure of artistic creation does not result in convincing clarity. This is particularly noticeable in the absence of any explanation of how the ideal model is modified to produce, in the case of acting, the specific portrayal required, and yet still retains its ideal stature. It is, perhaps, a perfect scheme for a theoretical and critical vision imposed on performance, in its combination of an authoritative terminology with an evocation of artistic discipline; but it does little to illuminate the practice of either Garrick or Clairon.[50]

The division of art from life, which has become a secondary subject of the *Paradox*, is effectively united with the contrast between discipline and feeling in the performer in a remarkable digression, in which Diderot scripts the actual and *sotto voce* exchanges of an actor and his wife alongside the words of the scene from Molière which they are playing. The two characters from *Le Dépit amoureux* are lovers engaged in a petulant comic quarrel, whose preposterous and mellifluous extravagance is punctuated in Diderot's script by the prosaic and staccato malice of the husband and wife who are playing them. The scene is presented by the First speaker as an anecdote, "a scene played publicly on the boards, just as I am going to give it to you, and perhaps a little better", and its effect on the Second speaker is one of great disillusionment [VE 323]. The opportunity the "simultaneous scenes" provide for the First speaker is rapidly and concisely exploited:

> If you maintain that this actor and this actress were 'feeling', I shall now ask you whether that was in the scene of the lovers, or in the scene of the husband and wife, or in both? [VE 326]

The illusion, once shaken, is thoroughly shattered by further revelations, as the First speaker parades the subsequent conversation of the actress and her lover to the Second speaker, with its discussion of dining arrangements and jealousies occasioned by a patron. The paradox is placed firmly between the two speakers, First and Second, as the First pretends that both were present at the performance:

> You exclaimed to yourself: "One must admit that this woman is a charming actress, that no one knows how to listen as she does, and that she plays with intelligence, grace, involvement, subtlety, and a rare sensibility...". And I was laughing at your exclamations.
> [VE 327]

The theorist exercises a firm control over the senses of the participants in the dialogue, with the Second speaker unable to hear the *sotto voce* exchange, and so dependent for a proof of the paradox on the First speaker, whose 'evidence' is unquestioned. This *tour de force* of specious yet imaginative argument leaves the paradoxical contention at a point of considerable confidence, on which the First speaker capitalizes by introducing the person of Garrick. The First speaker's claim to have heard the *sotto voce* 'text' of the performers is matched by his claim to have seen Garrick give a salon demonstration of his skills:

> Garrick puts his head in the gap between double-doors, and in an interval of four or five seconds his expression moves successively from ecstatic joy to moderate delight, from delight to tranquillity, from tranquillity to surprise, from surprise to astonishment, from astonishment to sadness, from sadness to despondency, from despondency to fright, from fright to horror, from horror to despair, and climbs back again from this last stage to the point from which it declined. Could his soul have experienced all these feelings, and have performed in concert with his expression this kind of tonal scale? I do not believe it for a moment, and neither do you.   [VE 328]

As a contradiction of a received opinion, the *Paradox* is meant to be shocking, but its extent cannot escape from the reiteration of its principal terms. In this respect a long-postponed definition of *sensibilité*, in its extravagance and signally theatrical applications, does little more than revive the potential objections to the central thesis:

> Sensibility, according to the sole meaning given to this term up to the present day, is as it seems to me that disposition which accompanies a weakness of organs, as a consequence of the mobility of the diaphragm, the vivacity of the imagination, and the delicacy of the nerves; which inclines someone to compassion, to nervous excitement, to admiration, to fear, to being disturbed, to tears, to fainting, to rescue, to flight, to shouting aloud, to a loss of reason, to exaggeration, to contempt, to disdain, to having no clear idea of the true, the good, and the beautiful, to being unjust, to being mad.   [VE 343]

The paradox cannot effectively leave sensibility behind because the term contains a potential description of the emotions involved in reception, which are insistent on embracing the person of the performer through the manipulative language of the poet. Rather than address these intricate problems of reception, and institute a challenge to the rule of sensibility in the *audience*, Diderot is content to remain within the limits of a single thesis. But despite the confidence of this paradoxical thesis, a tone of dissatisfaction predominates, in terms that are closely reminiscent of Rousseau:

> It is above all when everything is false that the truth is loved, above all when everything is corrupt that performances are most pure. The citizen who presents himself at the entrance to the theatre leaves his vices there to be picked up when he leaves. There he is just, impartial, a good father, a good friend, a friend of virtue; and I have often seen at my side villains profoundly indignant at actions which they would not have failed to commit had they found themselves in the same circumstances as those in which the poet had placed the character they were denouncing. [VE 354]

This is the language of the *Discourse on the Origin of Inequality* and of the *Letter to d'Alembert*. To his cynicism about the institution of theatre Diderot adds allegations of the over-bearing treatment of playwrights by actors. The public dotes on actors, but also despises them, and the effects of this contempt are passed on:

> The despotism that is exercised on them they exercise on authors, and I do not know which is the more despicable: the insolent actor or the author who puts up with him. [VE 356]

Dissatisfaction has ultimately little to offer except nostalgia, notably for the tragedies of Sophocles in which, it can be claimed, the language of drama is brought close to the tones of speech in society. The chosen example is that of Philoctetes, who recalls to Neoptolemus, in Diderot's highly compressed version of scenes from Sophocles' play, the high example set by his father:[51]

> *First*: Is there anything in this speech which you might not say to my son, or I to yours?
> *Second*: No.
> *First*: And yet it is fine.
> *Second*: Certainly.
> *First*: And does the tone of this speech pronounced on the stage differ from the tone in which it would be pronounced in society?
> *Second*: I think not.
> *First*: And would this tone in society be ridiculous?
> *Second*: Not at all. [VE 359–60]

Dialogue revives at a moment of reassertion for the reformist initiative, and yet the assertion fails to pass beyond the exemplary classic, and the sustained speech of the exemplary individual. The conclusion to the original 'observations' on Sticotti's pamphlet was on just this theme, that "the true tragedy is yet to be found, and with their faults the ancients were closer to it than we are." [VE 359]. In the *Paradox*, the Second speaker is drawn into advancing this contention; it is then supported, perversely, by Diderot's prose version of a lyrical ode by the Roman poet Horace. The First speaker transforms Horace's verse into a speech by the Roman general Regulus, haranguing the Senate on the decline of Roman virtue, and concludes his prose *précis* with the resources of the *tableau*:

> Such was his speech, and such his conduct. He refuses the embraces of his wife and children; he believes himself to be unworthy of them, like a vile slave. He fixes his stern gaze on the ground, and disdains the tears of his friends, until he has led the senators to a resolution which he alone was able to provide, and until he is allowed to return to exile.   [VE 361][52]

With this reversion to the exemplary virtues of antiquity the paradox is expended, although the 'paradoxical man', who senses he should stop, is loathe to do so.[53] What is gained is a convincing assertion of an objective discipline of performance, which by rejecting sensibility emancipates the actor from the cultural system in which the theatrical audience is enclosed. But the ambitions of Diderot's earlier theoretical vision cannot resolve the problem of the passage from feeling into language. People do not "come to see tears, but to hear speeches which draw tears, and the truth of nature is discordant with the truth of conventions" [VE 377]. Under the terms of this cynical yet perceptive aphorism, the pathos of extreme feeling, "nature at its finest", is left without an art:

> I shall explain myself. I mean to say that neither the dramatic system, nor action, nor the speeches of the poet would arrange themselves to my stifled, interrupted, sobbing declamation. You see that it is not even permitted to imitate nature, even nature at its finest, or the truth too closely, and that there are limits to which we must keep ourselves.   [ibid.]

PART TWO: ...AND AFTER

3

Brook and the Rhetoric of Theory

In this first chapter of Part Two, I shall consider the language of Peter Brook as theorist in *The Empty Space* and, more briefly, in *There Are No Secrets*. I have also included two further discourses that relate to Brook's work in Iran and Africa, which were not written by Brook, but which may be understood to complement his own writing. It is perhaps important to emphasize that I am not concerned, either here or in any of the discussions in Part Two of this book, to offer a critical commentary on particular productions or performances, or to contribute to any general assessment of these writers as practitioners.

3.1 Metaphor and dismissal in *The Empty Space*[1]

As far as I am concerned, Peter Brook's *The Empty Space* has held as much status as doctrine during my lifetime as any other argument on the theatre. This was obviously because the generation that preceded mine—as teachers, practitioners and audience-members—found the textuality of this short book a revelation. "What oft was thought, but ne'er so well expressed" would appear to summarize that reaction quite accurately. It would hardly be an exaggeration to regard it as the 'bible' of one theatrical generation in the UK. In what follows here I want to examine the language of Peter Brook in this influential series of what were originally lectures, delivered to audiences at the universities of Hull, Keele, Manchester and Sheffield. I will pay attention closely to metaphor as one device of composition, and also to the techniques and gestures of dismissal employed by Brook.

I have included these specific techniques in the general term of 'rhetoric', as the subject of analysis in this chapter, to draw attention to the combination of intention and method, of motive and means, in the texts of contemporary theory. For reader as well as writer, the text of theory is both persuasion and construction. In general, we sense the persuasion: from the beginning we are urged towards something, even if we do not know exactly what that something is. In the case of lectures—the original form of *The Empty Space*—the presentation takes the form of a series, often of a known extent: we are moved on to the next instalment, and in expectation to a conclusion, perhaps to a final revelation. In this process words are used and discarded, as persuasion surpasses its past moment in its present hold on us, in what amounts to the 'spell' of the speaker. But the present moment also almost always dislodges us towards the incumbent phrase and possibility, the 'idea round-the-corner', a promise which the evolution of the argument may continually withdraw to a tantalising extent. After all, if there was a final idea, a summation, we might want to dispense with the process, and have the idea not the means. To be frustrated of the idea enhances the means, and allows it to hold. Lectures do not always, or even normally, make good publication. Peter Brook's did, because in *The Empty Space* he withholds declaration in favour of enigma.

This beckoning quality of the discourse means that a book like *The Empty Space* can be read again and again for its content and its spell, without any firm critical faculty coming into play. Because Brook is so careful to seem not to want to 'add up' to anything, this 'seeming' can and does escape attention. But how is *The Empty Space* written? Is the speaking/writing simply casual, or is there care in it? Writing or rhetoric cannot be persuasion *without* being construction. But we do not usually look at the machinery while we are taking the ride.

There are two mechanisms that stand out for me in Brook's persuasion: metaphor and dismissal. By metaphor I initially mean grand display, the set-piece firework that explodes in front of us as part of the celebration, the obvious contrivance, an integral part of the pleasure. Here is Brook as oceanographer:

> Our relations with critics may be strained in a superficial sense: but in a deeper one the relationship is absolutely necessary: like the fish in the ocean, we need one another's devouring talents to perpetuate the sea bed's existence. However, this devouring is not nearly enough: we need to share the endeavour to rise to the surface. (36–7)[2]

From water to fire, or, rather, acid:

> I know of one acid test in the theatre. It is literally an acid test...When emotion and argument are harnessed to a wish from the audience to see more clearly into itself—then something in the mind burns. The event scorches on to the memory an outline, a taste, a trace, a smell—a picture.   (152)

The set-piece has two possibilities: it can either bemuse (Who or what rises to the surface, and why? What does it do when it has got there? Does it sink back down again?) and remain suspended, or it can lead on, to be developed fully later. The "acid test" might initially seem trite, but the concluding image, the mention of "picture", reveals itself in the "kernel engraved on my memory" of a few lines later. Engraving is certainly in Brook's mind, as it is in the "trace deeper than any imagery" of the same extended sequence on the aftermath of performance, although there is clearly a collision between the engraver's plate and the more familiar nut. It is curious how exact this figuration is, beneath the collision. The acid on the plate brings with it the notion of permanence. It is essentially ineradicable, and so susceptible of repeated imprints, unlike the fragility of most graphic forms before photography: "deeper than any imagery".

A sharp-eyed reader might also pick up an apparently casual connection here—in the idea of depth ("deeper")—between an otherwise unlikely pairing. I will return to that later, because it is in itself one of Brook's controlling metaphors, none the less formative and persuasive for being contained in a single word. But first some impression of the extraordinary metaphoric range should be given, and here there is no real substitute for a list. I have concentrated on metaphors that have some extension, and this includes the more elaborate set-pieces. From chapter one, "The Deadly Theatre": the theatre as a whore; the doctor and the lifeless body; the actor as an instrument; Broadway as a brutal machine; the actor as a master matador; generations of actors as shift-workers in a factory; footprints and signposts on the path to theatre; critics and practitioners as fish in the ocean (above); the author using literariness as a crutch for self-importance; Shakespeare as a peak in a mountain range; the modern playwright as an ostrich; the modern playwright in the prison of his seclusion; the director as a guide at night; the activity of theatre or culture as garbage disposal; the theatre as a toy made by slaves and given to children.

There is nothing particularly formidable in this range, although it is striking enough in review. The detail, of course, contains much of greater interest. Here is the figure of Shakespeare as the (pre-eminent) peak in full:

> Shakespeare was not a peak without a base, floating magically on a cloud: he was supported by scores of lesser dramatists, naturally with lesser and lesser talents—but sharing the same ambition... (40–1)

Whether it is vista and admiration, or the notion of attainment (climbing "ambition") that Brook is engaging here, he is clearly not thinking of the problem (of contending heights) that they have in the Himalayas, between Everest and K2. This is something more domestic, like the uncontested prominence of Ben Nevis or Snowdon. But it is important to note the subtlety of these relatively brief devices. This peak is "supported": one thinks, "naturally" enough, of shoulders, the shoulders of mountains or of people, and the picture immediately changes to one of human choice and will, of 'election', significantly by contemporaries, as in Ben Jonson's celebrated eulogy prefixed to the First Folio by its editors. This was placed, incidentally, opposite the Droeshout engraving of Shakespeare. A lot is achieved in a few lines; one cannot elude the effects of metaphor.

And the effects are cumulative. It is tempting, since the exercise will hardly be repeated, to draw out the full list of metaphors in this remarkable document. I shall, instead, make what is a brief but demonstrative selection. From chapter two, "The Holy Theatre": opera and ballet as adulterated wine; actors rubbed together like sticks to produce fire; Artaud as a prophet in the desert; the world of appearances as the crust of a volcano; the audience raped and "filled with a new charge"; bad 'Happenings' like a child mixing all the colours in a paintbox. From chapter three, "The Rough Theatre": obscenity and truculence as motors of revival; the stream of comedy branching and drying up; Chekhov as a skin surgeon; Chekhov as a tape-recorder left running; ironing Shakespeare into a typography of theatre; the Shakespearian play as a prism; *The Winter's Tale* as a musical composition, changing its keys; the dark, flowing current of *Titus Andronicus*. From chapter four, "The Immediate Theatre": the theatre as a magnifying glass, and a reducing lens; living events as dangerous electricity; the actor as Pavlov's dog; the actor like a garden with ever-growing weeds; the mediocre actor as a marksman who cannot hit the bulls-eye; direction as a dance (a waltz, in fact); direction following the principle of the rotation of crops; RSC touring groups like commandos; hunger and thirst in the audience; the theatre advancing crabwise; the theatre as an acid test; the theatre as a searchlight, a formula, an equation, as an arena, or as a slate wiped clean.

The list is descriptive, as well as selective: it does not attempt to reproduce the phrasing of the original. So by itself, it is perhaps just amusing, with no particular trace of the effects I have indicated in the initial examples I quoted. But is there a principle involved, apart from that of reliance (on metaphor as an ornament, for example) and of diversity? There are, even in the shortlist I have given, one or two indications of some sort of consistency in figuration: of flow, current, fire and light, and the iron of industry. I have already mentioned "deep" as a recurrent, single-word image, and there are in fact many of these—sometimes in associative groups—throughout *The Empty Space*. Their recurrence and consistency link the disparate parts of the discourse together, and provide a context for the more distinct, free-standing metaphors such as those listed above. Once again, I shall not attempt to be exhaustive.

A prominent group is of images of movement: words such as search, approach, path, way, goal. These words are purposeful: they (most usually) give a constructive view of theatre, and of the argument itself leading through to an end. So, to take an arbitrary selection of single-word and more extended metaphors from this group, we hear/read of the critic as a pathmaker (36), of shifting oneself from character to character (38), of steps to the answer (43), of the director as a guide (43–4), of searching for a new discrimination to extend the horizons of the real (108), of approaching the landscape of one's own emotions (132), of the passage of strong feelings (152), of truth in the theatre on the move (157). This sense of freedom and scope, and of achievement, is particularly applicable to Shakespeare: Shakespeare has "free passage from the world of action to the world of inner impressions" (97), it is he who is allowed to "roam the world" (97), and to "pass through many stages of consciousness" (98), in a particularly purple passage in chapter three.

Movement is also implied in a second group of images of flow, of "cascading words" (48), of streams, of currents, and of action that is "crystal clear" (92), of "tapping resources" (80), of a company (the Living Theatre) that without acting would "run dry" (69), of the "real main stream of art's essence" (89), of the stream of comedy (noted above). Romantic theatre, during the (second world) war, "came like water to the thirst of dry lips" (48), happy endings and optimism must "spring from a source", and they "can't be ordered like wine from the cellars" (53). Opera and ballet are, as I have noted, like adulterated wine (50), whereas Godard in the cinema "cracked into dead Illusion and enabled a stream of opposing impressions to stream forth" (91). There are related ideas: an actor may take a plunge (133) into a speech as well as a "running jump" (137), though since in the last case the speeches are "splendid slabs of storm music" this seems a little suicidal. There is also something usefully vague about nature: at one point "the indefinable stuff begins to flow" (122), at another "something flows more freely" (149). Perhaps this is "boiling matter" from the volcano (58), not such a flippant suggestion as it might seem, when actors and directors are potentially "explosions of human matter" (59–60).

It is important not to laugh—or, at least, not too much—at this accumulation of matter. After all, we do not laugh when we are reading the book. The listing is funny because devices *are* funny when they are seen as mechanical, much as Bergson determined for laughter, in the theatre or elsewhere. But the effect of them is perfectly serious: not only does an associative, repetitive group empower metaphors and lend them coherence and so persuasiveness, it also admits remarkable subtleties. If the audience has a need, a "thirst" (48) and a "hunger"(49), who then would give them the adulterated wine of opera and ballet, who would want "wishy-washy" poetic drama (54), the "sloppiest and thinnest plays" of Chekhovian extraction (89), or the "mish-mash of intellectual confusion" that is natural to modern England (94)? Metaphor deployed with consistency, and on this scale, allows a remarkable degree of control, and what we could justly call finesse. At the extreme, questions that are posed in Shakespeare can then recur "diluted" in life (101), which whatever else it may be taken to mean certainly puts life firmly in its place.

The aspirational metaphor of movement and the natural, romantic metaphor of streams and flows join with the industrial-electric version of "currents" and "charge" (undoubtedly the familiar 'electricity' of theatre), and with the crucial "living"/"deadly" axis, as the most predominant groups throughout *The Empty Space*. A critic may be "vital" (37), and so may be the theatre. Material may be "lively" (when it is Shakespearian, 41), theatrical experiences "vital" (74), roughness is "livelier" (108), we read of a "living flow" (128), "vivid…responses" (147), of the vital element in rehearsal coming from the director (156); and, conversely, of "lifeless" imitations (154), and the whole apparatus of "deadly" theatre. Similarly, the theatrical status quo may be "rotten" (36), and potential or actual "decay" engenders the scheme of healthy nourishment envisioned in "hunger and thirst" (49, 53, 64), in the craving for true experience (13), and in theatre-going "as an experience that feeds our lives" (51). This belief in sound nourishment is not just a matter of the right diet: it is also one of digestion. Artaud's writings, when "a tenth digested" (131), have done a great deal of harm to actors, and this leads to a naive belief, "fed further by ill-digested...bits of Grotowski" (132). Vitality has two obvious opposites: what is dead may smell ("a child can smell it out", 14), or it may be cold (73), "frozen" (17, 88, 125, 157), "rigid" (14), or "fossilized" (88, 125).

Of course, Brook—as the first-person of his own discourse—is inevitably the metaphoric doctor who determines life and death; but metaphoric conviction can be impulsive beyond the point where it is an effective aid to persuasion. This is the case with the emotive discussion of *Titus Andronicus*. Brook dismisses the idea that the play is "a string of gratuitous strokes of melodrama", and sees instead "a dark, flowing current out of which surge the horrors" (106). It is unusual for Brook to give a threatening tone to 'streams' or 'flows', or to his water imagery in general. I can think of some exceptions: one can have too much of a soaking (Poland is/was "drenched in both Communism and Catholicism", 94), and the enlivening (cold?) "douches of normality" brought by the clowns in *Measure for Measure* (99) contrast with the "emotional steam bath" of misunderstood *catharsis* (107–108), and with actors unfairly suspected (by outsiders) of "splashing about in self-indulgent euphoria" (126). In the case of *Titus*, "dark" in particular is distinctly ambiguous: it connects with the positive side of one potent axis (invisible/visible), although it also hints significantly at the language of psychology, which is "mushy, shifting, dark, imprecise" (87). But we are probably dealing here far more explicitly with the idea of "depth" as "truth", with "the unfathomable nature of man" (93). Since Brook also writes just above of beginning "to unearth the themes that Shakespeare so carefully buried" in *The Tempest*, and of *Titus* beginning "to yield its secrets", it is relatively clear that we should understand an underworld source for these floods. The pre-Christian Hades, with the gloomy river Styx, habitat of horrors and monsters, is a suitable provenance for the "powerful and eventually barbaric ritual" that Brook finds in the play. But the dilemma is then increasingly acute: how exactly are we meant to detach the word melodrama from the play, when these classical Stygian metaphors so strongly suggest the undoubtedly Senecan origins of this grim Elizabethan type?

Not that this dilemma matters: for we are already at sea if we have accepted the picture of the modern playwright as an ostrich, and of Shakespeare as a mountain. That is (and was) what is (and was) so exciting. *The Empty Space* is a glorious fantasy, and part of its attraction— in the 'headiness' induced by metaphor, and removed in an interesting experiment by Brook's actors from *Romeo and Juliet* (135–6)—is the fantastic opportunity for dismissal. Metaphor is the associative power of language, the "magic" that pervades this discourse and elicits conviction. But the true "force" of *The Empty Space* lies in its dismissals, for which the sense of power induced by metaphor is the "source". Metaphor orders the world, and it can also organize our contempt. I cannot list here everyone and everything put into place, or controlled *en passant*, by Brook in this elaborate display, but some examples may give the prompt to a re-reading alert to this device.

> The deadly spectator/the scholar (12–3); mediocre authors (13); the angry and impatient young actor (14); experts without first-hand knowledge (14); traditional actors (14); young and old actors at the Comédie Française (14–5); the Formosan Opera Company, "skimping...details" (17); grand opera (20); New York theatre, on Broadway (20–4); successful American actors (23); New York critics; an audience in Philadelphia (25–6); a girl at the Actors' Studio, "pouring her ardour and energy uselessly in the wrong direction" (31); the actor, as his career grows (32); the average actor (33); a permanent company, "doomed to deadliness...without an aim,...a method,...a school" (34); theatrical production—"the quantity of rubbish in our playhouses", scores of plays "betrayed by a lack of elementary skills" (35–6); theatrical personnel—"this art...served largely by casual labour" (35); the deadly writer (38); the author in the French theatre (38); new plays, in a catalogue of their failings (39); the present-day author, "locked in the prison of anecdote, consistency and style" (41); the director "serving an author" (43); the deadly director (44); designers and composers, "partners" of the deadly director (44).

These examples are drawn from the first, overtly dismissive chapter. But, there again, dismissal is Brook's own choice of opening, and some serious questions must remain: was the British theatre, for example, really this bad, this "deadly" and unskilled, by 1967–68? A decade or fifteen years earlier, perhaps; at least, arguably so. But the RSC, continuing activity at the Royal Court, the Mermaid, Olivier's company at the Old Vic, the decision to build on the South Bank of the Thames, and many other developments of the professional and national theatre in the UK belong to the sixties, as does a relatively historic regeneration of distinctly theatrical writing. This last fact is one of the few elements of contemporary reality that Brook allows (briefly, 39) to disturb his depressing domestic picture. But it is, characteristically, dismissed very quickly: "None the less, whether scholar or actor, too few authors are what we could truly call inspiring or inspired." (ibid.).

The list continues: Gordon Craig's predilection for painted trees and forests (50), "threadbare" ritual at Coventry Cathedral (ibid.), and, apparently, a similar 'deadliness' at Stratford—"when I first went to Stratford...every conceivable value was buried in deadly sentimentality and complacent worthiness" (51); the unfortunate guests at the celebration of Shakespeare's anniversary, the sterility of the theatre before the second world war in France, the theatre of the Absurd, followers of Artaud, bad Happenings, a child painting, "free form", the untrained man, most avant-garde and experimental groups, theatre architects, even German electronic music studios (74) cannot seem to get it right. Is there something very English about this summary disdain? Foreigners do not seem to come out of it very well, although there are some notable exceptions (Brecht, Weiss, Genet). Nor do actors, or designers content with "delivery of the sets and costume sketches" (114), "good painters" when they work in the theatre, Voltaire (who labelled Shakespeare as "barbaric", 98), matinée-goers who are pleased with little (106), flybynight impresarios in South America (93), Parisian intellectuals watching Genet (83), or Mozart's *Magic Flute* at the Metropolitan Opera, despite the accompaniment of an exhibition of pictures by Marc Chagall (148). Even Cunningham, Beckett and Grotowski, who come in for some initial approval in the chapter on Holy Theatre, are eventually "theatres for an *élite*" (67). Of British playwrights, John Arden's *Serjeant Musgrave's Dance* stands out as "remarkable", but then Brook directed the play; David Rudkin's *Afore Night Come* has some of the "disturbing" ritual qualities identified in *Titus* (53). Two seedy, spangled clowns in Hamburg (in 1946), the critic "exercising his vital function" (35–6; but "How many critics see their job this way?", 37), and psycho-drama in an asylum, which is "a necessary theatre" (150) also win some approval. But it is Brecht and Shakespeare—and people such as William Poel, "One of the pioneer figures in the movement towards a renewed Shakespeare" (75) or Peter Hall, in his cycle of Shakespeare's *Wars of the Roses*—who gain substantial appreciation.

A "*movement towards* a *renewed* Shakespeare": approach, attainment, vitality. Brechtianism is fine, at least in the Berliner Ensemble; in particular, "through alienation we could reach some of those areas that Shakespeare touched by his dynamic devices in language" (82). But outside that group, "Brecht is destroyed by deadly slaves" (86). Even the Berliner Ensemble drifts from approval when it alters the text of Shakespeare's *Coriolanus*: "a tiny defect that became for me a deep, interesting flaw." (92). And after the qualified approval for Artaud, Cunningham, Beckett and Grotowski, the way forward points inexorably back: "the model, as always, is Shakespeare" (69).

I will not expend much space on Brook's relatively transparent comments on actors, and the alleged generic shortcomings which amount to a dependency, even for guidance on what to read (work built on "fag-ends of doctrine", 131). But the actor is drastically subject to performance clichés (125, 130), is understood as a garden in which the "weeds always grow" (128), and is ultimately quite incapable of self-determination, unless his age and his reputation (Gielgud), or a close association with Brook (Scofield), demand respect. "The Immediate Theatre", Brook's final chapter, is incisive in establishing the theatrical need for its author. It is also dependent on a bewildering barrage of theatrical clichés, those lapsed metaphors that litter(ed) everyday practice in the theatre, but which do not make exciting reading: I counted something over three hundred in the work, of which over two hundred occur in the final chapter. But the techniques of dismissal present themselves most effectively in connection with the inadequacies of the (modern) playwright. The discussion I quote takes place after the mention of group creation, "which can be infinitely richer, if the group is rich, than the product of weak individualism", and after the determination of "compactness and focus" as the missing qualities in collective work.

> In theory few men are as free as a playwright. He can bring the whole world onto his stage. But in fact he is strangely timid. He looks at the whole of life, and like all of us he only sees a tiny fragment: a fragment, one aspect of which catches his fancy. Unfortunately, he rarely searches to relate his detail to any larger structure—it is as though he accepts without question his intuition as complete, his reality as all of reality. It is as though his belief in his subjectivity as his instrument and his strength precludes him from any dialectic between what he sees and what he apprehends. So there is either the author who explores his inner experience in depth and darkness, or else the author who shuns these areas, exploring the outside world—each one thinks his world is complete. If Shakespeare had never existed we would quite understandably theorize that the two can never combine. The Elizabethan theatre did exist, though—and awkwardly enough we have this example constantly hanging over our heads.   (40)

The general tenor of this passage is plain enough, and most of the strategic metaphors should be familiar: search and exploration, depth and the equivocal 'darkness' (Brook's language for the psyche), and a key axis, the unexamined 'inner/outer' antithesis, which clearly connects with 'invisible/visible'. But an analysis of the tactical construction may be useful.

Mention of the "group" has encouraged the definition of the playwright's activity as "individualism", and the buzz-word "rich"—always positive—has permitted the apparently consequential contrast in "weak". This construction is one version of the formula known technically as a *chiasmus*, a cross-over, which here deploys contrasting terms as if they were a logical antithesis. A similar construction is also apparent in the "in theory...free/strangely timid" formula, which introduces preliminary doubts concerning 'theory', and substitutes the more intriguing "strangely" for the more automatic "in theory/in fact". "Timid" is, of course, pejorative. The antithesis is then given just the degree of conviction it needs by an unmistakeable allusion to the familiar Shakespearian quotation: "All the world's a stage...". In this altered form the 'quote' does service as a subliminal suggestion about the qualities of Shakespeare's work. This should prepare us, and does, for the conclusion; it also aims to engage a justification for the immediate belittling of the playwright. The playwright—unlike Shakespeare—is "like all of us", and he can see only an "aspect" of a "tiny fragment" (of the whole of life). This is a clear case of a reduction-to-the-absurd ('a part of a tiny part of the whole'), which is made more effective by the emphatic repetition of the word "fragment". And "fragment"—as opposed to part—has the additional advantage here of suggesting that the 'whole' has in fact broken up, and so is now no longer really available.

The structure of the next two sentences needs little commentary: repetition between sentences ("it is as though..."—a proposition *inviting* acceptance, as a relief from a sequence of direct statements) and within them ("his..., his..."; "reality", repeated; "his...his..."; "what he...", repeated). The sequence of opening gambits ("In theory...", "Unfortunately...", "It is as though...", and "So there is...") is interesting in moving from a dubious certainty to a substituted conviction. The mention of "subjectivity" has been prepared for by the earlier "individualism"; the initial achievement in including "weak" with "individualism" in the preliminary definition also prepares for the suggestion of the playwright's delusion of "strength".

The climax is, of course, the elaborate antithesis of the two authors, exploring either "inner experience" or "the outside world", who suddenly appear split from the previously unified "he" of the argument so far; and it is noticeable that a strong notional negative ("darkness" and "shuns") is attached to each of them. The presentation, which offers a direct and unsatisfactory choice of alternatives, can then only be resolved by a transcendent term: Shakespeare. The introduction of "understandably" softens the dismissal of 'theorizing' through relieving the reader of responsibility for an error. But the final sanction is achieved by history-as-fact: "The Elizabethan Theatre did exist, though...", unlike the good modern playwright.

Throughout, the consistent male gender—the most striking of all the repetitions in this passage—has an important role to play: the "weak individualism" and "subjectivity" of the (modern—subsequent? younger?) male writer contrasts with the male 'completeness' (fully-formed? adult?) of Shakespeare. That this is meant to engage what we might call an Oedipal sense of inadequacy can hardly be doubted.

The rhetorical structure of *The Empty Space* is that of revelation. And this revelation ultimately takes the form of an exclusive devotion: "You shall not come to the father except through me".

3.2 The genesis of theory: the 'Theatre of Cruelty' season in 1964

The Empty Space seems to summarize Peter Brook's thinking in the sixties. The series of lectures began early in 1965, and the text was finally published in the autumn of 1968, following the collaboration with the poet Ted Hughes on Seneca's *Oedipus*, seen by most commentators as an Artaudian work. This was also the year in which Grotowski's *Towards a Poor Theatre* appeared in English translation, for which Brook provided a short preface, reworked from a summary introduction to Grotowski's significance written originally on the occasion of the performance of *US* in 1966. As theoretical reflections arising directly from directorial practice and ordered into one coherent presentation, the two works testify to the growing emphasis on the textuality of theory in the sixties. This tendency received a strong initial impetus from the English-language translation of Artaud's *The Theatre and Its Double* in 1958, was fortified by the publication of John Willett's translated collection *Brecht on Theatre* in 1964, and echoed in *The Presence of the Actor* in 1972, by Joseph Chaikin, director of the Open Theatre, who had been in contact with both Brook and Grotowski. In terms of a history of theory, this decade achieved a crucial transformation, because it united Anglo-American inclinations with a variety of European theory, and signalled an end to the professional pragmatism that had been prevalent in the UK, and to the virtual monopoly of methods derived from Stanislavski in the USA.[3]

The Empty Space has been linked to *Towards a Poor Theatre* by one leading Brook scholar, David Williams, who describes the books as "two of the seminal theoretical texts for the modern theatre", in his *Casebook* on Peter Brook.[4] In the organization of this collection of commentaries on Brook's practice, Williams determines the 1962 production of *King Lear* as "a major crossroads" in Brook's career; Albert Hunt, a collaborator with Brook on *US* in 1966, writing in 1975 of Brook's *The Ik* fixes on the *Encore* essays by Brook of the very early sixties as the point of departure for a new set of assumptions.[5] These testimonies carry considerable authority; but from the theoretical standpoint the conjunction of Brook with Artaud in the RSC's experimental 'Theatre of Cruelty' season early in 1964 provides an important marker. Brook's collaborator on that project was the director and critic Charles Marowitz, and both practitioners were interviewed by Simon Trussler, who was repeatedly sceptical about the relationship between the work in hand and the theories of Artaud.

In his replies to questioning, Brook reveals a number of concerns that establish unequivocally a continuum with the principal tenets of *The Empty Space*. His greatest interest is in what he calls "a theatre of synthesis", and after comments on the separation of the achievement of writers from that of performers, he adduces his theoretical model of the Elizabethan theatre:

> To relate this to one other thing: I think it's our job today to discover how we can make any contemporary theatre event as bold and dense as an Elizabethan event could be, facing the fact that the blank-verse device which the Elizabethans used no longer fits, and that we have to find something else. We're exploring what can take the place of blank-verse in the theatre: that is really the simplest summing-up of what we are doing.[6]

Brook also paradoxically conjoins, in partial explanation of his idea of "a theatre of synthesis", the modes and potential models advanced by both Artaud and Brecht—"the nearest thing to an Artaud theatre we have had was the Brecht theatre"—and then resolves this paradox in a manner that might readily be predicted by a contemporary reader of *The Empty Space*:

Brecht, by being both writer and director, could also create a completely formal structure, which had as complete an existence as a play of Shakespeare's has on the printed page. The contradiction...between the Committed Theatre and the Theatre of the Absurd is a false one.[7]

The transcendent quality of Shakespeare, as the textual paradigm of an Elizabethan model, is an unmistakeable component of this elaborate evasion, and it coheres with other, significant indications of a theoretical position. The modern and contemporary writer is largely disjoined from the project of experimentation, and his role only considered relevant when conjoined closely to that of the director. Brook did actually script a relatively successful piece for this season; but his comments are more interesting for their foreshadowing of the close collaboration between script-writer and himself, in the evolution of performance texts. This is noticeable in his relationships with Denis Cannan, Ted Hughes, and Jean-Claude Carrière, and produced performance works such as *US, Orghast, The Ik* and, more conventionally, *The Mahabharata*.

Equally striking in these summaries of aim is the emphasis on the absence of a paradigmatic theatrical language, one which might substitute for the blank verse of the Elizabethans. The word 'language' is, in fact, missing, and in its place stands "device". It is relatively clear, even here, that the intended replacement may well not be one of directly verbal, 'grammatical' speech. Artaud provides the inspiration for exercises, putting the performer, as Brook states, "in situations where, for instance, he has to take his first impulse and turn it maybe into a pure sound like an Artaud cry, maybe into formal gesture, maybe into a leap...".[8] This particular interpretation of Artaudian principles is echoed by Marowitz in his account of the work: "Little by little, we insinuated the idea that the voice could produce sounds other than the grammatical combinations of the alphabet.".[9] It eventually became far more than an experimental principle, because its theoretical importance is plain in accounts of the work with Hughes, notably in *Orghast*, as reflected in Smith's *Orghast at Persepolis*, but also in the expedition to Africa, recorded in Heilpern's *Conference of the Birds*: that is, with the experimental work with the International Centre for Theatre Research starting in 1970, to which I shall return.

In fact, what is remarkable about the brief 'Theatre of Cruelty' season, as it exists in the written record, is the relative stability of conceptual framework, working practice and institutional quality which it lays down. In terms of working method, Marowitz bears witness to the use of nonsense text (in auditions), and "of objects thrown out on to the stage", e.g. a toy shovel, and to interruption and disorientation: "When something has begun to develop, when the actor feels he is finally *on* to something, another object...is thrown out".[10] These methods—textual fracture or the use of non-semantic sound, and object-improvisation—are in their distinct ways the basis for *Orghast* and the methodology for Africa (in the improvisations known as "The Shoe Show" and "The Bread Show"), and the multiple accounts of rehearsal and production-preparation over many years of activity demonstrate their regular recurrence.[11] But perhaps even more significant, as a prediction of future developments, is the alliance of experiment, what Marowitz terms "a sort of laboratory situation",[12] with the selection of a specific group for the research, and the freedom from commercial pressures secured by blanket subsidy from extra-theatrical sources. Granted Marowitz's later and trenchant critique of Brook's work, the concluding comment to his summary of the short 1964 season carries a little irony:

> It is to the everlasting credit of Peter Hall and the Royal Shakespeare Company that it was understood from the start that this work required total subsidy.[13]

The money for the project came from the Gulbenkian Foundation, which joined with a prestigious list (the Ford and Anderson Foundations) in providing "unprecedented" funding for Brook's International Centre for Theatre Research in 1970.

3.3 Intertextuality: *The Empty Space* and *Orghast at Persepolis*

The establishment and the work of Brook's experimental group, the CIRT, have been recorded in publication, and, as I have stated, I do not intend to duplicate the detailed or critical accounts of his productions.[14] But I am concerned with Brook's theory, and the two substantial records that exist of his early projects, Smith's *Orghast at Persepolis* and Heilpern's *Conference of the Birds*, are of considerable value in this respect partly because of their narrative length, and partly because of their sustained, individual commentary.[15]

It is interesting, in reading Smith's *Orghast at Persepolis*, to note how quickly and how thoroughly *The Empty Space* established itself as a textual reference point, and a repository of dogmatic clarity. The account in Smith's introductory chapter of Brook's work from 1964 to 1970 is an excellent example of an intertextual narrative, in which chronological indications of activity are interwoven with regular citations from Brook's writing, and with confirmations given by Smith himself. In this respect, it is an interesting manifestation of Smith's invited role on the Centre's "Persian expedition", where it was suggested that he should act "not as an official chronicler, but as a writer concerned [himself] with the questions about theatre the Centre is asking.".[16] The role is curiously defined: official or unofficial, Smith, like Heilpern after him and the numerous recorders of Brook's exploratory or rehearsal work on productions, is a chronicler, and there are uneasy connotations in the idea of an "expedition" to Persia. Smith actually writes as if Brook has cited himself (from *The Empty Space*) as the textual authority for the privilege of privacy afforded to the group:

> Brook made one condition. Its premise is in his book, *The Empty Space*: "The work is privileged, thus private: there must be no concern about whether one is being foolish or making mistakes" (*E.S.* 140). I was not to record or comment upon the work of individual actors.[17]

Theory can have a binding effect, no matter how humanely expressed.

It is moderately clear from Smith's introductory chapter that he sees *The Empty Space* not only as a summation of Brook's achievements and conclusions in the hectic period of the mid-1960s, but also as a rubric for the research work set in motion by the foundation of the CIRT in 1970. To that extent, *The Empty Space* is a founding document as well as a theoretical treatise. In particular, Smith collates the experimental characteristics of the activity of the 1960s with religious imagery, and the idea of the group. Brook is identified with the scientist, with a need for research that exceeds his knowledge of the history of theatre:

> Brook...means a form of research much closer to that of scientists in an experimental laboratory: the search for processes, combinations, causes and effects hitherto unknown.[18]

This phraseology repeats that of Marowitz on the 'Theatre of Cruelty' season in the interview with Trussler, and Smith is sharp enough to observe that Brook's first production was of Marlowe's *Doctor Faustus*, the prototype of the research spirit, though he abstains from any mention of the obvious ironies.[19] *The Empty Space*, which was cited as evidence for Brook's knowledge of theatre history, is used as the source for summaries of the 'Theatre of Cruelty' experiment, for references to the quest for "a holy theatre" (*E.S.* 55), and for the telling commentary on the inadequacies of the actor and his existing resources (*E.S.* 125).

The Empty Space is also used by Smith to advance the notion of "sharing" in group activity, in an exemplary intertextual combination: a citation from *The Empty Space* (*E.S.* 118) on the "shared difficulties" of the *Marat/Sade* production is glossed with a comment from Smith on the discipline of sharing, and then reconfirmed by a further quotation from *The Empty Space* (*E.S.* 27), on the *US* production.[20] The passage then continues with observations on the fraught relationship with audiences, culled from diverse sections of Brook's lectures, and concludes with an extraordinary meld of Brook, Smith, Meyerhold and even D.H. Lawrence, illustrating what, for Smith, is "the truth of what Brook says in the case of tragedy":

> There are moments, often of great simplicity, when the drama, actors and audience melt into a shared experience that is greater than the sum of its parts. "From the fiction between the actor's creativity and the spectator's imagination, a clear flame is kindled", said Meyerhold. Unfamiliar levels of consciousness are opened up; the theatre's original purpose, sacred and healing, is manifest once more. The spectator, whose presence is essential to this biochemistry, becomes, in DH Lawrence's phrase, "a man in his wholeness wholly attending".
>
> However, such a phenomenon was not general among the audiences of *US*... .[21]

The combination of laboratory and religious imagery, notably of revelation, is remarkable for its levels of intoxication, which are made all the more striking by the sudden and almost comic return to objectivity and the world of plain fact.

The problematic presence of the audience, the inherent limitations of actors, the quest for 'holy theatre', and the concept of 'sharing' are significantly drawn together by Smith from *The Empty Space* in an indication of the directions to be taken by Brook, with the additional metaphor of the 'laboratory' and 'scientific' research apparently added by Brook himself. This programmatic reading of the foundation-text is then completed in direct relation to the *Orghast* project itself, and to the role of Ted Hughes. The involvement of Hughes in Brook's scheme is traced to the passage in *The Empty Space* (*E.S.* 39–40) where Brook observes, in relation to the collective work on *US*, that there is "eventually a need for authorship". Smith sees this theoretical maxim, which is more than a little equivocal in its original context of a severe critique of the theatre writer, as a prediction of the role assigned to Hughes, at first in *Oedipus* of 1968 (an adaptation by Hughes from a translation of Seneca's script), and then in the creation of the language which gave its name to the production known as *Orghast*.

The raw material for *Orghast* included the Greek of Aeschylus' *Persians*, the Zoroastrian language of the Avesta, the myths of Prometheus and Heracles, Persian legends, with the influence of Calderon's *Life Is a Dream*, and the sound patterns created by Hughes in the Orghast language itself (ORG—'life, being', and GHAST—'spirit, flame', as Smith explains).[22] The inspiration for the production, and for the new language, was undoubtedly Artaudian—the "pure sound like an Artaud cry" mentioned by Brook in the interview on the 'Theatre of Cruelty'— and this inspiration is given a programmatic context, as Smith sees it, in a passage from *The Empty Space*:

> Is there another language, just as exacting for the author as a language of words? Is there a language of sounds—a language of word-as-part-of-movement, of word-as-lie, word-as-parody, of word-as-rubbish, of word-as-contradiction, of word-shock or word-cry? (*E.S.* 55)

Brook's discussion of the 'Theatre of Cruelty' experiment at this point also contained a curiously biblical reference to "the illuminated genius" of pre-war France—"Yet in the desert one prophet raised his voice" (*E.S.* 54)—which would appear to foreshadow the 'expedition' to Persia, but is passed over by Smith. In the event, it is hardly surprising that the film of the *Orghast* production was finally justified by reference to Artaud, despite some objections and reservations. As Smith records, "it was pointed out what interest there would be now in, say, a film of Artaud's pre-war production of *The Cenci*".[23] The scientific and laboratory model here prevailed for some of the actors, "who argued that, as a privileged research company, they had some obligation to record their findings".[24] The continuity of theoretical reference was sealed by the inclusion by Brook himself of an extended passage from *The Empty Space* in the programme for performance at Persepolis:

> A word does not start as a word—it is an end product which begins as an impulse, stimulated by attitude and behaviour which dictates the need for expression. This process occurs inside the dramatist; it is repeated inside the actor. Both may only be conscious of the words, but both for the author and then for the actor the word is a small visible portion of a gigantic unseen formation. Some writers attempt to nail down their meaning and intentions in stage directions and explanations, yet we cannot help being struck by the fact that the

best dramatists explain themselves the least. They recognize that further indications will most probably be useless. They recognize that the only way to find the true path to the speaking of a word is through a process that parallels the original creative one. (*E.S.* 15)

In relation to the production concept and performance instance advanced by Brook and Hughes, there was an element of justice in alluding to the idea that "the best dramatists explain themselves the least", although, once again, the original context has been significantly altered: in *The Empty Space*, the reflections are made in connection with playing Shakespeare. But at the centre of this further occasion of an explicit intertextuality lies the transcending role and potency of metaphor, and the haunting if enigmatic polarity of the visible and the invisible. The paradoxical emphasis in the totality of the experiment that was *Orghast* lay on communication, although the proposed filmic record was actually to be made in the absence of an audience, which to Smith at least presented the concept of a 'record of research findings' with an awkward dilemma.[25] "What communicates on what level through what form?" was Brook's summary, thematic question in the festival debate after performance,[26] and it is initially awkward for theory to establish how an assessment might be made, or who exactly would be in a position to make it. But Brook's assistant director, on this as on other projects, was Geoffrey Reeves, and his belief seems to have been that the scientific model closed on the director:

> The problem with research work is that it is primarily a director's pursuit, it cannot ultimately prove as satisfying to an actor as engaging in what is called a finished work of art.[27]

These comments were made in relation to a performance in the village of Jar, which "ended in confusion, among loud conversations in the audience which were obviously not about the action but about the odd evening visited on Jar".[28] Yet Reeves, who perhaps rightly included himself in the category of 'director', was convinced of the reality of communication of much of this performance in the village, and experiences of that kind were to be given far greater prominence in the trip to Africa.

The general theoretical dilemma posed, but not satisfactorily resolved by *Orghast*, was one of a definition of theatrical 'language', which is central to Brook's relatively open concept of 'communication'. So we read, in Smith's concluding "Retrospect", that

> the basic theme of the work is the examining of forms of communication to see whether there are elements in the theatrical vocabulary that pass directly, without going through the stage once removed of cultural or other references.[29]

It is by no means clear that the concept of language, or of vocabulary, can be sundered from "cultural or other references" and retain its semantic value for discourse, theoretical or otherwise. Brook himself was to observe, in connection with a Kathakali performance, that he found the "hieratic gestures" represented "something mythical and remote, from another culture, nothing to do with my life", as Bharucha has acutely noted.[30] In respect of *Orghast*, Brook once again resorts to metaphor to facilitate conviction: the Greek of Aeschylus and the language of the Avesta are described as "atom-charged" and "energy-charged" in a renewal of the vitalist imagery, and of the groups associated with 'current' familiar from *The Empty Space*. Far more extreme dilemmas are opened in the substitution of "exchange" for the key-word 'communication' in one final summary:

> It was an experimental situation full of elements of pure observation and research, and I was all the time trying to discover what are the techniques by which a healthy exchange could take place in a limited period of time.[31]

The idea of "exchange" sits very awkwardly indeed with Brook's astounding comparison of his group to that of Cortez, "the tiny band that in some unaccountable way spread an influence through a vast nation".[32] I shall review the contention that 'interculturalism' involves exchange in *Part Three* of this book. For the moment, this conspectus of Brook's theory requires a consideration of the trip to Africa organized by Brook and the CIRT for the winter of the following year (1972–73).

3.4 Theoretical 'failure' and *Conference of the Birds*

In his conclusions on *Orghast* and the expedition to Persia declared to Smith, Brook had commented that the concept of Africa was, to him, "not geographical, but symbolic".[33] It is not clear how far this strange characterization related for him to the continent's proposed role in continuing research, experiment and theory; but Williams has commented, in relation to the CIRT, that "Brook saw Africa as the logical next step in their work".[34]

The major account of the journey through Africa across the Sahara and through Nigeria (but not of the return) by Brook and performers from the CIRT and their support team comes from John Heilpern in *Conference of the Birds: The Story of Peter Brook in Africa*. Heilpern, like Smith, was a chronicler, although unlike Smith he passes very little comment on his own initial involvement in the project, and, again unlike Smith, he is distinctly uninterested in any elements of explicit and stated intertextuality with *The Empty Space*. He is, instead, much more concerned with personalities, of the performers, crew and Brook himself, of whom he provides a sensitive pen-portrait. He is also, by degrees, far more outspoken.

The title of Heilpern's book, and the apparent theme of the African project, was drawn from a twelfth-century Persian poem by Farîd al-Dîn 'Attâr of Nîshâpûr, which exercised Brook's interest over an extended period.[35] In fact, a large amount of the work undertaken and performed in Africa centred on thematically unrelated improvisations, for one of which, 'The Shoe Show', Heilpern provided a working and non-verbal scenario.[36] Nonetheless, the importance of *Conference of the Birds* was far more than that attached to thematic material, as Heilpern's interpretative paraphrase of the poem makes clear:

> Brook was hoping to develop one particular performance in Africa—the Persian masterpiece, *The Conference of the Birds*. It's the story of a journey. And like many allegorical poems of the East the journey is a symbolic pilgrimage. A long search is undertaken only to find that what you're searching for can be found on your doorstep...
>
> In *The Conference of the Birds*, many birds meet for a conference to discuss how best to search for God. The Hoopoe, their leader and teacher, warns them that the journey abroad involves total discipline and sacrifice...
>
> At this the birds grow hesitant, which is very understandable. One by one they lose heart and excuse themselves for the journey. In return, the leader asks them to renounce all vanity and egotism, telling many parables and stories to reveal the timidity and self-deception of the birds. Ashamed of their weaknesses, the birds set out on the journey. But the leader warns them of many tests and trials that await them on the way...[37]

By the time he wrote this, Heilpern was probably aware of the allegorical tenor of his description, which derives from the allegorical status of the poem itself. The description certainly acts as a synopsis of Heilpern's extended narrative, and one can easily recognize the prominence of the 'search, journey' metaphoric group from Brook's active vocabulary in *The Empty Space*. When combined with the qualities of a 'holy' theatre, this metaphoric group readily accepts the notion of "pilgrimage", as an empirical and physical version of a "search for God". Conspicuous in Heilpern's review of successive presentations/performances is his use of the word "conference" to describe Brook's activities as group leader, in offering pragmatic solutions to difficulties or in providing a digest of work done: "There was always a conference after every performance" (80). Heilpern also chronicles with relentless attention the loss of heart and the despondency amongst the performers, which were often only countered by Brook's tireless energy and undaunted conviction.

But by far the most significant component of the synopsis is the role played by the attack on "the timidity and self-deception of the birds". This reintroduces, in a thoroughly forceful and theoretically far more integrated manner, the extended and negative directorial commentary of *The Empty Space* on the limitations and clichés of performers. Although alluded to by Smith, as I have mentioned, in connection with the 'Theatre of Cruelty' experiment, it is largely displaced in his narrative by the concept of "sharing", which is for him lightly allied to discipline. Discipline also takes its place in Heilpern's synopsis, with the religious weight attached to "tests and trials" (initiatory) and "sacrifice" (the symbolic communion between human and God). But a firm conviction of personal inadequacy will provide the essential psychological context in which repeated failure can be transcended and regarded as a positive experience. As Heilpern later observes, this conviction was certainly achieved: "Perhaps the best thing about Brook's actors is that they never blame anyone except themselves for a failure" (87). Brook's use of "parables and stories" can be interpreted partly along these lines, as his excessive and evasive use of question-for-question, which is a recurrent technique of reflecting light back in the questioner's eyes. Asked for his greatest fault, he replies "What is a fault?"; asked how to write a play without dialogue, he replies "What is a play?"; pressed on the meaning of sound, he repeats and rejoins "What does it *mean*? What's the meaning of Beethoven?" (19, 96, 178).

Perhaps as a result of continuous exposure to the fluctuating temperaments of the group, and perhaps because of a contrasting but urgent authorial drive to an objective, Heilpern maintains a remarkable grasp on failure. The varieties strike him afresh each time, but he is also continually aware of the master-discourse: "It's axiomatic in Brook's dogged approach to every aspect of his work that failure doesn't exist...Failure is progress." (197). Yet he also perceives that the emotional train of events that is the immediate human cost of failure is subject to translation into a group philosophy, or, more accurately, a philosophy for the group (of performers). He can, at moments, even absorb the tone of the master-discourse, in this case as the actors struggle heroically to achieve simplicity:

> And yet they falter and stumble, apparently unable to perform the simplest of things. Mere external effects can be no help to them. Truth, a truthful vitality, bursts from the centre. It is never the other way round. But to arrive at the centre the actors must undertake the most intense life of self-exploration. They must strip away their outward personalities, mannerisms, habits, vanity, neuroses, tricks, clichés and stock responses until a higher state of perception is found.   (157)

This incapacity stretches to the simplest exercise. They formed a circle. "An actor begins to make a movement", and the rest follow the lead. "Eventually, the actor next to him changes the movement". It was an exercise of great simplicity. The only complication was the direction of individual attention: "We were to watch the person directly opposite us in the circle", and not the person changing the movement. But "everyone got it wrong" (158).

Yet the theoretical status of disarming the actor is by no means trivial, or simply incidental or occasional. It plays a crucial part in the process of withholding an end or a conclusion, which is implied in the metaphoric chain 'journey, search, re-search (experiment)', and which I identified as a classic resource of rhetoric at the beginning of this chapter. This is strongly sensed by Heilpern in connection with the phrase and the concept of 'Work in Progress', in a more cynical moment. As he states: "The term...conveniently forestalls all conventional criticism. If the goal isn't yet reached, nothing is complete. If nothing is complete, it isn't open to final judgement." (193). Failure is process, and its insistent theoretical status contrasts inexorably with human experience:

> [Brook] put the emphasis on risking failure, failure in every direction, in the hope of learning something new. But for actors it can be a terrific strain. They understand what is expected of them, yet their natural instincts are to please and entertain. They volunteered for the Brook Experiment but they panic, lose all confidence, go through crisis after crisis, looking back to the good old days when there was such a thing as a well-made play, and a script, with dialogue. It's why Brook's critics often see him as the all-powerful mastermind using his actors as guinea-pigs.   (88)

Heilpern goes on to include the audiences, the musician, and himself additionally under the category of guinea-pigs, and even Brook. Certainly the audience, as he comments, was Brook's "searchlight—he often used the term" (70). But the degree of Brook's control over the experiment is implanted in discourse and practice, and is not confounded by an exposure to strenuous conditions:

> Brook is in the business of research—opening up questions. If he'd wanted to put on a successful show in Africa he could have prepared and perfected one...But this wouldn't have helped him find an answer to what he's searching for. Part of the demanding nature of the work is that the moment anything is a success it must be abandoned. If not, it becomes set and closed—unable to teach anything fresh. (ibid.)

3.5 A metaphoric formula

For Heilpern, the desert into which the group travelled in their Land-Rovers late in 1971 was one form of Brook's 'empty space': "Brook likes to begin work in empty places and voids: the Sahara Desert" (40). The trip down through to Nigeria and back was an "experimental journey"; but in place of the watch-word 'communication' which had permeated Smith's understanding of *Orghast*, Heilpern offers the concepts of 'necessity' and "a universal theatre". Indeed, this is his retrospective evaluation of the *Orghast* experiment, "a bold attempt to open up the fascinating possibility of a form of universal speech more powerful than anything we have known". (24). In particular, this most recent experience/ experiment defines Brook's 'search' as one for "a universal language of theatre". Unlike any normal language, this would have the energy and the power to reach and affect everyone: the discovery of the universal theatre "would be the equivalent in theatre of splitting the atom in science" (22).

This apparently slight shift in descriptive vocabulary has the uncanny effect of substituting a monistic 'universe' for the dialectical qualities implied in 'communication', and it points forward emphatically to one moment of unison. This is the exposure of the group, at Agades in Niger, to the performers known collectively as the Peulh. These were entrancing male dancers—"amazing, pretty, camp, vain and irresistible Peulh"—but it was their use of sound that became riveting for Heilpern and the CIRT members:

> There in one sustained note, a sound held for so long we weren't even aware of a voice behind it, a sound pure and simple, effortless, it was

> as if the meaning of everything that is so unintelligible and mystifying about life had somehow been shown to us. From where or how, I didn't know. But it was there and it was as if the sound had a life of its own. The sound merged with others, vibrating. It was as if the sounds weren't human. They were beyond art, beyond culture, beyond everything except dreams. They were beautiful. They were beyond the human.
> "Music", wrote Leonardo, "is the shape and form of the invisible". The Peulh could capture the invisible, and held the secret.
>
> (139-40)

The idea that the Peulh "could capture the invisible and held the secret" proved irresistible, and in the meeting arranged between the two groups the CIRT members under Brook's direction tried a variety of songs to charm the Peulh into attention. Finally Brook hit on the solution—"an 'ah' sound"—which had been worked on in Paris. The Peulh downed their mirrors, and joined in unison.

The conclusions that Heilpern draws from this encounter are those of an absolute calm following on from an ecstatic discovery. It is perhaps one of the very few moments when his own narrative drive can rest united with the conceptual research vocabulary that has shaped its existence. These are, of course, two groups of performers entertaining themselves, but there is something finite about the vocabulary in which the absolutes themselves are caught and held. Gathering round this 'ah' is an accumulation of expressions that suggest the fullness of theory. There is, unquestionably, an identity here for the universal language: "The Peulh music showed us that a universal language might be as simple as one note repeated many, many times." (144). The combination, and even the identity, of this experience with "the invisible" are confirmed by Brook; but its cancellation as a stable achievement is simultaneously demanded by the insistent mobility of theory, in the inevitability of 're-search':

> [Brook] knew at last that he was on the right road in the search for a universal language. Perhaps we were only beginning to understand. Spirits speak there, in invisible worlds. (ibid.)

The 'ah' of the Peulh clearly fulfils the requirements for a universal language without cultural referents, but only by an apparent—and extreme—process of reduction to the absolute status of a component of theory. The expunging of cultural reference seems also to entail the removal of art and what is human, in an illogical progress towards the paradoxical concept of a sound that has "a life of its own". The 'ah' had to be found: its theoretical importance is confirmed by the declaration that Brook and Swados, the group's musician, had discussed the possibility of "one note that can become a source, the purest of essence".

A reflex combination of words such as the 'invisible' and 'source' with the idea of inherent life and vitality suggests that we are very close, in this intriguing section of Heilpern's narrative, to a resolution of the metaphoric clusters in *The Empty Space*. Major groups there were found (in 3.1) to form around 'approach' or 'search', vitality, and 'source, flow, or current'; and there was one primary polarity apart from life and death, namely that of the visible/invisible antithesis. 'Depth' and 'richness' were also exploited with considerable regularity, and in an additional short series not previously discussed Brook deploys the concept of 'penetration', adopted from Grotowski's terminology, as Brook repeatedly acknowledges. Its definitive application is in the 'penetration' of the actor (*E.S.* 66, 123) by a role, but it is also applied by Brook to Shakespeare, who "penetrates a psychic existence whose geography and movements remain just as vital for us to understand today" (*E.S.* 97). It is an act of motion, a break-through to the inner from the outer.

In Heilpern's communion with the theoretical excitement generated by the Peulh he leads us unerringly towards the 'empty space' that is the resolution of Brook's thoroughly metaphorical theory. What Brook experienced at Agades confirmed his exploratory conclusions in Paris. These had included "shedding more and more outward forms" and the rejection of the external answer of Total Theatre for its opposite:

> The internal answer is an enriching process using minimum means: the empty space. And it's the best and most hazardous answer because it's like a razor's edge. It must penetrate in sharpness and depth. In theatre terms you must not even see the razor. Everything should appear to flow so naturally the magician shows the audience that he has nothing in his hands. (145)

Theory, of course, is not pragmatic: it is never in one's hands. But even if it is sustained through abundant metaphorical shift (and evasion) it is susceptible of resolution, if only into a verbal formula, to appropriate the scientific mode. The empowering term is that of perpetual or renewed motion, which transcends any 'momentary' realization. There are special moments, but they "can't really be explained" and "can't be repeated", according to Brook: "They can only be rediscovered" (146). So a principle of internal transcendence—transcendence of its own ends or conclusions—is the necessity of this theory, and of the scientistic re-search which it legitimates.

Postulated beneath this transcendent term of perpetual motion is a series of incidental realizations, of 'journeys', 'paths', or in the scientific mode, 'experiments'. Metaphoric discovery takes the form of the incidental search or approach (most abruptly, 'penetration') from the outer to the inner, which is 'deep' and 'rich', so breaking through the dividing line of that polarity. What is reached is the 'source', the 'essence' of vitality, which must also contain the term 'simplicity' because it is a unitary absolute, like all essences. And its inviolability, the absolute guarantee of theory, is its identity with the 'invisible'. This is the language that cannot be spoken, but can exist in theory: the 'universal language' of theory as revelation.

3.6 Mystery, but no secrets

Peter Brook's recent publications include *The Shifting Point*, a retrospective collection of interviews and occasional pieces, and *There Are No Secrets*, which contains adaptations of two short speeches given in Japan in 1991, with a longer transcript of a workshop held in Paris in 1991.[38] The published version of the workshop transcript carries the title "The Slyness of Boredom", and it is interesting that its unusual extent is apparently motivated by its status as a marginal commentary on *The Empty Space*. Discursively, Brook remains unprepared to dispense with metaphor even in the most perplexing conjunction with his stated subject: so "boredom", in the moment of its appearance, "is like a flashing red light" (35), and yet Brook means no more than a warning signal. Of course, similes do tend to announce their arrival: so, when an old theatrical "form" had been "broken", "a new one had risen spontaneously and naturally like a phoenix from the ashes" (49), in a comparison which surprises only in its omission of the renewing fire. But even metaphor fails to bring the enhancement to exposition, or to theory, that it had occasionally promised in the original text. The "alchemy" that turns an "empty object", a "banal object...into a magical one" (46) singularly lacks the quality it is describing, and the conclusion to the argument offers wearisome exercise to the calf-muscles, with little in the way of inducement: "There is always a ladder to be climbed, leading from one level of quality to another." (76).

One might argue at this point that Brook is merely demonstrating a fidelity to his own discourse, a refusal to discard the resources of metaphor when metaphor alone can indicate the revelation that is required of theory. Nonetheless, there are no guarantees in metaphor, and its extension or amplification can be counteractive. 'Purity' is a concern of "The Slyness of Boredom" from the early pages. But the restatement of the value of the "empty space"—which is required (presumably equipped with a ladder) "for something of quality to take place"—is not enhanced by the adjunct of the concept of 'virginity':

> no fresh and new experience is possible if there isn't a pure, virgin space ready to receive it. (4)

The theatrical initiative as aspiring *phallos* does not make a great contribution to the conceptual freedoms of 'purity', and Brook's metaphors fail him rather too regularly. It is true that some are simply familiar by a kind of indulgent recall, like the actor "who hides in his 'mechanical' shell" (25), but others are stunning in their lack of zest. The exact process envisaged in "To open oneself, one must knock down the walls" (23) may not matter, but one expects something more of an image for the self-discipline required of "the craft of the theatre":

> If the hand that wields the hammer is imprecise in its movement, it will hit the thumb and not the nail. (76)

The choice of steel or cuticle lends a momentary vitality, but substitution provides a quick and easy death for a wan definition of "true form":

> True form arrives at the last moment, sometimes even later. It is a birth. (24)

Sadly, the mysteries of generation and the joy of its timing are vulnerable to more mundane expectations: it might so easily have been a letter, a pay-cheque, or even the regular commuting train. The gnomic utterance is far too easily subject to even indolent activity on the part of the imagination, which is for Brook that "muscle that enjoys playing games", and which fatefully constitutes "the true meaning of audience participation" (27).

But if "The Slyness of Boredom" has a contribution to make to a reading of Brook's theory, it must be in the further examination to which Brook submits just one or two of his most familiar terms. The most prominent of these, in the transcript, is undoubtedly the "invisible". But Brook is also intent on asserting "life" and "vitality" for the theatre in what might seem to be a redundant theoretical prescription. The argument begins with the statement that the theatre "is about life":

> That is the only starting point, and there is nothing else truly fundamental. Theatre is life. (8)

Similarly, "the small spark of life must be present", and theatrical presentation must include "the one ingredient that can link it to its audience: the irresistible presence of life" (13–14). "Life" as "vitality" may, in fact, theoretically determine the design of the "empty space":

> a play in the round, or in any non-proscenium space where the audience surrounds the actors, often has a naturalness and a vitality quite different from what a frontal, picture-frame theatre can offer... (37)

With "life" and "vitality", access to "the invisible" may be possible in the predictable form of a "search" or "quest for the sacred":

> the elusive spark of life can appear within the right sound, the right gesture, the right look, the right exchange. So, in a thousand very unexpected forms, the invisible may appear. The quest for the sacred is thus a search. (60)

"The invisible" suffers some analysis. As "the sacred", it may be revealed in an explicitly religious setting, such as a performance of Ta'azieh in an Iranian village, which offers some interpretation of Brook's title:

> The secret was clear. Behind this manifestation was a way of life, an existence that had religion at its root, all-present and all-penetrating. (42)

Alternatively, it may be found in Shakespeare's use of verse, which is plainly prescient in its realization of "the great Freudian underworld" (58):

> Shakespeare, as a practical man, was forced to use verse to suggest simultaneously the most hidden psychological, psychic and spiritual movements in his characters without losing their down-to-earth reality. (11)

Brook is prepared to be quite precise about the material quality of what may give rise to "the invisible", which "may appear in the most everyday objects", such as a "plastic water bottle", a "scrap of cloth", or (less precisely) human beings:

> The life of a human being is the visible through which the invisible can appear. (60)

In fact, the "visible" and the "invisible" must merge, since

> an idea has to be given flesh and blood and emotional reality: it must go beyond imitation, so that an invented life is also a parallel life, which at no level can be distinguished from the real thing. (9)

But this initial tolerance of that which is material and visible must be qualified if 'the invisible' is to retain its theoretical validity. So, for this purpose, Brook insists on the concept of an enhanced 'visibility' which resolutely turns into its opposite:

> if we accept that life in the theatre is more visible, more vivid than on the outside, then we can see that it is simultaneously the same thing and somewhat different. (9–10)

In "The Golden Fish", "those who tie the knots are also responsible for the quality of the moment that is caught in their net" (84). But the imagery cannot rest, for the "net" may serve more than one 'mysterious' function:

> the making of a net is the building of a bridge between ourselves as we usually are...and an invisible world. (85)

Brook's metaphorical extravagance remains compatible with his enduring determination to confine the ineffable to a sacred text. So, even in Kyoto, the repetitive assertion that the theatre "exists to offer glimpses...of an invisible world" is related to Shakespeare. Shakespeare's theatre

> is religious, it brings the invisible spiritual world into the concrete world of recognisable and visible shapes and actions. (85)

The form of Shakespeare's theatre alone remains universal, as we might have gathered not just from *The Empty Space*, but also from the workshop-transcript earlier in the volume:

> It is surely obvious that Shakespeare was writing theatre for an infinite space within undefined time. (29)

In this context, it is hardly surprising that the final speech of the collection, which contains the unresolved paradox of the volume's title, is on *The Tempest*.

4
Theatre Anthropology

I have used the general heading 'theatre anthropology' to introduce a discussion of the theoretical writings of three individuals: Victor Turner, Richard Schechner and Eugenio Barba. Of these, Victor Turner was an ethnologist, anthropologist and ritual theorist who turned his attention increasingly to what he termed an 'anthropology of performance'.[1] A mutual influence existed between Turner and Richard Schechner, who directed his understanding of performance theory towards the relationship 'between theatre and anthropology' (as the title of one of his collections of essays reveals), and who has maintained an interest in ritual.[2] Eugenio Barba has elaborated a rather different scheme of thought, in a series of essays and manifestos, and in an 'anatomy of theatre', which has been translated into English as *A Dictionary of Theatre Anthropology*; the title of this last work follows Barba's earlier suggestions of 'theatre anthropology' as an 'hypothesis', and "a new pedagogical practice".[3]

Barba is working from a European context, while Turner and Schechner have written from positions in the United States; but all three figures have worked and researched extensively in other continents, and with individuals, groups and practitioners from other continents and cultures. I see no reason to challenge the general term as a heading denoting a distinct 'turn' in theoretical interest and expression; but apart from its use in grouping these three writers, I attach no particular significance to it of my own devising.

4.1. Victor Turner (1920–1983)

Victor Turner was an academic anthropologist, studying and teaching at Manchester University in England from 1955 to 1963 with Max

Gluckman, and then moving as a professor to Cornell University, and on from Cornell to Chicago (in 1968) and finally to Virginia (1977), where he remained until his death. As an anthropologist, he conducted research for the Rhodes-Livingstone Institute in Zambia, where he lived with the Ndembu tribe in the north-west of the country, between the upper Zambesi and the Lunga rivers.[4] His studies of the Ndembu, published as a series of papers for the Rhodes-Livingstone Institute and as a related series of books, concentrated particularly on their practice of ritual as what Turner called a 'social process'. From the beginning, Turner was concerned with a close analysis of the symbolism involved in the rituals, and he became convinced of the importance of an analogy with drama in understanding the 'performance' of certain categories of rituals. In the writings that followed, he extended his analogy with drama to social processes outside the immediate context of the Ndembu, and finally formulated a theory which linked ritual to what he termed the 'performative genres' in industrial and post-industrial societies.

In the discussion that follows I shall pay particular attention to those elements and aspects of Turner's writing that are concerned with theory, from the initial deployment of the analogy with drama to the fullest expression he gave of his understanding of an anthropology of performance. I shall not attempt a general assessment of his work as an anthropologist, nor of the value or validity of his detailed case-studies as an ethnographer. The invitation to consider Turner in some large part as a theorist of performance was made by Turner himself, and it is with this contribution, and its evolution in his earlier work, that I shall be concerned.

4.1.1 Symbolism and social process: ritual theory and the drama analogy

In his early studies of the Ndembu Turner found himself confronting the problems of "adjustment, adaptation and change" in "a society whose villages move widely and frequently over space and often tend to split, even to fragment, through time.".[5] As one result, his attention came to focus on the ritual activity of the Ndembu, and with an attention to ritual came a parallel concern with symbolism. Observations on symbols and symbolism began to exercise a strong presence in his work from the early 1960s, and they permeate or frame the two books he published towards the end of that decade on the ritual and religious processes of the Ndembu, *The Forest of Symbols* and *Drums of Affliction*.[6] The methodology espoused by Turner suggests a variety of modes of interpretation, starting with classification founded on the pragmatic description of symbols as "'storage units', into which are packed the maximum amount of information".[7] From this definition, which has its origins in a relatively unadorned communication theory, it follows that it is possible to make an inventory, and

> to record, in fairly complete form, what each symbol signifies to the average native informant and to the indigenous expert. We then have a quantum of information, which represents a set of 'messages' about a sector of socio-cultural life considered worth transmitting down the generations.[8]

But if the confidence in this electro-technological model seems initially untroubled, it is subject in Turner's expansive and intuitively open discourse to the profound and transcendental qualities of the "messages". The complexity of the transmission runs the risk of exceeding the simplicity of the model:

> we are concerned here with the crucial values of the believing community, whether it is a religious community, a nation, a tribe, a secret society, or any other type of group whose ultimate unity resides in its orientation towards transcendental and invisible powers.[9]

In fact, simplicity proves to be the last thing that can be assumed of the 'communication' achieved through symbols. For the creation of meaning is dependent "on the nature of the relationship between two or more symbols", and since symbols in ritual may be advanced or deployed by human participants, and may indeed be human participants, then meaning also depends on "interaction between human actors of roles". Behaviour, equally, may be symbolic in a ritual context, and the language of direct communication theory yields to that of codes, and code-cracking:

> Each society's ritual symbols constitute a unique code and each society provides a unique key to that code. I should say, rather, 'a bunch of keys', for some societies bring several systems of explanation to bear upon the symbols of ritual. These systems include: theology, dogma, doctrine, mythology, cosmology, allegory, parables, history or pseudo-history, and exegesis (or hermeneutics).[10]

Here the code and code-cracking model of analysis has been made subject to a formidable array of traditional modes of discourse, and it suffers still further from an apparently contradictory slide out of communicative language into the unspoken:

> It is not necessary for a symbol to be verbally explained to be comprehended; its significance is often understood at preconscious, or even unconscious, levels.[11]

This assertion receives some support from etymology in Turner's argument, for he reports that the Ndembu term for 'symbol' is *chinjikijilu*, a derivative from *kri-jikijilu*, to 'blaze a trail' in the bush to indicate the way back:

> The blaze or landmark, in other words, leads from unknown, and therefore in Ndembu experience as well as belief, from dangerous territory to known and familiar surroundings, from the lonely bush to the populated village. Ritual symbols have a similar function, for they give a visible form to unknown things; they express in concrete and familiar terms what is hidden and unpredictable. They enable men to domesticate and manipulate wild and wayward forces.[12]

Communication, expression, and ultimately revelation. The ritual symbol carries distinctly performative characteristics, which are virtually dramatic:

> One aspect of the process of ritual symbolization among the Ndembu is, therefore, to make visible, audible, and tangible beliefs, ideas, sentiments, and psychological dispositions that cannot be directly perceived. Associated with this process of revealing the unknown, invisible, or the hidden is the process of making public what is private or making social what is personal.[13]

In the absence of effective models symbology may be expressed more succinctly as "*multivocal*, i.e. susceptible of many meanings", and this description extends readily to ritual itself:

> This brings me to another important property of many ritual symbols, their polysemy or multivocality. By these terms I mean that a single symbol may stand for many things. This property of individual symbols is true of ritual as a whole.[14]

The degree to which Turner rested content with this theoretical summary is established by a passage from a late work on celebration, an introduction that Turner wrote to an exhibition with that title at the Smithsonian Institute in Washington DC:

> A symbol is something that represents something else by association, resemblance, or convention. Spoken or printed words, for example, are symbols. But celebratory objects are, first and foremost, material objects, though they represent ideas, objects, events, relationships, 'truths' not immediately present to the observer, or even intangible or invisible thoughts and conceptions. Such celebratory symbols, moreover, usually stand for many things and thoughts at once. Technical terms for this capacity are: *multivocal* (literally 'many-voiced'), 'speaking' in many ways at once; *multivalent*, having various meanings or values; and *polysemous*, having or being open to several or many meanings.[15]

This exhibition was composed, of course, of material objects, and in general Turner was concerned in his early writing to evaluate symbolic objects, although the suggestion of "interaction between human actors" points to a further dimension of ritual which he chose to examine under a different set of terms.

In studying and observing amongst the Ndembu, Turner believed that he was faced by the occurrence of what he called 'social dramas' or crises, "that lead to the application of ritual means of redress".[16] This perception provided him with an interpretative connection between the ritual process and the activity of the Ndembu in secular life, which could be expressed dramatically:

> In the social drama individuals don their social *personae* and become typical headmen, typical lineage heads, typical fathers, cross-cousins, sister's children.
> Ritual provides a stage on which roles are enacted and the conflicts of the secular drama reflected in symbol, mime, and precept.[17]

As the anthropologist Geertz has noted, terms such as 'role' and 'performance' had been current in anthropology from the 1930s.[18] But Turner turns what might have been faded metaphors resolutely into a theoretical scheme:

> When we study conflict in such societies, we are, I think, justified in applying the term 'drama' to public crises. For the minimal definition of drama would probably include the playing of roles, the employment of a rhetorical style of diction, and at least some sense of an audience. A drama also implies knowledge and acceptance of a single set of rules, and the expectation of a progress of events towards a climax. All these criteria are present in both the Ndembu social drama and ritual sequence.[19]

The application of the analogy with such resolution, in a scheme which conjoins secular activity and the symbolic ritual process, lends conviction to the introduction of the concept of artistic unity:

> The unity of a given ritual is a dramatic unity. It is in this sense a kind of work of art. It differs from the organized game or duel, though both are institutionalized processes, in that its rules leave little scope for competition, the outcome of which is uncertain.[20]

The relatively unexceptional drama analogy favoured by anthropology has here become something more than itself. If analogy is a form of comparison, it gains its force from a recognition of difference: strictly speaking, there is no analogy between things that are the same. But the suggestion of a "minimal definition of drama" and of the presence of "all these criteria" posits a congruence between the theatrical culture of the observer (and the reader) and ritual processes amongst the Ndembu, one which closes the gap which must be supposed in the 'reckoning' appropriate to analogy. If Turner's symbology has performative potential, but fails to extend satisfactorily to a theory of the individual-as-symbol, then the drama analogy supplies him with the unity of theoretical vision that he needs.

4.1.2 Further components of a performance theory: 'liminality', 'communitas' and the 'social drama'

In 1962 Max Gluckman, who had been director of the Rhodes-Livingstone Institute and was Turner's preceptor at Manchester, edited a volume of essays on the ritual of social relations which was dedicated to the memory of the Belgian anthropologist Arnold van Gennep.[21] In his introduction, Gluckman provided a brief explanation of the terms instituted by van Gennep in his analysis of rituals, and went on to criticize van Gennep's methods as a social scientist. Gluckman gave particular attention to what he regarded as the misapplication of van Gennep's identification of '*rites de passage*' in tribal societies to apparently similar phenomena in modern urban life. The volume followed the recent publication, in 1960, of an English translation of van Gennep's *Rites of Passage*, and Gluckman specified the concept of 'liminality' as central to van Gennep's "framework" of understanding:

> Van Gennep began his analysis by using 'territorial passages' for his framework, and he examined how when persons moved across borders,

or entered at the thresholds of houses and temples, they observed rituals.[22]

The adoption of the concept 'liminality' from the Latin *limen* ('threshold') had led to the determination of the triad 'preliminal', 'liminal', and 'postliminal', which van Gennep used to describe the sequence of phases before, during, and after the rituals of passage. This terminology became applied, in van Gennep's study, to rituals of life crises, of which the most prominent proved to be those of initiation.

In his contribution to this volume Victor Turner drew on his fieldwork with the Ndembu, concerning himself with the symbols involved in circumcision ritual, in a study closely related to the papers he published for the Rhodes-Livingstone Institute. The influence of van Gennep is implicit in the essay and its choice of subject, but perhaps for this reason Turner writes without theoretical reference to van Gennep's terminology, or to his methods of assessment and interpretation. Indeed Turner's essay is in some ways a model of what Gluckman found lacking in the Belgian's work, in its presentation of detail and clear sense of social relations, characteristics which dominated Turner's otherwise theoretically vacillating interpretation of symbols. The debt to van Gennep is all the more obvious in the title of a chapter—"Betwixt and Between: The Liminal Period in *Rites de Passage*"—from Turner's later book *The Forest of Symbols*. Writing of the "transitions between states" which provide the social context for his understanding of van Gennep's *rites de passage*, Turner clearly includes non-tribal categories in his definition of states:

> By 'state' I mean here a 'relatively fixed or stable condition', and would include in its meaning such social constancies as legal status, profession, office or calling, rank or degree.[23]

Yet the demands of the immediate subject, which is that of the Ndembu, return him to a further aspect of liminality, which is the equality or community of transitional beings, a temporary status which stands in direct contrast to hierarchy. Those in transition—in Turner's vocabulary, "neophytes"—have nothing, are often understood to be sexless or bisexual, and are socially "invisible": "Complete equality usually characterizes the relationship of neophyte to neophyte, where the rites are collective."[24] The liminal group "is a community or comity of comrades and not a structure of hierarchically arranged positions", and the liminal state has a critical function in relation to this "structure":

> During the liminal period, neophytes are alternately encouraged to think about their society, their cosmos, and the powers that generate and sustain them. Liminality may be partly described as a stage of reflection.[25]

Turner's apparent hesitation between elaborating a formal theory of symbolism or concentrating on the social aspect of the ritual process finds appropriate expression in *The Ritual Process*, his published version of the Henry Morgan Lectures he gave in 1966. In his preface to this volume, he effectively summarizes the divided attention that rules the order of the five essays it contains, which appear in two unmarked sections:

> The first deals mainly with the symbolic structure of Ndembu ritual and the semantics of that structure; the second, beginning about halfway through the third chapter, seeks to explore some of the social, rather than symbolic, properties of the liminal phase of ritual.[26]

In accordance with his promise in the preface, Turner begins to introduce a theoretical vocabulary and theoretical formulas for "the social...properties of the liminal phase of ritual" in the course of his third chapter, which carries the title "Liminality and Communitas". It is, in particular, the experience of "liminal *personae* ('threshold people')" envisaged as a group which prompts the development of a significant antithesis between liminality and the states or positions that pertain in society:

> The attributes of liminality or of liminal *personae* ('threshold people') are necessarily ambiguous, since this condition and these persons elude or slip through the network of classifications that normally locate states and positions in cultural space. Liminal entities are neither here nor there; they are betwixt and between the positions assigned and arrayed by law, custom, convention, and ceremonial. (95)

From the perception that neophytes form a "community or comity" advanced in *The Forest of Symbols*, Turner adduces a notional condition of "communitas", which takes its stand as a quality of liminality in the beginnings of an ambitious theoretical formulation. The result is a dialectical exchange between the influence of (social and hierarchical) structure and "communitas": "each individual's life experience contains alternating exposure to structure and communitas, and to states and transitions" (97). Earlier in the chapter, Turner had already rejected the assumptions of primitivism, of an absolute divide between "simpler" peoples and those, typically, of the investigator, anthropologist, or reader:

> in matters of religion, as of art, there are no 'simpler' peoples, only some peoples with simpler technologies than our own. Man's 'imaginative' and 'emotional' life is always and everywhere rich and complex.   (3)

So the condition of "neophytes" or "liminal *personae*" has much in common—through their lack of status, exposure to insult, anonymity and indeed sexual abstinence—with, for example, the characteristics of the religious life. In addition, the regular attribution of special powers to the weak may, according to this culturally expansive theory, create figures who are symbolically representative of "communitas". Turner cites monastic orders, and the court jester:

> These figures, representing the poor and the deformed, appear to symbolize the moral values of communitas as against the coercive power of supreme political rulers.   (110)

The historical examples are accompanied by a relatively easy transference, through millenarian movements, of the ritual properties of liminality to the contemporary social phenomena of opting-out, with the beat generation and the hippies. Included in the general formula are shamans and prophets, with the important theoretical dicta that "communitas can be grasped only in relation to structure", and that "it is often in the subjunctive mood", a linguistic analogy to which Turner repeatedly returned in his later writings.

Although it was apparent, initially, that "communitas" was bound to the assertion of a 'community' of initiands, its considerable status in a provocative antithesis with "structure" ultimately demands a tripartite scheme to embrace all the phenomena to which Turner alludes. The spatial metaphor contained in the concept of the 'threshold' is accordingly extended to a description of a universal thesis:

> Communitas breaks in through the interstices of structure, in liminality; at the edges of structure, in marginality; and from beneath structure, in inferiority.   (128)

This expanded scheme results in what is probably Turner's most complete theoretical formulation to date, combining his observations on symbolism and his nascent willingness to link religion and art with the potential of the pervasive drama analogy:

> Liminality, marginality, and structural inferiority are conditions in which are frequently generated myths, symbols, rituals, philosophical systems, and works of art. These cultural forms provide men with a set of templates or models which are, at one level, periodical reclassifications of reality and man's relationship to society, nature, and culture. But they are more than classifications, since they incite men to action as well as thought. Each of these productions has a multivocal character, having many meanings, and each is capable of moving people at many psycho-biological levels simultaneously. (128–29)

Perhaps the most curious feature of what is at first introduced as a dialectic of "alternating exposure to structure and communitas" is the note of diachronic pessimism which follows this dynamic description of the "action" of "communitas":

> Exaggeration of communitas, in certain religious or political movements of the leveling type, may be speedily followed by despotism, overbureaucratization, or other modes of structural rigidification. For...those living in community seem to require, sooner or later, an absolute authority, whether this be a religious commandment, a divinely inspired leader, or a dictator. Communitas cannot stand alone if the material and organizational needs of human beings are to be adequately met. (129)

Communitas may be "existential" or "spontaneous", a "happening" in contemporary jargon; or "normative", taking the form of "a perduring social system"; or it may be or become "ideological", creating "utopian models of societies based on existential communitas" (132). The pessimistic tenor of this scheme calls upon the strictly non-theoretical and non-scientific concept of fate, in an historical vision of a "decline and fall":

> Both normative and ideological communitas are already within the domain of structure, and it is the fate of all spontaneous communitas in history to undergo what most people see as a 'decline and fall' into structure and law. (132)

Partly through the complications posed by the concept of communitas, liminality has been moved from its position in a terminology of ritual to a place in a general theory of culture. Despite the ambition of this theory, the performative characteristics and potential of liminality remain largely unrealized; compensation comes in the re-direction of

Turner's burgeoning theoretical interest to his own, original concept of the "social drama".

In a subsequent volume, *Dramas, Fields, and Metaphors* Turner for the first time calls into question the use of metaphors in social philosophy, and expresses considerable doubts about the organic metaphor of "becoming" when applied to society.[27] These reservations do not inhibit him from a re-presentation and partial justification of his own choice of terms. What he was studying amongst the Ndembu were "public episodes of tensional irruption" arising from conflict, and if time gave them a form that was "essentially dramatic" then the very fact of conflict might also lend these social dramas a "tragic quality". The dramatic metaphor is above all justified by its capacity to suggest the dynamism of "social processes", providing a methodological approach to the data that draws attention away from static models of social structure.

> I would like to stress as strongly as I can that I consider this processual approach decisive as a guide to the understanding of human social behavior. Religious and legal institutions, among others, only cease to be bundles of dead or cold rules when they are seen as phases in social processes, as dynamic patterns right from the start. We have to learn to think of societies as continuously 'flowing', as a "dangerous tide...that never stops or dies...And held one moment burns the hand", as W.H. Auden once put it. The formal, supposedly static, structures only become visible through this flow which energizes them, heats them to the point of visibility—to use yet another metaphor. (37)

Metaphor is a means-to-an-end in the revelation of what is invisible. Whether the invisible world would then be described in other than metaphorical terms is left open, as indeed is the question of whether anything other than the "formal...structures" themselves can actually be the subject of revelation.

The subsequent pages of the opening chapter of *Dramas, Fields, and Metaphors* provide a clear and detailed description of Turner's theoretical scheme for the social drama, one to which he returns repeatedly in later writings. He distinguishes four main phases in social dramas: (1) a "*breach* of regular, norm-governed social relations"; (2) the phase of consequent "*crisis*", which has "liminal characteristics", but is thoroughly public, not "thrust away from the centers of public life"; (3) "*redressive action*", which "may range from personal advice and informal mediation or arbitration to formal judicial and legal machinery, and...to the performance of public ritual"; (4) "*reintegration* of the disturbed social group or...the social recognition and legitimization of irreparable schism" (38–41). Both the second and the third phases of the scheme have "liminal characteristics" or "liminal features", and the design as presented is clearly indebted to van Gennep's categories for the ritual process of *separation*, *margin*, and *re-aggregation*, cited by Turner in the concluding chapter of *The Ritual Process*.[28] Turner seems confident that the drama analogy is sufficiently convincing to accept additional refinement: the social drama may be expected to culminate in a "climax", and this is in keeping with Turner's "explicit comparison of the temporal structure of certain types of social processes with that of dramas on the stage, with their acts and scenes" (43). In this comparison, the phases correspond to acts, and the scheme permits an analysis of "processual units" that can respond to time: "'Processualism' is a term that includes 'dramatistical analysis'" (43).

The theoretical purpose of *Dramas, Fields, and Metaphors* is to carry the concept of social drama away from its specific origins in fieldwork studies to (or towards) universal applicability. As his principal examples Turner selects social dramas from the European middle ages and from the early nineteenth century in Mexico, and follows these with a language study from West Africa. In the earlier historical example, that of Becket and Henry II in England, Turner traces the four phases of the drama carefully, but in the second, despite references to "a complex and dramatic liminal period" and to Mexico's "*rites de passage* to nationhood", the phases become indistinct in a general narrative of betrayal and sacrifice. The problem is, essentially, that Turner introduces a new concept, a "root paradigm" of self-sacrifice and symbolic martyrdom, which largely absorbs his interest in both accounts, and leaves its relation to his primary scheme substantially unclear. As a result, the social drama does not really emerge from the confines of the drama analogy, although the principle of extension over three continents and historical time is at least avowed, if not thoroughly demonstrated. Turner declares his interest in pilgrimage, which he believes to have characteristics of liminality and communitas, at the beginning of the chapter on Becket. Significant in the discussion of pilgrimage is the introduction of a contrast between obligation and voluntariness. The obligation of ritual entails communitas, and engenders reflection on "structure". So voluntary pilgrimages

> seem to be regarded by self-conscious pilgrims both as occasions on which communitas is experienced and as journeys towards a sacred source of communitas, which is also seen as a source of healing and renewal. (203)

It is this universal property of communitas, whether experienced through obligation or choice, which receives most attention and theoretical development in the closing chapters of *Dramas, Fields, and Metaphors*. Communitas "strains towards universalism and openness", and in its relationship to structures it is "the *fons et origo* of all structures, and, at the same time, their critique" (202):

> Structures, like most species, get specialized; communitas, like man and his direct evolutionary forebears, remains open and unspecialized, a spring of pure possibility as well as the immediate realization of release from day-to-day structural necessities and obligatoriness.   (202)

The organic, biological metaphor of which Turner was so wary in his introduction is here required to communicate the co-extensiveness of communitas with the activity of the species, and its universalism is essential to the formation of theory:

> Communitas is a fact of everyone's experience, yet it has almost never been regarded as a reputable or coherent object of study by social scientists. It is, however, central to religion, literature, drama, and art, and its traces may be found deeply engraven in law, ethics, kinship, and even economics. It becomes visible in tribal rites of passage, in millenarian movements, in monasteries, in the counterculture, and on countless informal occasions.   (231)

Considerations such as these extend the concept of liminality, through the intervention of a universalist presentation of communitas, into final links with religious mendicancy and the counterculture.

4.1.3   From 'liminal' to 'liminoid'

The final component of Turner's cultural theory of performance rests in the brief allusion to the liminoid genres found in the preface to *Dramas, Fields, and Metaphors*. Introduced there, without further explanation, as "literature, film, and higher journalism", this concept receives full theoretical expansion and treatment in an essay published in 1977 in a collection devoted to the contentiously paradoxical subject of 'secular ritual'.[29] Turner's contribution, undemonstratively titled "Variations on a Theme of Liminality", resumes a number of his observations and conclusions on ritual, liminality and communitas under an initial acknowledgement to van Gennep. But it also contains an extremely precise comparison of the 'liminal' to the 'liminoid' in a discussion which modulates, in accordance with the expanded scope of his developing theory, between tribal societies and those which the reader might regard as the product of history. This (by now) established change of emphasis in his work is summarized by Turner himself in the opening of the essay:

> My theoretical focus has...shifted from societies in which rituals involve practically everyone, to societies in which, as Durkheim puts it, "the domain of religion", if not perhaps of ritual, has "contracted", become a matter of individual choice rather than universal corporate ascription, and where, with religious pluralism, there is sometimes a veritable supermarket of religious wares. In these societies, symbols once central to the mobilization of ritual action have tended to migrate directly or in disguise, through the cultural division of labor, into other domains, esthetics, politics, law, popular culture, and the like. (36)

The proposed division in this paragraph is between "preindustrial societies" and "complex", large-scale civilizations, and central to Turner's discussion here are the concepts of work and leisure, with 'play' acting as an element potentially common to both. Dominating and provoking the whole discussion is the leading question, "whatever happened to liminality in *post*tribal societies?". Turner answers this programmatically by stating that "cultural phenomena...may either be shown to have descended from earlier forms of liminality, or are, in some sense, their functional equivalents" (39). In theoretical terms, this is an extremely strong proposition, and it rests on the reinstatement of methods of explanation that Turner had mistrusted and hoped to surpass. The importance to this proposition of the organic metaphor of 'descent', and the reliance on structural functionalism both confirm Turner's insecurity in making this final leap of theory, from one set of phenomena to another.

The essay is, in some senses, a model of clarity for those hoping to follow the 'construction' of Turner's cultural criticism, because it provides summaries of established concepts and resumes suggestions introduced but not elaborated in earlier writings. So, in his discussion of 'work' as a possible description of ritual, Turner includes his earlier comments on ritual as 'obligation' in a concise and persuasive synthesis, which then contrasts these aspects of ritual to the voluntary quality which he first identified in certain post-tribal liminalities, such as pilgrimage. The conciseness of the argument at this point demonstrates the ethnologist's self-confidence:

> In tribal and archaic societies what people do in ritual is often described by terms which we might translate as 'work'...Bantu-speaking peoples

in Africa use the same term for a ritual specialist's activity as for what a hunter, a cultivator, a headman, or today a manual laborer does.   (39)

Etymology (in examples from Greek, Old English and Indo-European) is also adduced as evidence, but Turner's confidence is composed from a close integration of theoretical terms with generalized description:

> I could cite many other examples, but the point I wish to make is that the ritual round in tribal societies is embedded in the total round of activities, and is part of the work of the people which is *also* the work of the gods. We are dealing with a universe of work, in which the whole community participates, as of obligation not optation... Communal participation, obligation, the passage of the whole society through crises, communal or individual, directly or by proxy, these are the hallmarks of the 'work of the gods' and sacred human work. Without sacred work profane human work would be, for the community, impossible to conceive.   (39–40)

The definition of 'work' in tribal societies is moved away from "what we, from our stance on the hither side of the Industrial Revolution and perhaps the Protestant Ethic, might regard as 'work'", because "it includes what we might think of as 'play'":

> in many tribal rites, there is built into the liturgical structure, a good deal of what we and they would think of as amusement, recreation, fun, and joking; furthermore, there is the actual 'playing' of games...   (40)

This description of ritual as "sacred human work" which includes both "play" and "experimental behavior" concludes with a repetition of the original question: "whatever happened to liminality, and to the richness, flexibility, and symbolic wealth of tribal ritual?" (ibid.). Put in this form, the question firmly suggests impoverishment as a quality of the culture of both writer and reader, and one senses the moral regret or indignation seemingly latent in anthropology since its creation as a theoretical discipline by Rousseau. Noticeably, at this point, Turner avows his Christianity, and associates impoverishment with "deliminalization", and the departure of "the powerful play component" from the liturgy. This absence is not confined to Christianity—"Other religions of the book, too, have regularly stressed the solemn at the expense of the festive" (41)—and the imperative registered in the repeated question is best understood as an absolute instruction to relocate liminality. For this purpose, ethnographic or even generalized anthropological description offered to the reader as compensation for a 'lack' is inadequate: it is theory that must perform the "sacred work" of substituting presence for absence.

According to the preliminary discussion, "experiment" and "play" are components of ritual liminality in tribal society. Work conceived "on the hither side of the Industrial Revolution and perhaps the Protestant Ethic" might be contrasted to play, or alternatively to leisure. As Turner defines it, following research by Dumazedier, leisure is the product of urban conditions, which are most pronounced in "industrial and industrializing societies":

> Here work is organized by industry, by clocking in and out, by office hours, and so on, so as to be separated from 'free time', which includes, of course, in addition to leisure, attendance to such personal needs as eating, sleeping, and caring for one's health and appearance, as well as familial, social, civic, political, and religious obligations. (41)[30]

This separation provides a clear contrast with the "work–play sacred–profane continuum" found in tribal societies, and an acceptable definition of leisure would contain physical relaxation from work-rhythms "on the beaches and mountains, and in the parks and game reserves provided as liminoid retreats", with those opportunities that are available to enter the "symbolic worlds" of games, entertainments and "diversions". The notion of play is readily rediscovered in both of these groupings, but in the second it is relocated away from the physical connotations of relaxation abruptly into authorial and artistic activity. Leisure is

> freedom, indeed, to play—with ideas, with fantasies, with words (in literature, some of the 'players' have been Rabelais, Joyce, and Samuel Beckett), with paint (think of the Pointillistes, Surrealists, Action Painters, and so forth), and with social relationships (new forms of community, mating, sensitivity training, and so on). (42)

The diversion seems abrupt, because although these particular categories of 'leisure' connect at least coherently with the liminoid genres of the preface to *Dramas, Fields, and Metaphors* ("literature, the film, and higher journalism"), the sustaining context here is that of physical relaxation and games, and this chosen emphasis continues:

> And now we are getting closer to our lost liminality, for in this modern 'leisure', far more even than in tribal and agrarian rituals, the

experimental and the ludic are stressed. There are more options in complex, industrial societies: games of skill, strength, and chance...Football, chess, and mountaineering... (ibid.)

Such games are optional, and since they are pleasurable they contrast with "alienated" industrial work. Through these instruments, leisure proves "capable of releasing creative powers, individual and communal".

The association of recreational and physically relaxing activities, easily understood as contrasting to work in industrial societies, with certain kinds of writing and painting is enhanced by a brief reference to the "professionalization of the arts and sports", which Turner declines to discuss. He does, however, allude in passing to

> the notion that art itself is a quasi-religious vocation, with its own asceticism and total dedication—exemplified by Blake, Kierkegaard, Baudelaire, Proust, Rilke, Cézanne, Gauguin, Mahler, Sibelius and so on. (ibid.)

"And so forth", "and so on" are provocative codas to exemplary lists embracing "players" of this notoriety or stature. But Turner's important categories remain merely suggestive, suspended before the announcement of the major theoretical intention of the essay:

> Here I wish to draw attention to some similarities between the *leisure* genres of art and entertainment in complex industrial societies and the *rituals and myths* of archaic, tribal, and early agrarian cultures. (42–3)

According to Turner, leisure—"a betwixt-and-between, neither-this-nor-that domain"—has liminal characteristics which may be framed, as the liminal is in the ritual process, between two states of 'structure': as an intermission in work, or as an activity placed between "occupational" and "familial and civic activities". This clear declaration of theoretical intent by Turner is followed by an explicit theoretical statement of the relationship between leisure, liminality, and the "liminoid genres":

> We have now seen how tribesmen *play* with the factors of liminality, with masks and monsters, symbolic inversions, parodies of profane reality, and so forth. So also do the genres of industrial leisure: theater, ballet, film, the novel, poetry, classical music, rock music, art, pop art, and so on, pulling the elements of culture apart, putting them together again in often random, grotesque, improbable, surprising, shocking, sometimes deliberately experimental combinations. But there are

> certain important differences between the tribal genres, relatively few in number, of liminality, and the prolixity of genres found in modern industrial leisure. I have called the latter 'liminoid' by analogy with *ovoid*, '*egg-like*', and *asteroid*, '*star-like*'. I wish to convey by it something that is akin to the ritually liminal, or like it, but not identical with it. The 'liminoid' represents, in a sense, the dismembering, the *sparagmos* of the liminal; for various things that 'hang together' in liminal situation split off to pursue separate destinies as specialized arts and sports and so on, as liminoid genres.   (43)

The "liminoid" genres are the "genres of industrial leisure", and the range has now expanded from the short-list given in *Dramas, Fields, and Metaphors*, dispensing, it seems, with "higher journalism". Comparison is the explicit theme of this theoretical statement, introduced mildly by the connecting and potentially performative notion of "play". But the corollary of comparison is contrast, which also occupies a central position in the statement, where the "certain important differences" between liminal and liminoid include those of number ("few in number", as against "prolixity") and an open distinction between "tribal" and "modern". The diachronic scheme implied in this last distinction remains hidden and complex: if the contemporary Ndembu are the source of Turner's research into tribal liminality, they are no less "modern" than the history of such liminoid genres as theatre, ballet or—the vaguest category—art. 'Likeness' is asserted in the suffix "-oid", and comparison is supported by an allusion to anthropological terminology in the use of "akin", "like" but not "identical". But what is at stake here is no idle or arbitrary comparison, nor even analogy deployed as a rhetorical ornament, or in support of a sustained argument. The theoretical relationship is essential, and is registered in the coinage of "liminoid" from "liminal". In answer to Turner's repeated question, liminality has to be found in "modern" or industrial societies, and theory plays with the mode of comparison and attendant contrast as a distraction from the awkward task of proposing a relationship of essence. This relationship is expressed, finally, in the Dionysiac imagery of the *sparagmos*, the "dismembering" of a ritual animal or human being (Pentheus in Euripides' *Bacchae*) that identifies the liminoid genres as 'limbs' of the liminal body. But this evocative version of the organic metaphor has to be rescued from theoretical futility—a severed arm has little potential for growth—by what appears to be a swerve from anatomy to molecular or atomic science. So these components of the natural body that "split off" from it may then, as is required by theory, "pursue separate destinies".

The awkwardness of establishing the crucial relationship is apparent in subsequent expressions of the supposed change in or transformation of liminality that theory requires, a transformation which Turner chooses to imagine in terms of movement, with its connotations of relocation and extent over time. So, in the following paragraph, "many of the symbolic and ludic capacities of tribal religion have...*migrated* into nonreligious genres", and "symbol and ritual have *gotten into* drama and poetry", an expression that plainly suggests that these (pre-existent genres) did not have these components or qualities 'before'. The implied scheme in both cases is radically different from the imagery of the *sparagmos*, because it accepts an existent host location (of nonreligious genres?) which can receive the 'migration' from the liminality of ritual. The choice of solution achieves two things: it satisfies a latent requirement for an account of time, perhaps as a sequential chronology ("tribal" and "modern"), and it suppresses the potential problem of the (prior) existence of non-liminal or non-liminoid ('artistic') genres, by raising it briefly only to ignore it resolutely. This effect is compounded by the embracing theme of secularization, which complicates the analytical possibilities to the particular advantage of theory. If "the liminoid is very often secularized", as Turner proposes, then the chronology of change becomes extremely complicated. By suggesting an analytical scheme of change that is too elaborate to be explained fully—what the liminoid genres were before they became secularized is manifestly puzzling—Turner encourages the reader into a reliance on the relief of familiar organic and mobile metaphors, and into an acceptance of *some* relationship or kinship between his two categories, flexibly but firmly expressed in the simple suffix of liminoid.

This elaborate but elusive initial statement of a theoretical relationship is followed by a major series of comparisons, which act as definitions of "liminal phenomena" under the general headings of "contrast" and "distinctions" (44–5). In three successive paragraphs "liminal phenomena" appear as "collective", and concerned with "cycles or rhythms", whether "natural or sociocultural"; as "centrally integrated into the total social process"; and as "generalized and normative". By contrast, "liminoid phenomena" are, respectively, "characteristically produced and consumed by known named individuals", and "are not cyclical but continuously generated"; they "develop most characteristically *outside* the central economic and political processes, along their margins"; and they are more idiosyncratic and quirky", and "are often subversive, representing radical critiques of the central structures and proposing utopian alternative models". In addition, liminoid phenomena are also "plural, fragmentary, and experimental", where "fragmentary" refers to "the total inventory of liminoid thoughts, words, and deeds", which suggests a contrast with an unstated 'singularity' of liminal phenomena.

The peculiarity of this major series of distinctions is that the theoretical objective of establishing a relationship between two sets of phenomena is achieved by means of contrast. 'Likeness', after all, is Turner's profound concern, and this series serves as an assertive form of negative analogy at a crucial point in the construction of a cultural theory. Comparison between two different entities or sets ordinarily relies for its force on our conviction of a lack of identity; and analogy concentrates, for its role in persuasion, on a reckoning of likeness against this conviction of difference. What Turner achieves is remarkable, because it is a conviction in the reader of a fundamental, theoretical relationship between two sets of phenomena which is produced by sustained attention to their differences. As a rhetorical mode of argument it is both subtle and sophisticated: by concentrating on manifest or plausible distinctions, Turner encounters and answers the objections that would accrue were the argument reliant on the positive factors of overt comparison or analogy. In this respect, the occasional qualifications to the set of distinctions reveal the binding quality of the argument as a whole. So liminoid phenomena, although distinguished as individualistic, "may be collective", but when they are so they "are often directly derived from tribal liminal antecedents". Similarly, although liminoid phenomena are, in the set of distinctions, 'marginal' in contrast to the 'central integration' of the liminal, "liminoid ideas and images may seep from these peripheries and cornices into the center". These qualifications are placed, as an aside or parenthesis that is in fact a nucleus, in each of the first two paragraphs. In the third, liminal phenomena "may, on occasion, portray the inversion or reversal of...social structure", a statement that promotes a similarity with the liminoid that was explicitly rejected in the primary contrast between "normative" (liminal) and "subversive" (liminoid) phenomena.

Constructed in this paradoxical manner, the general theoretical intent can take advantage of the objections that the distinctions might readily provoke. These are not only contained in his qualifications, which redirect the reader to a relationship between his two terms, but might— as Turner embarks on a change of readership with an address to cultural studies—be expected to be supplied by the readers themselves. So, for example, it would take very little to anticipate the citation of liminoid phenomena that appear to be "normative" rather than "subversive", or those that appear to take their place in the "cycles or rhythms" of society. But in so far as these objections can be anticipated, by their resolution of difference, distinction, or contrast they will support the conviction of a profound similarity which theory requires. The construction of cultural criticism is as much the work of the sophisticated reader as it is the result of an imposing or determining argument.

If there has been a suggestion of temporal change, of a theoretical scheme of chronology contained in the idea of 'migration' or of the pursuit of "separate destinies", then this suggestion of one component of the theoretical relationship can also be qualified. So Turner accepts, in passing, that "even in so-called tribal societies, there is an easily recognized '*liminoid zone*' of culture" (45). Similarly, "there is a well-marked '*liminal zone*' in our own culture" (ibid.), an assertion which, at the same time as it significantly qualifies a chronological scheme, allows for a concentration of attention on the social aspects of (modern) liminoid activity. Turner has in mind here the rites set up "when a group of liminoid artists constitutes itself as a coterie", and this specific link between liminal and liminoid in contemporary society will later justify Turner's increasing emphasis on the exemplary qualities of the (theatrical) avant-garde. The fact of recurrence, of a blending of liminal with liminoid phenomena in different degrees in different societies, apparently does not affect the central conviction of a differential relationship based on the primary characteristics of 'tribal' and 'modern', which is expressed in a familiar cliché of time:

> despite the coexistence of liminal and liminoid phenomena in all societies, it remains true that in complex societies today's liminoid is yesterday's liminal. (46)

Turner's argument has rendered suggestion into an art of persuasion, in which the development of the liminoid genres from the 'body' of liminality provides a general context for the specific recurrence of liminality as what might be called 'epiphenomena'—'groups' or 'coteries'—in contemporary societies. Turner's quest for the liminal in "post-tribal societies" is satisfied in two ways: by a theoretical scheme, vague in its demonstrations but firm in its assertions, which constitutes the category of liminoid genres for cultural criticism, and by the determination of liminality in the social formations associated with that category. In the conclusion of the essay the emphasis shifts from cultural to social theory, as Turner resumes his tripartite scheme for communitas (spontaneous, normative, and ideological), and notes that

> one of the social aspects of 'liminality' is probably to produce optimal conditions in small-scale preindustrial societies for the emergence of communitas among liminalities, particularly among those jointly undergoing initiation. (47)

This observation leads to a further distinction between "the tribal-liminal and the industrial-liminoid", which are understood here as social formations. In the former, "the whole group is engaged" in the process leading to the emergence of communitas, whereas

> in our society, it seems that the small groups which nourish communitas, do so by withdrawing voluntarily from the mainstream not only of economic but also of domestic familial life. (ibid.)

This final distinction would seem to deny communitas to the performance of the liminoid genres in the general theoretical scheme, permitting its emergence only to the chance collocation of the liminal with the liminoid. It is a conclusion that Turner does not make explicit, but it explains the tenor of his later work.

The publication of *From Ritual to Theatre* under the auspices of the *Performing Arts Journal* signals a major change in Turner's address to a readership, and this change is accompanied by several prominent attempts to find new theoretical models for what is already a developed thematic vocabulary of cultural studies. The problem raised by these attempts is intrinsic to anthropology, and is addressed by Turner in the distinction between "emic" and "etic" models, or forms of analysis: those which are understood to be, respectively, either 'internal' or 'alien' to the culture or the cultural materials under discussion. So in a relatively resolute reference to the authority of Aristotle in connection with his concept of the social drama, Turner strives to combine the advantages of possessing a theoretical model in European thought to his denial of "etic" imposition on the culture of the Ndembu:

> The fact that a social drama, as I have analyzed its form, closely corresponds to Aristotle's description of tragedy in the *Poetics*, in that it is an "imitation of an action that is complete, and whole, and of a certain magnitude...having a beginning, a middle, and an end", is not, I repeat, because I have tried inappropriately to impose an 'etic' Western model of stage action upon the conduct of an African village society, but because there is an interdependent, perhaps dialectic,

relationship between social dramas and genres of cultural performance in perhaps all societies. Life is, after all, as much an imitation of art as the reverse. (72)

The justification Turner presents for this universal relationship is what contemporary analysis might call the 'intertextuality' of story-telling and the "rhetoric" of the social drama itself amongst the Ndembu. Turner's assertion here, for which unfortunately he offers no example, is that a Ndembu story may be heard in childhood and then may later help to "frame" a social drama when the auditors are adult:

> Just as the story itself still makes important points about family relationships and about the stresses between sex- and age-roles, and appears to be an emic generalization, clothed in metaphor and involving the projection of innumerable specific social dramas generated by these structural tensions, so does it feed back into the social process, providing it with a rhetoric, a mode of employment, and a meaning. (ibid.)

The plausibility of this statement is supported only by reference to the 'paradigm' of martyrdom, which Turner had outlined in his earlier argument concerning the social dramas of Becket and Hidalgo in *Dramas, Fields, and Metaphors*, and it sits uncomfortably with another attempt at theoretical association with White, the theorist of histori-ography. The second chapter of *From Ritual to Theatre*, "Social Dramas and Stories About Them", from which the above quotations are taken, is itself 'framed' or introduced by a consideration of the potential analogies between White's paradigms of European historiography and the qualities of Turner's analysis.[31] Turner sees White's "theory of the historical work" as relevant to "ethnographies as well as histories" (66), but his suggestion of relevance is eclectic, and directed to particular ends. Most prominently, Turner chooses to select from White's four categories of 'formism', 'organicism', 'mechanism' and 'contextualism' as modes of composing a historical narrative those two which he sees as most applicable to his "voyage of discovery". So the 'structural-functionalism' in which Turner was trained as an anthropologist is understood to be equivalent to the 'mechanistic' in White's scheme, and Turner declares his own likely allegiance to 'contextualism', since the social drama is an example of an event which may be the source for contextual investigation. The advantages of determining this allegiance for his earlier ethnography, and for the essays on historical social dramas in *Dramas, Fields, and Metaphors*, are relatively clear. But contextual investigation is not apparent in the propositions of the wider cultural theory, which specifically evades or transcends the confines of an immediate, local context. Similarly eclectic is Turner's interest in White's distinction—for historiography—between chronicle and story, to which Turner is attracted because White's 'story', like Turner's concept of the social drama, is a process with an (Aristotelian) beginning, middle and end.

This kind of selective and relatively inconsequential allusion to distinguished authorities, contemporary and classical, in the field that Turner has determined as 'liminoid phenomena' is understandable, but it fails to qualify or redirect terminology or discourse in *From Ritual to Theatre*. A similar criticism should be levelled at the introductory discussion of the hermeneutical philosopher Wilhelm Dilthey (12–15), whose theory of the 'expression' of "experience" (*Erlebnis*) Turner adduces to validate the performative potential of the 'redress' phase in the social drama. Turner's representation of Dilthey's theory concentrates on the culminating cultural expression of experience, which he divides into "ideas", "acts" and "works of art", associating the social drama with "acts" (15). The degree to which Turner's representation is or is not a misrepresentation is not at issue here, because Turner's Dilthey serves merely to link "acts" with "works of art" in a scheme which permits, but makes no specific contribution to, Turner's unaltered emphasis on the performativity of the redressive phase in the social drama.[32]

Turner's general failure to adduce further theoretical models or authorities in *From Ritual to Theatre* may be a result of his particular adherence to the structural scheme proposed by van Gennep. Yet, curiously, it is in what he believes to be his rejection of Marx that he discovers a metaphorical resource whose attractions he cannot resist. Initially, in the collection of essays, Turner dismisses the idea of "mirroring" as an appropriate or useful metaphor for the liminoid:

> the liminoid can be an independent domain of creative activity, not simply a distorted mirror-image, mask, or cloak for structural activity in the 'centers' or 'mainstreams' of 'productive social labor'. (33)

Turner makes it plain that he is here contradicting the view of "the superstructural" he assigns to Marx:

> the connotation of a distorted mirroring, even falsification or mystification of the 'structural' or 'infrastructural', which is, in his

terms, the constellation of productive relations, both in cohesion and conflict.   (32–3)

By contrast, Turner's "independent domain of cultural activity" permits a more active role for "antistructure" and liminoid phenomena:

> To call them a distorting mirror is to identify liminoid productions solely with apologia for the political *status quo*. 'Antistructure', in fact, can generate and store a plurality of alternative models for living, from utopias to programs, which are capable of influencing the behavior of those in mainstream social and political roles (whether authoritative or dependent, in control or rebelling against it) in the direction of radical change, just as much as they can serve as instruments of political control.   (33)

Yet this dismissal ultimately, in the final essay of the collection, conflicts with Turner's consistent interest in making use of the concept of 'reflection'. As early as the analyses of ritual processes amongst the Ndembu in *The Forest of Symbols*, Turner had provisionally identified 'reflection' with 'liminality':

> During the liminal period neophytes are alternately forced and encouraged to think about their society, their cosmos, and the powers that generate and sustain them. Liminality may be partly described as a stage of reflection.[33]

Similarly, in the concluding essay of *From Ritual to Theatre*, theatrical performance "cannot escape reflection and reflexivity":

> This proximity of theatre to life, while remaining at a mirror distance from it, makes of it the form best fitted to comment or 'meta-comment' on conflict, for life is conflict, of which contest is only a species.   (105)

Yet the theoretical distinction between 'liminality' and the 'liminoid genres', of which theatrical performance is one—a distinction which is so crucial to Turner's argument—is not expressed in any analysis of the idea of metacommentary, which Turner here claims to be adopting from the anthropologist Geertz.[34] Instead, 'reflection' is relocated firmly in its origin as image, on a variable surface that flattens theatre to a creation of post-industrial silvering:

> In a complex culture it might be possible to regard the ensemble of performative and narrative genres, active and acting modalities of

> expressive culture as a hall of mirrors, or better magic mirrors (plane, convex, concave, convex cylinder, saddle or matrix mirrors to borrow metaphors from the study of reflecting surfaces) in which social problems, issues, and crises (from *causes célèbres* to changing macrosocial categorical relations between the sexes and age groups) are reflected as diverse images, transformed, evaluated, or diagnosed in works typical of each genre, then shifted to another genre better able to scrutinize certain of their aspects, until many facets of the problem have been illuminated and made accessible to conscious remedial action.
>
> (104–105)

Culture as remedy-through-distortion, or theory bemused by the light from its own imagery? The choice is not as difficult as one might have hoped by this stage of the development of a cultural theory.

4.1.4 Some case studies from an anthropology of performance

Turner applied his theory in a number of later essays, many of which were published in two posthumous collections.[35] I shall conclude this critique with a brief consideration of three case studies, two of them related to contemporary Brazil and one discussing the Indian theatrical form Kutiyattam. I shall take the leading essay of *The Anthropology of Performance* as an introduction.

The title of the opening essay of the collection *The Anthropology of Performance*—"Images and Reflections: Ritual, Drama, Carnival, Film, and Spectacle in Cultural Performance"—seems designed to embrace almost all the themes composed by Turner into his cultural theory of the liminoid, but Turner's starting point is that of "cultural performances", a term borrowed from Singer. Singer's "units of observation" in the Madras area of India included "plays, concerts, and lectures", but also "prayers, ritual readings and recitations, rites and ceremonies, festivals, and all those things which we usually classify under religion and ritual rather than with the cultural and artistic".[36] Singer represents, in Turner's discourse, a relatively simplistic view of the activity of these performances through their media, which relies on a concept of untroubled "communication". Turner isolates phrases from Singer such as "combined in many ways to express and communicate the content of Indian culture" and "the ways in which cultural themes are communicated" in order to insert his correction. This is, fundamentally, that cultural performances are not simple reflectors of culture or even changing culture but may themselves be active agencies of change... (24)

This corrective statement organizes a number of disparate attempts that Turner makes to describe the relationship between culture and its performances: "My thesis is that this relationship is not unidirectional and 'positive'...but that it is reciprocal and reflexive" covers the proposal that "performance is often a critique, direct or veiled, of the social life it grows out of" (21–2). Turner also returns to mirrors, in connection with the variety of different media:

> The result is something like a hall of mirrors—magic mirrors, each interpreting as well as reflecting the images beamed to it, and flashed from one to the others. (24)

An alternative suggestion is that the different genres are like "instruments", whose full reality is in their 'playing', and in this case music offers what appears to be the most comprehensive analogy:

> The master-of-ceremonies, priest, producer, or director creates art from the ensemble of media and codes, just as a conductor in the single genre of classical music blends and opposes the sounds of the different instruments to produce an often unrepeatable effect. (23)

Turner also considers the linguistic or grammatical analogy offered by the homophony between 'reflective' and 'reflexive', attributing the perception here to Babcock.[37] In "performative reflexivity" agents

> bend or reflect back upon themselves, upon the relations, actions, symbols, meanings, codes, roles, statuses, social structures, ethical and legal rules, and other sociocultural components which make up their public 'selves'. (24)

The list offered here is exhaustively impressive, almost astonishing, but the nature of the relationship involved remains elusive, beyond the governing metaphors of 'bending' or 'turning'. Performative reflexivity "is not mere reflex", but "is highly contrived, artificial, of culture not nature". Turner suggests that a natural reflex would result in a kind of pictorial realism; but the "*dominant* genres of cultural performance" are not like that, and his closest formulation of the process involved "rests on the principle that mainstream society generates its opposite". In this reflexive process the self is divided, becoming "something that one both is and that one sees and, furthermore, acts upon as though it were another". The final contrast suffers some elaborations: we read firstly of "acting upon the self-made-other in such a way as to transform it", and then of actors who

> can be so subdivided as to allocate to some the roles of agents of transformation and to others those of persons undergoing transformation. (25)[38]

The definition of cultural performances hesitates ambiguously between what Turner would earlier have divided into liminal and liminoid, with the vocabulary functioning suggestively in the mode of the 'drama analogy' and, at the same time, in that of the technical profession of theatre. Yet although the technical language approaches more closely to theatre, in the 'allocation' of "roles" to "actors", it is paradoxically all the more difficult to apply the resultant statement to dramaturgical practice or theatrical performance. It is as if Turner has confronted the disjunction implicit in all forms of comparison, where the similar dislikes and rejects the appropriation involved in equation. The more intricate the dramatic analogy within a discourse of anthropology or social studies, the greater the resistance to the act of incorporation from phenomena that will not be 'taken in'. What is similar, or even grossly dissimilar, will admit comparison: but it will not suffer the imposition of homogeneity, even under the imperatives of theory.

That Turner senses this dilemma, and finds it intractable, seems apparent from the remaining body of the essay, which includes a curious review—almost a listing—of "dramatic forms or movements", which Turner rather mysteriously claims that he hopes "to scrutinize".[39] The promise is certainly not fulfilled in the immediate argument, which proceeds in a desultory manner from a résumé of Turner's observations on liminality and on the "subjunctive mood" to considerations of the origins of drama, on which Turner refuses to commit himself or his argument. Statements that drama is "a matter of raising problems about the ordering principles deemed acceptable in real life", and "is never really complete...until it is performed" (27), leave drama relatively untroubled by new critical contentions. Similarly, Turner's insistence that a full understanding of aesthetic drama must take into account "social, political, and economic factors", that our preoccupation should be with "text in context" is hardly innovative. Possibly more interesting is his assertion that "Artaud's Spiritual progeny, the Theatre of Cruelty and the Theatre of the Absurd" are the "archtheatre of what I call the liminoid" (29). Turner seems to approve of Artaud's call for "some kind of real metaphysical inclination" in theatrical activity and creation. But the argument leaves the term "archtheatre" unexplained as Turner concludes with a brief commentary on film, the last of "the range of topics available" for a scrutiny of "the ongoing reciprocal relationships between the sociocultural process and major genres of ritual and dramatic performance" (32). In the case of film, the relationship is apparently contained in the approximation of cinema to ritual "in the great length of time and elaborate organization needed". It is difficult to see the critical or theoretical value of observations like these, which might as well—to be irreverent but fair—be applied to the filing systems in the local town hall as to any of Turner's specifically distinguished liminoid genres.

In the second essay of the volume, "Social Dramas in Brazilian Umbanda: The Dialectics of Meaning", Turner returns to his concept of the social drama, which he reviews under the function of narrative. His first project is to acknowledge that his own composition of the social dramas of the Ndembu did constitute a narrative, and was dependent on his own observations, rather than on the narratives that arose indigenously from the dramas. His second project is to affirm that narrative is a part of the third, or redressive, phase of his scheme for the social drama, notably in the jural or divinatory "narratives" that are themselves attempts at "'establishing the facts'". These significantly contextualize the events leading up to and constituting the crisis, eliciting in certain cultures the hidden motive impelling the actors (39). But these projects are components of an *apologia*, which may defend the concept of the social drama from complaints within the profession of anthropology that its author "is imposing the metaphor of drama on sequences of social relations where...it is inappropriate" (37). The form of the argument seems to be that if narrative is an integral part of the process observed, then a narrative about the process is not a purely "etic" imposition. It remains unclear how this affects the complaint about the model drawn from "a stylized, aesthetic construct, the drama", as Firth put it;[40] but Turner appears to be eluding the criticism of his model by substituting narrative as the mode of conjunction between observer and observed. So Turner's own anthropological narrative finally merges, in his argument, with those (a third category) that are consequent upon the conclusion of the social drama, which he sees as a

> process of 'mythologization' or 'fabulization' at work, beginning from

> my own observations of social dramas and continuing into the collection of narratives about these social dramas. Even participants produced different accounts. (40)

The "relationship between social dramas and narrative", or "the interplay between social drama and narrative", provides the theme for the study of the Umbanda religion in a suburb of Rio de Janeiro, for which Turner draws on the account by the anthropologist Velho, who had applied Turner's methodology.[41] Turner's initial thesis is that "in all cultures social dramas provide the 'raw stuff'...from which less existentially embedded cultural genres escape", and this thesis returns him to his mirror imagery:

> Social dramas may draw their rhetoric from cultural performances; cultural performances may draw on social dramas for their plots and problems. Genres of cultural performance are not simple mirrors but magical mirrors of social reality: they exaggerate, invert, re-form, magnify, minimize, dis-color, re-color, even deliberately falsify chronicled events. (42)

His immediate objective, in conformity with this thesis, is to search for the "intrusion of mythological and other narrational structures" into accounts from those "implicated in the events" (44). The drift within the term "cultural performances" is noticeable, with "cultural genres" standing for the earlier "liminoid genres" and "genres of cultural performance", which included, elsewhere in the preamble, "myths and rites" as well as "folk epics, ballads, dramas, and *Märchen*" (42). Further forward, in the main body of the discussion of Umbanda ritual and a specific social drama arising from the foundation of an Umbanda *terreiro* (cult-centre), the emphasis lies on the "performing of ritual", how Turner and his wife "experienced a particular performance" of Umbanda (50), with a passing allusion to "the great popularity" of the "performative genres" in Brazil. These last are classified by Turner, with some reservations, under 'celebration' as "the generic term", with 'ritual' and 'ceremony' dividing transformative from confirmatory processes. Masses, Corpus Christi processions, "performances of Umbanda, Con-domblé, or Batuque" cults, *Carnaval*, the Independence Day military parade, and *Futebol* are gathered in a list of "performative genres" that shows no trace of the "liminoid" as it existed in Turner's cultural theory of performance. Turner seems to stray from his thematic attention to narrative, but he is repeatedly interested instead in the urban context of Umbanda, how the cult enables its mediums to "play out...fantasies of being other than their circumscribed lives in urban slums and factories allow them to be" (59). The principal conclusion has little obvious connection with narrative, and that is "that the whole Umbanda complex is a standardized mode of redress for interpersonal and intra-personal conflicts", and is "not seen primarily as a collective redressive instrument for mending its own corporate fissions" (69). In fact, the theme of 'schism', and the constituent 'Africanity' of Umbanda posit links with Turner's earlier ritual ethnography, and his final definitions insist on the identification of the sessions at the *terreiro* as a ritual, "a transformative performance, 'a symphony in more than music'" (70).

In "Carnaval in Rio: Dionysian Drama in an Industrializing Society", Turner allows himself some brief theoretical comments before reviewing and eventually discarding the applicability of Caillois' classification of play.[42] The "soupçon of theory", with which Turner prefaces his account of Caillois and of Carnaval, is the reciprocal influence of the social drama and the performative genres:

> Underpinning each type of performance are the social structures and processes of the time; underlying the social drama or 'dramas of living', the Dreyfus cases and Watergates, are the rhetorics and insights of contemporary kinds of performance—popular, mainstream and avant-garde. Each feeds and draws on the other...One of the modes in which they do this is play—including games and sports, as well as festivals.   (124)

This, of course, is 'reflexivity', as Turner observes, but it is the general topic of reflexivity treated as a theoretical bond between the social drama and the liminoid genres, viewing them as "dialectical dancing partners", in the phrase Turner borrowed from Grimes.[43]

Turner's objection to Caillois is not specifically to details of his categories of play, but to his failure to grasp its "dialectical nature", how it "moves from structure to antistructure and back again to transformed structure" (127–8). Turner regards Caillois as a social evolutionist and a positivist, and concentrates on Caillois' contrast between "primitive" and "rational" societies, a contrast which is established, according to Caillois' scheme, by the kinds of play that predominate in them. For Turner, Carnaval is "antistructure" and "childlike", and it contains "*all* Caillois' components" of play "at once" (130). To maintain this anti-structural profile for Carnaval Turner has to dismiss, in the process of personal and derivative documentation, the evidence of structure in the bureaucratic organization of the event, and the ruling presence of a "military oligarchy" (131). As unqualified antistructure, or "the creative antistructure of organized modernity", Carnaval can then be seen as paradigmatic, as an offering from Brazilian culture to the anthropologist of performance:

> *Carnaval* is made to serve as a kind of paradigm, or model, for the whole modern and postmodern world.   (137)

Significantly, in this immediate context, Carnaval is "mostly glad", and is "the reverse of fiction or fake", and "no-one can feel embarrassed in the many-dimensioned world of carnival" (ibid.). According to Turner, only the middle class flees the city of Rio, "dreading the carnivalesque reversal of their hard-won bourgeois values".

It is an emotive and polemical picture—"the Golden Age really does return"—but it is not clear from Turner's discussion how Carnaval relates to the social drama, and so how it illustrates the thesis of the opening of the essay. What Turner presents is the enthusiastic triumph of a certain kind of documentation over the exigencies of classification; and what emerges is a relatively insistent rejection of any categorization of play that does not conform to the theoretical imperative of "antistructure". The theme of the return of the Golden Age in the spectacle open to the eyes of the theorist recalls Rousseau's aspirations in the *Letter*. As a child, Rousseau is on the verge of participating in the celebrations of St Gervais, but for Turner the carnival itself is childlike— "Even the evident sexuality...of *Carnaval* has an infantine quality" (129), and the contemporary theorist does not have Rousseau's anxieties of cultural and national identity to keep him from participating fully.

Critique and theatre are the two subjects of Turner's review of research by Richmond and Richmond on the south Indian performance convention, Kutiyattam, which for Turner is, crucially, "a transitional form between ritual and theater".[44] Turner's examination of the form through the Richmonds' account is directed and sustained by what might be described as a set of 'asides', which translate the phenomena of the Richmonds' discourse into elements of theory. Turner's forthright statement that Kutiyattam is dependent on "plays" written in "Sanskrit and Prakrit, languages known and understood by only a few priests and scholars who witness the performances" (238), fails to provide any indication of the lapse of time. The minor addition of 'now' to the phrase (as, for example, in 'now known and understood by only...') might have drawn more assiduous attention to an earlier theatrical context for the scripts. But the contemporary obscurity of the main body of the texts is used by Turner to highlight the contribution of the clown, or Vidusaka, which is in "the local language Malayalam". This existent contrast, in the contemporary performance constituted by Kutiyattam, promotes the theoretical connection with ritual:

> You will recognize in this opposition between actors and clown the opposition typical of ritual liminality in initiations between the perennially sacred and the perennially sacrilegious... (ibid.)

Turner is aware of the objection that if the clown engages in "detailed commentary on the conduct and mores of contemporary personages", as he does, then this can hardly be an example of the "anti-temporality of the liminal domain", in the phrase Turner uses of its separation from the everyday. So the solution offered to this awkward contradiction is that the clown's apparent commentary is in fact a "metacommentary".

The violence of cosmogony in the Richmonds' account of Vedic belief, which results in the order of the universe and of the temple, is subject to theory because it is, in Turner's words, "homologous with the movement of the social drama from the phase of crisis to that of redress, when indeterminacy is reordered" (240). "You will have recognized that..." is Turner's rhetorical instruction here, as Kutiyattam is encouraged to reveal its theoretical import, and the instruction is salutary when Turner brusquely alludes to "the etymological link between cosmetic and cosmos", which in fact belongs to the Hellenic ancestry of his own language. It is not a convincing discussion, but the resultant theoretical enthusiasm is unrepentant, even potentially innovative:

> Clearly, Kutiyattam is the firstborn child of ritual, perhaps even a younger sibling. (242)

Kutiyattam, as theatre, 'is and is not' ritual in the same manner as liminoid 'performance' is and is not liminal 'performance'. The text continues:

> Nevertheless, though still oriented to the sacred, it is already...an 'exhibition', 'something shown', an emergent from true ritual liminality, which engrosses its participants existentially, catching them into the inner momentum of a society's life. Already there is an element of voyeurism, an increase in reflexivity, especially in connection with the hypertrophy of the vernacular clown, and the split between actors and

> audience. Cognitive detachment is growing: the spectators witness divine, demonic, heroic, and anti-heroic deeds and their denouements; they are no longer kinetically engaged in them. (ibid.)

"Exhibition", "voyeurism", and "witness": the theatre is, according to this definition, a revelation of religious *sacra* carrying a strong sexual charge, and these key terms approximate theatrical performance to religious ritual as insistently as "split" and "detachment" argue for a contradictory sundering. The dilemma of comparison, in sameness and difference, must be expressed as process—Kutiyattam is "an emergent from true ritual", there is "an increase in reflexivity", and "cognitive detachment is growing"—and yet Kutiyattam "is already" something other than ritual. Turner's Kutiyattam participates in both ritual and theatre because it is a substantiation of the principle of comparison: to fulfil its theoretical function it must be both, either, and neither.

The abstraction that Turner's Kutiyattam has become is dependent on a number of factors. Turner's own perception is that it has, as he receives it from the account by Richmond and Richmond, been deprived of its context:

> Richmond does not, as I would have done, place a specific performance in its social, cultural, and political processual contexts in a well studied community. (238)

As a contemporary performance, it nonetheless represents, for Turner, "a transitional form...which has held its own for a thousand years" (ibid.), and its even greater antiquity is implied by its Sanskrit texts. Understood as a "transitional form", it belongs both to the past and to the present, in a permanent liminality of its own that prepares it for theory. As an example of "Oriental theater", it will be represented in western discourse as an object of ethnographic or cultural research. Ageless, lacking context, redolent of 'otherness', it is unable to protest its own freedom from 'transition' in its cultural or social stability, and what it 'lacks' in the context of western discourse will be supplied by the complementary requirements of theory. In this respect it is idle to debate whether Kutiyattam 'is' ritual, or 'is' theatre, or is 'betwixt and between' these two components of theory: it is what a western, and indeed an orientalizing, theoretical discourse wishes it to be.

4.2 RICHARD SCHECHNER (1934–)

Richard Schechner has been writing on the theatre for over thirty years, a period which has included tenure at Tulane University and the Tisch School in New York, and two, long-divided sessions as editor of *Drama Review*, from 1962 to 1969 and then from 1986.[45] Prevented from directing at Tulane by his contract, Schechner had founded the New Orleans Group in 1965, and in New York he founded The Performance Group in November 1967.[46] Schechner is a prolific writer, as he himself notes at the head of the "Acknowledgements" in his most recent book:

> My writings usually exist in versions or variants. My writing isn't finishable. My strategy is to rehearse, rework, revise. I publish at various stages of working, not being too neat about precisely when a constellation of ideas gets into print.[47]

More precisely, Schechner's books are regularly collections of essays, which may appear in more than one volume, and which may be revised, altered or extended. His first collection had the title *Public Domain*, and this was followed by what is, to date, his only book-length study of a single subject, *Environmental Theater*, an account of the work of The Performance Group in its first four years.[48] In addition to these studies, I shall be drawing on chapters from the revised edition of *Performance Theory*, published in 1988,[49] and on two essays which were both published in two related collections: *Performative Circumstances* of 1983, published in India, and *Between Theater and Anthropology* of 1985, published in the USA.[50] The essays, "Restoration of Behavior" (originally of 1977) and "Performers and Spectators Transported and Transformed" (originally of 1979), are important constituents of Schechner's anthropological performance theory. Later essays have been collected in *The Future of Ritual*, which, despite its title, is rather less theoretical in orientation than these earlier volumes.

4.2.1 The eye of theory in *Public Domain* and *Environmental Theater*

In his "Six Axioms for Environmental Theatre", which he had republished (from *Drama Review*) in *Public Domain*, Schechner had taken as his starting point John Cage's definition of theatre as "something which engages both the eye and the ear. The two public senses are seeing and hearing...", and claimed that he found Cage's exclusion of taste, touch, and odor "unnecessarily restrictive".[51] As one consequence, contiguity, the characteristic of those three senses confined to "intimate situations" by Cage, became substantial to the first of the Six Axioms: "primary transactions" between and among performers and audience, and secondary "interactions" between these and "elements" in the production. A complementary component was the relationship, or interaction, between the total production and the space in which it takes place. Schechner then concluded with a fundamental point:

> The final exchange between performers and audience is the exchange of space, the use of the audience as scene-makers as well as scene-watchers. This will not result in chaos: rules are not done away with, they are simply changed.[52]

The legislative and prescriptive tone is marked, and this holistic definition of environmental theatre was corroborated in the next three axioms, which dealt with the removal of "fixed seating and the bifurcation of space" (second axiom), with a totally "designed" space as in intermedia (third axiom), and with the organization of space "so that no spectator can see everything" (fourth axiom). The fifth axiom subordinated the performer to the general concept: "The performers may be treated as mass and volume, color, texture, and movement, not as 'actors', but as part of the environment".[53] The sixth adopted John Cage's idea of using "past literature as material rather than as art", in the relatively conventional terms of the avant-garde: as Schechner put it, "The repertory—from Aeschylus to Brecht—clogs rather than releases creativity".[54]

The removal of the restriction of theatre to a limited engagement of eye and ear, and its consequent extension to contiguity, strongly suggest liberation, but the text of "Six Axioms" does not encourage a sense of greater freedom. There is a strong hand of control in the concepts of a totally pre-designed space and/or of spatial "organization", as there is in the language of "rules", the "use" of the audience, the performers "treated as" impersonal perceptual qualities. Quite whether this hand is subjective (that of a director or designer) or not is also unclear: the language of "relations", "primary transactions", "exchange", and "interaction" is distinctly sociological, and as it emerges environmental theatre might be subject as much to a discipline of thought (e.g. sociology or anthropology) as to a specific mentor. What is clear is that the spectator is to some extent deprived of sight, the performer of a customary prominence, and the script-worker of a determining influence. As with Brook in *The Empty Space*, one senses that the dismissal (if no more) of immanent skills has an important function in clearing the ground for the new proposition. But there is an ill-defined or hidden 'first-person' for the activity of dismissal or clearance entailed by the rhetoric, which differs firmly from Brook's explicit subjectivity. This is the voice of impersonal clearance ("is", "are", "will be", "should"), and the reader finally enters the playground of metaphor when the axioms have all been established:

> The text is a map with many possible routes. You push, pull, explore, exploit. You decide where you want to go...You don't 'do' the play, you 'do with it'—confront it, search amongst its words and themes, build around and through it...and come out with your own thing.
> That is the heart of environmental theatre.[55]

The "search", the "routes", the 'exploration' and even the activity of 'building' are trite enough as metaphors; only the heart gives us a living body for the new theatre.

The 'environment' for Schechner suggests something more than sight and sound. An attention to environment offers a firm location for the myth of corporeal 'presence', the same insistent living priority as can be attributed to speech. But there is an inevitable agony for the legislative 'voice' in writing, and that is writing itself. Schechner attempted to face this problem in the Foreword to his subsequent book, *Environmental Theater*, which is, in its full extent, a small masterpiece of evasion. I quote briefly from the opening:

> Why write a book? Shouldn't work be its own justification? Sometimes the people I work with suggest that I direct plays so that I can write about them. But if this book has value, it is because in it I can do something that I cannot do in the work. What then is the relationship between "the work" and "the book"?
> This book is about where I have been and what I have done between roughly 1967 and the present.[56]

Schechner raises these questions only to ignore them, or perhaps to summarize his answer to them in the one word "about". But more importantly, he reveals (as it seems) the nature of the hesitant and undeclared subject for the pronouncement of the earlier Six Axioms:

> My studies of anthropology, social psychology, psychoanalysis, and gestalt therapy are the bases of my belief that *performance theory* is a social science, not a branch of aesthetics. I reject aesthetics. (ibid.)

That we should read *performance theory* as the anthropological determinant for the Axioms on environmental theatre becomes quite certain from the following paragraph, which, nonetheless, contains a remarkable shift from its opening to its concluding statements:

> Environmental theater is a way of working that has grown more precise over the past fifteen years or so. It is a particular style of theater in Europe and America. I consider much of the work of Jerzy Grotowski, Peter Brook, Eugenio Barba, Ludovico Ronconi, the Théâtre du Soleil, the Living Theater, the Bread and Puppet Theater, the Open Theater, and the Manhattan Project to be environmental theater. Across much of Asia, Oceania, and Africa *all* theater is environmental. Because, in a way, this whole book is an exposition of environmental theater, I will not elaborate. (ibid.)

The concept has proved remarkably elastic: a "way of working" (New Orleans Group, The Performance Group), a selection of parallel European and American practitioners and groups, and the theatre of the three remaining continents. Elasticity is, obviously, one of the primary capacities of metaphor, and the associative tendencies of 'environment' begin to tell strongly. But there are further advantages: a definition fixed in a metaphor of global elasticity—from the close topography of the Performance Garage out and around the theatrical traditions of the Old World—is more effective than most in its inclusion of mobility. If purposeful movement—path, search, etc.—was only one of the evocative groups deployed by Brook, then for Schechner it acts to justify the path taken by work as writing, which will include intercontinental research. In this movement, the book itself plays a vital role:

> This book grows out of my conviction that the only way to move ahead is to know where I have been. To scrutinize my former work, to be free from the obligation to defend it, to move beyond it: to reject it, every last bit. Rejection is not denial. It is the liberty to select what is to be kept, using criteria other than "that's what I've done—so I'd better keep on doing it.". (viii)

The criteria remain undeclared. Schechner dismisses aesthetics, but 'speaks' of identifying "a style such as 'environmental theater'" (ibid.). The environment, and environmental theatre, take their place in the metaphoric shift as the objective, self-leaving 'movement away', always onwards, and as the style that is no style in the absence of aesthetics, but a science. Schechner is 'speaking' of a phenomenon, not writing it into existence: "I am not (I hope) writing a manifesto but describing a phenomenon called into existence by social circumstances." (ibid.). That 'hope' is ill-founded: environmental theatre, and Richard Schechner, categorically exist as writing.

Environmental Theater is indeed a detailed and highly personal description of the work of The Performance Group from *Dionysus in 69* and *Makbeth* in 1969–70 to the production of Shepard's *The Tooth of Crime* in 1972–3. Its chapters include meditations on Space, Participation, Nakedness, Performer, Shaman, Therapy, Playwright, Groups, and Director in what is one of the most articulate and specifically thorough documents of the work of an experimental group in its period. Schechner is open and forthright about problems in the group, and with outsiders, such as the playwright Shepard: a median is established by the therapy sessions led by Tom Driver, of which there is an account in the chapter on "Participation", because it was in that area of the work that the problems arose. In many respects Schechner is keen to identify the problems of the Group as those of internal politics. Schechner began the Group because he wanted to continue work he had started with the New Orleans Group, and because he wanted to apply some of what he had learnt from Grotowski's New York University workshop in November 1967. The choice of myths for the constituting productions (Pentheus and Macbeth) strongly suggests a need to explore the concepts of leadership and destruction, and the shift from individual leadership to the collective is the obvious advertisement of the book as a whole.

In point of fact, the political discourse is inadequate. The problems faced by Schechner and by The Performance Group as a whole were those already entailed by an insistence on the excluded senses in "Six Axioms...". In the opening chapters of *Environmental Theater*, Schechner activates his release of the strictly corporeal senses of touch, taste and smell:

> I believe there is an actual, living relationship between the spaces of the body and the spaces the body moves through, that human living tissue does not abruptly stop at the skin. Exercises with space are built on the assumption that human beings and space are both alive. (12)

The metaphor of life is transferred, through contiguity, to the space. Touch leads to the two remaining internal senses:

> In the spring of 1969 TPG explored the relationship between the snout—the nose and mouth, the cavities of the sinuses and throat—the gut, and the larger spaces in the theater... (15)

Schechner links this exploration to Artaud, in the creation of a fruit-eating, communal ritual, and establishes what he terms the "visceral space-sense". Yet, curiously, he cites Artaud's *visions* in Mexico: rocks with the shape of women's breasts, "heads, torsos in agony, crucifixions, men on horses, huge phalluses, and other images impressed on the rocks or rising from them" (17). Participation, the subject of his second chapter, is also corporeal, and contiguous: spectators are kicked into the circle for *Commune* in a "paradigmatic and unsettling scene of audience participation" (46-7), and the "ardor" of some participators in the "Caress" scene of *Dionysus in 69* apparently proved an annoyance to performers. According to Schechner's own account, the performers were dissatisfied with participation, and to some extent with Schechner himself. This was partly due to uncertainty:

> Participation voids destiny and fortune, throwing drama back into its original theatrical uncertainty: re-introducing elements of the unrehearsed into the smooth ground of the performance. (78)

The myth of 'origins' is combined here with the spatial metaphor ("ground") in order to counteract the force of fear, repugnance and disruption. But repugnance and reluctance can be dismissed theoretically with something far more powerful and immediate. "Nakedness", the subject of his third chapter, gets to "the heart of environmental theater", by adding 'eros' and the mystical reliability of the inner/outer polarity to the now familiar, additional senses:

> I propose that the body state of environmental theater—the spatial mood—is erotic: the inside-outness of the body translated into theater architecture. Orthodox theater spaces emphasize the eyes and ears: environmental spaces emphasize the nose and mouth. (105)

Schechner's evasions, as they accumulate in these chapters, conceal the evidence that his environmental theatre of touch, taste and smell is ultimately controlled by vision. But it is not the spectator who sees, nor the voyeurs who haunted *Dionysus in 69* as he readily acknowledges. The environmental theatre entails the removal of the aesthetics of audience reception in favour of the observation of a social event: as Schechner notes, "audience participation takes place precisely at the point where the performance breaks down, and becomes a social event" (40). As early as "Six Axioms..." Schechner had relished the prospect of dismantling the view of the audience: "The space is organized so that no spectator can see everything.".[57] The effect of environmental theatre is to dislodge the audience from its role as constituting subject, and transform its members into yet more performers:

> The orthodox theatre-goer is snuggled. He can keep his reactions to himself, and he is more likely to get utterly wrapped up in the experience on stage.[58]

This objective is actually the basis of Schechner's scarcely concealed violence against the critic, who intractably insists on fulfilling a traditional function of seeing, and it is also the meaning of Schechner's rejection of aesthetics.[59] The ideal spectator in environmental theatre is observed, not observing, and with the performer is translated into an object of performance theory:

> People come up to me and say, "I couldn't keep my attention focused on the play." Or, "I was moved by some of it, but I kept thinking my own thoughts. Sometimes I lost track of what was going on." Or, "Sometimes I felt good, but at other times I felt threatened." Or, "You know, I watched the audience so much I lost part of the play." Or even, "I fell asleep." I think all of these responses are splendid.[60]

Environmental Theater provides a good account of the transformation of theatre practice into "a social event", and as an extended piece of writing answers the originally unanswered questions of its own Foreword. The removal of aesthetics, of the audience and the spectator, is the removal of independent judgement, substituting the event as the object of theory for the director-and-the-cast as the object of unwelcome criticism. "Performance theory is a social science", as Schechner states, and it can only be achieved in writing, as an unending movement 'ahead' across the printed page.

4.2.2 The discursive figures of performance theory

"Approaches" was first presented (with the fuller title "Approaches to Theory/ Criticism") at an interesting moment in Schechner's first period as editor of the *Drama Review*. Of the two versions available—the original in *Drama Review*, and the revision in the second edition of *Performance Theory*—I shall use the text and numeration of the second, which is probably more accessible to most readers.

The essay starts from the assimilation by an American scholar, Francis Fergusson, of theories of the ritual origins of Greek drama advanced by the school of thought known as the Cambridge anthropologists. These writers—Jane Harrison, Gilbert Murray, and Francis Cornford—took their bearings from the work of James Frazer, *The Golden Bough*, published towards the end of the nineteenth century, and Schechner summarizes their proposals as an assertion of the existence of what he terms a "'primal ritual'", from which Athenian drama was derived. Schechner's contention is that this assertion is "highly speculative" and tendentious, and he insists that the proposal has been so influential because it "can be compressed, codified, and generalized", and "seems to explain everything" (5). To this preliminary survey Schechner appends an uncompromising and arresting theoretical announcement, which substitutes attention to the horizontal axis—"what each autonomous genre shares with the others"—for that normally given to the "vertical or originary" axis in "the study of the performative genres". Schechner rejects theories of origin comprehensively—"Origin theories are irrelevant to understanding theater"—and in place of the binary system 'ritual/drama' substitutes "several activities related to theater". Ritual, play, games, sports, dance, and music are to be located alongside theatre.

> Together these seven comprise the public performance activities of humans. If one argues that theater is 'later' or more 'sophisticated' or 'higher' on some evolutionary ladder and therefore must derive from one of the others, I reply that this makes sense only if we take fifth century BCE Greek theater (and its counterparts in other cultures) as the only legitimate theater. Anthropologists, with good reason, argue otherwise, suggesting that theater—understood as the enactment of stories by players—exists in every known culture at all times, as do the other genres. These activities are primeval, there is no reason to hunt for 'origins' or 'derivations'. There are only variations in form, the intermixing among genres, and these show no long-term evolution from 'primitive' to 'sophisticated' or 'modern'. (6)

According to this statement, the act of 'derivation'—indicating or determining an origin—is a disfranchisement, granting 'legitimacy' to the derived form and denying it to the "originary". Schechner is also clearly thinking of certain kinds of unspecified value judgement that find expression in the contrasting terms "primitive" and "sophisticated": these might be cultural, racial or ethnic, or possibly aesthetic and intellectual, but all would refer in an exclusive manner to the 'judging' subject. So his confusing reference to "the only legitimate theater", when 'theatre' is in his scheme only one of a full seven "genres" of performance, should presumably be rephrased to read 'the only legitimate performative genre, namely theatre'. In fact, the reference to "intermixing among genres" suggests that the apparent use of "theater" as just one category amongst seven conceals a broader theoretical scope for the term. If "theater" is a vacillating category, one of seven theoretical phenomena but also a universal term, then evidence may always be found for 'its' existence. In the argument that follows Schechner actually conflates "dance", "music", and "theater", naming all three as the "aesthetic genres", and confines his main discussion to a heading that includes only five of the seven proposed "performative genres": "play, games, sports, theater, and ritual" (ibid.).

The essay determines four "basic qualities...shared by these activities": these are "a special ordering of time", "a special value attached to objects", "non-productivity in terms of goods", and "rules" (6). Schechner refers to "clock time...adapted from day–night and sensory rhythms" as a contrast to the three varieties of "performance time", which are "event time", "set time" and "symbolic time". Intercultural juxtaposition is the main function of the three categories, with baseball and hopscotch aligned under "event time" with rain dances and "scripted theatrical performances taken as a whole", and with theatre and "rituals that reactualize events or abolish time" aligned with "make-believe play and games" under "symbolic time". In this latter case, Schechner seems averse to using the word 'drama', which undoubtedly is the more exact point of contrast (in "symbolic time") with the extent of theatrical performance (in "event time"). He gives most prominence in his three categories to symbolic time, which 'happenings' discard, but which is normative in "orthodox theater":

> Symbolic time, seemingly absent from happenings and the like, is actually most difficult to banish. Once action is framed 'as theater' spectators read meanings into whatever they witness. Orthodox acting and scenic arrangements stress mimesis with its symbolic time...   (8)

The tone of regret—"most difficult to banish"—may be dependent on the uncontrolled 'readings' of spectators in the conventional aesthetics of "orthodox theater", a companion to the theoretical hostility I noted in section 3.2.2 above.

The section on 'objects' is more cursory, with the contrast lying between their "market" or "material value" and their "extreme importance" in performance, when they may be "as in theater and children's games...decisive in creating the symbolic reality" (9). The third of the "basic qualities", that of "non-productivity", involves him in some slight difficulty:

> The separation of performance activities from productive work is a most interesting, and unifying, factor of play, games, sports, theater, and ritual.   (ibid.)

Schechner briefly cites Huizinga and Caillois, but acknowledges an obvious contradiction to his own proposition in the massive involvement of money in some of these activities, and offers no resolution to the problem. The fourth 'quality', of "rules", operates universally because Schechner allows it to include traditions and conventions:

> What rules are to games, traditions are to ritual and conventions are to theater, dance, and music. If one is to find a better way to perform, this better way must conform to the rules.   (11)

This is a strange description of many periods of invention in "theatre, dance, and music", but Schechner is here aware of an implicit contradiction in the activities of the avant-garde:

> The avant-garde is apparently a rule-breaking activity. But actually, experimentation in the arts has its own set of rules.   (ibid.)

Whatever they are, they remain undeclared, but Schechner contrasts drastic technological change with the comparative stability of the avant-garde "over the past seventy years". A final and additional 'quality', making a provisional total of five, is constituted by "performance spaces", which Schechner distinguishes as "uniquely organized so that a large group can watch a small group—and become aware of itself at the same time" (13). This formula has some weaknesses. In the initial context of Greek drama, the Athenian political assembly had a comparably "organized" design to that of the theatre, and it is more than a little difficult to consider Schechner's earlier example of hopscotch in accordance with the prescription.

The essay contains nine diagrams (figs 1.1–1.9 in the revised edition of *Performance Studies*), which punctuate and illustrate the argument. I shall briefly describe and discuss a limited number of them, as they relate and are related to the discursive text. The first is a simple arrow-and-line, vertical development of tragedy and comedy from the "Primal Ritual" at the base, through two of an indefinite number of intervening "rites" (fig. 1.1, 3). The diagram itself is clear, and unequivocally figures

Schechner's representation of the amalgamated thesis of 'the Cambridge anthropologists'; but it is, according to Schechner's discursive text, the figuration of a misleading argument. According to Schechner, the straight lines leading from the "Primal Ritual" to the intervening rites, and then upwards as arrows from two of those rites to tragedy and comedy, are not justified by the available evidence. The diagram is a figure of a theoretical fallacy, but our understanding or acceptance of it in that capacity is dependent on conviction or assertion sustained in the accompanying text. As a graphic illustration, it cannot or does not declare its own quality, and does not function independently. The figures that Schechner uses, like other 'figures' of speech or writing, are directed by the discursive strategies or tactics of argument, and are a part of the main text of persuasion. For this reason I shall continue to give a verbal description of them when appropriate, in a method which confronts their illusory neutrality, and returns them to their place in discourse.

Schechner's second figure (fig. 1.2, 12) is a 'table' which adopts the characteristics of a questionnaire. The five "performative genres" or "activities" (play, games, sports, theatre and ritual) displayed on the horizontal axis each 'answer' to the five basic qualities (time, objects, non-productivity, rules and space) on the vertical axis, to which eight other 'qualities' have been added, making a total of thirteen 'questions' for each "genre" to answer. These eight others have had no specific introduction, and are more or less self-explanatory: they appear as "appeal to other", "audience", "self-assertive", "self-transcendent", "completed", "performed by group", "symbolic reality", "scripted". The 'answers' given by the "genres" are mostly "Yes" and "No", but "not totally" and "not necessarily" and "usually" also occur. So, for example, "theater" is asked the thirteen questions, and answers "Yes" to ten of them. As with all questionnaires, the 'subject' appears to be making clear statements about itself.

Schechner's introduction to the figure is brief: it is a "performance chart", with which he will "summarize the formal relations" between his five categories of activity. His principal conclusion from it immediately follows the introduction:

> Referring to it, we see that theater has more in common with games and sports than with play or ritual. (13)

It is not clear how this conclusion is drawn. If the "basic qualities" are equally "basic", and the affirmative or negative a reliable indication to the reader, then the "formal relations" should indeed be apparent from the figure. But while "theater" has ten occurrences of "Yes", a descending scale on the affirmatives has "ritual" and "sports" with six, "games" with four and "play" with three. On the clear negatives, "play" has three, "games" and "sports" two, "ritual" one and "theater" none. On both these calculations, "ritual" and "theater" are in fact the closest of all five. Two further conclusions added by Schechner at this point are also extrinsic to the table or "chart": "happenings", which are not included in the figure, are stated to "relate more to play than anything else", and play is affirmed to be "the ontogenic source of the other activities" (13). This discord of text and figure is followed by a statement which confirms the assertions made in the text at the same time as it subverts the figure:

> The definitive break between games, sports, and theater on the one hand, and play and ritual on the other, is indicated by the different quality and use of the rules that govern the activities.   (ibid.)

So the category of "rules" is clearly more "basic" than the other listed qualities, but the only 'indication' of this on the chart is the use of exceptional 'answers', which Schechner has not discussed. The answers in the chart aligned with "rules" are neither direct nor qualified affirmatives or negatives: instead, "play" has "inner"; "games", "sports" and "theater" have "frame"; and "ritual" has "outer". From the text, and a subsequent diagram (fig. 1.3, 13), it becomes apparent that in play "one makes one's own rules" (= "inner"), whereas "ritual is strictly programmed" (= "outer"), and that "games, sports, and theater (dance, music) mediate between these extremes" (= "frame") (13–14). The Freudian seal for this tripartite division of the performative genres is expressed in figure 1.3 in a contrast between the "pleasure principle" (or Eros, or the "id") for "play", and the "reality principle" (or "Thanatos", or the "superego") for "ritual"; the remaining three activities or genres achieve a balance between the two principles.

The degree of conviction achieved by these two figures (1.2 and 1.3) in their conjunctions with, and disjunctions from, the discursive argument rests finally in mathematical symbols. Between the plus-sign attached to play and the minus-sign attached to ritual in figure 1.3 is the combined plus-and-minus ($\pm$) attributed to the other three genres of theatre, sports, and games. This leaves these three firmly fixed in their central location by a convention to which we are all visually as well as conceptually obedient. Ultimately, in the organization of both diagrams, ritual and play are driven apart from the central three activities in order to isolate theatre, sports and games as most appropriate to the methodologies of "mathematical and transactional game analysis":

> The indication that theater has more in common with sports and games than with ritual or play should be the cue to explore work in mathematical and transactional game analysis as methodologies for the study of theater. (15)

The "indication" has not been achieved by the figure or by the text, but it is apparent in the collusion between them, which passes responsibility from one to the other. As a consequence, it is not surprising to find that the recommended forms of analysis emphasize the value of figures for theory:

> One thing game theory and transactional analysis teach is the advantage of constructing models. These are—as they apply to theater—simple, graphic representations of the structure of the action(s) of a play or scene. Models have the double quality of brevity and precision.
> (16)

The "brevity and precision" of figures encourage Schechner to proceed from a critical analysis of the *Oresteia*, past a short digression on *Hamlet*, to a discussion of paradigmatic "post-dramatic drama" (in Beckett's *Waiting for Godot* and Ionesco's *The Lesson*), to a conclusion that posits a transitional role for Chekhov (in *The Three Sisters*). The initial model used (fig. 1.5, 16) is that of an equilateral triangle, which is taken to represent conflict between "forces, groups, or individuals" (ibid.) in the two corners of the horizontal axis of the triangle, and resolution at its peak. The *Oresteia* of Aeschylus is then, in a three-dimensional projection of this geometry, represented as a triangular pyramid (fig. 1.6, 17), with the stage action as "just one face of a more complicated structure", and "all the faces of the pyramid operative on stage" only in the final play of the trilogy: the previously hidden faces are those of the "state" and the "gods", the open face is that of the "family" (17). The transformation of the two-dimensional triangle (of fig. 1.5) into a triangular pyramid (fig. 1.6) is apparently necessary because of "the complexity of the trilogy", and the discursive dialectic between "simple, graphic representations" and dramaturgical "complexity" is mystifying: how 'simple' does a model have to be to represent relative complexity, for example, and what exactly is "the advantage of constructing models"? The answer is, perhaps inevitably, that the figures support the figurative critical language on which Schechner chooses to rely: so he writes of "basic lines" in the trilogy (18), of basic (at the base, beneath or chthonic) conflicts, and of a "deeper look at the model" (19), which would indeed be problematic were it a triangle rather than a pyramid in projection. Similarly, "a plumb line" may be dropped from the apex of these figures, which "can be called the line of reason". Yet, conversely, were this line followed "there would be no drama" (20): an excess of figure over the capacities of discursive argument results in the collapse or disintegration of the figure itself. Its independence and value, even as a critical adjunct, is no more than illusory.

The principal objective of "Approaches" is to divorce theatre from a dependence on ritual as its origin, and to associate theatre with games and with sports. In so doing, and despite some of his own practices in the essay—commentaries on *The Maids*, the *Oresteia*, *Hamlet*, *Waiting for Godot*, and *The Three Sisters* form part of the presentation—Schechner can theoretically discard literary criticism in favour of "other tools, other approaches" (27). These "will prove fruitful", and will "urge explorations of horizontal relationships among related forms":

> They will also situate theater where it belongs: among performance genres, not literature...The possibility exists that a unified set of approaches will be developed that can handle *all* performance phenomena, classical and modern, textual and non-textual, dramatic, theatrical, playful, ritual.   (28)

This 'ontogenesis' of performance theory relies on figures to distract attention from its lack of demonstration or consistency in argument. But the conspicuous failures of precise achievement should not obscure the rhetorical gains: these are programmatic and prescriptive, concerned with the kinds of freedom that manifestos regularly declare, even if they do not aim to justify them fully. One of the freedoms is made explicit:

> The accepted methods and vocabularies are inadequate for the analysis of both orthodox and new theater.   (27)

The other is almost completely suppressed: if ritual is released from its subordinate, circumscribed and culturally-demeaning role as an 'origin' for 'sophisticated' theatre, it is then theoretically available for re-association in a new set of relations to an ensemble of "performative genres".

"Drama, Script, Theater, and Performance" of 1973 contains a bizarre thesis, which is nonetheless part of Schechner's incipiently anthropological theory of theatre and performance. Much of the essay is devoted to an *apologia* for Schechner's fraught relations with Sam Shepard on the occasion of The Performance Group's production of *The Tooth of Crime*, which, in another presentation, order some of the narrative in his study *Environmental Theater*.[61] The attractions of anthropology in the essay are those of prehistory, rather than of modern or near-contemporary documentation. Schechner's formative dismissal of a ritual origin for theatre becomes entangled with a claim for the universality of the subject(s) of performance theory:

> The phenomena called either/all 'drama', 'theater', 'performance' occur among all the world's peoples and date back as far as historians, archaeologists, and anthropologists can go. (68)

The emotive evidence for this equivocal proposition is that of the caves that preserve the marks of palaeolithic culture. Schechner quotes La Barre's interpretation of the preservation of footprints in the obscure and obstructed interior of Tuc d'Audoubert as those of "ancient dancers", and begins his cultural reconstruction:

> This cave is not the only one to make difficult, if not altogether inaccessible, its performance space. These earliest theaters—or shall I call them temples?—are hidden in the earth, lit by torch, and the ceremonies enacted therein apparently concerned hunting-fertility. (ibid.)

In the accompanying photograph (plate 3.1, 69) a chamber at Lascaux is "A paleolithic cave performance space...", and the general evocation soon becomes that of "the dancer-shamans of the Paleolithic temple theaters" (70). Schechner's desire to reconstitute the space and the activity demands a dubious exactitude:

> Extrapolating from the prehistorical and historical evidence, as well as modern experience, I assume that the dancing took a persistent (or 'traditional') shape which was kept from one event to another... (70)

The activity of "the avant-garde in the west" is then related to this construct in two ways. The first involves the evolution of drama as writing from the unwritten code which ordered these cave dances:

> Potential manifestations previously encoded in patterns of doings were later encoded in patterns of written words. (ibid.)[62]

This is the "drama" that has preoccupied "the great tradition of the west" from the Greeks and then the Renaissance "until very recently". It is the avant-garde that is responsible for discarding the emphasis on writing, and this perception serves to introduce the conflict of interest between the playwright Shepard and The Performance Group led by Schechner. A second reference to the caves later in the essay returns briefly to the issue of evidence, but with a diminished sense of certainty:

> There is some hard evidence pointing to dancing ceremonies accompanying the visual representations in the Paleolithic caves...These are interpreted as footprints of dancers. (92)

This is the Tuc d'Audoubert again, but in the account of a second source.[63] Schechner is, on this occasion, more tentative in a rhetorical question he puts to the reader, but at least as ambitious in the assumptions contained in the question:

> If ancient humans drew and carved beings who combine the physical attributes of humans and animals can we not assume that actual costumes were created; and can we not further assume that the paintings on the cave walls are either of dances, or at least in their own way 'accompany' dancing? (ibid.)

The important conclusion is that these theoretical dances were those of hunters: "The dances were probably both evocations of animal spirits and emulations/ transformations of animal movements" (ibid.). This permits a connection to be made with play, because "play belongs mainly to carnivorous and omnivorous species: hunters" (98). If play is "what organizes performance, makes it comprehensible", then "hunting is inherently...theatrical/dramatic", because it necessitates a co-ordinated sequence of actions, involving signals and communication, and results in a climax (98–9). So it follows that the origin of drama, or its recurrence, lies "among certain peoples who have consciously made a connection among hunting, warfare, human and/or animal sacrifice, and play" (102). This applies to China, Japan, Korea, India, America and Greece, and both shamanism and story-telling were combined in the creation of drama.

I have called this thesis bizarre because it reduces the agriculturalism of history and prehistory (in the post-glacial period from *c*. 10,000 BC) to a minor intrusion on the theatrical "cartography" (91) drawn by Schechner. Agriculture plays no part in the evolution of drama:

> Agricultural societies develop spectacles organized around ceremonies whose function it is to entreat the regularity of the seasons, the falling of rain, the warming of sun. (103)

Dionysus is the god of the cultivated vine in the Athenian dramatic festivals, as well as the god of the ritual *sparagmos*. But, in the second of his connections between the paleolithic and the present, the avant-garde offers for Schechner a refuge from aggression, a "laboratory" in which drama—"Drama develops in cultures for whom hunting is especially important" (103)—may be ritually dismembered in the controlled "environment" of the workshop/cave. Schechner concludes with the idyllic associations suggested by this theoretical 'fancy':

> And if I may end on a somewhat fanciful note: I associate the workshop environment with those ancient, decorated caves that give evidence of singing and dancing, people celebrating fertility in risky, sexy, violent, collective, playful ways. (104).

If Schechner's early arguments and essays in performance theory are often tendentious, then that tendency, which is to establish a charter for the activity of the avant-garde, is at least increasingly pronounced and consistent. The charter, seemingly, has a local validity—America, the USA, Los Angeles possibly, New York certainly, the Performance Garage in particular—but there is a need to appeal to more than the exemplary authority of Artaud and Grotowski. The method used is not so much demonstrative as associative, and readers are assumed to be satisfied with this because they are satisfied that there is a need for such a charter. Ritual, theatre and performance can remain indefinite and universal, available for appropriation in a discourse persistently sensitive to the diversity of experimental praxis. This at least is the role assumed by Schechner: the hope of the theorist that theory will satisfy the conditions in and for which it is formulated. Theory of this kind would seem to have a divided profile: attached to its immediate context for the purposes of generating conviction, it can also become engaged with the risk of conceptual isolation. Schechner's multiplying figures are an image of this perplexity: in order to be pleasing, they may detach themselves from meaning, and though dependent on the discourse they must not, even then, confirm irrevocably any single proposition in it.

4.2.3 Cultures and theories transported and transformed

"Towards a Poetics of Performance" was originally a paper composed in 1975 for a conference on 'Ethnopoetics'. The paper/essay is divided into presentations on four topics, of which the first and longest on "Hunting circuits, ceremonial centers, and theaters" offers a summary anthropology of theatre, while the second, "Transformances", is an adaptation of Turner's theory of the social drama. This is followed by a series of propositions on ecstasy and trance, and the paper concludes with a few, largely empirical, observations on rehearsal.

The opening argument returns to the paleolithic caves, on whose use Schechner is once again prepared to speculate: in this presentation, the caves function as one exemplary location for the gathering or "concentration" of hunting bands. This interpretation is given support by reference to the (contemporary) !Kung of the Kalahari and to Aboriginal corroborees, to the ceremonies in Highlands New Guinea, and to "pilgrimages, family reunions..., potlatches, and 'going to the theater'" (154). Subsequently, human behaviour is linked to that of primates. A modern reassessment of a nineteenth-century report, which according to the revisers had relied on "native hearsay", seemingly accepts the application of the term "carnival" to the periodic behaviour of chimpanzees in the Bundongo forest of Uganda.[64] The original report included reference to chimpanzees making a "drum" from clay, which the modern researchers apparently did not witness, although they refer to "calling and drumming" (154). Schechner's attention is clearly drawn to their tentative suggestion that the behaviour "seemed to be associated with the meeting at a common food source of bands", although the researchers in principle declared that "it was not possible" to establish the reason decisively.

Schechner is distinctly less hesitant—"Aren't these 'carnivals' prototypes of celebratory, theatrical events?"—and he lists four noteworthy qualities of them: (1) a gathering of bands, (2) the sharing of food sources, (3) "singing, dancing (rhythmic movement), drumming, entertainment", and (4) the use of a place for the gathering "that is not a 'home' for any group" (155). The application of cultural terms in the third 'quality' is of great importance to the argument by association, but it seems almost inexplicable following Schechner's own caveat a few lines earlier:

> The nineteenth-century report indicating some kind of entertainment (singing, dancing, drumming) apparently romanticized and anthropomorphized the gathering of chimpanzees. (154)

The end result of a warning disregarded by its author is the introduction of both entertainment and carnival to the argument: paleolithic caves and primates are established as validating prototypes for a theory of performance that will concentrate on 'gatherings'.

Universality also seems to require origins in the second stage of the presentation, which insists that the "theater place did not arrive late in human cultures...but was there from the beginning" (155–56). The definition of "theater place" is achieved by reference to the art of the paleolithic caves or the landmarks of the Aborigines, which are "means of transforming natural spaces into cultural places: a way of making theaters" (155). Transformation is accomplished by "writing", which may not be literal or even visual, but can be oral, as in the Aboriginal culture. So according to this strategy of definition, the "first theaters were ceremonial centers", and "the transformation of space into place means to construct a theater" (156). This insistence entails an elision between ceremony and theatre, which is strongly marked in the uncertainties about the kinds of performances involved:

> The functions of the ceremonies—the performances—at the ceremonial centers, and the exact procedures, cannot be known precisely.   (157)

"Functions", "exact procedures", and "known precisely" suggest the temporary modesties of scientific investigation, but in fact Schechner has no more evidence to offer on this topic than the paleolithic "heelmarks left in clay in at least one of the caves" (ibid.). But drawing briefly on the idea of "ecological rituals" in New Guinea, proposed by Rappaport, Schechner is prepared to consider that conclusions on New Guinea and his own attempt "to reconstruct performances of Paleolithic hunters...both bear on patterns within modern and postmodern societies" (ibid.).[65] The gatherings of hunting bands which occasioned "performances at the ceremonial centers" had the three functions of maintaining friendly relations, exchanging goods or techniques, and showing or exchanging "dances, songs, stories" (ibid.). The rhythms of these performances were tripartite: gathering, "playing out an action or actions", and dispersing (157–58).

> In other words, people came to a special place, did something that can be called theater (and/or dance and music because all these genres are always performed together in such situations), and went on their way.   (158)

Here, as in "Approaches" of a decade before, "theater" as a category subsumes dance and music/song, and "theater" has become "playing out an action or actions", and not the "cultural place" established from "natural space" of the preliminary argument of the essay.

The presentations in "Towards a Poetics of Performance" are made in what might be called sense-blocks. The subsequent sense-blocks on this initial topic are concerned with two kinds of gatherings in what Schechner terms a "'natural' theater"—"eruptions" and "processions"—and with a brief history of conventional or orthodox theatre. Accidents or street events are the principal examples of a gathering around what Schechner calls a "hot" event or "eruption" surrounded by a "cool" crowd. "Parades, funeral corteges, political marches, and the Bread and Puppet Theater are processions" (160), which have a "goal" in a concluding event which is "well-planned for, rehearsed, ritualized" (ibid.). These two kinds of "'natural' theater" can be theoretically combined:

> Understood as a coherent system they form a bipolar model of the performances that took place in the ceremonial centers which arose at points where Paleolithic hunting bands, moving across the terrain on their seasonal treks, met.   (159)

The relationship of the two model poles of the "coherent system" to the heelmarks in the paleolithic cave(s) remains undemonstrated, although the meeting of the Bundongo chimpanzees is stated to be "both eruptive and processional", occurring at a "known place in a known circuit", occasioned by an "abundance of food":

> It is my belief that a roughly similar thing happened countless times on the hunting circuits of Paleolithic humans. Out of these hunting circuits developed ritual circuits, meeting places, ceremonial centers, and theaters.   (161)

This kind of belief leads to the final sense-block, which deals cursorily with the Greek, or Athenian, theatre, the proscenium theatre, and with the "liminal" contemporary theatre. The Greek theatre is portrayed diagrammatically (fig. 5.4, 160), as a concentric pattern of alternating bands of contest (or *agon*, in the Greek term) and solidarity, with solidarity represented by the altar of Dionysus, the chorus, the audience, and the *polis* (the city-state, or community of citizens), and contest by "the agonistic actions of the actors", and the competition for prizes by actors and poets. This image, composed of conceptually disparate entities in an imposed circular pattern, is termed a "sociometric design", which is contrasted to a less contentious ground-plan of a proscenium theatre (fig. 5.5, 162). Schechner notes the class divisions in the proscenium theatre, contrasting the visibility of "almost every space" in the Greek theatre with the concealment of the backstage area in the proscenium theatre. He concludes, by means of analogies with the "factory" (backstage) and the "store" (house), that "the proscenium theatre is a model of capitalism" (164). In the contemporary theatre, "as capitalism evolves into corporation", corporatism is represented by "cultural centers and regional theaters", whereas "environmental theaters...exemplify a resistance and alternative to the conglomerates" (ibid.).

The second topic, "transformances", is an appropriation and realignment of Turner's theory of the social drama. Schechner's immediate response to the drama analogy of Turner's scheme of social process is to return it redundantly to the originating context of performance:

> The replication of the redressive action phase is, of course, a theatrical performance, a formal restaging of events. The four-phase process as a whole is a drama in the Euro-American tradition—this scheme can be determined in Greek tragedies, Shakespearian plays, or the dramas of Ibsen or O'Neill. It is less easy to find in Chekhov, Ionesco, or Beckett— but it is there; the way it is distorted gives an insight into dramatic structure. (167)

To avoid what may be, by his own admission, "just an elaborate tautology" (168), Schechner adopts the device of subsuming Turner's four-part scheme under the central term of his own proposal, namely "performing" (ibid.). The problem with this conjunction is that it remains completely unclear whether it is social process (Turner) or the structure of dramas (Schechner) that is contained under "performing". The equivocation appears to be intentional in the summary that follows, leaving "performance" with the ambivalence required by performance theory:

> Conflict is supportable (in the theater, and perhaps in society too) only inside a nest built from the agreement to gather at a specific time and place, to perform—to do something agreed on—and to disperse once the performance is over. (168–69)

Arguments from primate behaviour recur in "Ethology and Theater", an essay from *Performance Theory* marred by Schechner's acceptance in the first edition of particularly lurid accounts of cannibalism and the sexual abuse of corpses in New Guinea, which he partly retracts in the second. Previously an example of the aggressive and sexual behaviour 'displaced' by performances, these accounts in Schechner's revision are theoretically reordered to act as "displays of fact-mixed-with-fantasy", analogous to contemporary filmic violence, and so themselves displacements. Lorenz (on aggression) and Freud (on jokes) are two principal theoretical sources, but Schechner's most pronounced contribution is made in the preamble, when he returns to primate behaviour.[66] The chest-beating of gorillas, as a display, provides an opportunity to express a theoretical relationship:

> The function of discharging excitement among gorillas is parallel to the cathartic function of theater proposed by Aristotle and Artaud, an ancient, persistent, and robust therapeutic tradition of performance. (208)

Schechner here is expressly using the "theatrical paradigm" to advocate that the "continuity of behavior from animals to people" proposed by Darwin should also be applicable to culture. So the displays by chimpanzee Mike in Goodall's account are understood by Schechner to be "rehearsals" for a challenge to the 'alpha male', and Mike's discoveries through this process are analogous to those made by Grotowski, Brook, Chaikin and The Performance Group.[67] Characteristically, the potential qualifications to this association are not allowed to control the discursive argument. In this case, their acknowledgement is delayed, and the connective value of the concept of a "threshold" ensures that they are minor. Animal performances generally lack special performance places and properties:

> But by the time we get to chimpanzee Mike's performance with the kerosene cans we are at the threshold of human theater. It only remained for Mike to do his act with another chimp playing Goliath while Goliath looked on, for us to have a chimp version of Hamlet's mousetrap. (215)

If the substantial differential in the act of comparison is pushed "aside", then one behaviour can seem "very much like" another:

> Aside from its non-repeatability and the lack of an audience, Mike's display is very much like human dance-theater. (ibid.)

It is a perception that has, in the UK at least, guided the advertising of one major tea consortium for a good many years, which has conquered the problem of "non-repeatability and the lack of an audience".

Schechner's interest in behaviour and transformations/transformances as components of an anthropological theory of performance dominates the collection *Between Theater and Anthropology*.[68] This was published in 1985, but two of the essays contained in it, "Restoration of Behavior" and "Performers and Spectators Transported and Transformed", date in their origins to the later seventies (1977 and 1979 respectively). Of these two, the "Restoration of Behavior" is a complex meditation on the rehearsal process which presents itself as a modal definition of the concept of performance:

> Restored behavior is used in all kinds of performance from shamanism and exorcism to trance, from ritual to aesthetic dance and theater, from initiation rites to social dramas, from psychoanalysis to psychodrama and transactional analysis. In fact, restored behavior is the main characteristic of performance.   (35)

The argument refers almost immediately to another figurative model (fig. 2.1, 38), which is a square divided into quarters, posing a dichotomy in the horizontal division between "Past" (left) and "Future" (right), and in the vertical division between "Indicative" (lower) and "Subjunctive" (upper). Further signification is made numerically, and interpreted by explanations in the discursive text, which are only gradually supplied.

Placed at a point in the centre of the square is the number "1", which is "Me rehearsing", and this numeral relates diversely to others placed in their quarters. Number "3" in the 'past indicative' quarter (lower left) is "Event", and number "4", in the 'future indicative' quarter (lower right), is a "restored event", or public performance, as the text eventually makes clear. In the upper quarters of the 'subjunctive', the 'past subjunctive' to the left contains number "5a", which stands for the fictive or suppositional past that may be implied in and by a performance. Number "5c", in the 'future subjunctive' quarter to the upper right, is the "Unpublicly performed restored non-event", which occurs in "workshops that are never shown publicly" and in "paratheater and non-public happenings" (39). The lower right quarter of the 'future indicative', which must contain public performance, has two further numbers in addition to "4": of these, the first is "2", indicating "Someone else", and an arrow from "1" to "2" is schematic for "trance" (41). The second number is "5b", which is interpreted as a "Restored non-event" (39), which is placed in the 'future indicative' quarter because it is publicly performed, although it must be made to refer to its fictive origins in the 'past subjunctive' quarter (upper left) of "5a".

The concept of the "restoration" of behaviour which presides over this figure introduces its own clear contradiction in "the restoration of a past that never was". This is designated in the figure by the movement from "5a" in the 'past subjunctive' quarter to "5b" in the 'future indicative' quarter, which contradicts both the concept and the dichotomy represented by the figure. Yet it is exactly "this performative bundle" of invention, as he terms it, that is for Schechner "the most stable and prevalent performative circumstance" (39). That the overall scheme for performance is set 'four-square' is a suggestion that is graphically represented in the figure, but it is one that is further contradicted by the introductory discussion of "3" ("Event") and "4" ("Restored event").

The examples chosen by Schechner of the connecting, rehearsal-into-production process "1→3→4" are a "'living newspaper'", or, alternatively, a "Wild Animal Park" such as that at San Diego (42). Yet this notional process in the supposedly 'indicative' mode, as Schechner himself notes, has already been "transformed by specific cultural values" into the "restoration of a past that never was", the type of the relation "1→5a→5b". On either interpretation of the "Wild Animal Park", speculation on the absolute role of "1, Me rehearsing" remains relatively endearing. But the inherent contradiction in both concept and figure becomes more explicit with their application to conventional, and probably aesthetic performances. The initial discursive statement is forthright, and unqualified:

> Many traditional performances are 1→3→4. So are performances that are kept in repertory according to a strict adherence to the original score.   (43)

Schechner's examples here are the Moscow Art Theatre in the 1960s, the Berliner Ensemble (presumably post-Brecht) and classical ballets. But the theoretical connection between textual example and numerical formula proves to be "unstable", as particular numbers demonstrate an unarithmetical capacity to represent and to displace each other:

> But even the strictest attempts at 1→3→4 frequently are in fact examples of 1→5a→5b. 1→3→4 is very unstable: it is always becoming 1→5a→5b.   (43)

Schechner's predominant interest in the "performative bundle" of inventive (or 'subjunctive') performance leads him to the example of Noh drama, which is "both 1→3→4 and 1→5a→5b simultaneously and consciously", notably in the initiative reserved to the *shite*, or leading performer, in any given instance (44). In an act of theoretical association, the proposed instability between the two leading formulas is also applied to "some contemporary experimental theater in New York", which includes "the restoration in a subjunctive mood of a past that is demonstrably factual" (45). The fact that this past is that of "actual sound tapes" of the performer Spalding Gray interviewing his mother, and that the 'past' of Noh is that of past performances of the received "score" does not help to resolve the problem of the instability between "3→4" and "5a→5b", but further complicates it with differences between different kinds of instability. The additional example of Robert Wilson's "work with Raymond Andrews, a deaf boy, and Christopher Knowles, a brain-damaged boy (or one unusually tuned to experience, depending on one's view of the matter)" introduces behaviour which may not be 'restored' at all, but may be "raw, the unrehearsed or untreated" (ibid.): in which case the theoretical process marked by the arrow, between "3→4" or "5a→5b", would seem to be deconstituted. Schechner seems to be closer to the kind of example he wants in his consideration of Shaker dancing, researched into a 'modern' choreography by Doris Humphrey in *The Shakers* of 1931, and reconstructed into the objective of authenticity by Robin Evanchuk. But the problem is that the Shakers had stopped dancing by 1931, and so both realizations are "actually 1→5a→5b", which leaves "3" and "4" as notional entities, and the dichotomies of the general scheme dissolved by the theory they are supposed to figure.

> Technically the Moscow Art Theatre production of Chekhov, the Berliner Ensemble productions of Brecht, and the Limon Company's production of *The Shakers* are 1→3→4,. But in actuality—in the immediacy of their being performed now—all these performances are 1→5a→5b. (50)

The 'indicative' qualities of the concept of "restored behavior", figured in the model diagram 2.1, appear to be subject to the 'subjunctive'. The model is acknowledged by Schechner to be "drawn from a Euro-American perspective", but the intention is to "apply it to events that are not Euro-American" (51). In doing so Schechner calls attention to an examination of "the rehearsal process":

> how the single behaved behaviors of ordinary living are made into the twice-behaved behaviors of art, ritual, and the other performative genres. (52)

"Event" and the "single behaved behaviors of ordinary living" have survived the collapse of the indicative into the subjunctive, but Schechner's application of his conceptual scheme to a performance in Papua New Guinea returns them to confusion. In his account of a dance in the village of Magendo, which he represents from the reports of John Emigh, Schechner seems undecided about the status of the boy-figure Wok honoured in the dance.[69] Wok is "credited by the villagers with teaching them how to build better canoes, how to catch fish, and how to plant crops" (53). A quotation from Emigh provides an additional cultural context to the involvement of a bird in the story of Wok:

> The dancers imitate birds because the clan the story is significant to is a bird clan, has a bird as its totem.

The preparation of the dance is described by Schechner as a "rehearsal", which "looks backward to Wok and forward to a finished performance", but neither "event" nor "ordinary living" are apparent in the "restored behavior" of the men and women "dancing as birds":

> Wok's dance, like rituals everywhere, disguises itself as a restoration of actual events when it is in fact a restoration of earlier performances. (54)

Since Wok is a "virtual or nonevent", performance theory demands his subordination (as "5a") to the 'indicative' future-present of "5b":

> It is not because of Wok that the people of Magendo dance; it is because of their dance that Wok (still) lives. (ibid.)

The sole value of Schechner's scheme to what the anthropologist Geertz has called "the interpretation of cultures" would seem to lie in an assertion of the 'indicative' of actual performance over the 'subjunctive' of infusing culture. The possibility of here identifying an example of "the single behaved behaviors of ordinary living...made into the twice-behaved behaviors" of art, ritual, or a performative genre seems even more remote.

Nonetheless, reiteration exists as a resource for theory:

> The model offers ways of comparing performances—and from comparison the means of developing a theory that includes both aesthetic and ritual performances. (ibid.)

So the process described as "trance", numerically represented as "1→2", is "ritual in the ethological sense"; while the process represented as "3→4", so dubiously alleged to be a characteristic of the dance of/for Wok, is reinstated as a second formula for ritual:

> The repetition of a given or traditional performance score, 1→3→4, is ritual in the social and religious sense.   (ibid.)

Ultimately, inconsistencies or plain contradictions may be resolved by theory's baffling claim to a validity which is not dependent on the differentiating propositions from which it has been constructed:

> These differentiations of performance types occur along a continuum. There is no need to specify a given performance as all this or that. A performance can be between modes...   (55)

What is certain is that a performance is a performance, because by that designation it may be submitted to comparison, a function on which the discourse of an anthropological performance theory totally depends.

The importance of the concept of "restored behavior" to the universality of performance as a transcendent category is evident in the opening of the essay "Performers and Spectators Transported and Transformed". In support of this universalism, Schechner posits the existence of "a wide variety of performative rituals, games, sports, and hard-to-define activities that lie between or outside established genres" (118). Consensus about an "established genre" records the fact that something "has found its place", while in relation to "performance activities" as a whole the concession must be allowed that "there will always be a certain proportion of them in the process of transformation, categorically undefinable":

> But all performances—defined and undefined—share at least one underlying quality. Performance behavior isn't free and easy. Performance behavior is known and/or practised behavior—or 'twice-behaved behavior', 'restored behavior'...   (ibid.)

In this broad categorization, the important factors are those of rehearsal, learning from childhood onwards, revelation during the performance, or the presence of rules governing the activity. In executing behaviour that "isn't free and easy" the performer may be subject to external direction, to the intervention of chance or "accident", or to the adjustment consequent upon the requirement of repetition.

The substance of the essay depends on two distinct but related qualities of performance within what is, once again, a "continuum of performance types" (125). The essential division lies between the permanence of transformation, which may be effected in "initiation rites and 'rites of passage'", and those performances in which the performer "is transported and returned to his starting place" (ibid.). The distinction between the two terms, which appears at first to be exact, permits complication. A performer may be temporarily "transformed" in the process of being transported, while a continued status in a relatively fixed role may effect a partial "transformation" from "transportation":

> Thus each separate performance is a transportation, ending about where it began, while a series of transportation performances can achieve a transformation. (126)

Cultural differences are suppressed within the scope of this reciprocating terminology. So, for example, "trance" and "character acting" may appear to present a contrast between "involuntariness" and 'self-control'. Yet Schechner 'suspects' that he finds both of these qualities present in each of these "kinds of transportation":

> I suspect that the differences between the kinds of transportation have been overemphasized...The difference between these kinds of performance may be more in labeling, framing, and cultural expectations than in their performance processes. (127)

But the theoretical need for suppression of a cultural context provokes awkward contradictions. So in the discussion of initiation rites, in which "transformation performances are clearly evidenced", the *process* of initiation is given the purely material *status* of a "machine that works the changes transforming boys into men" (129). But the resultant status, in the given example of the initiation of Gahuku boys, "is fundamentally social, public, and objective" (ibid.). Nonetheless, with the subordination of cultural considerations the theoretical "continuum" of the concept of performance can substitute for discarded categories and distinctions:

> People are accustomed to calling transportation performances 'theater' and transformation performances 'ritual'. But this neat separation doesn't hold up. Mostly the two kinds of performance coexist in the same event. (130)

In a ritual such as that of the Gahuku the men who assist the boys at the ceremony "were transported not transformed" (ibid.), and in a process of this kind "the transported is identical to the actor" (131). The term "actor" can be used as a referent within Euro-American discourse because, traditionally, "the actor in Euro-American theater is an example of a transported performer":

> For reasons that will be made clear later, the Euro-American theater is one of transportation without transformation. Many performance workers, especially since 1960, have sought to introduce into the Euro-American performing arts the process of transformation. (ibid.)

With this indication of collusion, Schechner's "model of transportation/ transformation performance" can be posited as "open", one that "can be applied across cultures and genres", and those cited are Gahuku initiation, Greek tragedy, Sanskrit theatre, Noh drama, the Broadway production of *The Elephant Man*, and Schechner's own *Dionysus in 69* (133).

Schechner's characterization of Greek and Sanskrit theatre fixes upon one specific attribute of each: the *agon*, or contest in the Greek theatre and the theory of *rasa* as applied to Sanskrit theatre in the *Natyasastra*. For the Greek theatre, with prizes offered to playwrights, a separate competition for actors, and the role of judges/critics in this arbitration, Schechner insists that competition was preferred to aesthetics. With this bias, the Greek theatre theoretically lends itself to one particular variety of "transformation", which has its origin in an "experience...of confrontation: the radical separation of audience and judges/critics on one side and performers, playwrights, and other theater people on the other":

> This basic confrontation leads to the accumulation of 'values' by which artists are transformed into winners and losers. Again, much of the experimental work during the last twenty years has been directed— through devices of audience participation, environmental staging, and collective creativity—at abolishing this agony. (135)

The word-play—*agon*/"agony"—decorates an extreme compression of theatrical history, in which the Greek mode of theatrical production is the immediate and contrasting antecedent to off-off-Broadway. The religious and cultural context of the 'competition', in which all contributions were presented as offerings to the presiding god Dionysus, is ignored by Schechner in favour of a humanist discrimination between skills. Theoretically, the most significant conjunction is that of the audience with "judges/critics", which subsumes and conceals the extended activity of reception under the final act of judging. Diversely from the title of the essay, no theoretical attention is given to what might have 'happened to' the Greek "spectators", despite the existence of a strong theoretical tradition (e.g. the emotional theory of *katharsis*) stemming from the culture itself.

In contrast, Schechner draws for his observations on Sanskrit theatre from the theoretical treatise the *Natyasastra*, and concentrates on the principal metaphor of reception that it contains . Equally contrasting is the sense of cultural history, of "a flourishing theater-dance tradition long before extant Sanskrit dramas" (which might with equal validity have been applied to Greece) and of a "style which is at its core not literary but theatrical" (137). Theoretically, the Sanskrit theatre presents characteristics which are distinct from the Greek, which are summarized in the fact that it is not similarly competitive. Correspondingly, the theoretically suppressed religious context returns for the Sanskrit and Indian theatre, understood together as a continuity:

> The gods are frequent characters in the plays, as well as spectators of the human and divine show. In Ramlila of Ramnagar long poles topped by effigies represent the gods on high looking down at the performance. (137)

The theoretical contrast implied is spurious: Dionysus, the god of the Greek festival, is a character in the *Bacchae*, which Schechner himself adapted in *Dionysus in 69*, as well as in the *Frogs*, in which 'Dionysus' seeks refuge with his priest, who was centrally placed in the auditorium. A procession carrying an ancient image of the god preceded the Greek dramatic festival, and all twelve Olympian gods take seats to observe the Panathenaic festival on the frieze that surrounded the temple of Athene on the acropolis, the Parthenon.[70] But if Greek theatre in theory is 'confrontational' because 'competitive', Sanskrit and 'Indian' theatre is contrastingly religious: "The performance is sometimes thought of as an offering" (138).

The concept of *rasa* also provides an integrative rather than a confrontational quality, since *rasa* is translatable as "flavor" or "taste", and thus connected with food, or "*prasad*": "Natya is theater is *prasad*" (137). This permits an appreciation of reception denied to Greek theatre:

> Indians use the word 'taste' with a great deal more subtlety and range of socioaesthetic signification than we do. If some theater needs an audience to hear it, and some needs spectators to see it, Indian theater

needs partakers to savor it. I don't have the space here to discuss exactly
how *rasa* is used. (138)

The requirements of an otherwise unnoticeable brevity determine no
'discussion' of the functional constituents of *rasa* in the *Natyasastra*,
which are, in the translation used by Schechner, the eight "sentiments"
or *rasas* with their "complementary psychological states", or *bhavas*.
These are the sentiments of the "Erotic, Comic, Pathetic, Furious,
Heroic, Terrible, Odious, and Marvellous", to which correspond the
"durable" *bhavas* or psychological states of "love, mirth, sorrow, anger,
energy, terror, disgust, and astonishment".[71] As in the Aristotelian
concept of *katharsis*, a governing metaphor controls an emotional theory
of reception, with the distinction that in the *Natyasastra* the metaphor
is carefully exposed and explained, in answer to a supposed enquiry:

> just as well-disposed persons while eating food cooked with many kinds
> of spice enjoy its tastes, and attain pleasure and satisfaction, so the
> cultured people taste the Durable Psychological States...
>
> Just as by many articles of various kinds, auxiliary cooked eatable is
> brought forth, so the Psychological States along with different kinds
> of Histrionic Representation will cause the Sentiments to be felt.[72]

Despite his awareness of the presence of metaphor—"Noh drama in
Japan works in a similar way, except that the root metaphor is gardening
and what is shared is *hana* (flower)" (138)—Schechner continues to
display a feast:

> The experience of the performance is like that of a banquet where the
> cooks and servers must know how to prepare and serve, but the diners
> must know how to eat. (138)

'Participation' is the theoretical quality extracted from the "banquet",
and by a dubious route the influence of the *Natyasastra* may be found
in Brecht:

> This Indian system of participant enjoyment—a system exported to
> Southeast Asia, China, and Japan—is one of the main things that
> attracted Brecht to Asian theater. (ibid.)

The generalities, "Indian", and now "Asian" theatre, are accumulating
imposingly in this migration of theoretical influence, and the 'flavour'
of theory attaches itself confidently to Brechtian *Verfremdung*. In the
culturally pervasive "Indian system"

> some spectators can savor one part of a performance, others another; a performer can be absorbed into his role at one moment and detached from it at another. Brecht took from Asian theater this technique of independently variable elements and developed from it his theory/practice of verfremdung (alienation or distance). Let me emphasize again how close this system is to the way fine food is eaten. (139)

The conclusions drawn from this extended argument seem to exceed the principal thematic concern with "transportation" and "transformation". The theme is summarily addressed ("according to the *Natyasastra*, both performers and partakers are transported, and no one is transformed", 140), but the "Indian system" Schechner presents sustains a further theoretical purpose in its contrast with the "Greek system". This subsidiary purpose is figured in a diagram (fig. 3.9, 141) featuring a pair of images, in which "Greek" appears to the left as an arc of arrows connecting geometric shapes (the square, triangle, rectangle and circle) representing the "causal chain" leading from "Beginning" to "End" through "Production details", "idea", "climax" and "resolution". "Indian" appears to the right as a random interlacing (what Schechner terms "strands" in a "braid") of five sinuous lines each marked by arrows from "Start" to "Finish", in which plurality there is no primary or dominant causal principle to equal the single arc of arrows in the "Greek" image. The amalgamation of Sanskrit theatre and drama with "much contemporary Indian theater" and "folk traditions", apparently including the Ramlila, permits the visual generalization that "Indian" performance does not have any definite 'beginning' or 'end', and is "not supposed to go anywhere" (141). Theoretically, however, it does, because it is required for a predictable act of association:

> Like postmodern performances in Europe and America, the Indian system is a braid of several strands of activities: these require that performer and partaker attend together to the here and now of the ever-changing relations among the strands. (140)

The concept of 'performance' requires the subordination of cultural referents, and the exploitation of ambiguities in its central terms—notably 'theatre' and 'performance' itself—to sustain the dignity of a universalizing theory. The elision between ritual and theatre, between non-western and postmodern 'performances', has been used repeatedly by Schechner to provide a conceptual charter for the activities of experimental theatre. Yet the relationship with the practising avant-garde has been uneasy since the publication of "The Decline and Fall of the (American) Avant-Garde" at the beginning of the 1980s, and the uncertainty affecting the exact engagement of performance theory is apparent in Schechner's most recent collection of essays.[73] In the introduction to *The Future of Ritual*, Schechner includes a discussion of five forms of the avant-garde. These avant-gardes are the "historical", the "current", the "forward-looking", the "tradition-seeking" and the "intercultural". The "historical" and the "current" offer an attractive, single division, which Schechner had once advocated in the form of the "historical" and the "experimental" in "The Decline and Fall...".[74] Here he rejects that simple division (10) in favour of what might seem to be a subdivision of the "current" category into "forward-looking" and "tradition-seeking", with such as LePage and the Wooster Group, and Grotowski and Barba as the respective examples. Schechner fixes on Grotowski's 'Theatre of Sources' and Barba's interest in Asian practice and in a 'theatre of roots', summarizing this as a search for the "traditional", with a particular attention to Asia. The explanation of the fifth category of the avant-garde apparently ignores the intercultural claims of the 'researches' of both Grotowski and Barba in what is a most demanding prescription:

> Engaging intercultural fractures, philosophical difficulties, ideological contradictions, and crumbling national myths does not necessarily lead to avant-garde performances. Intercultural performances occur across an enormous range of venues, styles, and purposes. What is avant-garde is when the performance does not try to heal over rifts or fractures but further opens these for exploration. (17)

It is hard to belong to the intercultural avant-garde. Brook's *Mahabharata* fails the test—it "was intercultural, but not avant-garde"—because he assumed "that certain works operate at the 'human' rather than the cultural level" (18).

Yet, paradoxically, after these strictures and this renewed and extended exercise in classification, Schechner decides that the term 'avant-garde' "no longer serves a useful purpose. It doesn't really mean anything today." (ibid.). The explanation for this lapse is given in terms of exhaustion, or lassitude, since there is "little artists can do, or even ought to do, to shock":

> And why try to shock? There are no surprises in terms of technique, theme, or approach. (ibid.)

The future, instead, lies in the possibilities made available in a "neo-medieval" or "neo-Hellenistic" period by an emphasis on 'ritualizing':

> To recycle, reuse, archive and recall, to perform in order to be included in an archive (as a lot of performance artists do), to seek roots, explore and maybe even plunder religious experiences, expressions, practices, and liturgies to make art (as Grotowski and others are doing) is to ritualize; not just in terms of subject matter and theme, but also structurally, in form.   (19–20)

Referring to the work of ethologists and psychologists, Schechner affirms that the new understanding of ritual "as a process applying to a great range of human activities" has "punctured" the boundaries between the "various spheres of performance" (20). What now remains is the "big project" of the study of "performative behavior, not just the performing arts" (21), and presumably both are included in the "four great spheres of performance—entertainment, healing, education, and ritualizing" (20). It is a perception which, characteristically, carries with it a programmatic uncertainty:

> Each of the performance spheres can be called by other names.   (20)

Nonetheless, despite this reformulation of the scope of performance theory, Schechner confesses that he is "at least of two minds regarding all this" (ibid.), an ambivalence expressed in his doubts about a functional "conversion" to Hinduism and in the uncertainties of his final essay. In "The Future of Ritual", theory makes its appearance as a species of indecision, notably in relation to the theoretical and discursive concept of ritual itself. On the one hand, it is indefinable, or unstable in its definitions:

> Even to say it in one word, ritual, is asking for trouble. Ritual has been so variously defined—as concept, praxis, ideology, yearning, experience, function—that it means very little because it means too much.   (228)

But, alternatively, ritual may be figured as a certain scheme of "evolution", most conventionally as a tree ("The ritual tree": fig. 7.1, 229). In this diagram, "ritualization" is the base of the bole; passing up the 'trunk', we read of three short branches that refer to "insects, fish" ("genetically fixed"), "birds and mammals" ("fixed and free"), and "nonhuman primates" ("social ritual"). At the top of the 'trunk' is "human ritualization", and the branches that form the 'crown' of the tree are "social ritual", "religious ritual" and "aesthetic ritual", all 'stemming' from "human ritualization". All three are subdivided: "everyday life", "sports" and "politics" come from "social ritual"; "observances, celebrations" and "rites of passage" from "religious ritual"; and "codified forms" and "ad hoc forms" from "aesthetic ritual". The figure recalls that which first illustrated the fallacious theory of the "primal ritual" of the Cambridge anthropologists in "Approaches".[75] In that essay, Schechner had introduced performance theory with a dismissal—"Origin theories are irrelevant to understanding theater"— and insisted on a "horizontal" exploration of the performative genres. In this essay, the multiplicity of definitions for 'ritual' is resolved into a figurative 'vertical' scheme, with the equivocating "ritualization" substituting for the "primal ritual" as a concept which is prior to its realizations in animal form: an essence, or theoretical 'origin'.

Establishing the figure permits movement among the branches. There are, granted the flow of sap upwards from ritualization, inevitably connections between different branches:

> Nonhuman primates such as chimpanzees and gorillas behave in some respects very much like humans. Some of their actions closely resemble human performance. (229)

Although "nonhuman primates" lack speech, and lack even the capacities for speech in musculature and brain, "they can express and communicate feelings", and this "expressive behavior

> might be closer to human ritual and its associated "behavior arts" (theatre, dance, music, some kinds of painting) than anything rational or cognitive the 'higher apes' are capable of. (ibid.)

But the principal distinction is, perhaps significantly, between a lower branch on the tree and the nexus of "human ritualization". For insects, such as bees, everything is "genetically determined" ("genetically fixed", on the lowest branch of the diagram) whereas human performance is "founded on contingency" (230). What exactly Schechner means by "contingency" is unclear: "human behavior" is also described as "paradoxical, a practised fixity", and it seems likely that the idea of "restored behavior" is active. But when this idea does appear, the initial distinction has changed to include animals with humans, and one part of one part of "aesthetic ritual" is adduced to describe not only the 'crown', but the whole of the tree above its first branch:

> Both animal and human ritual actions are very close to theatre. In theatre, too, behavior is rearranged, condensed, exaggerated, and made rhythmic.　(230–31)

The crucial relationships remain rather as they were, figuratively suspended in a tree.

4.3　EUGENIO BARBA (1936–)

Eugenio Barba's professional biography has been compiled in some detail on a number of occasions, and I shall repeat only the institutional history here.[76] After winning a scholarship to study at the Warsaw State Theatre School, Barba became an assistant to Jerzy Grotowski between 1961 and 1964, visiting Kerala in southern India in 1963. In October 1964 he founded Odin Teatret in Oslo, and in June 1966 the company moved on invitation to Holstebro in Denmark, where it has remained.

Adopting the precedent of Grotowski's Institute for Research into Acting, Barba established the Nordisk Teaterlaboratorium for Skuespillerkunst ('The Scandinavian Institute for Research into the Art of the Actor') during 1966–7. Gatherings of the Third Theatre, a concept formulated by Barba, have been held in southern Europe and Latin America after an initial meeting in Belgrade in 1976. ISTA, The International School of Theatre Anthropology, was established in 1979 in Bonn, and has since held meetings repeatedly in Europe.[77]

In this critical discussion, I shall confine myself to a selection from Barba's published writings in English, with particular attention to the development of his concept of theatre anthropology, and related theoretical observations.

4.3.1　Barba and Grotowski: theatre in the laboratory

One of the most significant acts of Barba's earlier years in the theatre was the organization and presentation of what the scholarly and theatrical world outside Poland came to know of Jerzy Grotowski. Barba was responsible for the editing and publication of *Towards a Poor Theatre* in 1968, and it is clear from accounts (notably the excellent one by Watson) that Barba had acted as a publicist, almost an international manager, for Grotowski throughout the decade.[78] Barba has on more than one occasion referred to Grotowski as his 'master', and there are, besides, many marked indications of influence, institutionally and theoretically. Barba published a study of Grotowski's theatrical quest in Italian in 1965, and a presentation by Barba and Flaszen, Grotowski's literary manager, appeared in *Drama Review* in the same year.[79] In his personal contribution, "Theatre Laboratory 13 Rzedow", Barba's leading idea was that of purification:

> The 'intellectual adventure of the twentieth century' is a sudden awareness of the unexploited possibilities of the arts...a deep conviction that art must change its structure and even its function. All the arts have purified themselves, eliminating the intrusions of other arts; they have rejected everything that was not necessary and vital to their own intentions.[80]

Earlier attempts at "reform" by Appia, Craig, Meyerhold, Vakhtangov and Piscator had had "negligible" results, "There is no purification, no effort to develop (or rediscover) the essence of theatre", and Witkacy and Artaud had carried out "paper revolutions", in their call for "laboratory theatres in which to explore the means of theatrical production" (153–54). The language of "reform" (partial and inadequate) and "paper revolutions" contrasts unfavourably with that of "purification" and "essence", that which is "necessary and vital", and which may only be subject to 'rediscovery' in the hitherto unrealized project of a "laboratory". The dismissal of deficient attempts is a preliminary to the announcement of the quest for origins:

> Grotowski wished to create a modern secular ritual, knowing that primitive rituals are the first form of drama. Through their total participation, primitive men were liberated from accumulated unconscious material. The rituals were repetitions of archetypal acts, a collective confession which sealed the solidarity of the tribe...The shamans were masters of these sacred ceremonies, in which every tribesman had to play a part.   (154–55)

In the collaborative article by Barba and Flaszen that follows Barba's essay the quest initiated by Grotowski is provided with a more expansive definition:

> This type of theatre could be compared to an anthropological expedition. It goes beyond the civilized territories into virgin forest. It ignores clearly defined rational values and challenges the darkness

> of the collective unconscious. Our culture, our language, and our imagination are rooted in this darkness which science has called by many different names: "savage thought" (Levy-Strauss), "archetype" (Jung), "collective representations" (Durkheim), "categories of the imagination" (Mauss and Hubert), "elementary thoughts" (Bastian).
>
> In the theatre laboratory, the spectators are made to face the most secret, the most carefully hidden part of themselves. (174)

The notion of secrecy and the model of anthropology will be retained by Barba, although the emphasis changes: the subtitle to the English edition of *A Dictionary of Theatre Anthropology* is *The Secret Art of the Performer*.[81] Language in Grotowski's theatre reflects the anthropological quest for origins, and for a totality:

> Inarticulate groans, animal roars, tender folksongs, liturgical chants, dialects, declamation of poetry: everything is there. The sounds are interwoven in a complex score which brings back fleetingly the memory of all the forms of language. (182)

Other achievements by Grotowski are clearly related to contemporary forms of practice. The "stage/audience dichotomy" is eliminated in the work of the Laboratory, as actors and spectators are brought together in "a return to the sources of primitive theatre" (174). The action of performances is distributed "all over the theatre and among the spectators", in a phrase that may have left its mark on Schechner, the editor of the journal, and there are "no 'sets' in the usual sense of the word" (180). But the topical primitivism espoused by the account collapses into stagy banality with the "theatrical magic" of the "actor sorcerer", which hardly conjures up the picture we know of the severe and bespectacled Polish practitioner directing his ascetic performers.

The idea of a "ritual theatre" is repeated in Barba's documentation of "The Kathakali Theatre" in the same journal two years later, and Barba is explicit about the purposes of his studies in Kerala in 1963:

> This essay is neither an aesthetic analysis of Kathakali nor a study of its origins or its relationship to other forms of Indian theatre, for my main purpose in studying Kathakali was to acquaint myself with a specific technique and assess the possibilities of adapting it for the training of European actors.[82]

The training concerned would have been intended at the time for Grotowski's Laboratory Theatre, although it was only a short time after the visit that Barba established his own company in Oslo. The idea of ritual allows for a definition of "stylization" which removes performers and spectators from the human to the supernatural world:

> If the adjective 'human' is understood as meaning natural, ordinary, belonging to everyday life, then we can say that the Kathakali technique aims at a complete dehumanization of the actor. The reality of the play is pushed through the sieve of stylization. The ritual value of the spectacle guarantees the involvement of the audience...Unaware, the spectator slips into the 'magic time' of the ritual and drifts into a stream which lifts him out of the world of phenomena into the supernatural world where gods and demons fight the archetypal battle of our human adventure. (42–3)

How far Barba was viewing Kathakali through the work of the Laboratory is hard to judge, since his account of the work of the Laboratory may have been affected by his view of Kathakali. But the distinction between "everyday" human behaviour and the trained technique of the actor is a component of Barba's performance theory that finds expression here in English for the first time. The succeeding comparison between "Oriental" and "European" theatre seems superficially unaffected by the involvement with the Laboratory:

> The importance of visual language is one great difference between the Oriental and the European theatre. The use of signs, make-up, colors, motions, and costume instead of words is possible because the stories are already known to the audience, which is mostly interested in the physical virtuosity of the actor. (44)

This virtuosity becomes the object of Barba's most detailed attention, and the descriptive phrases insist on great severity. "The incredible physical discipline" includes exercises which "no matter how painful, are necessary" (48), and acting is "not a profession, it is a form of priesthood" (49) in a training which is "harsh almost beyond endurance" (50). Performing in this ritual theatre is transcendental and mystical:

> He who wants to come near the gods, must move away from what is human; his technique is a means to reach the metaphysical. It is also an offering and a consecration like that of the Karma-Yoga. For the Kathakali actor, acting has an intrinsic value and is its own reward. It is a form of prayer and a true method of psychic transmutation. (50)

Indeed, Barba writes of "the hermetic mysticism of the Oriental theatre", and the generalization and his insistence are both motivated by an absolute, and similarly severe theoretical sundering: "Any attempt at comparison between the European actor and the Kathakali actor would be absurd" (ibid.). Dedicated from childhood to the art, with "no fixed salary", in many cases an 'indigent', "the actor-priest of the Kathakali offers his body to the gods" (ibid.). The absolute division, which permits Barba as potential practitioner-trainer to divorce himself theoretically from European precedents, is expressed evocatively as an "abyss":

> After studying the rigorous training of the Kathakali actor, his humility in front of his art, his reverence for everything pertaining to the theatre, and his willingness to give without expecting reward, we can measure the abyss which separates him from his European colleague. (ibid.)

That the "abyss" may be bridged is an idea that is only subliminally contained in the ultimate concession of "colleague".

An emphasis on training preoccupied further reports on Barba himself in the same journal, although attention was directed to his work with Odin. Inevitably, Barba was conscious in these pages of his relationship as a "disciple" to Grotowski, and firm in his avowal of it: "If there is one man I consider my master, it is Grotowski".[83] But there was a marked change in vocabulary from the early documentations, as Barba distanced his current practice from an easy association with religion or ritual, while retaining the idea of a theatrical study of—or enquiry into—'man' in 'nature':

> What we now consider the 'naturalness' of the man in the street possibly isn't so natural after all. Perhaps when that man in the street finds himself overcome by some deep, violent feeling and instinctively assumes a 'strange' or hieratic attitude, he may be closer to nature than when he sits back and puts his feet up on the table. Above all, our search is psycho-physiological, and the scientific spirit in which we work precludes any falsification of our findings, even though they may remind some people of religious rites. [84]

The overt contrast between "the scientific spirit" appropriate to a 'laboratory' and the excitement of "religious rites" requires some kind of resolution:

> if theatre can draw from the human sciences such as anthropology, psychiatry, and sociology, it's still a fact that more than any of these

sources, theatre is ethically and subjectively engaged. Theatre can't identify with science any more than religion can.[85]

The discipline of study approximates to the name of a science, but is theoretically withdrawn from it, in a motif which will recur in the later definitions of Barba's "theatre anthropology". The debts of the discipline of training at Odin to the biomechanics of Meyerhold were registered in the second of the two pieces, which was published in 1972.[86] This article, like "A Letter from Barba in Southern Italy" which appeared in 1975 in the same journal, was later republished in the first English-language collection of Barba's writings, *The Floating Islands*.[87]

Much as Barba had organized the presentation of Grotowski in his editing of the writings collected in *Towards a Poor Theatre*, Taviani provided introductions and a vocational scheme for Barba's written work in *The Floating Islands*, which he followed with the documentation of productions by Odin. The scheme divided Barba's writing into three sections: "Theatralische Sendung: Laboratory" ('Theatrical Mission...'), "Lehrjahre: Training" ('Years of Learning...'), and "Wanderjahre: Barter" ('Years of Travelling...'). In his introduction to the first section, Taviani at times adopts a critical tone—he recalls Planchon's warning of the "fundamentally reactionary tendencies" of Artaud's "mysticism"—and at times seems to be merely repeating what is identifiable as the language and thought of Barba:

> An actor who trains daily and doesn't limit himself to rehearsals and performances is totally unknown, or known only in the context of the distant oriental civilization rooted in traditional values. [88]

"The distant oriental civilization rooted in traditional values" is an inscrutable phrase, which seems most likely to be part of an institutional ideology which has not been subjected to much critical exposure. A similar ideological origin is also most plausible for the genealogy of the 'laboratory' which Taviani provides:

> In the history of theater one remembers the 'laboratories' of Stanislavsky, Vakhtangov, Meyerhold, and the laboratory of Copeau, the latter more like a real theater school. (16)

This is very much like the list of failed attempts given by Barba in his report on Grotowski, and it is indeed followed by the outstanding precedent of the "Theater Laboratory of the Thirteen Rows" in Opole. Taviani also refers to an interesting ideological model cited by Grotowski in *Towards a Poor Theatre*, which was that of the Bohr Institute. Taviani quotes from the beginning of Grotowski's short essay, "Methodical Exploration", as Grotowski introduces the Bohr Institute:

> It is a meeting place where physicists from different countries experiment and take their first steps into the 'no man's land' of their profession.[89]

Grotowski in fact went on to record that the Institute "has fascinated me for a long time as a model illustrating a certain type of activity", and further quotation from the essay suggests how exact is Barba's debt to Grotowski, as Grotowski speculates on the role of methodical research into acting:

> An institute which devotes itself to research of this kind should, like the Bohr Institute, be a place for meetings, observations, and the distillation of experiments collected by the most fruitful individuals in this field from different theatres in every country. Taking into account the fact that the domain on which our attention is focused is not a scientific one and not everything in it can be defined (indeed many things must not be), we nevertheless try to determine our aims with all the precision and consequence proper to scientific research.[90]

Grotowski had also suggested that to engage in research of this kind was "to place oneself on the borders of scientific disciplines such as phonology, psychology, cultural anthropology, semiology, etc.".[91] The lack of exact identification with any one scientific discipline is the authoritative precedent for Barba's hesitation, which may be reassuring to the ecologically minded.[92]

4.3.2 Isolation and the "social cell": the Third Theatre

The severity of the 'Theatrical Mission: Laboratory' in the *The Floating Islands* is apparent in Barba's short 'call-to-arms' on self-discipline, "Waiting for the Revolution", addressed to the young who have chosen the theatre:

> Let them attain, with their own personalities and by their bodies and their souls, the ultimate judgement on themselves as representatives of this society which still proclaims: thou shalt love thy neighbour.   (35)

But it is more fully expressed in the stern, magisterial tones of the

"Letter to Actor D", which an explanatory note reveals "has often appeared in books and magazines in different parts of the world, either to illustrate the Odin's vision of theatre or to present, in more general terms, its attitude to a new actor" (37). Barba has "been struck by a lack of seriousness" in the work of this anonymous reprobate, which is the accompaniment to a lack of commitment. Actor D has suffered "humiliations" and "degradation", and is believed to have "guilt", a "need to love" and a "longing for a lost paradise hidden in the past".

> Everybody present with you in this space will be shaken if you succeed in rediscovering these sources, this common ground of human experience, the hidden fatherland. This is the bond that unites you to the others, a treasure that lies buried deep within all of us, never unearthed, because it is our only comfort, and because it hurts when we touch it. (37–38)

The "hidden fatherland" is a curious image, which associates human nature with land ("the common ground of experience") only for it to be reassociated with the "treasure" that is "buried deep within all of us". The actor's person is certainly the mine for this exploration, or even excavation, and depth is eventually allied with a fierce, and characteristically absolute, condemnation of the (social) world:

> But in a world where people around us either no longer believe in anything, or only pretend to believe in order to be left in peace, he who digs deep within himself to reach a clarity about his own situation, his absence of ideals, his need for spiritual life, will always be called fanatic or naive. In a world with cheating as a norm, he who seeks his own truth is taken for a fraud, a hypocrite. (38)

But even if the exploratory actor is surrounded by a dispirited world, what the actor produces in the "space" is a form of social confrontation:

> No matter which personal and hidden motives have led you to the theatre, once you are within, you must find a meaning which, stretching beyond your own person, confronts you socially with others. (38–9)

The enquiry the actor conducts on the self is, in this expression of theory, "socialized":

> Your work is a sort of social meditation upon yourself, your human condition and the events that touch you to the quick through the experiences of the age. (38)

The section of writings on training includes "Words or Presence", republished from *Drama Review*, and a series of "Questions on Training" (put to Barba by the theatrical semiologist Franco Ruffini) which relate directly to Barba's initiatives in the 'Third Theatre'. The 'manifesto' on the Third Theatre is included in the third section of the book, which concentrates on "Journeying: Barter", and which also contains the "Letter from the South of Italy", which had first appeared in *Drama Review* of 1975, as I have noted. The significant dates are those of 1974, when Odin visited southern Italy for the first time, and 1976, when the Third Theatre constituted itself at a meeting in Belgrade. The third section concludes with further reflections on the Third Theatre between the years 1976 and 1979, which were originally written for the Mexican magazine, *Arte Nuevo*, and published in 1979 in the same year as *The Floating Islands*. All these pieces contain new formulations of considerable significance, and I shall deal with them in chronological succession.

The "Letter from the South of Italy" is preceded in *The Floating Islands* by a short interview from 1974 on the Odin's stay in Carpignano in southern Italy, in which the term 'barter' is introduced. The trade involved was "cultural", and the exchange is differentiated by means of this term from the normal act of selling theatre, or of performing for free:

> This was the barter: we did not give our goods away, nor did they give theirs.   (117)

What the "Letter from the South of Italy" makes clear is that the adoption of the practice of 'barter' was a response to the act of visiting a culture in which there was no awareness of theatre. As the Odin performers performed, so the villagers themselves wished to perform, and did so. This reciprocation became a mode of acceptance that happily replaced the possibility of complete rejection:

> It is not the village that should be the object of study, but the theatre group...It is no longer the theatre that wants to conquer the village, but the village that wants to seduce the group, and in this attempt reveals the need for theatre, something of which they were ignorant before, and which, had it been presented from the outside as a kind of gift, would have been felt as something alien, belonging to another planet.[93]

The encounter in southern Italy provided an abrupt contradiction to the principle of "social meditation" advanced to Actor D, to the discovery of a "meaning" which would confront the actor "socially with others":

> How can theatre concretely affect something which is outside of theatre? How can it open a breach—in fact not in words—in the wall that, even though dividing us from others, lets us live freely?
> To do it, it is necessary to return to humble crafts: things that one really can have an impact on are always much smaller than those one can talk about. Even so, trying always to break out, we run the risk of losing our way.[94]

For Barba, the activity of 'barter' is a substitute for theatre, in one sense at least a 'destruction' of theatre:

> Our stay in the South of Italy was to be for us proof that it is not the performance—a result which is limited in time—that counts, but the group with its behavior, with its vision realized in work filling the entire day...
> A small group of foreign actors, seemingly not well-grounded in social and political questions, had destroyed the theatre, but they had brought to light the ore hidden in that mine.[95]

The "theatrical situation" may appear to have lost its quality of a "social meditation" for the actor, but Barba acknowledges a desire for "something that will leave a mark on the political and social situation of the place". This was found at Monteiasi, where people were asked to bring a book when they attended the "dances", because a "group of young people" had the intention of turning a small room into "a library for everyone". But Barba finds the incident "paradoxical": "why not pay in money instead of coming with a book?".[96]

Ultimately, Barba equivocates in his presentation and formulation of 'barter'. In one brief image, 'barter' is compared to an octopus to which Barba would like to give "tentacles capable of clinging to a small piece of rock and breaking it off", and in an extended, lavishly organic metaphor the theatre is compared to a "body continually losing blood":

> Each time that it descends into the streets and encounters reality, it suffers blows, loses blood from wounds that do not heal. The body of the theatre cannot live on its own blood. Its hemophilia requires it to nourish itself on blood that comes from other bodies. It always needs new blood, it cannot survive on its own. There is a hemophiliac theatre that denies its condition: white as a larva, in its crystal tower, surrounded by authorities and interpreters who proclaim it everlasting,

> and undertake operations of reinvigoration through diagnoses and theories.
>
> But there is a theatre conscious of its hemorrages, which separates itself from the protective circle of its learned men and seems to lose itself in a reality that ignores and degrades it, has no use for it, and that in collision with this reality, bleeds.
>
> It is necessary to survive. Transfusions sprinkle the brain with a blood that cannot come from the body of theatre, but from other bodies, until now ignored and held at a distance, rejected as treacherous and dangerous.[97]

The tone is one of a heroic isolation, which seems perverse coming from the era of street theatre, happenings, performances in factories, and a general revival of popular and political theatre. More significant is the rhetoric of absolute condemnation, in which the "body" of the theatre is briefly concealed in the image of the "white...larva". What Odin achieves in 'barter' is and is not "theatre", and the practice of Odin as it is contained in 'barter' may be a part of, or apart from, an understanding of theatre practice, according to the discretion of the discursive theorist. The emotive, rhetorical question retains this option:

> In these unknown places, amongst these uncelebrated people, will the actors lose the drive they seemed to possess? Will they lose the intransigent commitment to their own art that seemed to give them bearings and which allowed them to present themselves only at the summit of their own work, of their own experience?
>
> In our last performance it was as if seven young people had abandoned the skin of their being as actors.[98]

The "skin of their being as actors", not their metaphorical body. Acting reserves the right, in this account, to withdraw its "intransigent commitment" from the alien, social world that Actor D had the duty to confront. Like the Hindu *Alvars*, who are the *"fools of God"* in their search for "truth" and "unity", the performers may be "controlled by a searching will that wants not to be shut up within the applause of a ring of spectators".[99]

Barba's rhetorical dismissal at this juncture of "authorities and interpreters" who "undertake operations of reinvigoration through diagnoses and theories" predates by some few years his foundation of the ISTA, and his later insistence in interview that his collaborators in that environment were "super-intellectuals".[100] This summary designation is expanded in the closing pages of *A Dictionary of Theatre*

Anthropology, which contain a massive list of experts headed by the names of the "pedagogical committee":

> ISTA's research team is made up of biologists, psychologists, psycholinguists, semiologists, theatre historians and anthropologists, but also, and especially, of masters and performers from various cultures and theatrical traditions.[101]

'Authority' and 'interpretation' are presumably not alien to many of these figures. Nor might the governing concept or the text of the *Dictionary* itself be easily divorced from an operation of "reinvigoration through diagnoses and theories", a phrase which readily describes the task of 'purification' originally envisaged by Barba. In his Introduction to the second section of *The Floating Islands*, Taviani reports on what has been a repeated judgement of Barba, "Barba seems to have an iron-clad—and some say dictatorial—authority" (44), and most recently, Watson summarizes the proceedings of the ISTA succinctly:

> ISTA's public sessions bring together traditional Eastern master performers and their Western counterparts, as well as relatively young, inexperienced actors and directors from the Euro-American tradition, and a team of intellectuals, including theatre scholars, anthropologists, psychologists, biologists, and critics.[102]

Watson has, early in his Preface, informed the reader that Barba has "read every word" of his book, and our unremarkable conclusion should be that rhetoric and the attitudes it may convey can be reversed without undue dismay, according to the demands and the purposes of the occasion.

In his introduction to the third section of Barba's writings in the collection, Taviani recorded the seventy-per-cent leap in the price of oil in 1973, and added that "the Odin performed, and still does perform, in a room" (95). In 1976, Barba presented the short document "Third Theatre" to the participants of the gathering of theatre groups in Belgrade. In it, he attempted to locate and define what he believed had been ignored, and introduced the image of a group of islands:

> A theatrical archipelago has been forming during the past few years in several countries. Almost unknown, it is rarely subject to reflection, it is not presented at festivals and critics do not write about it. (145)

The image was repeated to identify relatively isolated groups on a variety of continents:

> Like islands without contact between themselves, young people in Europe, North and South America, Australia and Japan gather to form theatre groups, determined to survive. (146)

The image might appear to carry connotations of the 'third world' situated between the two ideological blocs of the era: a 'developing' and not yet 'developed' grouping, perhaps located in specific geographical areas. But the second paragraph of the document reveals that the implied 'first' and 'second' theatres are distinguished in a different manner. If the "third theatre" is "the anonymous extreme of the theatres recognized by the world of culture", then the 'first theatre' is the "institutionalised theatre, protected and subsidised because of the cultural values it seems to transmit, appearing...even as a 'noble' version of the entertainment business". The 'second theatre' is opposed to this:

> on the other hand, the avant-garde theatre, experimenting, researching, arduous or iconoclastic, a theatre of changes, in search of a new originality, defended in the name of necessity to transcend tradition, and open to novelty in the artistic field and within society. (145)

The suggestion of an opposition, of 'left' and 'right' hands, can be taken to imply a closed system, and makes the task of achieving a satisfactory definition for a 'third' theatre difficult. Barba adopts a topographical image:

> The Third Theatre lives on the fringe, often outside or on the outskirts of the centres and capitals of culture. (ibid.)

The problem with this definition is that it might apply—and had, indeed, regularly been applied—to all kinds of 'alternative', 'fringe' and avant-garde performances and groups. Barba draws from the experience of Odin, which was founded from people who had been rejected as candidates for formal theatrical training. The workers of the Third Theatre

> have seldom undergone a traditional theatrical education and therefore are not recognised as professionals.
> But they are not amateurs. Their entire day is filled with theatrical experience, sometimes by what they call training, or by the preparation of performances for which they must fight. (ibid.)

The "phenomenon" of Third Theatre is assimilated to Barba's repeated emphasis on the severity and thoroughness of training, what was originally the point of absolute distinction between "oriental" and 'European' performers.

If the definition is imprecise in terms of geographic location or cultural formation, except that the model seems to be Odin, it is given greater exactitude by reference to the 'experience' and 'choice' of those who are taken to constitute it. What Barba attempts to do is to reconcile the idea of social change with that of the "personal needs" of the Third Theatre workers:

> Different people, in different parts of the world, experience the theatre as a bridge, constantly threatened, between the affirmation of their personal needs, and the necessity of prolonging them in the surrounding reality.
>
> Why do they choose the theatre in particular as a means of change, when we are well aware that other factors determine the reality in which we live? Is it a question of blindness, of self-delusion?
>
> Perhaps for them, the theatre is a means to find their own way of being present—which the critics would call 'new expressive forms'—to seek more humane relationships among men, with the purpose of creating a social cell inside which intentions, aspirations and personal needs begin to be transformed into actions. (146)

The concept of a "social cell" is a reformulation of the idea of "social meditation" for the (individual) Actor D, and as a repetition it is of considerable theoretical importance. The "surrounding reality" may well be as consistently alien as the negative view presented to Actor D, and the "more humane relationships among men" clearly refers to the relationships established in the group itself. The 'path' left open for the initiative for "change" is a "bridge", but it is "constantly threatened". In fact, the "change" may well be largely confined to the foundation of the group itself, with the activity of theatre acting as a guarantee against total isolation:

> One cannot dream only in the future, waiting for a total change which seems farther away at each step we take, and which nevertheless gives free reign [rein?—GL] to all the alibis, compromises, and to the impotence of waiting.
>
> One wants a new cell to be formed immediately, but without isolating oneself in it.
>
> To submerge oneself, as a group, in the universe of fiction, to find the courage not to pretend...Such is the paradox of the Third Theatre. (147)

The naming of the Third Theatre provoked a firm response, from groups wishing to possess a collective definition, and from critical interest. The "Questions on Training", from the second section of the collection, were put to Barba by Ruffini, and submitted in a report to UNESCO on the Belgrade gathering. With his first question Ruffini is concerned to know whether the term 'training' should be included in "a glossary of the Third Theatre", to which Barba's response was that he believed it to be "a fundamental term" (81). His particular reason for this once again relates the Third Theatre to the original distinction between "oriental" and European theatre practice, with the term "traditional theatre" clearly not referring to Asian models:

> While in traditional theater you have two phases: rehearsal and performance, in the Third Theater you have three phases: training, rehearsal, and performance.   (81–82)

Ruffini does not question Barba on how far this model for the Third Theatre derives from the practice established by Barba for Odin, and/or how far it describes the activity of groups in the Third Theatre. But Barba has a further distinction to make, which might clarify that issue:

> Many groups have a training that has nothing to do with the rehearsal for the performance. There are two parallel rails: one is the training. The rehearsals and the performance are the other. These two parallel rails allow the train—the group and its activity—to advance.   (82)

What interests Ruffini repeatedly is the idea that "training has a tendency itself to become performance", and he uses the term "spectator" for one who looks at training as well as at performance. Barba's responses are that training offers the performer a greater freedom, and he provides no direct answer to Ruffini's questions on training as a "performance". He does introduce the idea that training 'colonizes' the performer's body, "imposing a new form of culture upon it from the outset", but the implications of the term "culture" are left unexplored. At the close of the interview, Barba comes close to a more direct response to Ruffini's interest in the separation of a 'performance' of training and performance itself, by returning to the idea of "sociality":

> Training concerns only the actor who is doing it and his colleagues. It is the first step towards sociality, towards creative work. The performance is the second and final step, in that it also involves those who do not participate in the training: the spectators.   (84)

In his final question, Ruffini insistently returns to his principal concern:

Then could we say that training without performance is an incomplete socialization?

The response is equivocal:

> Yes, precisely. Unless you use training consciously, as we have done in our group, as a situation of socialization.   (ibid.)

Barba suggests that training contains "a form of elementary dramatic content", but that in performance "the dramatic content is much more complex":

> While in the training it can provide a series of limited images and associations, the dramatic content of the performance is rooted in a historical context.   (85)

What Ruffini fails to determine, despite repeated efforts, is whether the definition of the Third Theatre by way of the addition of the term 'training' implies simply one more part of a continuous process, or a profound distinction in the separate value of 'training' as another kind of 'performance', which may itself be observed. Barba's single, explicit reference is to Odin (to *The Book of Dances*), and as a consequence the definition of the Third Theatre as a collective entity seems tied to the model established by Barba for and with Odin.

In the final essay of the collection, "Theatre-Culture", Barba appears to integrate the concept of 'barter' at least implicitly with the situation of the Third Theatre:

> In order to understand the social value of theater, it is necessary to look not only at the wares, the performances produced, but also at the relationships established by producing performances.   (149)

The kind of 'sociality' Barba has in mind is partly clarified when he responds to the problem that the Third Theatre, by accepting its own situation, may be accepting the "ghetto". The ghetto allowed for "the freedom to follow one's own cult, to speak one's own language, to live according to one's own norms" (152), and it was the home of philosophers and physicians, and of technical invention. The discriminatory separation of the ghetto "implied the limitation of certain elementary liberties", but, Barba insists, it was not a separation from society:

> The separation of the ghetto meant separation from one's neighbours. It was not separation from society, from history, from the deepest transformations of one's own era.   (153)

The figure of the ghetto, which Barba understands as representative of an idea of diversity, is replaced in the later part of the essay by the figure that provides the title to the collection, "the floating islands". In the section with this heading, 'sociality' becomes subject to a far more drastic critique and revision than Barba has admitted in his writings up to this point:

> Critics, ideologists and men of theater have for years ignored this ascertainment: that the theater has lost its character of deeply functional use for a determined social rank, for a determined community.
>
> In various countries of the world, especially among the younger generations, an unexpected meaning has come to be given to the encounter with theater: not the need to *receive theater*, but the need to *do theater*, to create new relationships, as actor and as spectator. (159)

In this definition, 'sociality' is relocated to the theatrical group, and only marginally extended beyond it in the final concession of "as spectator". The emphasis on the "individual" is also marked:

> These groups do not dream of themselves as a vehicle for great words, great messages, for great debates, but seek a way to make the individual come into contact with the individual, the different with the different. (ibid.)

The redefinition of sociality announced as a general thesis was achieved in the particularities of the experience and organization of Odin:

> All the fundamental traits—from the actor's technique to internal organization, from its ethics to its way of resolving economic problems, finally to its performances for few spectators and not based on the understanding of a text made up of words—all these are the answer to a situation that seemed to condemn us to impo-tence. (ibid.)

It is this common situation that provides a collective identity to groups in the Third Theatre, and not some kind of common, linear purpose or motivation. According to Barba's discourse, which he distinguishes from that of the "masters of writing", there is a common emphasis on "individual needs", and a different kind of "dream":

> The groups that I call Third Theater do not belong to a lineage—to a theatrical tendency. But they do all live in a situation of discrimination:

personal or cultural, professional, economical or political. The masters of writing are the ones to decide the validity of what they are doing.

They are thus groups forced into daily verification of the need for an 'anti-historical' obstinacy: the need to persevere, even in isolation, in the search for an answer to one's own individual needs.

They are the people who, through theater, pursue the dream of building their own lives.   (160–1)

The metaphors of "isolation" and "building" are combined in a complex and sustained image, which directs Barba's discourse away from the polarity of European and "oriental" towards the Aztecs, and the historic topography of Mexico City. To reach this location for his imagery, Barba adopts an idiosyncratic figure for the "dreamer", which takes him into the water:

What image do we have of the dreamer?
A person who goes away from the land and takes to water. But not just to discover or to reach other regions.
Some, although they seem to isolate themselves far out in the water, nevertheless wish to remain close to others. They try to build upon the lake fragments of land. These are the floating islands.   (161)

The Aztecs were Barba's originative 'dreamers', and, significantly, his originative 'sowers'. They occupied "lake fragments of land", but also made their own gardens:

The Aztecs also built rafts of reeds on which they spread earth and planted seeds. From these floating gardens slowly grew a village, whose name would have a long destiny: Mexico—Tenochtitlan.   (161–2)

That the figure of the "dreamer" has no colonial motive for movement across the waters, and that the "floating islands" are Mexican, confirm the impression that, for Barba, writing of the Third Theatre carries connotations of the 'third world'. But ultimately it is the experience of Odin that determines the discursive situation of the Third Theatre, and that appropriates the imagery to its own "courage":

From the letters I receive, from the visits, from the encounters that I have, I realize that the sense of Odin lies not only in its theatrical results. It is in its very existence, in its survival as a tangible sign that a group of excluded people, from different countries, of different religions, with different languages, in reality a group of misfits, had the courage to leave the mainland, where men seemed to be usefully working the soil. On to a raft they brought their own bags of soil and

> worked obstinately, without following the culture of the mainland, adapting themselves to the currents that carried them far away.
>
> This is the value of the Odin, of other groups, of other people who by now have spent almost an entire life sowing on water. (162–3)

This definitive experience, a point of reference for the collective identity of the groups "that lived in the same situation as us", encourages the admission of an initial "asociality", and the determination of theatre as a "bridge" across which passage may be made to the "social":

> But if in spite of everything one succeeds in surviving, then paradoxically one's 'asociality' transforms itself into something social. Thus theater becomes a means of not remaining alone, of forming a bridge, of creating ties without renouncing one's own dreams.
>
> Theater also becomes the shrewdness, the trench that protects and hides what we hold as essential. (163)

The image of the "floating islands", the collective "isolation" within the waters of the lake, can offer a definition of what it might be to be "social"; but the dogma of "asociality" calls the dream back to an embattled position on dry land.

Part of the rhetoric of self-encouragement in the essay is given to an enhancement of the small against the large: Barba's choice of image here is that of microbes, which were initially "a conversation piece, a curiosity whose existence had no weight", but which were later recognized to be potentially "more dangerous than the tiger" (164). This imagery of ignored or suppressed power justifies, in different ways, subsequent aphorisms, including the two different formulations that "It is necessary to transform oneself from a sub-culture to a culture" (165) and that "It is illusory to believe that only big organisms provoke big changes" (166). Yet the rhetoric of assertion does not displace the continuing problem of the 'social' and 'sociality' in Barba's discursive theory:

> What sort of theater does today's society need?
>
> Often, latching on to a Political Theater means escaping from the problem of pursuing, with theater, a policy.
>
> He who does not accept a society and a culture that is imposed upon him, but seeks a different society and his own culture, must invert the question. He must ask what he wants, through theater, from society. (166)[103]

What this "he" might want is not at all clear, but Barba obscures a direct enquiry with a repeated and emphatic concern for 'defence', and for the choice of a site for theatre that is placed "out of range", 'naturally' defended by performance:

> The theater-culture cannot be a defenceless theater...
>
> Those who built a new village would look for a site that best allowed for community life, and at the same time the site best defended by the mountains, the water, and the forest.
>
> The performance is our mountain, our water, our forest.
>
> Its capacity to impose respect and to fascinate even those who should not or will not accept us, not only permits us to live, but places us out of range.   (167)

In the light of this image, the subsequent claim that theatre "is the rock onto which we have clung and that...makes us social", as an attempt to return to an equivocal 'sociality', is distinctly weakened, because theatre appears more clearly as a means of "escape":

> Theater is waste, but it is also a socially-accepted activity. It is apparently non-productive, but it justifies group-work. You can project onto it your dreams and obsessions, giving them a body, reaching down to the others without skimming over the surface of common language.
>
> It is a means to escape the reasoning of the tamers, to break the circle of solitude.   (171)[104]

4.3.3 Going beyond technique: the discourse of a theatre anthropology

The publication of *The Floating Islands* in 1979, with its attention to the innovative concept of the 'Third Theatre' established in 1976, was followed closely by the first meeting of the International School for Theatre Anthropology in Bonn, in October 1980. The earliest document available in English is Barba's "Theatre Anthropology: First Hypothesis", dating from a conference held in Warsaw in May 1980. A further, more extensive document entitled "Theatre Anthropology", "summing up the experience" of the ISTAs of 1980 and 1981, was published in journals in 1982.[105] Both documents were later published together, in a revision of *The Floating Islands*, with the title *Beyond the Floating Islands*.[106]

The surprising choice of disciplinary title for the School's activities is quite clearly connected to the crucial addition of training to the definition of the 'Third Theatre', an addition which had immediately attracted Ruffini's attention. In "Theatre Anthropology: First Hypothesis" Barba addresses the subject of training through the idea of "laws" of bodily performance subject to research and observation, which may then be associated with a 'pedagogy':

> The point of departure for ISTA's research activity was the study of the basic laws which govern the particular use of the body in a performance situation.[107]

This is the language of an empirical ("particular use") and then theoretical ("basic laws") science, and the ISTA is constituted as the validating and concluding institution for the observations made in the research 'laboratory'. Whether or not this 'laboratory' is to remain the training practised by Odin is not apparent. But the principles of the 'pedagogy' are consistent with an attempt to bridge the "abyss" that had separated the Kathakali actor from "his European colleague". Barba is concerned with an assimilation of these "basic laws" into the body of the "individual" and "western" actor:

> a pedagogical situation based not on imitation and reproduction, but on personal observation, on comprehension, and on the individual challenge of rediscovering and developing analogous processes in their own 'western' bodies.[108]

The idea of 'rediscovery' recalls Barba's early subscription to a ritual theatre in the Laboratory of Grotowski, which he had understood to be founded on the premise that "primitive rituals are the first form of drama".[109] That theatre he had compared to "an anthropological expedition", and in his early commentary on the work of Odin he had accepted that in the "scientific spirit" of its research and training the theatre might draw "from the human sciences such as anthropology, psychiatry, and sociology".[110] The qualification then exercised that the theatre "can't identify with science" is less obtrusive in the more formal setting of the ISTA:

> On the one hand there is the fascination of using the insight of the natural sciences in theatrical work, and on the other hand there is the challenge of using a new pedagogical practice. The future will show whether theatre anthropology was but a dream and a suggestive hypothesis.[111]

The three "laws" that Barba introduces in the "First Hypothesis" are those of "the alteration of balance", of "opposition", and of a "consistent inconsistency" which is subsumed in the principle of an "extra-daily" bodily technique for the performer. The exposition of these laws, with the full text of "Theatre Anthropology", was absorbed into the publication in 1983 of *Anatomia del teatro: un dizionario de antropologia teatrale*, which was republished in English translation in 1991.[112] I shall discuss the presentation in the English edition of this book, in which the 1982 article on "Theatre Anthropology" appears as the Introduction, and the texts on 'balance' and 'opposition' appear at the beginning of the 'dictionary' entries with those titles.

The exposition of the discipline of "Theatre Anthropology" in the Introduction to *A Dictionary of Theatre Anthropology* opens with a confirmation of the role of Barba's new pedagogy in supplementing a theoretically assumed lack:

> Where can performers find out how to construct the material bases of their art? This is the question which theatre anthropology attempts to answer.[113]

In the earlier version of the essay, published in *Beyond the Floating Islands*, "the western actor" appears in place of "performers", in a polar emphasis which conforms to the principles of the pedagogy expressed in the "First Hypothesis".[114] But the text in both versions then proceeds to contradict the advocacy of the study of "basic laws" advanced by the "First Hypothesis":

> Theatre anthropology seeks useful directions rather than universal principles. It does not have the humility of a science, but an ambition to uncover knowledge which can be useful to a performer's work. It does not seek to discover laws, but studies rules of behaviour.[115]

Barba's equivocation about the status of research, or of a "theatre", which "draws on the human sciences of anthropology, psychiatry, and sociology" abruptly returns here after the scientific and theoretical confidence of the "First Hypothesis". The uncertainty is made all the more awkward by the annotations which introduced the earlier English version of the essay in *Beyond the Floating Islands*, and which noted that the programme of the second ISTA "was greatly expanded in all respects, but particularly in the scientific area". Prominently included in the "research teams" listed in these annotations were a neurophysiologist from Copenhagen University Hospital, and a psychologist from the University in Giessen, West Germany, who conducted specific studies. The essay itself actually offers a behavioural determination of the scope of 'anthropology':

> Originally, anthropology was understood as the study of human beings' behaviour, not only on the socio-cultural level, but also on the physiological level. Theatre anthropology is thus the study of human beings' socio-cultural and physiological behaviour in a performance situation.[116]

'Theatre anthropology' in Barba's formulation is and is not a science, because it reverts to the origins of science.

Granted this equivocation, there is, unfortunately, no clear reading of Barba. Much as the problem of 'sociality', mediated through the experience of Odin, confused a discourse explicitly dedicated to the collective identity (and so the definition) of the 'Third Theatre', so the problem of the status of theatre anthropology troubles the discourse that presents it. In the English edition of the *Dictionary* the Introduction to "Theatre Anthropology" proves inadequate for a resolution of the problem, to which an additional preface on the ISTA has to be dedicated. In this preface, Barba draws attention to the variety of 'anthropologies' (cultural, criminal, philosophical, physical, and palaeoanthropic), commenting that "partial homonyms" are not confused by researchers with "homologies", and distinguishes 'theatre anthropology' in the work of the ISTA in particular from "cultural anthropology". What both 'anthropologies' share is "the questioning of the obvious (one's own tradition)":

> By means of a confrontation with what appears to be foreign, one educates one's way of seeing and renders it both participatory and detached. (5)

What this formulation fails to register is the problematic nature of the situation of the 'observer' of "what appears to be foreign" in either anthropology, while the use of "appears" suggests that differences are in some fundamental sense illusory. Yet by stating that "theatre anthropology" is not concerned with "the application of the paradigms of cultural anthropology to theatre and dance", nor with "the study of the performative phenomena in those cultures...traditionally studied by anthropologists" Barba aims to "avoid equivocation". "Theatre anthropology" is also distinct from "the anthropology of performance". A positive definition then follows:

> Again: Theatre Anthropology is the study of the behaviour of the human being when it uses its physical and mental presence in an organised performance situation and according to principles which are different from those used in daily life. This extra-daily use of the body is what is called technique. (ibid.)

The principal difficulty with this definition is that it has dropped or discarded the original and apparently significant emphasis placed by Barba on "what appears to be foreign". This elimination of the 'cultural' also affects our understanding of "an organised performance situation", which in the context of the paragraph might readily be taken to apply to sports, and so to the "anthropology of performance" with which Barba expects us to be familiar. One reason for the elimination of the 'cultural' becomes apparent in the introduction of the potentially universal term "transcultural" in the following paragraph. Barba insists that "a transcultural analysis of performance" will reveal "three aspects" of the performer's activity: these are their "personalities" and their "unique and once-only" individual characteristics; "the particularities of the traditions and socio-historical contexts" which manifest these personalities; and "the use of physiology according to extra-daily body techniques" (ibid.). Of these three aspects, the first two are different kinds of particularity, but the third presents the possibility of universality:

> The first aspect is individual. The second is common to all those who belong to the same performance genre. Only the third concerns all performers from every era and culture. (ibid.)

"Transcultural" clearly has two different applications: it may be applied to the (extrinsic) "transcultural analysis" of performance work located in different cultures, or it may be applied in the concept of (in-trinsic) "transcultural principles". These are identified by Barba as the 'base' on which all "extra-daily body techniques", his third and non-particular "aspect" of performance, are founded:

> The recurrent and transcultural principles on which these techniques are based are defined by Theatre Anthropology as the field of pre-expressivity. (ibid.)

The assertion of universal "principles" may not be the act of a 'science', but it is the familiar prerogative exercised by theory. Theory, although distancing itself from science in a denial of "equivocation", also returns immediately to a scientific analogy, which appears to have the status of an organic metaphor. The third aspect "can be called the performance's 'biological' level":

> The first two aspects determine the transition from pre-expressivity to expression. The third is the *idem* which does not vary; it underlines the various individual, artistic and cultural variants. (ibid.)

This, of course, is the determination of 'invariables' amongst the unordered plethora of variables in the 'laboratory', which permits theoretical, if not scientific, formulation. This "level" may also be expressed as what constitutes "the performer's 'presence', or scenic *bios*", as Barba makes an etymological connection with the metaphor of 'biology' and the performer's 'life'. A theory of this kind allows observation to be more than pragmatic, because it lays claim to theoretical "knowledge":

> Knowledge of the principles which govern the scenic *bios* can make it possible for one *to learn to learn* rather than to learn a technique. (ibid.)

"Theatre anthropology", as the theoretical discourse that validates the work of the ISTA, allows the work of the ISTA to transcend the value of the master-class in a particular discipline of performance, or, as Barba phrases it, "to go beyond the limits of specialized technique". But the final promise is mystical, rather than theoretical:

> This is a question of understanding not technique but the *secrets of technique*, which one must possess before one can go beyond technique. (ibid.)

In the essay on "Theatre Anthropology" which forms the Introduction to the *Dictionary*, Barba substitutes the notion of "recurrent principles" for the "laws" of the "First Hypothesis", and creates problems in the ordering of his discourse:

> The first task of theatre anthropology is to trace these recurrent principles. They are not proof of the existence of a 'science of the theatre' nor of a few universal laws. They are nothing more than particularly good 'bits of advice': information useful for scenic practice. (8)

This is a comforting dictum, but it cannot hold:

> To speak of a 'bit of good advice' seems to indicate something of little
> value when compared with the expression 'theatre anthropology'. But
> entire fields of study—rhetoric and morals, for example, or the study
> of behaviour—are likewise collections of 'good ad-vice'. (ibid.)

Yet even the word "advice" must be integrated, theoretically, into the systematic division between the "Occidental" performer, who does not have "an organic repertory of 'advice'", and the "traditional Oriental performer", who has a "base of organic and well-tested 'absolute advice'". What interests Barba is the possibility of a theatre "which can be open to the experiences of other theatres", and this possibility requires the determination of "recurrent principles", and the intervention of "theatre anthropology": "Theatre anthropology seeks to study these principles" (9). Granted the dangers of "sterility" in "a closed performing style" of "Oriental theatre", and of "arbitrariness and an absence of rules" in "Occidental" performance, the first "bit of good advice" may well be the adoption of a discipline which has dogmatically determined the undeclared 'needs' of both groups.

It is the third "aspect" of performance—the "use of physiology according to extra-daily body techniques" or "pre-expressivity"—with which Barba is concerned, and he finds confirmation for this concept in terms declared to him by the Odissi dancer Sanjukta Panigrahi. These are *lokadharmi* ('daily-life/behaviour') and *natyadharmi* ('dance/behaviour'), and this distinction prompts a renewal of the theoretical division between east and west:

> In the Occident, the distance which separates daily body techniques
> from extra-daily techniques is often neither evident nor consciously
> considered. In India, on the other hand, the difference between these
> two techniques is obvious, even sanctioned by nomenclature:
> *lokadharmi* and *natyadharmi*. (9)

Barba's choice of dance as his paradigm here is either careless or misjudged, because his observations on the "Occident" clearly do not apply either to traditional dance (ballet) or to mime. Nor is his later citation of Craig's judgement on Irving ("Irving did not walk on the stage, he danced on it") particularly helpful, because it recalls the possibility that the histrionics of European performance may well have included many modes in which the "behaviour" was "extra-daily". But the theoretical distinction between "Occidental" and "Oriental" serves to establish the most general of the "recurrent principles", and the absolutism of that distinction is all the more apparent when Barba attempts to define "daily" and "extra-daily" in non-cultural terms:

> The purpose of the body's daily techniques is communication. The techniques of virtuosity aim for amazement and the transformation of the body. The purpose of extra-daily techniques, on the other hand, is information: they literally *put the body in form*. Herein lies the essential difference which separates extra-daily techniques from those which merely transform the body.   (10)

Apart from the supposed illumination of the pun, the meaning is obscure, particularly in relation to movement or walking, which one might uncontentiously take as a form of locomotion rather than "communication".

Walking does, in fact, appear as one of Barba's prime examples of the extra-daily "balance" deployed by ("Oriental") performers, and movement in general is a major point of distinction:

> The performers of the various Oriental traditions deform the positions of the legs and knees, and the way of placing the feet on the ground, or they reduce the distance between one foot and the other, thereby reducing the body's base and making balance precarious.   (11)

In a quotation from the "First Hypothesis" which introduces the entry on "Balance" later in the *Dictionary*, Barba's examples are those of Noh, Kabuki, Odissi, "Balinese theatre" and Kathakali, while *commedia dell'arte* can be assimilated, through illustration, to Odissi. The theoretical departure of the "Occidental theatre" from the first of the "recurrent principles" is recorded tersely:

> In the most recent Occidental theatre tradition, in which the functions of actor and dancer have been separated, one finds this alteration of balance only in such strongly codified techniques as mime or classical dance.   (34)

The 'separation' of acting and dancing, however dubious as an analysis of its history, condemns the "recent Occidental theatre tradition" to a 'lack', while the remnants of what theory must suppose as a once unified tradition can only be found in the current enclaves of ballet and mime. That Barba is aware of difficulties is apparent in a 'disclaimer' in the text of the Introduction:

> The reader should not be surprised if I use the words actor and dancer indiscriminately, just as I move with a certain indifference from the

Orient to the Occident and vice-versa. The life principles which we are searching for are not limited by the distinction between what we define as theatre, dance or mime. (12)

But the discourse of "theatre anthropology" apparently is "limited", at least in relation to the "Occident". Barba's view of the "Occidental" 'separation' of theatre and dance in the Introduction is open to exceptions, but just as resolutely negative:

> The tendency to make a distinction between dance and theatre, characteristic of our culture, reveals a profound wound, a void with no tradition, which continuously risks drawing the actor towards a denial of the body and the dancer towards virtuosity. To an Oriental performer, this distinction seems absurd, as it would have seemed absurd to performers in other historical periods, to a jester or a comedian in the sixteenth century, for example. (ibid.)

The "wound" and the "void" (both, presumably, 'gaping') are emotive terms, and they conceal the probability that the "tendency to make a distinction" is justified in relation to European theatre history. That Barba fails or refuses to study the techniques—even the "extra-daily" techniques—of the European actor is the responsibility of his own theoretical inclination, which dismisses them from the universality of "recurrent principles" in his own determination of "performance".

A confrontation with this exclusion is postponed until what was, in the "First Hypothesis", the second "law" has been expounded, that of "opposition". This "principle" is first expressed in general terms:

> We have seen in fact that although extra-daily techniques are different from daily techniques, they maintain a tension with them without becoming isolated and separated. The performer's body reveals its life to the spectator by means of a tension between opposing forces: this is the principle of opposition. (ibid.)

The phrasing suggests that Barba may be referring here to the "alteration" or "distortion of balance" which had formed his first principle. But clarification is afforded by a polarity drawn from "Balinese dance", much as the initial contrast between "daily" and "extra-daily" was sanctioned by the terms used in Odissi:

> All the forms of Balinese dance are constructed by composing a series of oppositions between *keras* and *manis*. *Keras* means strong, hard, vigorous. *Manis* means delicate, soft, tender. *Keras* and *manis* can be

> applied to various movements and positions of different parts of the body in a dance, and to successive movements in the same performance.   (ibid.)

This analytical or theoretical "opposition" seems very different from Barba's leading example, which is drawn from Peking Opera, and which is expressed in "the principle that every movement must begin in the direction opposite to that in which it will ultimately be carried out".[117] Further examples introduce a third interpretation, which is that of the "ease in unease" of mime, according to Decroux, and the pain that accompanies a "correctly assumed" position, according to a "master" of Japanese Buyo. The examples, and divergent interpretations of the single principle of "opposition", are then conflated:

> Indian dancer Sanjukta Panigrahi, the masters of Peking Opera, classical ballet or Balinese dance, all reiterate the same idea. Unease, then, becomes a means of control, a kind of internal radar which permits performers to observe themselves while in action.   (13)

The principle is variable, and yet a composite: "The dance of opposition characterizes the performer's life on many levels" (12). In its concluding variation, it resumes the contrast between "Occidental" and "Oriental" performers, with an interesting qualification placed in brackets:

> When Occidental performers want to be energetic...they use huge movements, with great speed and muscular strength. And this effort is associated with fatigue, hard work. Oriental actors (or great Occidental actors) can become even more tired almost without moving. Their tiredness is not caused by an excess of vitality, by the use of huge movements, but by the play of oppositions.   (13)

This uncompromising formulation replaces an earlier and more tolerant concession, in which the "principle of opposition" was allowed to be "also part of the Occidental performer's experience" (12).

Subordinate to the principle of "opposition" is the principle of "simplification" or "omission", which refers to "the omission of certain elements in order to put other elements into relief" (13). Despite admitting the relevance of this concept to the conventional notion of an actor's "stage business" (15), Barba interrupts his discourse with an Intermezzo, which acknowledges the evident inclinations of "theatre anthropology":

> At this point one might well ask if the principles of the performer's art

which I have described do not take us too far from theatre and dance as it is known and practised in the Occident.   (ibid.)

What "one might well ask" is represented by Barba as a sequence of rhetorical questions, which he is prepared to accept are "binding", although his 'answer' to them is something less, or other, than direct:

> Are these principles actually 'good advice', useful for performing practice? Does drawing attention to the pre-expressive level of the performer's art blind us to the Occidental performer's real problems? Is the pre-expressive level perhaps only verifiable in theatrical cultures which are highly codified? Is the Occidental tradition not perhaps mainly characterised by the lack of codification and by the search for individual expression? These are undoubtedly binding questions, but rather than demanding immediate answers, they invite us to stop and rest for a moment.
> So let's talk about flowers.   (ibid.)

I have commented before that rhetorical questions are more favoured in the asking than in the answering, and in this case the suggestion of a suitable 'postponement' (for the weary) is nothing more than an embellishment of the standard procedure. Nothing in Barba's long exposition on art as a 'flower', and on its representation in the figure of the *ikebana*, which Barba draws from Japanese graphics, addresses any of his "questions". The acknowledgement that they are "binding" grants a reprieve to "theatre anthropology", which exists in the written space between their deposition and the promised, non-"immediate" answers, whose deferral remains at the discretion of the theorist.

The absence of "answers" to these questions, or the assumption of their constant deferral, is one part of the theoretical constitution of "theatre anthropology". The second part also exists in a constant deferral or postponement, which is implicit in the determination of the "abyss" between "Occidental" and "Oriental", the cultural 'difference' which sustains and continually renews the discourse. At the close of the essay Barba writes of the songs and dances presented at the end of the Bonn meeting of the ISTA by Sanjukta Panigrahi and Iben Nagel Rasmussen. Panigrahi and Rasmussen are determined as theoretical representatives of Barba's constant polarity of cultural difference:

> The Oriental actress and the Occidental actress seem to be moving far apart, each one deep in her own culture. Nevertheless, they meet.   (22)

Discursively, "theatre anthropology" identifies and yet promises the transformation of difference, repeats and retains the polarity on which it insists while suggesting its transcendence:

> They seem to transcend not only their own personalities and sex, but even their own artistic skills, and show something which is beyond all this. (ibid.)

In Barba's tripartite formula from the Preface on the ISTA, performances like personalities are "particularities" (5). Theory alone has the capacity to reveal the individual personality-in-performance as a set of "recurrent and transcultural principles": "They seem to...show something which is beyond all this." This revelation may occur in the occasional and institutional context of the ISTA, but the hidden term of "theatre anthropology" which manifests the transcendence proposed by theory is the Odin Teatret, directed by Barba:

> A theatre can, however, be open to the experiences of other theatres, not in order to mix different ways of making performances, but in order to find basic common principles and to transmit these principles through its own experiences. (9)

The theoretical discourses of the Third Theatre and theatre anthropology have this in common, that they seem to function as validations of, or charters for, the 'presence' and particular practice of Odin Teatret.

4.3.4 Revising the anatomy of theory: later essays

A paradoxically high degree of integration for a theatre founded on the principle of 'isolation' and "asociality" has resulted in the continual revision of theoretical propositions by Barba, notably in a series of essays published in the leading English-language journals, *New Theatre Quarterly* and *Drama Review*, but also most recently in *The Paper Canoe*.[118] Of these revisionist writings I have selected two, which purport to offer a definition of a "Eurasian Theatre" and to address the problem of reception. In addition, I would refer the reader to the exchange between Zarrilli and Barba published in *Drama Review*, in which Zarrilli presented a critique of terms advanced at the 1986 ISTA, and of Barba as pedagogue and writer, to which Barba then replied in an open letter.[119]

Included in the same volume of *Drama Review* as Barba's response to Zarrilli is the essay "Eurasian Theatre", in which Barba offers a third term which might transcend the apparent polarity of "Asian" and

"Western", or "Occidental" and "Oriental" in his earlier writings. In this essay, Barba argues that the "undeniable embarrassment" that the "exchanges" between "Western" and "Asian" theatre "might be part of the supermarket of cultures" may be removed by renaming the theoretical concept of "pre-expressivity". The activity of "comparison" with which Barba started his researches may be appropriate to the "epidermises" of cultural conventions and genres.

> But if I consider that which lies beneath those luminous and seductive epidermises and discern the organs which keep them alive, then the poles of the comparison blend into a single profile: that of a Eurasian theatre.[120]

The 'anatomy of theatre' must penetrate beneath the skin, and in its theoretical rigour must not be distracted by the "seductive" appearances of cultures and performances. To justify his choice of the term "Eurasian", Barba writes of a "transcultural dimension", in the language previously used for theoretical "pre-expressivity", but he applies the term here to the concept of "a 'tradition of traditions'" (ibid.). This evocative notion he identifies in examples taken from a relatively 'normal' European theatrical history, in which the Renaissance fascination with antiquity and the romantic interest in the medieval and renaissance theatres demonstrate how attempts at an "'anti-traditional'" theatre have drawn from the "tradition of traditions". The proposition is carefully asserted for "the East" as well as "the West", but there are no examples given for "the East", and the application of the term "trans-cultural" to the "tradition of traditions" remains puzzling. Is this a phenomenon that occurs *within* 'cultures' to a similar extent in "East" and "West", and so might be called "transcultural"? If this is the argument, it seems to have little connection with Barba's belief in a transcendence of the obvious "exchanges" between "Western" and "Asian" theatre, in "a Eurasian theatre".

The "transcultural dimension" and the "tradition of traditions" are displaced in the argument by a series of questions which resume aspects of the polarity between "Occidental" and "Oriental" theatre familiar from earlier writings. The series asks "why" there is a 'specialization' of the actor in "the Western tradition", as "actor-singer", "actor-dancer", and "actor-interpreter"; "why" the actor "in the West" tends "to confine herself within the skin of only one character"; and, in a less familiar question, "why" it is that "the use of words whose meaning the majority of the spectators cannot understand" is confined to opera "in the West", when it is evident in "so many forms of Oriental theatre" (127). The series is confirmed to be rhetorical, leaving the 'questions' as unexamined statements:

> Clearly, from the historical point of view, there are answers to these questions. But they only become professionally useful when they stimulate us to imagine how we can develop our own theatrical identity by extending the limits which define it against our nature. It is enough to observe from afar, from countries and uses which are distant, or simply different from our own; to discover the latent possibilities of a Eurasian theatre. (127)

"Different" and "distant" are descriptions that recur in the open letter Barba wrote in response to Zarrilli; here they are conjoined with "countries and uses", while in the letter they are conjoined with "craftspersons".[121] In both formulations, the conventional notion of 'cultural identity' as a point of distinction between performance genres is discarded, effaced in favour of a "transcultural" principle which will not be "against our nature". This is a restatement of the theory of "pre-expressivity", which now appears under the new name of the "Eurasian theatre".

That "pre-expressivity" is involved is made explicit by a reference to the ISTA, and the gathering there of "masters of both Eastern and Western theatre, to compare the most disparate work methods, and to reach down into a common technical substratum":

> This common substratum is the domain of pre-expressivity. It is the level at which the actor engages her own energies according to an extra-daily behavior, modeling her 'presence' in front of the spectator. At this pre-expressive level, the principles are the same, even though they nurture the enormous expressive differences which exist between one tradition and another. (128)

This concept of "tradition" seems to depend on the individual and cultural "particularities" familiar from Barba's earlier writings. But, as such, it must be distinct from the elusive "tradition of traditions", which is applied to the theoretical transcendence of these "particularities":

> Defining one's own professional identity implies overcoming ethnocentricity to the point of discovering one's own center in the tradition of traditions. (ibid.)

Barba observes that in the course of years he has come to discount the differences between 'dance' and 'theatre', to reject 'character' as "a unit of measure of the performance", to accept cross-gender playing, and to "exploit the sonorous richness of languages" in a communication that goes "beyond the semantic" (128–29). By means of this "series of practical solutions" he believes that Odin Teatret has achieved characteristics that are "equivalent to some of the characteristics of Oriental theatres", except that those of Odin "were born of an auto-didactic training". Odin is again the transcendent term in a polarity that remains as absolute as it had been in any earlier writings, expressed resolutely in the contrast between *logos* and *bios*, between the primacy of the written text and that of the "living" presence of the actor:

> On one hand, then, stories that are unstable in every aspect but the written; on the other hand, a living art, profound, capable of being transmitted, and implicating all the physical and mental levels of actor and spectator, but anchored in stories and customs which are forever old. On the one hand, a theatre which is sustained by *logos*. On the other hand, a theatre which is, above all, *bios*.   (128)

The transcendence of this polarity resides with Odin, who, as "foreigners", faced the "impossibility of being like other theatre people", and the theoretical role ascribed to Odin by theatre anthropology returns to its author in the form of a new identity:

> For all these reasons I recognize myself in the culture of a Eurasian theatre today.   (129)

So *logos* and *bios* may be combined in the work that occurs at the "professional village" of the ISTA. But the 'sociality' involved in this "necessary theatre"—"Eurasian theatre is necessary today as we move from the 20th into the 21st century"—includes a strictly delimited category of "spectators". There are "few spectators capable of following or accompanying the actor in the dance of thought-in-action", while "the Western *public*" finds this particularly difficult. For the "few", the experience of work arising from research undertaken in the laboratory is one of "ritualization":

> Beyond the public there are, in the West as well as the East, specific *spectators*. They are a few, but for them theatre can become a necessity.
> For them theatre is a relationship which neither establishes a union nor creates a communion, but ritualizes the reciprocal strangeness and the laceration of the social body hidden beneath the uniform skin of dead myths and values.   (130)

In the exchange between Ruffini and Barba on the 'performance' of training, problems of reception were discussed inconclusively, and it is interesting that Barba's most notable essay on this subject may be a response to another study.[122] That study, by the semiotician de Marinis, was published in 1987 with the title "Dramaturgy of the Spectator".[123] De Marinis introduced a number of distinctions and topics which seem to be recalled in an essay by Barba, "Four Spectators", published three years later in the same journal.[124] De Marinis was interested in "the problem of reception in the theatre", and his first distinction was between the spectator "in a passive or, more precisely, an objective sense" and "in an active or subjective sense": the spectator as a "target" for the activity of theatre and its personnel, and as a subject engaged in the activities of "response".[125] De Marinis also envisaged a situation in which the concept of a "Model Spectator" might be inappropriate, and the results of reception anomalous: this would be the case with "the behavior of an adult at a children's performance", for example (103). In particular, de Marinis was attracted to the notion of "open performances", which might exaggerate the "relative independence" to be allowed to the spectator by theory:

> Open performances make a point of addressing themselves to a receiver who is neither too precise, nor too clearly defined in terms of their encyclopedic, intertextual, or ideological competence. (ibid.)

De Marinis thinks in this connection of "the example of many non-Western theatre traditions, where the normal practice is to leave plenty of interpretive freedom to the audience", and this unexamined assertion leads him to introduce Eugenio Barba and the Third Theatre. Despite Barba's repeated, written insistence on the limited number of spectators for his theatre, de Marinis makes "a real increase in the number of 'authorized' spectators" a point of contrast between the avant-garde and the Third Theatre as defined by Barba. The avant-garde has often produced "esoteric works reserved for a select band":

> However, in Barba's 'Third Theatre' the aim—though not always achieved—has been to create performances which might allow a real plurality of reception or viewings which are equal to one another. (104)

De Marinis' use of Eugenio Barba and the Third Theatre as theoretical components in a continuing semiotics of theatrical communication offers an interpretation which can hardly be supported from Barba's writings, and which is admitted to be doubtful in practice or 'achievement'.[126] But his distinction of the Third Theatre from the avant-garde, although presented in the different terms of a theory of reception, confirmed Barba's own determination of a separate category of 'groups' and "situation" in the theatre. Barba's later essay, "Four Spectators", introduces the problem of the spectator in a different manner, but involves some related formulations. In the preamble, Barba makes it clear that his interest in the spectator is dependent on the spectator's capacity to combat characteristics of 'the theatre' itself. The negation of the theatre's "ephemerality" is assumed by Barba to be a responsibility or a duty: "to negate the theatre by doing it."[127] By opposing "the unavoidably transient nature of theatre" we are brought "to a discovery of its meaning", and by hiding "the negation in the heart of a work" we are able "to transmit the meaning of the revolt without naming it, simply by means of technical principles and professional attitudes" (ibid.). The composition, rather than the sequence, of thought is complex, notably in the changing status of the word "meaning": "negation" leads us to the "meaning" of theatre, yet the act of "negation", in the concept of "revolt", also has its own "meaning", which "we" may seek to hide. In fact, the term "meaning" seems to signify its own absence or indeterminacy in this argument, and what are apparent, by contrast, are the "technical principles and professional attitudes" in a given performance, "which must above all be 'well-done'". There is also an important theoretical tension between "the theatre", understood as a conceptual entity, and individual performances:

> It is the performance, not the theatre, which lasts only a short time. The theatre is made up of traditions, of conventions, of institutions, of habits which endure throughout time. The weight of this endurance is so heavy that it often prevents life from emerging and replaces it with routine.   (ibid.)

In this formulation it is the theatre's "ephemerality" which effectively saves it from itself; when "it" combats its ephemeral nature by means of continuities, it risks theoretical disapproval, as continuities are represented as "habits" and "routine". Opposing "the unavoidably transient nature of theatre" must, therefore, not "mean" protecting "tradition"; nor should "film and electronics" be allowed to "seduce" the theatre. These conserve performances unchanged, but

> they obscure the awareness that the essential dimension of the theatrical performance resists time not by being frozen in a recording but by changing itself.

> The extreme limit of this transformation is found in the individual memories of the individual spectators.   (ibid.)

Barba's interest here is in a theoretical spectator guarding, through memory, a theoretical essence—"the essential dimension"—of theatre, which is realized in the "transformation" achieved by 'naturally' ephemeral performances. This 'essence' of theatre is undoubtedly related to what Barba means by "meaning", and it requires "memories" for its 'reception' and sustenance. The distinction is between theories of theatrical reception which adopt an empirical attitude to the theatre, in the reception of particular performance events, and a theory of reception in which "the theatre" is itself, primarily, a theoretical entity. To this complex Barba adds his own rejection of "the public" in favour of "individual spectators", in a confirmation and clarification of his emphasis on "the few" in "Eurasian Theatre":

> The necessity of distinguishing between public and spectators derives from the will to consciously exploit an inevitable condition: even though some or many reactions can be unanimous and common (these are the public's reactions), communion is impossible. Intense relationships can be established, but they are based upon reciprocal estrangement.   (97)

The theoretical insistence on the priority of "estrangement" over "reactions" that may be "unanimous and common", which displaces the "public" from theoretical importance, has a corollary in the kind of performance that may be constructed:

> Instead of trying to construct a performance as an organism which speaks to all spectators with the same voice, one can think of it as being composed of many voices which speak together without each voice necessarily speaking to all spectators.   (ibid.)

Barba records the fact that Odin's performances have "contained fragments (sometimes entire sequences) which are directed to certain specific spectators", but then accepts that he has cited "an extreme case". There is an opposite pole, "where everything must be equally decodifiable by the maximum number of people", and an 'exploration' of the "gamut of possibilities" between these two poles allows one

> to cross barriers of language, of social and cultural divisions, of different levels of education—not because the performance is 'universal' and says something acceptable to everyone, but because at some moments

it speaks to all while at other moments it speaks differently to each individual. (ibid.)

What Barba offers "the spectator" is not a discovery of the "'real meaning'" of "a story", but the opportunity "to ask her/himself questions about the meaning". "Meaning" once again removes itself, from event into essence, from perceptive faculties into memory: "The performance is the beginning of a longer experience."

This complex and contentious theoretical preamble is followed by Barba's introduction of the 'four spectators' whom he instructs the director to envisage. The director must be loyal both to the actors and to "the spectators", and the latter term contains a theoretical mandate, in the separation of "spectator" from "public":

> Loyalty to the spectator consists of assuring that each spectator is not patronized by the performance, does not feel treated like a number or like 'a part of the public', but experiences the performance as if it were made *only for her/him*, in order to whisper something personal to her/him. (98)

This is an extreme rendition of the "asociality" of theatre, expressed in the "whisper" passed to an audience of "individuals". The skills of the director must include those techniques which are necessary "to break up the unity of the public on the mental level", and included in those techniques is the skill of "de-composing the spectators' possible behaviors into certain basic attitudes" (ibid.). Barba then identifies his 'four spectators':

> —the child who perceives the actions literally;
> —the spectator who thinks s/he doesn't understand but who, in spite of her/himself, dances;
> —the director's alter ego;
> —the fourth spectator who sees *through* the performance as if it did not belong to the world of the ephemeral and of fiction. (99)

The director must justify all moments of the performance in relation to these four spectators, and each "individual" may be thought to combine all four "in differing proportions". Barba's explanations of the first two spectators simply confirm his brief formulas; the third spectator, it seems, is one who "is minutely informed about all the contents of the performance", and granted Barba's admission that "the actors and director are also spectators", it would seem that this category includes involved practitioners. The fourth spectator sees "that which no spectator can materially see": the embroidery hidden from immediate view which is there because "it has a value for the individual actor and the director", and the left hand of the performer when the right hand is displayed. In at least one sense, the fourth spectator is not a spectator at all:

> S/he sees the 'well-done' work even when it is secret and s/he recognizes if the actor is doing it because of a necessity which goes beyond any spectator's exigencies.   (100)

Beyond technique, beyond the public, and even beyond the spectator. The theory of theatre anthropology transcends the theatre, negating its "ephemerality" in order to find its "essential dimension":

> The fourth spectator is the collaborator who helps us negate the theatre by doing it.   (ibid.)

PART THREE

5

Some Observations on Stanislavski and Brecht

In accordance with the objectives of this book, I do not intend to give a detailed commentary on what has been conventionally known as "the theory of the modern stage" or, more succinctly, as 'modern theory'.[1] What I offer in this chapter is a short set of merely marginal observations to that reception, which may be taken to comply with my interests in the discourse of theory, as these have been expressed in Parts One and Two of this book.

5.1 STANISLAVSKI

In the English-speaking world, any dependence on 'modern theory' has been for most a dependence on translation, and as I have observed elsewhere, the period from the late 1950s to the late 1960s was decisive in creating a canon of modern theory for consumption and influence.[2] To this period belong the substantial initiatives in the translation of theatre writings by Artaud, Brecht, and Grotowski, with the English-language publication of Stanislavski's "system" completed in the same years. Although Grotowski does certainly belong, as a practitioner and theorist, to the period of general liberalization in Poland from the later 1950s, it is relatively plain that much that was received as 'new' at this time was simply unknown in the English-speaking countries, rather than new.[3] The circumstances in which Artaud and Brecht had initiated their practice and interventions were, at the time of the translations of their written theory, already historic, but this did not inhibit a widespread response. The composite reception established at that time has encountered objections, but in general they have come too late (and have been made too infrequently) to have had much effect on the creation of an English-language 'Brecht' and an English-language 'Artaud'. Even the objections can propose, as an alternative, a method of supposedly 'simple matching', which does not seem adequate to the scale of the problem:

> Much epic confusion...could be avoided if those looking at a Brecht play of any period would simply match it up with Brecht's theoretical pronouncements of that same period.[4]

This is the Brecht-scholar John Fuegi, who has done more than most to revise conventional thinking about the composite 'Brecht', most significantly in terms of authorship.[5]

A contemporary revisionism, in relation to the Anglo-American 'Stanislavski', has placed an accent on a restored awareness of the textual history of the translations and Russian editions of his system. A new set of translations, based on the amended Russian edition, will provide the Anglo-American reader with an "uncensored and unabridged" version of the theorist, thus removing the apostrophes from 'Stanislavski'.[6] But the difficulties with the system plainly do not end there, since, of the three books which contain it, only the first—*An Actor Prepares*—was published during Stanislavski's lifetime. The textual history of the English-language translations has been one of controversy from that time, and the arguments and emendations prove that 'Stanislavski', like 'Homer' according to many authorities, is still being written. In some respects the revisionism must be welcome, but in others it seems to detract from an attention to the nature of the discourses associated with the name and the system. The curious absence of a critical, even a stylistic analysis in English of the three systematic books may actually have been determined by these uncertainties, which at the same time have not inhibited a relatively gross reception and adoption of them as prescriptions for a method of training. The historic facts are disturbing, because the system has had the unique characteristic of contributing to the formation of standard principles in what were the dominant nations of two blocs for much of the twentieth century.[7] If this remarkable characteristic is firmly rather than casually acknowledged, the importance of the intriguing issue of translation and emendation must surely diminish, perhaps even to the point where it reveals itself to be a distraction. Whatever may be significant about the text of the written discourse that constitutes the system, it cannot be a matter of the relationship between a 'pure' source and its contamination, because the significance is as much contained in the contaminated as in the pure. It might be an unnecessary sophistication to claim that the significance is actually contained in the confrontation of the two, one in which claims to priority (on the American side, for the earlier works) and to the undeniable authenticity of a native language mark the struggle over the ownership of an essence of theatrical creation.

Yet this intriguing possibility of Stanislavski as the cultural site of an ideological confrontation does not exhaust the issue of the figure-as-system. Stanislavski also continues to exist as biography, and here there has been a further exchange, which might also be ascribed to a confrontation of the claims of authenticity with those of an alien, yet hosting language. I refer most immediately to the succession of biographies by Magarshack, Polyakova and Benedetti, in which the Moscow publication by Progress Publishers of Polyakova in translation appears perhaps as an intervention, now superseded by Benedetti.[8] What is remarkable in both these instances, of a 'life' and a 'system', is that reception has sustained the discourses established by the 'master'. I do not make this point in order to extend the controversy, painfully, over the composition and compilation of the systematic books, but to draw attention to the peculiar priority of autobiography over biographies. One of the plainer certainties in the textual history is that Stanislavski, faced by pressing financial needs, did dictate *My Life in Art* to an assistant, and that it was "translated chapter by chapter".[9] As an index of authenticity, autobiography might in other circumstances seem to exercise a firm authority; but nothing to do with 'Stanislavski' can evade the textual agony of rewriting, since the author himself conducted revisions of the text for subsequent Russian editions.

The textuality of *My Life in Art* is not, however, to be deduced solely from its textual history, which it shares in some respects, though less contentiously, with the systematic works. That the succession of biographies has been continued is in itself an implicit acknowledgement of the need for a writing-over of the discourse of autobiography, a kind of palimpsest of a 'real life' account by a 'real' life. Scholars may rightly point to a defective memory on the part of the autobiographer, to matters of accuracy, and to a demand from attentive readers for amplification, for greater or supplementary detail. But the effect is to pronounce this autobiography not, irreverently, as a form of fiction as opposed to fact, but as a text which has to be read in some way 'outside' its own explicit subject: whatever *My Life in Art* may be, it is not an authentic substitute for biography. Perhaps the best analogy is Wagnerian: *My Life in Art* is the prelude to a great trilogy of theory, separated yet intimately connected. Yet if it is connected, how do we read the whole great work? Do we understand the written system, like *My Life in Art*, to be fact in a discursive form that has some of the attractive and conventional qualities of fictional narratives? Or, to place the accent on the beginning rather than the end of composition, does *My Life in Art* have to be understood as a prelude to a theoretical fiction: an autobiographical discourse itself as theoretically directed and ordered as the system to which it is already dedicated?

I would propose that *My Life in Art* be read as an allegory of power. That the discourse of the system itself was conceived allegorically is probably too well known to need comment from me:

> He had originally intended to use the typically eighteenth-century contrivance of giving his characters unlikely but significant names: Rassudov [from the Russian word for reason—Tr.], Chuvstov [emotion], Tvortsvov [creator]...Later, however, he made subtle changes, transforming Tvortsvov to Tortsov, Chuvstvov to Shustov, and so on.[10]

My Life in Art begins with "Old Russia", and ends with the discovery of "the streak of gold", the hope dependent on divine help ("May the Lord aid me in this task!") to "describe in a well-balanced system all that I have reached after long researches".[11] In the penultimate chapters the War, the Second and the Third Revolutions (both of 1917) are recorded, and the account closes in chronological terms in 1919, but is surpassed by the future-present promise of the 'disclosure' of the "secret of our art". The text of political evolution and revolution is paralleled by the text of personal and theatrical 'history', to an extent that exceeds any requirement for an historical panorama. I can cite here two prominent examples, that of the foundation of the first Studio and the divergence between Nemirovich-Danchenko and Stanislavski, which have an almost ludicrous correlation to the grander political sphere. In the first instance, the fortunes of the Studio, its temporary realization of the aspiration of its founders, and its final "liquidation" accompany the premature aspirations of the First Revolution of 1905 (*My Life in Art*, 425–38: "The Studio on Povarskaya"). In the second instance, the split between Nemirovich-Danchenko and Stanislavski, between the Theatre and the second Studio, is placed towards the end of the narrative, and the record of the War and the Revolutions of 1917. Stanislavski's "system" was "accepted in part by the Theatre", while the Studio and the later succession of Studios became the historical site of the progress of his principles. The division between Theatre and Studio is related by Stanislavski to the disintegration of the "quiet and balanced life of Russia", as a succession of generations preceded the moment of final overthrow: "The pillars of government were beginning to tremble" (533, in the context of the general narrative, 525–41).[12] The text, as it is composed, is open to diverse readings, with conflicts between factions associated with Kerensky and Lenin, or between Mensheviks and Bolsheviks for later Soviet readers, providing the satisfactions of allegory.

What might have induced the creation of this Lilliput of art for the satisfactions of first an American and then a Soviet readership? On the one hand, one might be inclined to sense a salutary deference to the forces and powers of 'historical necessity': one that for an American readership would acknowledge the pre-eminence of disturbing but undeniable historical events, and for a Soviet readership would signal the subordination of art to the (equally undeniable) imperatives of political change. There are further purposes: by allowing his 'life' to be overtly 'historical', Stanislavski can secure the final independence of his 'art' from either history or politics, in the postponed realization of a systematic theory. But as an allegory of politics, and of the evolution of power to a point where principles culminate in practice, *My Life in Art* can also conceal the truth about that culminating "truth" of the art of acting, which is that "the principles were always the same" (534). This is the intended quality of Stanislavski's artistic revolution, and the proper objective of the constant state of aspiration which forms most of the discourse of the autobiography; the theoretical "system" will ensure that nothing will change. What remains to be written will not be merely the tabulation of a method, but the guarantee of stability, a "gold" standard. So the allegory extends itself. What has come to pass in Russia has come to pass in the theatre, and through the "life in art" of this historic practitioner, and that is and will be the permanence of a system. What is reserved, through the apparent deference of allegory, is the issue of whether the two systems—artistic and political—will correspond.

My Life in Art is also a collection of fables, for which the allegory of the evolution of the theatrical art as a political history serves as the grand narrative. There is, as a prelude, the fable of rejection, of the *recusatio* or refusal of other disciplines. So Stanislavski, the 'stage name', passes through drama school, the ballet—"The ballet is a beautiful art, but not for us, not for dramatic artists" (102), the Conservatoire and the Russian Musical Society, through operetta and opera, which all prove unsatisfactory. There is also the fable of the utopian community, of the fullness of a 'life as art' for actors meeting "in nature, in common work on the soil, in fresh air, in the light of the sun", as well as "on the stage" (538). "Creative work on the soil" in the spring and summer, and even in the autumn, would match and support their creative life in the theatre. But these were "dreams" of completeness, "unrealizable", which "had to wait for a better time". The principal reason why this was "nothing but a dream" is revealed in yet another, masterful fable, which is that of the paradox of the "primary importance" of actors and of their constitutional inadequacy. This paradox is presented as a fable of discovery, which leads inexorably to the conclusion of a 'life in art', and which requires an accumulation of perceptions. Early experience is the pedagogue:

> These performances seemed to be created for the purpose of showing the primary importance on the stage of the actor himself and the entire lack of necessity of the whole production and all beautiful scenery in the absence of the most important person in the theatre—the actor.   (143)

This "primary importance" of "the actor" is inalienable, but it proves to be a responsibility for which actors are inadequate. The sharpness and the temerity of a fundamental reproof are first mitigated through the experience of Stanislavski himself as an actor, who accepts criticism from Ernesto Rossi for his portrayal of Othello. The perception on this occasion is that 'talent' and "natural gifts" are not enough: "one needs ability, technique, and art" (287). Perceptions are delayed in this fable, but they are ordered to a distinct and uncompromising conclusion, which renders the banality of these first reservations disproportionately significant. The foundation of the First Studio in 1905, of which the account comes after some four-fifths of the total narrative, provokes a new perception in an adjusted formula:

> I was convinced again that between the dreams of the stage director and their realization there is a tremendous distance, and that the theatre is first of all intended for the actor and cannot exist without him. For the new art new actors were necessary, actors of a new sort with an altogether new technique.   (437)

This formula prefigures the failure of the later utopian "dream", in the substitution of a "tremendous" theoretical "distance" for the physical immediacies of "realization" in an ideal community alternating between work on the land and work on the stage. Discursive attention to the actor's inadequacies from this point begins to be insistent. A perception that "the failure of the actors was hidden by the successful performance of the other workers in the theatre", that "the actors were protected by the other artists" is fixed to the year 1907, well after the productions of Chekhov's plays. It is followed relentlessly by the full, magisterial condemnation, which is also a prescription for a remedy:

> The production had only one good thing about it—it showed me in practice the complete inadequacy of our art and of our actors, who were to be taught from the very beginning in their art and made to create fundamentals for it.   (481)

The mastery that finally condemns the actor is not merely incidental to the outcome of the narrative. 'Stanislavski' is, as a figure of his own stage, both actor and stage director, and much of the drama of *My Life in Art* is composed of the tensions between these two personalities of the autobiography. Two aspects in particular are registered in the early "life": the requirement of the actor for attention and praise from the stage director, and the crucial distinction between the contributions of actor and stage director. What is important about praise from the stage director is that it should not simply be a variety of "general" applause, but should have the specific and intimate capacity to unite with the "moment" of "inner satisfaction":

> It was not enough for me that after the act was finished I received general praise from all for all of my work. How important it would have been to receive the stage director's praise during the very moment of my inner satisfaction. But stage directors did not, it seemed, recognize the importance of that yet.   (172)

"Yet" is prophetic and promissory, a discursive device that renders a perception into part of a fable, a constituent and continuing part of the larger narrative. In a production of 1896 Stanislavski both acts and directs, not for the first time, but here he chooses decisively to allocate the responsibility for 'creation' to the stage director. In his judgement on his own powers, the 'scales' fatefully incline to one side of the balance:

> But who had created these strong moments, the stage director with his production or the actor with his playing? Of course, it was the stage director, and the laurels were his rather than the actor's. And

> the preponderance of usefulness was also in the balance cup of the
> stage director.   (244)

The "primary importance" initially asserted for the actor begins to be qualified, as 'the actor' is prepared for an historic transformation from being the subject of the stage into being the object of theory.

The transformation has, in part, a mythical status, of the child who discovers on his quest a crock of gold. Autobiography is perhaps never quite what it seems, because it is, in linguistic terms, little more than the free play of the subject to order its own objects. For Stanislavski, the discourse of autobiography allows him to situate himself as both actor and director, and so finally to dispose of 'the actor' as he chooses. But the disposal is prior to the actual composition of the text, in much the same way as a 'life in art' may already be read as a political allegory of the events it could not predict, or as an allegory of power in general. Power is the decisive determination of an 'other' as object, but as we now know from many analyses, it also exists by writing itself on both subject and object. For Stanislavski, as the child of his own narrative, there is a terrible absence of power, marked by the abdication of the father from his responsibilities over language and silence. The incident is introduced as an example of his own obstinacy, when he replies to his father's correction with a repetitive and impotent threat (ch. III, 21–31, particularly 25–8). His recalcitrant "I won't let you go to Auntie Vera" becomes symbolic, through its numerous repetitions, of the incontinence and futility of the actor's speech when it fails to encounter the expected and foreclosing authority of 'direction'. The possibilities of delivery become endless as well as impotent, and end in 'powerlessness' and fear:

> I repeated the same sentence insistently, and almost impudently, changing the intonation of the words each time.
>   I hammered at him in dull and obstinate anger, powerless to combat the evil force which had carried me away. Feeling how weak I was in its grasp, I began to be afraid of it.   (26)

The mimicry of the recusant director's gestures and movements provides no solace, and when remorse comes it is too late. *My Life in Art* is the tale of the child who discovered the "secret", hidden by past generations and "jealously guarded", which alone might combat "this so dangerous circumstance for the actor" of "empty theatrical self-consciousness":

> I want to compare myself to a gold-seeker who must first make his way through almost impassable jungles in order to find a place where he may discover a streak of gold... (571–2)

The required power over the actor finds its charter in the founding of the Moscow Art Theatre, which occupies a central position in the narrative, compared as it is to the "peace conference at Versailles" (294). This pointed, if partly flippant, anachronism carries plain connotations of a new order, and brings an emphasis to bear on the last in Stanislavski's list of artistic "questions", which is that of the "mutual relations" between Nemirovich-Danchenko and himself (ibid.). As Stanislavski remarks, the division of powers, accompanied by veto, which gave him authority "in matters of stage direction and artistic production" took into account his life 'outside' art (297). He was, without demur, willing to recognize Nemirovich-Danchenko's "superiority" in administration:

> Besides, it was enough that I did administrative work in my factory and my business office, for I was a director and chairman of a manufacturing and trading company. I was forced to continue this work parallel with my acting and stage direction throughout the whole course of my scenic activities, and right up to the very beginning of the Soviet system. (296)

The settlement included the proscription of some actors, alongside the selection of others, and the arrangement—the principles are stated at this time—of warm and clean working conditions for the company. The price of this 'accommodation', according to the narrative, was a severe set of "artistic ethics", which were entered "into the minutes" (298). In these, the theoretical "primary importance" of the actor ensured a diminution of standing. "'There are no small parts, there are only small actors'" carries the magisterial tone, and the onus lies on the actor to "'love art, and not one's self in art'" and to "'become an artist'". The corollary of this is that shortcomings will be eliminated, and the list of 'selfish' and 'inartistic' failings offers a model for resolute correction:

> 'Lateness, laziness, caprice, hysterics, bad character, ignorance of the role, the necessity of repeating anything twice are all equally harmful to our enterprise and must be rooted out.' (298–9)

In some respects the "peace conference" of Nemirovich-Danchenko and Stanislavski put an end to the "despotism" of which Stanislavski repeatedly and prominently accuses himself, because it regulated it. In other respects, the regulation of an abundant power made it more instrumental. In particular, Stanislavski begins to direct attention more noticeably to his struggle with the actor's will, as the "old, obstinate, experienced actors" refuse to be instructed in "the fundamentals of our art" (306–7). The tactics on this occasion are to expose the "obstinate actors" to the achievements of their "younger comrades" in rehearsal, and this shock-treatment has its effects:

> I remember that after one such rehearsal which saw the brilliant failure of an experienced actor, he was so shaken by what had happened that he came to my home...in the middle of the night and awakened me. I came out in my night clothes and we talked far into the dawn. At last he was listening to me like a scholar that had failed at an examination, and he swore that he would be obedient and attentive in the future. (307)

The question of the will becomes paramount as those "fundamentals of our art"—and we should recall that "the principles were always the same"—are transformed narratively into a "system". When he begins to "put the results of my new experiments into practice", Stanislavski encounters "great resistance", and only gradually understands "the real reason" for his lack of success (526). Actors are "energetic in the sphere of purely physical work":

> But if you touch their wills ever so lightly, and put before them inner spiritual problems, so as to call forth their conscious or superconscious emotions, you will be met with a rebuff, for the will of the actor is not well exercised; it is lazy, capricious. (ibid.)

The magisterial condemnation of the actor as 'lazy' is succeeded by an analysis which identifies the need for an "inner technique" which induces a "proper creative mood" in the will:

> That inner technique of which I preached and which is necessary for the creation of the proper creative mood is based in its most important parts on the process of will. (527)

What the stage director and artistic therapist requires are "the right words that build a road not to the mind but to the heart of the actor, to his superconscious intuition". As theorist, he will require far more:

> The words that were still unrealized by myself the actors understood with their minds, but not with their feelings, and this satisfied neither

them nor me. Besides, my system cannot be explained in an hour or in a day even. It must be systematically and practically studied for years.   (529)

As a system of production, which Stanislavski in his "life in art" understands under the dignities of the word 'creation', the "system" is historically decisive in removing the actor's art from the control of the actor, and associating it with the novel power of the stage director. The masterful discourse of theory aims to inhabit the will of the performer throughout a 'life in art', and the theoretical model is—in its assumed historical innocence, and its triumphant convictions—resolutely managerial. The expropriation of the "will" as the "superconscious" has its plain analogies in the Freudian expropriation of the soul as the "unconscious"; but the analogies are those of a masterful discourse, rather than of method. Derivation or influence are not in question: Stanislavski's "system" is not a therapy of any sort, because the supposedly required correction is a premise of the system itself. What is fascinating about its achievement is that Stanislavski's artistic 'revolution' projected the authoritarian presuppositions of a Moscow burgher into the Soviet doctrine of 'socialist realism'. The political allegory of *My Life in Art* is illusory, because the expropriation of the old "principles" does not finally produce an equation of system with revolutionary system, but retains production in the control of a regulated director. Yet this in itself makes *My Life in Art* another kind of allegory of power, as the course of theatrical evolution signals to the discerning reader the stability and productivity of a bourgeois model of management. What cannot, in material terms, be practised after the Third Revolution may be sustained in art and secured by theory.[13]

5.2 BRECHT

Recent commentaries on Brecht have produced two themes, which may be related to what is described as the pervasive "Brecht-*Müdigkeit*", or 'Brecht-weariness'. The first of these is a renewed concern for the issue of pleasure in Brechtian theatre, which is particularly prominent in recent statements made in defence of Brechtian aesthetics. The second is a concern to achieve a 'postmodern' definition of Brecht's activity and status, which can be connected to the belief that Brecht's "productivism" is an "ethic that is now totally outmoded".[14] This was the opinion of Tatlow in an essay with the title "The Way Ahead: Brecht and Postmodernism", which dates from the mid-1980s, and Tatlow foresaw a constructive role for Brecht in the "formulation" of "postmodernist positions":

> Re-reading Brecht might involve realising a neglected potential with the capacity not merely to relate passively to postmodernist positions but to contribute to their formulation.[15]

Reconstituting Brecht is not a matter for casual initiative, and it is interesting that this proposal was made in the influential *Yearbook* of the International Brecht Society, which was formed "on the model of Brecht's own unrealized plan for the Diderot *Gesellschaft*", as its programme regularly announces. The Diderot Society, as Brecht envisaged it, had as its aim "to gather together the skilled experience of its members to create a terminology, to control scientifically the theatrical conceptions of the human community", and it was to include figures such as Auden, Eisenstein, Jean Renoir and Piscator.[16] The scheme of regulation is inherited, with Brecht himself substituted for the Encyclopedist, and the scholarly community for the community of practitioners. So Brecht becomes the authority for monitoring the criticism and reception of his own theory and practice, and the primacy of Brecht must remain evident in any reconstitution of that critical reception. A 'postmodern Brecht' must be found, at least in principle, to validate any 'postmodern' reading of Brecht.

This task was undertaken by Wright in the later 1980s in what she termed a "re-presentation", which found Brecht to be "sceptical of what Jean-François Lyotard called the great narrative", and to be a "deconstructionist *avant la lettre*":

> In common with the poststructuralist writer/critic, Brecht proclaims that the author is not the creator of an original work.[17]

The first claim is certainly contentious, since Lyotard's concept of the "great narrative" unquestionably included exactly those narratives of emancipation and Marxism to which Brecht subscribed. The second claim has achieved ironies unintended by Wright with the publication of Fuegi's study of the multiple authorship of 'Brechtian' work;[18] but Wright's principal challenge was to what might be called the orthodox liberal reception of Brecht. Rejecting the "tripartite" scheme of development advanced by Esslin, which posited an evolution from an "anarchist/nihilist" early Brecht to a "rationalist" middle period to a final "resolution" achieved in the major dramas, she advocated a relativist reading:

Would it not be better to read, teach, and stage Brecht as a source of discontinuous insight, extracting from his theory and practice what seems most valuable at the time, rather than continue to purvey the three-phase package?[19]

The difficulty with this proposition is that it appears to be pragmatic, and Wright leaves the words "better" and "valuable" unexamined. In suggesting that the early plays (specifically *Baal* and *In the Jungle of the Cities*) might provide the means for the project of "co-opting" Brecht "as postmodernist", Wright alluded to a concept of a "political use-value":

> if they have any political use-value it is perhaps more likely to be found in their formal properties than in any uniform conceptual view.[20]

The expression is tentative, and does not clarify whether a "political use-value" is really understood by Wright to be important in the context of postmodernism, nor what exactly is meant by "political". This can hardly be a redundant question, granted the strong association of Brecht with a particular political philosophy, and with a particular political regime in the German Democratic Republic.

Wright's few explicit definitions of 'postmodernism', or 'the postmodern' do not provide much help in understanding the central proposition. In relation to Brecht's aesthetics, an emphasis on "individualism" seems a paradoxical choice:

> If modernism is to be characterized as breaking with tradition while still retaining an individualist stance, then postmodernism can be seen as calling into question both tradition and individualism.[21]

Yet this supposedly Brechtian critique of "individualism", which must be represented in the early plays if Wright is "to turn the early Brecht...into a postmodern Brecht", has to be reconciled with what Wright describes as "a move away from soliciting any kind of collective perception" in just those same plays.[22] The same kinds of apparent contradiction make it difficult in reading the book to understand how the *Messingkauf Dialogues* can be "Brecht's most distinguished achievement", when "his most radical ideas" were developed "in his early and most marginal works".[23] It may possibly be a different thing to be "radical" and to be "distinguished". But if this is the case, then at least two parts of the rejected tripartite scheme of an orthodox Brecht seem to be still in place, if we read "distinguished" for the "resolution" of the later works. The examples that Wright selects for "the Brechtian postmodern" are the work of Bausch, Müller, and Wilson, yet their exemplary status is confusing. Much of Wright's emphasis seems to be placed on the considerable differences between Bausch and Brecht, and the same becomes true of the discussions of both Wilson and Müller. "Where Brecht attacks in full consciousness, Müller undermines via the unconscious" is a statement that would leave the 'postmodern' meaning little more than 'very different', and some attention to "the historical process" results in a similar, and similarly intractable distinction:

> Brecht was trying to reconceptualize the historical process at a public level; Müller is reconceptualizing it at a private one.[24]

In fact, in the course of the argument, Wright presents a confusing and apparently contradictory conflation of Müller's preferences, which allocates to 1977 his "paramount interest in...the Lehrstücke", and then disarmingly notes that in the same year "Müller categorically rejected the Lehrstück as Brecht conceived it".[25] The first part of this paradox is in fact drawn from an interview given by Müller in 1975:

> At the moment, the Lehrstücke and one or two fragments are the most important thing in Brecht for me. It seems to me that the early plays are, at the present time, more interesting than the so-called classic plays.[26]

Subsequently, in 1977, Müller wrote the "farewell to the Lehrstück" which was noted by Wright in a letter to the Brechtian scholar Steinweg:

> I have sought with growing reluctance to pick out something remotely useful from the word-sludge (the sludge is my part) of our conversation on the Lehrstück. The search has been a failure; nothing occurs to me any more about the Lehrstück.[27]

The "farewell" was given a significant context, in which Müller rejected the notion of himself as a theorist:

> Today more than in 1957, plays are written for the theatre instead of for a public. I am not going to twiddle my thumbs until a (revolutionary) situation comes along. But theory without basis is not my trade, I am not a philosopher, who needs no ground for thought, nor am I an archaeologist, and I think we must say farewell to the Lehrstück until the next earthquake.[28]

With this declaration Müller marked a significant division between theatrical tendency and critical tendency, for the addressee Steinweg—as Wright records in her first chapter—was responsible for producing a critically favourable re-assessment of the Lehrstücke. It is Steinweg's re-evaluation that provides Wright with a model for her advocacy of a relativist or pragmatic 'postmodern' reading, as well as for "a radically different theatre of the future":

> The actors, all amateurs of one kind or another, occupy a double role of observing ('spectating') and acting, working and reworking a communal set text which is perpetually alterable, the object being to turn art into a social practice, an experiment in socially productive behaviour.[29]

Wright's intention was plainly to combine both critical and theatrical tendencies, despite their apparent opposition, in activity for a "postmodern Brecht". But if Wilson and Bausch are dubiously Brechtian, Müller for his part is emphatic in his contempt for 'the postmodern':

> *Question:* Could you explain what in your opinion would constitute a Postmodern drama, a Postmodern theatre?
> *Answer:* The only Postmodernist I know of was August Stramm, a modernist who worked in a post office.[30]

The respondent here is Müller; the only recourse for a postmodern analysis would appear to be to accuse him of 'false consciousness'.

Pleasure is a sensitive topic in the contemporary reception of Brecht, not solely for aesthetic reasons, but also because of decades of production and favour which have resulted in the Brecht-*Müdigkeit*. Contributions from directors of the Berliner Ensemble in the volume *Re-Interpreting Brecht* drew attention repeatedly to the social function of pleasure in Brechtian and contemporary theatre. Wekwerth considered that the "role of pleasure" might make the function of theatre "more complex and at the same time more concrete", and Tenschert allotted to pleasure the significance of being the "prime aim of the theatre":

> The prime aim of the theatre, then, is to convey pleasure in the vitality of human beings in an entertaining way. The intention is to increase people's joy in living and to strengthen their will to live.[31]

Wekwerth was concerned that, with regard to Brecht, people "assume the primacy of edification over amusement, clarity over emotion".[32] A similar reaction was expressed more recently by Brooker, who wrote of

> the (unfounded) charge that Brecht outlawed feelings and amusement when in fact he wished to prevent empathy (one type of feeling) and encourage instead the broad pleasures, whether high or low, of a productive life—including the pleasures of learning and the passions of a committed, critical attitude.[33]

In his summary of attitudes to Brecht in France during the 1980s, Dort also concludes that "he is generally thought to be dull, that is, when he is not dismissed as old hat". Völker, the biographer of Brecht, contrasts productions by the Berliner Ensemble unfavourably with a production by Strehler which he describes, in terms that are intentionally 'non-Brechtian', as a "brilliant Cinemascope soap opera...a bright, festive socio-romantic musical".[34]

The "productivism" which Tatlow described, in his view of the "way ahead" for "Brecht and postmodernism", as "an ethic that is now totally outmoded" is explicitly involved by Brooker in the Brechtian conception of pleasure. It is, to summarize briefly, present in formulations throughout Brecht's written theory. So, in 1927, "theatre, art and literature...have to form the 'ideological superstructure' for a solid, practical rearrangement of our age's way of life", a relatively simple and coercive Marxist prescription.[35] With the advancement of proposals for a "critical" method of acting, and the introduction of a "critical attitude into art", the notion of "productivity" in "enterprises that improve people's lives" retains its place:

> A critical attitude of this type is an operative factor of productivity; it is deeply enjoyable as such, and if we commonly use the term 'arts' for enterprises that improve people's lives why should art proper remain aloof from arts of this sort?   (*Brecht on Theatre*, 146–7)

The comparison made through the common term "arts" is of the 'fine' arts such as theatre with the technical arts, and it offers an instrumental definition of theatre as a function of production. This functionalism involves the notion of pleasure, but under a more precise analysis it also includes a reference to feelings and "impulses":

> We need a type of theatre which not only releases the feelings, insights, and impulses possible within the particular historical field of human relations in which the action takes place, but employs and encourages those thoughts and feelings which help transform the field itself.   (190)[36]

It is this kind of formula which is responsible for the emphasis placed by Tenschert on the intention to "increase people's joy in living and to strengthen their will to live"—Wekwerth also writes of "the increase in humanity's capacity for enjoyment"[37]—and by Brooker on "the pleasures of learning and the passions of a committed, critical attitude".

The problem facing these delightful and apparently justified interpretations—counter-claims are "unfounded", according to Brooker—was neatly expressed by Völker, when he recalled Brecht's comment to the Berliner Ensemble in 1955: "True art is not pleasing."[38] The solution to this apparent dilemma is by no means obscure. In *A Short Organum for the Theatre*, Brecht recapitulates arguments he had made incidentally on many earlier occasions, and compares his "aesthetic" to the increasing possibility of "an aesthetics of the exact sciences" (179–80). Pleasure becomes the opening topic of the discussion, in a formula that identifies pleasure as an Aristotelian 'final cause' of the theatre, which exists and acts with "a view to entertainment". The procedure of the discussion is supposedly scholastic, a supposition which contrasts intentionally with the occasional and at times polemical presentations of the earlier arguments:

> Let us treat the theatre as a place of entertainment, as is proper in an aesthetic discussion, and try to discover which type of entertainment suits us best. (180)

"Entertainment" has always been the "business" of the theatre, and the theatre is not elevated in status by the introduction of a moral purpose: "Nothing needs less justification than pleasure." Brecht seeks his authority in Aristotle, and his interpretation of Aristotelian catharsis is accordingly hedonistic, "a purification which is performed not only in a pleasurable way, but precisely for the purpose of pleasure" (181). The important distinction that follows, between "higher and lower degrees of pleasure" and correspondingly "weaker (simple) and stronger (complex) pleasures" in artistic creations is a conflation of Greek propositions, as its immediate context makes clear. The concluding part of the argument contains a summary theory of 'modernity': what is required of the theatre and this enquiry is the 'discovery' of "the special pleasures, the proper entertainment of our own time". To the satisfaction of this requirement the established forms of theatre are an obstacle—"we and our forebears have a different relationship to what is being shown" in the theatre—because these forms do not provide the proper definition of "ourselves" as subjects and objects of representation:

> For when we look about us for an entertainment whose impact is immediate, for a comprehensive and penetrating pleasure such as our theatre could give us by representations of men's life together, we have to think of ourselves as children of a scientific age. (183)

The revised integration of pleasure into theatrical activity takes account of the equation of "science" with "productivity":

> But science and art meet on this ground, that both are there to make men's life easier, the one setting out to maintain, the other to entertain us. In the age to come art will create entertainment from that new productivity which can so greatly improve our maintenance, and in itself, if only it is left unshackled, may prove to be the greatest pleasure of them all. (185)

I am not here, in this summary restatement, specifically concerned with the quality of Brecht's argumentation, but with the apparent dilemma in Brecht's theoretical attitude. Nonetheless, some notes are worthwhile. A "productive attitude" is the disposition appropriate to "productivity"—"that productive attitude in face of nature and society which we children of a scientific age would like to take up pleasurably in our theatre"—and the analysis determines that a "productive attitude is a critical one" (ibid.). We have, apparently, a "great passion for producing", and this predisposition takes the place held in Aristotelian theory by the natural inclination to *mimesis*. "Productivity" in "itself" may become, "in the age to come", the "greatest pleasure of them all", in a prophetic promise of the equation of "productivity" with "pleasure" that might "prove to be" a discursive substitution of the one term for the other. In the meantime, "productivity" and "pleasure" can only meet in theory through the "productive attitude" which "we...take up pleasurably in our theatre". It is a tenuous suggestion, but on it depends such assertions that the theatre may "find enjoyment in teaching and inquiring", and that "the theatre can let its spectators enjoy the particular ethic of their age, which springs from productivity". In the invitation to take up productivity "pleasurably in our theatre" is a curious patriarchal metaphor, that of "the children of a scientific age". The imperative of theory, such as it is, is reliant on a discursive formulation of the "scientific age" as the father, with theory representing the instruction he offers. To adduce a religious model, "productivity" is the son-as-spirit of the "scientific age" as father, with theory as revelation and text, the theatre as church, and joy as the prophetic promise. Banal as this might seem, it may not necessarily be a forced comparison.

What is plain from Brecht's arguments elsewhere is that the appropriate congregation can be closely defined, and this should remove many of the disingenuous difficulties or propositions about the Brechtian notion of pleasure. Most bluntly, the category Brecht has in mind is that of "a fighting people that is changing the real world", and "pleasure" in learning will correspond to a position in the class struggle: "Enjoyment of learning depends on the class situation" (109 and 132).[39] "Criticism of society is ultimately revolution" (146) because the "critical attitude" characteristic of the epic theatre pertains to a revolutionary movement:

> It demands not only a certain technological level but a powerful movement in society which is interested to see vital questions freely aired with a view to their solution, and can defend this interest against every contrary trend.   (76)[40]

In Brecht's understanding, one precondition for a "modern theatre" was the 'completion' of "the theatre's equipment" by technology, and this conjoins with the concept of the "productivity" of the "scientific age" in confirming a specific historical moment for the practice of epic theatre.[41] The requirements of the last formulation are exacting: a "movement" that is "powerful" enough to "defend" its "interest" in a "critical attitude" "against every contrary trend". Any allowance for diversity in the potential audience is categorically related to the issue of allegiance to this movement. So the actor, in "A Short Description of a New Technique of Acting" of 1940, "prompts the spectator to justify or abolish these [social] conditions according to which class he belongs", and a simple division of interest in the theatrical audience is repeatedly assumed in the written theory. The apparent dilemma in the concept of pleasure does not lie in the difficulties of determining an appropriate subject for the "critical" attitude. The problem is the fraught relationship between the "critical" and the "productive attitude" and pleasure. Aristotelian catharsis was "performed...precisely for the purpose of pleasure". But the prophetic Brechtian equation between "productivity" and "pleasure" is postponed through the intervention of "labour" and "terror" in the necessity of *praxis*:

> Let us hope that their theatre may allow them to enjoy as entertainment that terrible and never-ending labour which should

ensure their maintenance, together with the terror of their unceasing transformation. (205)

In this respect, the conclusion of "A Short Organum" is no less formidable than the final dictum of 1955.

The conclusive rule of "terror" in the Brechtian discourse of theory should hardly be surprising, because it can be related to his reading of Lessing and Aristotle. In this set of marginal observations I can draw attention only to two aspects of that reading. The first is that Brecht ascribes to both Lessing and Diderot the conviction that the theatre should combine learning with pleasure:

> Bourgeois revolutionary aesthetics, founded by such great figures of the enlightenment as Diderot and Lessing, defines the theatre as a place of entertainment and instruction. (131)[42]

This representation of the two writers suggests the immediate context of the *Hamburg Dramaturgy*, and Lessing's extended consideration of Diderot's theorizing on comedy and comic character in its later chapters. The reader will not find there any prescription of the kind suggested by Brecht. But Lessing did, in his discussion of tragedy in the same work, dismiss the translation of the Aristotelian *phobos* by the word *Schrecken*, or "terror":

> The word that Aristotle uses means fear; fear and pity, he says, should be evoked by tragedy, not pity and terror...
>
> Fear has, as I have said, been interpreted as terror by our modern translators and expositors, and by this substitution they succeed in picking the strangest quarrel imaginable with the philosopher.[43]

"Terror", in the example of Shakespeare's *Richard III*, provokes only amazement and shock.[44] The problem with "terror", according to Lessing's critical review of commentaries, is that it is an emotion which might be activated indiscriminately, and not just in respect of "virtuous persons", or "equals". In contrast, Lessing interpreted Aristotle as specifying for tragedy a

> fear that we ourselves might thus become objects of pity. In a word this fear is compassion referred back to ourselves.[45]

The Brechtian resumption of "terror" contrasts the "never-ending labour" of "unceasing transformation" to the "pleasure" of the Aristotelian catharsis of pity and fear, which does not entail an "unceasing transformation". Brechtian "terror" eludes the Aristotelian closure with an ironic gesture to a mistranslation, but as one consequence it must also elude the stabilizing, Aristotelian certainty of pleasure.

Through Lessing Brecht became aware of what he might, with motivation, have regarded as a potential component of a theatre of "instruction", in Diderot's attention to the idea of "conditions" replacing characters:

> He [Diderot] therefore proposed that classes instead of characters should be brought upon the stage and desired that their treatment should form the especial labour of serious comedy. He says, "Until now character has been the chief work of comedy and class distinctions were something accidental; now however the social standing must be the chief consideration and the character the accidental...If the character was a little exaggerated, then the spectator would say to himself, this is not I. But he cannot deny that the class represented is his class, he cannot possibly mistake his duties. He is forced to apply that which he hears to himself.[46]

Brechtian "terror" and 'amazement' substitute for Diderot's concept of 'duty' in a context of "transformation" which extends beyond the individual's responsibility for himself. What is implicit and unexamined in the theories of both Diderot and Brecht is a concept of 'will', that commitment to a process of "learning" which, in the case of Brecht, will lead from "terror" to "pleasure". For Brecht in *The Messingkauf Dialogues* "insecurity is at the root of a desire for knowledge", and it is that "desire of the audience for knowledge" on which the Philosopher in those *Dialogues* himself wants to base his theatre.[47] The congruence of "desire" and 'will' (*Wunsch* and *Will*) in the spectator and the directing 'philosophical' intention leads, in this exchange between Dramaturg and Philosopher, to the question of whether it "is possible to enjoy insecurity". The contention of the Philosopher is that "People want to be made just as insecure as they really are":

> *Dramaturg*: You don't want to get rid of the element of insecurity in art, then?
> *Philosopher*: Not by any manner of means.
> *Dramaturg*: So it's back to pity and terror after all?[48]

By a curious irony, the translation of *Furcht* (in "*Furcht und Mitleid*") in this standard English version of the text appears as "terror". At the close of this exchange in *The Messingkauf Dialogues*, the Philosopher is insistent that the Dramaturg should not "jump to conclusions"; but the immediate dangers of a "pleasure" or "joy in insecurity" ("*Freude an der Unsicherheit"*) are evidently those of a reversion to the Aristotelian formula. The imposing Aristotelian closure of emotion, adopted and adapted as it has been by "bourgeois aesthetics", requires of its Marxist counterpart in *A Short Organum* the emotional universality of terror. "True art is not pleasing" is the inevitable conclusion to a 'revolutionary aesthetics' that demands of its spectators a "never-ending labour" of "transformation".

That the Brechtian theory and practice of theatre is inherently rhetorical has been argued briefly by Eagleton, who is precise in his identification and characterization of the will and motivation of the appropriate spectator. Concentrating on the Brechtian concept of the "gest" or "*Gestus*", Eagleton summarizes the achievement of Brechtian presentation in terms assimilated to current criticism:

> Another way of putting this is to claim that Brechtian theater deconstructs social processes into rhetoric, which is to say reveals them as social *practices*.[49]

According to Eagleton, "the revolutionary questioner" entailed in the theoretical practice of Brechtian theatre "accepts that all justification is in this sense rhetorical", but reserves the right to "do something else for a change".[50] But in his analysis of this 'revolutionary question', Eagleton identifies a negative and a positive will, which constitute the "question" itself as "rhetorical in its turn":

> Since such a question is not of course simply requesting historical information, it is rhetorical in its turn—both in the sense that it implies its own answer (we *shouldn't* rest happy with such practices), and in the sense that like the discourses it addresses it is therefore animated by malice, scorn, insecurity, hostility, the will to reject.[51]

This description provides a specific characterization of the appropriate spectator entailed by both Brechtian theory and practice. But it also draws attention to the rhetorical quality of the theoretical discourse that defines both theatre and spectator. I should like to conclude these few observations on Brecht with a brief analysis of "The Street Scene", which Brecht presents as "A Basic Model for an Epic Theatre".

The thesis of this particular theoretical presentation is summarized most clearly at the conclusion to the argument:

> Reflecting along these lines we see that our basic model will work. The elements of natural and of artificial epic theatre are the same. Our street-corner theatre is primitive; origins, aims and methods of

its performance are close to home. But there is no doubt that it is a meaningful phenomenon with a clear social function that dominates all its elements. (*Brecht on Theatre*, 128)

The analogy of the "street-corner theatre" to the "epic theatre" is intended to be a charter offered by the former to the latter. The charter is provided by two characteristics of the "street-corner theatre". Firstly, it has "a clear social function", which the "epic theatre" must also have: the emphasis here lies on "clear", because such a function for the "epic theatre" might be less "clear", or be doubted. The second assertion is that of 'nature' and of 'origins': the "street-corner theatre" is both "natural" and "primitive", and this confirms for theory its authenticity. Accordingly, if the "elements of natural and artificial epic theatre are the same", then the "epic theatre" will also be "natural" and 'original', as Brecht maintains towards the close of the presentation:

> The epic theatre wants to establish its basic model at the street corner, i.e. to return to the very simplest 'natural' theatre, a social enterprise whose origins, means and ends are practical and earthy. (126)

From the beginning of the presentation the "street scene" of the title becomes a chosen "example", with that discursive choice transforming "an incident such as can be seen at any street corner" into an "example of completely simple, 'natural' epic theatre" (121). The "scene" as "theatre" is contained in the 'demonstration' made by an "eyewitness" of a traffic accident to "bystanders", who are defined in two ways: they may not have seen the accident, or they may "simply not agree with him". The "eyewitness" in the discursive transformation becomes the "demonstrator", who takes specific roles—"acts the behaviour of driver or victim or both"—in order to allow those present "to form an opinion about the accident" (ibid.). Brecht is insistent that "the incident is clearly very far from...an artistic one" and that "the demonstrator's performance is essentially repetitive", that the demonstrator "should not transport people from normality to 'higher realms'". Yet despite this insistence, the "demonstration" has a "socially practical significance", which is understood to be dependent on the motivation of "the demonstrator":

> Whether our street demonstrator is out to show that one attitude on the part of driver or pedestrian makes an accident inevitable where another would not, or whether he is demonstrating with a view to fixing the responsibility, his demonstration has a practical purpose, intervenes socially. (122)

The dependence of the "street scene" as "demonstration" on the "demonstrator's purpose" engages the problem of the "engendering of illusion", which Brecht had paradoxically insisted be "excluded from our street scene":

> The demonstrator's purpose determines how thoroughly he has to imitate. Our demonstrator need not imitate every aspect of his characters' behaviour, but only so much as gives a picture. (123)

In the final analysis, the "demonstrator's purpose" replaces the "traffic accident" as the true subject of theory; and theory instructs the demonstrator to 'adopt' the "natural attitude" which presents the "street-corner theatre" as a "repeat" of the "street scene":

> He behaves naturally as a demonstrator, and he lets the subject of the demonstration behave naturally too. He never forgets, nor does he allow it to be forgotten, that he is not the subject but the demonstrator. (125)

'Nature' is a discursive figure, as the "street scene" itself—"natural" and "primitive"—is from the moment of its introduction a figure of theory. But theory insistently removes itself: "There was nothing fabricated about our street accident" (127). Art is not art when theory, and the social 'purposes' sustained by theory, hide behind the scene:

> It will have been observed, not without astonishment I hope, that I have not named any strictly artistic elements as characterizing our street scene and, with it, that of the epic theatre. (126)

6

The Significance of Theory

A series of close readings of this kind should not aim to have any particular conclusion consonant with a personal thesis, nor indeed is there any perceptible end to theory. The objectives of this book remain, at its close, what they were at the beginning, and as a consequence it is obvious that there can be no summary of what was not included. But in this final chapter, I shall offer a discussion of 'interculturalism' as a term, referring to leading presentations by Schechner, Bharucha and Pavis (in 6.1), and a 'modest look' at the ambitions of semiotics as a discourse (in 6.2). In concluding, I shall attempt to fulfil some at least of the implications of the title of this chapter by making suggestions about the possible significance of theory as discourse (in 6.3). Once again, these will rely substantially on readings, in this case, and marginally, of Lacoue-Labarthe and Goffman. The book ends with some reflections on power as it relates to theory, and with some tentative morals for reading theory. That seems to me to be most appropriate: after all, the 'significance of theory' must presumably be understood to lie in the reading of it.

6.1 Disposing of interculturalism: Bharucha, Schechner and Pavis[1]

Bharucha collected a number of essays and studies in his book *Theatre and the World*, of which the earliest was a polemical critique of "attitudes to the Indian theatre" demonstrated by Craig, Grotowski and Schechner in particular.² The book itself was first published in India, and its opening essay, to which I have just referred, appeared in its original form in the *Asian Theatre Journal* for 1984. In the choice of title, which in his book is "Collision of Cultures: Some Western Interpretations and Uses of the Indian Theatre", Bharucha was apparently referring to a phrase of Schechner's from the essay "Performers and Spectators Transported and Transformed".³ My opening concern here will be with both Schechner's and Bharucha's constructions of 'interculturalism', whose currency as a discursive term in performance and theatrical theory dates most decisively from this time, in the later 1970s and the early 1980s.

In a compilation of extracts from his own writings which Schechner made in 1989 entitled "Intercultural Themes", Schechner gave as his first entry on this theme a section from his 1974 essay "From Ritual to Theater and Back" on tourism, in which his interest primarily lay in "the exchange between what's left of traditional performances and emerging tourist shows".⁴ The term 'interculturalism' was not used, but Schechner did refer to tourism as "a two-way street":

> Travelers bring back experiences, expectations, and—if the tourists are practitioners—techniques, scenes, and even entire forms.⁵

But despite writing of "today's cross-cultural feed", in a phrase he was to repeat, he did not extend his discussion of this "two-way street" beyond a brief set of references to "the impact of communal-collective forms on contemporary Western theatre". Interculturalism as a term, and potentially a theoretical concept, appeared prominently in a series of essays beginning in the late 1970s, a number of which Schechner collected in his volume *The End of Humanism*, and in his introduction to an issue of the *The Drama Review* dedicated to "Intercultural Performance", for which Schechner was the guest editor.⁶

In "The Decline and Fall of the (American) Avant-Garde", Schechner retrospectively introduced 'interculturalism' as a characteristic of the American experimental theatre between 1950 and 1975. This was a theatre that was "engaged" and committed to "a network of struggles: political, social, aesthetic, environmental":

> A theatre that was genuinely intercultural, drawing its techniques and examples from within the Euro-American culture area, and from without—from Africa, Asia, Native America, Micronesia: everywhere.⁷

The encomium was followed immediately by an interesting qualification:

People didn't question too much whether or not this interculturalism—this affection for Kathakali exercises, the precision of Noh drama, the simultaneity and intensity of African dance—was a continuation of colonialism, a further exploitation of other cultures. There was something simply celebratory about discovering how diverse the world was, how many performance genres there were, and how we could enrich our own experience by borrowing, stealing, exchanging.[8]

At this point in the essay the concept occasions no further consideration, and so it remains subordinate to the discussion of the American avant-garde in its "heroic" period. Indeed, this experimental theatre movement is plainly the subject of whatever 'interculturalism' is taken to mean (note "our own experience"), and despite Schechner's gesture of qualification, his presentation is unsatisfactory. This is largely because a strong and positive assertion is implicit in the authoritative description of a "theatre that was genuinely intercultural": a form of the 'genuine' that is hard to reconcile with the lack of 'questioning' on which the subsequent paragraph insists. Later in the essay Schechner briefly mentions the reciprocal influence of Western and Asian "modes" of theatre on Asian and Western experimenters, but confines that influence to "technique".[9] Nevertheless, despite its marginal intrusion into the extended analysis, "interculturalism" proves to be Schechner's final selection from a long list of discarded "-isms" in the essay, which includes "Formalism", "Frontalism", "Nihilism", "Personalism", "Narcissism", and—in the conclusion itself—"nationalism", "state capitalism", "corporatism", and "international socialism". Schechner's thesis here is that "the world seems to be learning how to pass from its national phase to its cultural phase", and that "at a fundamental level interculturalism operates in the postmodern world".[10] In fact, "learning" is an inappropriate word, since we must "unlearn what is blocking us from returning to the intercultural":

> From as far back as we can look in human history people have been deeply, continuously, unashamedly intercultural. Borrowing is natural to our species.[11]

The thoroughly rhetorical triad of adverbs is in itself disturbing, alerting the reader to a rhetorical function assigned to the new term. So, indeed, is the assertion of an 'original' status for "interculturalism" in the scheme of decline and consequent revelation. The restoration of a primeval state is the promise of theory, rather than the result of analysis, and inevitably in this kind of scheme current society is to blame for the suppression of what is otherwise 'natural' to the species:

> Only with the advent of a particularly virulent form of Western Euro-American exploitative nationalism, and its ideological outgrowths (including Soviet Marxism) was interculturalism foreclosed. We must work to make this foreclosure temporary. Thus, I am arguing for both an experiment and a return to traditional, even ancient, values.[12]

The question that remains, of course, is quite why "interculturalism" should now be growing and already "operative" when those same relentlessly 'foreclosing' conditions responsible for its theoretical demise show no obvious sign of ameliorating in its favour. A programme is supposedly required for the avant-garde, but it is notably one that will readily permit the subjection of practice to theory, and "interculturalism" as a concept functions in exactly this manner. It is, accordingly, theoretically determined before it has been adequately examined or explained, acting curiously as an anachronistic compliment to the historical American avant-garde at the same moment as Schechner dismisses that ephemeral avant-garde in favour of the permanence of writing.

In the conclusion to this essay Schechner insists that "interculturalism" is "a theme I've presented in several writings". Of those listed, the introduction to the *Drama Review* issue carried much of the same text as this revised conclusion to "The Decline and Fall...", and "The End of Humanism" does not discuss the concept of interculturalism. In "The Crash of Performative Circumstances" Schechner is primarily concerned with the "postmodern", as he had been in "The End of Humanism", and "interculturalism" appears there as only one of "ten qualities of this postmodern subjunctively projected future".[13] Here the thesis is that "Interculturalism is replacing—ever so tenderly, but not so slowly—internationalism":

> The nation is the force of modernism; and the cultures—I emphasize the plural—are the force (what word can replace force?) of postmodernism.[14]

As in "The Decline and Fall...", one '-ism' is supposed to succeed to another, although here the play on the prefix 'inter' replaces a rejected "nationalism" with a (similarly rejected but undefined) "internationalism". In this expansive mode, Schechner does not immediately discuss different forms of performance, but draws attention to the idea of "cultures of choice", in a social context in which "people will choose cultures the way many of us now choose what foods to eat".[15] In a characteristic qualification, he acknowledges that there may not be that much "choice" involved in the case of immigration. Yet immigrants, because "they are 'almost at home' in more than one culture" can be alleged to be "in the position of performers", since "they are always learning 'how to be' in whatever cultural situation they find themselves".[16]

Once it had been theoretically proposed, "interculturalism" continued to play an intermittent role in Schechner's conference papers and writings, appearing in the introductory essay to the volume *Between Theater and Anthropology*, where "intercultural" was linked to "interdisciplinary".[17] Once again, "interculturalism" was a distinctive feature of the future-present of a concluding charter, and Schechner confined his attention to some of the "intercultural companies" he had mentioned earlier in the essay, which proved to be those of Brook, Grotowski and Barba. As had been apparent from the passing reference in "The Decline and Fall...", Schechner was also interested in an 'interculturalism' of performance techniques, which formed the subject of a subsequent essay in this volume, "Performer Training Interculturally". It was in the conclusion to "Performers and Spectators Transported and Transformed", which Schechner began to compose in 1979, but which was revised for publication in different volumes, that Schechner had written of "a world of colliding cultures no longer dominated by Europeans and Americans".[18] This conception was allied to the wordplay on the prefix "inter-":

> Soon enough, as the changed relations among peoples are manifested, the term 'international' will be replaced by 'intercultural'.[19]

Although in the final published version Schechner wrote of the "intercultural phase of history" in this connection, the immediate referent for this "collision of cultures" in all the published versions was distinctly more local, much as it was for 'interculturalism' in "The Decline and Fall...":

> Today there is a quiet in the American theatre. But the surface calm lies. Tectonically there is a movement bringing a collision of cultures. And where traditions collide—or separate radically—up bursts creative magma.[20]

In the introduction to the critical essay "The Collision of Cultures" which he revised for his book *Theatre and the World*, Bharucha chose to identify Schechner as the promoter of the term "interculturalism":

> In fact, it is Schechner who has been largely responsible for the propagation of 'interculturalism', both as a concept and a practice, much more so than Craig or Grotowski, who have merely confronted other cultures without systematizing their experiences. (13)

In the original version of the essay, Bharucha had written more obscurely of the "tensions and contradictions in his [Schechner's] writings which illuminate...the innate intricacies of interculturalism in the theatre".[21] His stated objective in the revision is to "examine the phenomenon of interculturalism in the theatre by focusing on some western interpretations and uses of the Indian theatre", and he introduces his polemic by quoting Schechner's description of the American avant-garde in "The Decline and Fall..." as "genuinely intercultural". Bharucha places his emphasis on Schechner's subsequent qualification about the lack of 'questioning' in the avant-garde at that time, and formulates his own polemical intentions in connection with that silence:

> In this essay, I raise precisely those questions which were not confronted by the American avant-garde in relation to their 'celebratory' use of other cultures. This 'use' amounts, in my view, to a naive and unexamined ethnocentricity. (14)

These polemical intentions finally come to rest in a phrase from the paragraph he has just quoted from Schechner's essay:

> Quite simply, I would like to show that borrowing, stealing and exchanging from other cultures is not necessarily an 'enriching' experience for the cultures themselves. Interculturalism can be liberating, but it can also be a 'continuation of colonialism, a further exploitation of other cultures'. (ibid.)

It is remarkably difficult in the first instance to resolve the critical relationships suggested by this close intertextuality between the two writers. But it is apparent that "interculturalism" as a "phenomenon" is not denied by Bharucha, although he is firmly of the belief that it may be 'propagated' "both as a concept and a practice". This acceptance of the term corresponds to the general tenor expressed in both preface and introduction to *Theatre and the World*, in which "time" is seen to be the major obstacle to the formulation of a "valid theory of interculturalism":

> I am more convinced now than when I wrote this book that it is both premature and somewhat presumptuous to assume that *a* theory of interculturalism can be written at this point in time. From whose pont of view do we see this scenario of colliding cultures?...A valid theory of interculturalism can be initiated only through a respect for individual histories out of which a 'world' can be imagined in which the colliding visions of theatre can meet. (x)

Similarly, the "discourse on the subject" is "simply" to be varied by another, although significantly non-"western" contribution, and in principle confirmed by the acceptance of a distinction between the accepted "phenomenon" and its accompanying "critical discourse":

> Like the phenomenon of interculturalism itself, the discourse on the subject has been overwhelmingly dominated (if not monopolized) by western theorists and practitioners. My book in its own way is an attempt not to provide a more 'balanced' view on the subject, but simply another view, another voice responsive to the particular contradictions of a post-colonial history in which interculturalism is not an issue but a burning reality. (ix)

In his Introduction to the book, Bharucha writes of "this cultural phenomenon of our times", and it is the "phenomenon" rather than the suggestion of a concept which is to be questioned, despite the repetition of elements from Schechner's rhetorical scheme:

> Substituting, however nebulously, the older category of internationalism, interculturalism is opening up new possibilities of relationships between cultures that seem to transcend the specificities of history, race, language and time. (1)

The 'substitution' is, of course, that originally established by Schechner's wordplay, and it is no more convincing in repetition. What Bharucha brings to his discussion immediately is a mixture of a strong sense of a material context, and an equally strong sense of an alternative subject. "Interculturalism" is a "symptom" of a "world-unifying order" of information systems, and has been "promoted both as a philosophy and a business" in America and technologically advanced societies. But as an Indian, Bharucha understands that "the implications of interculturalism are very different for people in impoverished, 'developing' countries" (ibid.). The introduction also anticipates reference to Schechner's phrase "cultures of choice":

> In the case of India, the exposure to 'other' cultures has not always been a matter of choice. Colonialism, one might say, does not operate through principles of 'exchange'. (1–2)

This alternative subject for the term prompts a decisive assertion that this kind of cultural "colonization" is "undeniably different in its orientation from the exposure to cultures that the American avant-garde experienced during the 1960s" (2). The Americans were "free to pursue their 'cultures of choice', and an imbalance of economic and political power has "constrained, if not negated the possibilities of a genuine exchange":

> In the best of all possible worlds, interculturalism could be viewed as a 'two-way street', based on a mutual reciprocity of needs. But in actuality, where it is the West that extends its domination to cultural matters, this 'two-way street' could be more accurately described as a 'dead-end'. (ibid.)

What exactly is "interculturalism"? The close intertextuality with Schechner's writings assumes a familiarity which the Indian publication of Schechner's *Performative Circumstances* might assure for the Indian publication of Bharucha's book in 1990. But in relegating Schechner's local context (the American theatre, and its avant-garde in particular) for "interculturalism", Bharucha ignores the fact that Schechner had not established a wider context of 'intercultural' practice in any substantial detail. The problem is not reduced by Bharucha's subsequent delimitation of his critique to "interculturalism" as it had developed in the "Euro-American theatre of this century" (ibid.). The "Euro-American" is another of Schechner's casual constructs, which Bharucha accepts uncritically, and it is interesting that the "confrontation of interculturalism" which Bharucha promises is confined to "Euro-American uses and constructions of the Indian theatre" (ibid.). As an alternative subject himself, Bharucha is conscious of a restricted competence, since he will not attempt to speak "for all the performance traditions in the East". But his short-list of artists who have engaged in "interculturalism" has only one significant addition to that offered by Schechner, namely Craig. In the first section of Bharucha's book, separate chapters are devoted to Grotowski, Barba and Brook, whom Schechner had specified in connection with "intercultural companies" in the introduction to *Between Theater and Anthropology*. In that brief discussion Schechner had commented mostly on the "exchange of techniques" practised by Barba, and on the diversity in provenance of Brook's performers, and of teachers and participants in Barba's International School. Company practice in the "exchange of techniques" is the explicit theme, and Schechner was dubious, here as elsewhere, of the degree of "exchange" accomplished by Brook's 'trips'. Although distinguishing between the "particularities" of the "visions" of those practitioners he is to discuss, Bharucha is content to write uniformly of "interculturalism" and "interculturalists".

Despite his extensive prelude on "interculturalism", it is interesting that Bharucha's criticisms of "western perceptions of Indian performing arts" in his chapter "Collision of Cultures" are quite specific, and proceed without further reference to the term. The essay concludes equivocally, in a resolution of a discursive problem that expects to be able to divide the possibility of an equitable "interculturalism" from "the priorities of Euro-American interculturalists". Bharucha is willing to make his own demand:

> If interculturalism in the theatre is to be more than a vision, there has to be a fairer exchange between theatrical traditions in the East and the West. At the moment, it is westerners who have initiated (and controlled) the exchange. It is they who have come to countries like India and taken its rituals and techniques (either through photographs, documentations, or actual borrowings). (38)

That "interculturalism" includes "exchange" is an assumption which Bharucha's description hardly sustains, commenting as he does on the "sheer poverty, if not destitution of most performers in India", and an "exchange" of reciprocal appropriation hardly constitutes an attractive brief for the concept. The conclusion to the revised version of the essay offers a brief indication of an alternative for the local, if extensive, context in which Bharucha is now situated:

> Perhaps, instead of interculturalism, what we need in India is a stronger awareness of our intracultural affinities. It is only by respecting the specificities of our 'regional' cultures that we in India can begin to understand how much we have in common. (40)

In the original version of the essay Bharucha had called for "a more sustained dialogue and exchange of ideas, techniques, and performance skills between performers and scholars from India and the western world".[22] In the revision, if "interculturalism" is conceptually accepted, it must be submitted to an appropriate change of discursive subject:

> If we in India need to pursue a study of interculturalism in the theatre, we need to contextualize our research within the inner necessities of our history. The last thing we need is to assume (as Schechner does) that a Euro-American perspective on interculturalism is applicable and acceptable to everyone. (41)

It is, in some senses, an alternative charter, one which Bharucha implements through the discourse of his book, and continues to advocate.[23]

If there has been a critical debate on 'interculturalism', this is largely due to the early intervention made by Bharucha, significantly in the first issue of the serial *Asian Theatre Journal*, published by an American university with a long-standing interest in Asian studies. In contrast, Pavis is a semiotician, and his collection of essays *Theatre at the Crossroads of Culture*, published in an English version in 1993, proposes to reconcile an interest in 'interculturalism' with a semiotic discipline of analysis and reception.[24] For Pavis, "interculturalism" is "the most complex case of theatre production", and in the opening essay of the collection, "Towards a Theory of Culture and *Mise en Scène*", he regards "intercultural theatre" as a useful subject with which to resolve the issue of performance analysis (4–5). The essay poses an initial problem, attempts to define terms, and suggests that "intercultural theatre" places a particular emphasis on *mise en scène*. The initial problem is that of bewilderment:

> Never before has the western stage contemplated and manipulated the various cultures of the world to such a degree, but never before has it been at such a loss as to what to make of their inexhaustible babble, their explosive mix, the inextricable collage of their languages. (1)

It is not a particularly consequential statement, although the exaggeration is plainly calculated, as an opening gambit, to make its readers grateful for any relief that analysis or theory may offer. But Pavis is an evasive and dilatory writer, and this essay contains only one significant proposal, which is that *mise en scène* in "intercultural theatre" should be understood as "a mediation between different cultural backgrounds, traditions, and methods of acting" (6). Pavis is tentative, because he regards *mise en scène* as "itself a recent notion", which he proceeds to reify, detaching 'its' "conscious" activity from the specific projects of named practitioners, but preparing for the additional concept of an "intercultural *mise en scène*:

western *mise en scène*, itself a recent notion, has made use of these meetings of performances and traditions in a conscious, deliberate manner only since the experiments by the multicultural groups of Barba, Brook, or Mnouchkine (to cite only the most visible artists that interest us here). (7)

What is "interculturalism"?:

> The term *interculturalism*, rather than *multiculturalism* or *transculturalism*, seems appropriate to the task of grasping the dialectic of exchanges of civilities between cultures. (2)

It is a bizarre and whimsical definition, but it leaves little doubt about the importance of the prefix 'inter-' in a "dialectic" or 'exchange', and an extensive note 1 (20) includes related definitions for the "*transcultural*", the "*ultracultural*", and the "*precultural*". The last of these is "what Barba calls the pre-expressive", "the common ground of any tradition in the world"; the "*transcultural* transcends particular cultures and looks for a universal human condition", which would appear to bring it close to Brook's view of 'universality'; and the "*ultracultural*" is the "mystical quest for the origin of theatre, the search for a primal language in the sense of Artaud", for which Pavis cites Brook's *Orghast*. What is signally lacking is any attempt to correlate these terms, to determine—for example—the distinction between ideology (or manifesto) and practice, between theoretical proposition or description. The proliferation is awkward, because the references to specific practitioners obscure Pavis's initiative in terminology, and in part confuse it: the "transcultural dimension" is a phrase used by Barba in his writings, who, conversely, does not refer to the "precultural", which is associated with his writings by Pavis through play on a prefix.[25] The "ultracultural" appears to be an invention by Pavis, who does not offer a definition of "multiculturalism", although the groups of Barba, Brook and Mnouchkine are described as "multicultural". It may be that Pavis has been provocatively decisive in his separation of the "intercultural company" itself, which concerned both Schechner and Bharucha, from the "dialectic of exchanges of civilities [in and through performances?] between cultures". It may be, alternatively, that the task of definition and all that it entails, substantially relegated to a footnote, does not much concern him.[26]

That *mise en scène* is the general beneficiary is apparent from the titles of two later essays in the collection, in which it is closely conjoined—

as the preliminary essay suggests it will be—with "interculturalism". The longer of these two essays considers four productions by Pavis's named practitioners, Brook, Mnouchkine and Barba. Yet "Interculturalism in the Contemporary *Mise en Scène*: the Image of India in the *Mahabharata*, the *Indiade*, *Twelfth Night* and *Faust*" begins with what seems, in the circumstances, to be a rather disingenuous disclaimer:

> There is something presumptuous or at best naive in proposing a theory of interculturalism in contemporary *mise en scène*, given the complexity of the factors at stake in all cultural exchange and the difficulty of formalizing. (183)

Whether or not Pavis is correctly surmising the diffidence of the reader, he can surely have no one else to blame for the proposal itself. His remedy for diffidence in this case is the image of an hour-glass (fig. 1.1, 4, and fig. 8.1, 185), in which the sands of one culture filter through the neck of adaptation and become the sands of another. This figure occasioned the scorn of Bharucha in the Afterword to his book:

> Not only is this image almost pedantically quaint, it totally restricts, to my mind, the larger dynamics of intercultural exchange. To imagine 'grains of culture' trickling through filters from one bowl to another and then collecting in particular formations and conglomerations at the bottom is just too neat a construction.[27]

Unfortunately, Bharucha's alternative choice of figure seems equally preoccupied with mechanical forms of time-keeping, and equally inept at demonstrating this elusive concept of 'exchange':

> Ideally, interculturalism evokes a back-and-forth movement, suggesting the swing of a pendulum rather than a downward movement through the narrow trajectory of filters by which the 'source culture' is emptied while the 'target culture' is filled.[28]

A course in graphics, or even holography, seems to be required. Bharucha rightly draws attention to the fact that Pavis has determined that he will discuss "situations of exchange in one direction from a source culture, a culture foreign to us (westerners) to a target culture, western culture" (7). Whether this means that Pavis regards "interculturalism" as a phenomenon of just this kind, descriptively, is not clear. As Bharucha (again rightly, and pointedly) demands: "Where then are the crossroads of culture?"

The initial summary by Pavis of the process involved in this hourglass is hardly satisfactory, but its inadequacy is subsequently explained by a creed. The summary is distinctly vague in what one might with justice call its 'outlines':

> We thus assume the position of the audience receiving a foreign culture that has gone through a series of operations and transformations, which facilitate its transfer and adaptation.   (184)

The creed is, by contrast, magisterial and insistent, because the discourse has finally located its controlling, primary term of analysis:

> The source culture reveals itself through the mediation of a form, that is a semiotic system and model...Culture can be grasped and described only in the form of a semiotic system whose mode of functioning must be established; without this, we will pick up only superficial and isolated traits, which would not have the complexity of a cultural system, and would not deserve the name of culture.
> (185–86)

The reference to the "mediation of a form" connects with the role assigned to *mise en scène* in the first essay, a role that was seen to be decisive in the case of "intercultural theatre". 'Revelation' is a function of a "semiotic system", which automatically presupposes the existence of—and theoretical requirement for—a semiotic analysis; "without this", we shall be left with detecting 'superficialities'. The *mise en scène* is, by this decree, automatically "semiotic", and as a "cultural system" it will deserve the name of "culture". The extreme conclusion to this ecstatic declaration of faith would seem to be that without "semiotics" there can be no "culture", and certainly no "interculturalism".

6.2 A modest look at the discourse of semiology and semiotics: Pavis and de Marinis

The prior allegiance of Pavis to semiotics could hardly be more marked than it is in his engagements with interculturalism in *Theatre at the Crossroads of Culture*. Less immediately obvious from the essays in that volume, on first reading, are the problematic and promissory qualities of (theatrical) semiotics as a theoretical discipline. As this critique comes to a close, I shall consider just two examples of these qualities extremely briefly, those of Pavis himself in his earlier collection of essays, *Languages of the Stage*, and of de Marinis in *The Semiotics of Performance*.

In his Foreword to *Languages of the Stage* Pavis adopted an apologetic stance for the discipline of thought and analysis he was promoting, and perhaps the most striking phrase is the "transmutation of theoretical space into a narrower pragmatic one", which Pavis employed to describe what his book will accomplish.[29] It is a strange disclaimer for a theoretical discipline, but it concludes an opening presentation which makes little of the 'universalism' normally attributed to theory:

> Today there is still no agreement on *the* model of *a* semiology of dramatic art. To see this as a failure would be wrong; rather there exists a healthy state of suspicion about any universal model and a concomitant desire to make 'attempts' on specific objects—a *mise en scène*, a decor, an acting style—using methods inspired by semiology. (9)

The 'pragmatics' in this last statement are noticeably "inspired" by a theory, whose existence 'behind the scenes' of specific analyses is not in doubt, no matter how pronounced the *apologia*. But the modesty is tactful, as lack of "agreement" and accompanying "suspicion" dictate that it should be and that semiology should take its place within critical methodology, alongside "other critical attitudes" (10).

In "A Possible Definition of Theatre Semiology" Pavis offers the reader the comforting suggestion that the "performance text" can be read, in an activity obligingly related to that of reading theory. Furthermore, the creation of meaning in production is "syncretic", combining the "'readerly' production reading of the director and the 'productive' reading of the spectator" (15–16), whose eyes are plainly directed to this exclusively lexical end. As a consequence, semiology is a discourse concerned with a discourse:

> Semiology is concerned with the *discourse of staging*...It investigates the organization of the 'performance text', that is, the way in which it is structured and divided. (20)

According to this interpretation, the activities of practitioner and analyst can be appropriately co-ordinated:

> The director interested in semiology...may move slowly towards a generalized rhetoric of staging (or at least of a particular staging). The semiologist should mark (and sketch) the rhetorical figures that regulate the production of meaning resulting from sign systems. (19)

It sounds like a very pleasant club, with few claims to universality. Yet the concluding ambit is contrastingly expansive in tone:

> The present tendency is not toward exclusivity and isolation. On the contrary, semiology is gradually recovering everything it formerly excluded from its methodological field. It is, therefore, now concerned with *the problem of discourse*, speech acts, theory of possible worlds, presuppositions, socio-semiotics. (20)

Of course, the classic form of theoretical *apologia*, in the impersonation of Socrates by Plato, used modesty to advance assertions of comprehension. Semiology has "a clear desire to set up a poetics or rhetoric of theatre forms", and will not be confined to "the genre that is specifically theatre" but will 'encompass' "all types of performance" (ibid.). While tactfully (one must recall that "state of suspicion") declining the title of a "science", semiology modestly accepts the title of a science of a science:

> Rather than a new science or virgin field of study, theatre semiology appears to be most widely accepted as a propaedeutic or epistemology of 'performance science', a reflection of the link between the dramaturgical plan and the scenic realization. (ibid.)

These particular claims are repeated throughout *Languages of the Stage*, alongside the occasional assertion that semiology is only an "attitude". It is, in fact, characteristic of Pavis's mode of presentation that claim and disclaimer should be juxtaposed. So, in his "Discussion on the Semiology of Theatre", semiology may not be "an autonomous discipline" but "rather a method and an attitude towards the performance" (25), in a thoroughly commendable pluralism which is not compromised by the reservation to semiology of a rather more ambitious, validating role:

> It would be at the same time the propaedeutics and epistemology of the various *theatre studies*, reflecting on their conditions of validity, and the possibility of using the results of one area to interpret the other. (25–6)

Criticism, in particular, has no "explanation of its analytical procedures" (26), and so criticism is later required to submit to the unique claims of semiology to control its discourses:

> No critical writing can exist without a metacritical, hermeneutical and epistemological reflection on its own mechanisms, and semiology seems the best equipped to supply it with such a methodology. (106)

Yet, despite this confidence, Pavis is constantly dubious about the "idea of 'codes'", which he regards as "mechanistic" (16), and about the practice of "notation", which is critically reviewed in "Reflections on the Notation of the Theatrical Performance". His reservations are firmly expressed:

> Whatever the system of notation used, it is readily acknowledged that the notation of the performance simplifies it to the point of impoverishment.   (111)

Similarly, video-recording imposes on performance a "limited and *partial* vision", and Pavis writes generally of the "mythical projects" of notation (124), and of "mythical attempts to discover a means of notation of performance" (127). Such attempts—amongst which Pavis cites Artaud—are trying to become "a kind of ultimate book", and yet Pavis himself insists on "the principle of semiotization which transforms every theatre act into a sign" (127–28). The conclusion for semiology is unavoidably problematic: "One cannot help coming to a rather skeptical and disillusioned halt" (129).

In *The Semiotics of Performance*, which was originally published in 1982, de Marinis engages in a related problematic with far less hesitation or apparent scepticism.[30] His "Introduction: Theater or Semiotics" is challenging and explicitly uncompromising, and he initially characterizes his research as "a rejection of all arbitrary or metaphorical extensions of the 'linguistic model' to the field of nonverbal semiotics" (1). More precisely, he declares an "aversion toward the equally arbitrary and metaphorical concept of a language of theater or the like", and offers a gesture of tolerance towards a theoretical pluralism for theatre studies, in the

> conviction that the study of theater *sub specie semioticae* does not exhaust all aspects of theater. Like every other cultural object, theater is not *only* signification and communication, even if it can be understood more fully if one approaches it from the standpoint of signification and communication...   (ibid.)

It is plainly a "conviction" that intellectual or theoretical pluralism, once complimented, can be quite as casually discarded. De Marinis's aversion to the "linguistic model" for "non-verbal semiotics" does not extend to the appropriation of the term "text", which he regards as a "new theoretical object" to be 'constructed' (2). The concept of "text" unites theory with this "object", as a note explains:

> ...the term /text/ will generally be used in the course of this volume in both of its accepted meanings, i.e. to designate concrete discursive

occurrences (aesthetic, pictorial, literary, scenographic, or performance texts) as well as the theoretical construct that permits the analysis of these occurrences in their semiotic functioning.   (189)

To constitute that "theoretical object" which is the "performance text", a performance must have "completeness and coherence", since "not all performances can be considered automatically as performance texts" (3). This insistence on the categorization of performance as a "text" plainly derives from a methodological desire to make performances analogous to other "texts". So de Marinis's concern for the value of "pragmatics" is expressed in his inclusion of "the relationship of the *text to its receiver*, which includes the act of reading and interpretation" (ibid.). In other words, reception is reading, and the "spectator" is a grammarian:

> The spectator always judges the performance's *grammaticality*...on the basis of the genre to which it belongs.   (6)

It is a contention that is exceptionally difficult to reconcile with de Marinis's declared "aversion toward the...arbitrary and metaphorical concept of a language of theater".

Critical, or theoretical, pluralism seems to fare no better in the course of this programmatic introduction, because the ambitions of the semiotician cannot be contained by the initial expression of 'aversions' or 'convictions'. The language, if I may dare to call it such in the face of those aversions, resembles that of Pavis, since semiotics apparently has "a metadisciplinary function in providing an epistemology of theater studies" (8), and is, besides, a "scientific discourse" (10). In addition, we must understand "theater semiotics"

> as a *metascience*, i.e., as a discipline with the goal of verifying, and of recreating when necessary, the scientific statutes of traditional theatrical disciplines by offering access to powerful theoretical tools framed within a unified apparatus of categories and terms.   (7)

An engineering "*metascience*", clearly, with "powerful theoretical tools", which then engages in the "construction" of its "theoretical object". Theoretical primacy for semiotics is supposedly guaranteed by this kind of "utterance", but the 'pragmatic' quality of this "scientific discourse" is also secured by its averred relationship with some "forms of theater":

> Theater semiotics...can nevertheless contribute to forms of theater committed to asking questions about the languages and techniques they use...   (13)

Potentially a large contribution, one might feel, but the scope is actually confined. So the examples are

> the experiments of the American avant-garde of the 1960s (R.Foreman, R.Wilson, the Structuralist Workshop, the Squat Theater, M. Monk, L. Childs)... (ibid.)

and

> experimentation by the so-called third theater, and above all its leading figures (J. Grotowski, E. Barba, P. Brook, P. Schu-mann)... (14)

Conceived in this way, semiotics offers a kind of symbiotic existence for a select few, which in its discursive aspect is not in the least afraid of inconsistency, since we read that these practitioners "conceive of performance...as a meditation on, and deconstruction of, the languages of the stage" (ibid.).[31]

6.3 The significance of theory

I shall conclude with a short series of disparate observations, which may or may not accord with individual or consensual convictions of 'significance'. The first observation must be concerned with the continuity of theory. Theoretical abstraction, in first principles, aims to establish concepts as a product of argument, and the concepts are often remembered despite the manifest inadequacy or failure of arguments. That this is the case with *mimesis* hardly needs any special demonstration from me here, since I have alluded incidentally (throughout this book) to the recurrence of the concept. The process of conceptual acceptance begins with Aristotle, and in any useful construction of the significance of theory we should at least note that there is something distinctly casual about it, ominously so, if our concern in the first instance is with the theatre. Let me put it this way: there is something in theory, and in critical theory—the kinds of criticism that depend tendentiously for certainty on arguments that are meant to be 'better' than arguments—which has required or even desired the doctrine of *mimesis*. Something similar may be observed with *katharsis*. Almost arbitrary examples will perhaps demonstrate this proposition best.

For Auerbach, *mimesis* provided the title for a monumental study of 'realism', to which the subtitle was "the representation of reality in western literature", and for which the concluding summary of the subject was "the interpretation of reality through literary representation or 'imitation'".[32] Despite the intensely problematic qualities of the relationships proposed in these descriptions, Auerbach was content not to submit the doctrine of *mimesis* to any examination. The inherent value of criticism was apparently understood to be a satisfactory substitute for any attempt at a close definition of terms. But if we interpret this as no more than a convenience, a gesture, so to speak, towards a prevalent consensus, then we do no justice to the contradictions to Platonism that Auerbach is concerned to reveal in his studies, and to his tribute to them. The reliance on *mimesis* is nominal, paradoxical, and possibly even irritating, but it is prescribed. More recently, Walton has demonstrated something of the same unconcern: his *Mimesis as Make-Believe* makes us believe that we can dispense with *mimesis* while still retaining it, in a sophisticated version of an everyday expression that cannot be assumed to carry connotations of the Platonic, or Aristotelian, doctrine.[33] His lengthy study offers no analysis of the concept that *appears* to preside over its re-evaluation: it is, without dismay, taken for granted.

The concept of *katharsis* has a similar pertinacity, although the motivation for re-examination is at least pronounced in a survey such as that by Wiles, who offers an interpretation of the leading 'modern' theorists of the theatre in accordance with it. But, in particular, I should draw attention to the work of Lacoue-Labarthe, and to his intricate assessment of the thesis of Girard. Girard has proposed what is probably the most impressive of all recent revisions of both *mimesis* and *katharsis*, and through Girard it is easy—at this point—to allude to the influence of both Freud and Lacan. The theatrical and specular quality of Lacan's psychology only declares more explicitly (despite a tortuous prose) the extraordinary reformulation of classical theory that is apparent in that of Freud. So it is perhaps sufficient here to observe that the 'classical' psychotherapy of our era would be inconceivable without a concept of *katharsis*. I do not intend to discuss Girard here, and would refer the reader instead to the impressive analysis by Lacoue-Labarthe.[34] But in the context of conceptual continuity some commentary on Lacoue-Labarthe himself may be helpful, since his interests in dialogue, paradox, and mimesis are appropriately conjoined in the essay on "Diderot's Paradox and Mimesis", to which reference was made in the notes to Part Two of this book.[35]

Lacoue-Labarthe's principal concern in this essay is with the 'paradox' of the subject in Diderot's dialogue, who is both a narrator and a character, as the enigmatic conclusion to the *Paradoxe* would seem confirm. This secondary paradox of criticism is left unresolved by the conclusion of the essay; but in the course of the discussion Lacoue-Labarthe has satisfied himself with an important re-rendering of *mimesis*. I use the term 're-rendering', rather than 'revision', because Lacoue-Labarthe proposes the detection in an Aristotelian text of two kinds of *mimesis* in Aristotelian theory. In a discussion of "art" or "skill" in the *Physics*, Aristotle clearly distinguishes between the kind of artistry that produces a house or a bed, which are not already present in nature, and that which is *mimesis*: "In sum, skill either brings to fulfilment what nature (*phusis*) has not accomplished, or it imitates" (*Physics* 199a). Lacoue-Labarthe's interpretation of this statement abolishes the distinction, and renders it into an exposition of a double Aristotelian *mimesis*:

> There are thus two forms of mimesis. First, a restricted form, which is the reproduction, the copy, the reduplication of what is given (already worked, effected, presented by nature)...
>
> Then there is a general mimesis, which reproduces nothing given (which thus reproduces nothing at all), but which *supplements* a certain deficiency in nature...It is a productive mimesis, that is, an imitation of *phusis* as a productive force, or as *poiesis*.[36]

Readers of Derrida, with whom Lacoue-Labarthe has been closely associated, and who wrote the preface to this volume of translations by Lacoue-Labarthe, will recognize the concept of the 'supplement', which provides Lacoue-Labarthe with a magic charm as he makes this remarkable amendment. The substitution of *mimesis*—in either a "restricted" or a "general mimesis"—for Aristotle's common subject of "art" or "skill" is made without apology, offering a version of mimetic theory which may seem plausible. The conclusion is even more so:

> Theatrical mimesis, in other words, provides the model for general mimesis. Art, since it substitutes for nature, since it replaces it and carries out the poietic process that constitutes its essence, always produces a theater, a representation. That is to say, *another presentation*—or the presentation of *something other*, which was not yet there, given, or present.[37]

"In other words" ("*autrement dit*"): this particularly telling parenthesis might apply as well to Lacoue-Labarthe's rendering of his own first statements as it does to his re-rendering of Aristotle. In this conclusion, "theatrical mimesis", which is clearly a synonym for Lacoue-Labarthe's "restricted" *mimesis*, appears as "representation". This familiar formula is then rendered into "another presentation—or the presentation of something other", which leads "theatrical *mimesis*" into a direct correlation with "general *mimesis*". The distinction Lacoue-Labarthe had originally drawn, between a "restricted" and a "general" *mimesis*, is dissolved in a more acceptable or plausible rendition of the established term.

Now I have no wish to penalize Lacoue-Labarthe for an impressive critical interest in the inherited concept of *mimesis*, which extends well beyond this essay, still less for suggesting that the theatre might be best considered under the general term of 'presentation'. But the intricacies, even the duplicities, of his argumentation here are an appropriate witness to the longevity of conceptual abstractions. Lacoue-Labarthe does not dare to replace the desperately exhausted philosophical concept of 'representation' by 'presentation' without the most elaborate evasions; and even then does not fully dare. To be exact: the innovative and underivative concept of 'presentation' has to be advanced not only under *mimesis*, in the allusion to the passage from the *Physics* as a kind of 'secret' revision to the *Poetics*. It has also, in the final rendering by Lacoue-Labarthe of his own proposition, to be integrated, in confusion, with 'representation'.

The term 'performance' has a unique value for the contemporary discipline of theatre studies, offering as it does a kind of demarcation from studies of the dramatic script as literature. The question that might follow from that demarcation is whether 'performance' has a sufficient theory to validate the distinction, and it is relatively plain that both semiotics and performance theory have presented themselves to fulfil that function. I have written above, repeatedly, of the 'drama analogy' that had established itself in anthropology and sociology perhaps before that requirement was strongly felt, and of how that analogy was at times reversed for the anthropology of performance and performance theory. So Schechner may claim that "performance theory is a social science", and in particular both Schechner and Turner repeatedly allude in the moments of that 'reversal' to the work of Goffman. For Schechner, the existence of the "theater in life" is a given, and for Turner the concept of 'acting' "can mean doing things in everyday life, or performing on the stage or in a temple".[38] The phrase "everyday life" marks the allusion to Goffman's study *The Presentation of Self in Everyday Life*, and that allusion is found, in a variation, but with a similar function, in Schechner: "Performativity—or commonly, 'performance'— *is everywhere* in life, from ordinary gestures to macrodramas".[39] In this respect, and in view of his collaboration with both Schechner and Turner, Goffman's discursive presentation of the drama analogy has a significance for our contemporary interests which its author may not have intended.

For Goffman in his preface to *The Presentation of Self in Everyday Life*, the theatre offered a "model" for a socio-psychological enquiry that was not necessarily adequate, but which was preferred to any other:

> The perspective employed in this report is that of the theatrical performance; the principles derived are dramaturgical ones...In using this model I will attempt not to make light of its obvious inadequacies. The stage presents things that are make-believe; presumably life presents things that are real and sometimes not well rehearsed.[40]

One particular 'inadequacy' was announced in the preamble, because it conflicted with a concept which Goffman had already established, that of "interaction".[41] Goffman is conscious that, if the analogy were strict, then the existence of the audience as a third party to the "interaction" of characters in the theatre would have to be acknowledged. An adjustment is needed:

> In real life, the three parties are compressed into two; the part one individual plays is tailored to the parts played by the others present, and yet these others also constitute the audience. Still other inadequacies in this model will be considered later.   (9)

What this admission conceals is that there may be inadequacies in the concept of "interaction" itself, which explicitly includes an emphasis on exchange, what Goffman defines as "the reciprocal influence of individuals" (14). Although Goffman later draws on memoirs of the *ancien régime*, on observations in Mayhew's classic study, and on some illustrations from contemporary working-class life, his report seems to be co-ordinated on professional and commercial practice, with the 'customer' (who is, in many examples, an institutional 'patient') fulfilling the function of the 'audience'. The "presentation of self" does not seem, in these circumstances, to be completely compatible with the concept of "interaction", and as Goffman observes, it is "the moral character of projections that will chiefly concern us in this report" (24).

I shall return, briefly, to other qualities of the concept of "interaction", notably its definition as "ritual", in connection with an early paper by Goffman "On Face Work". For the moment, two other aspects of the drama analogy, with or without the inadequacies noted by Goffman, are of immediate interest. The first is the question of a division between 'performer' or actor and 'character' within the analogy. The difficulty that Goffman's discourse encounters lies in the issue of motivation or purpose in the "expressions given off" (14 and 16) by one individual to another. Goffman writes of the "promissory character" of the individual's behaviour to another, which would appear—by analogy—to refer to the activity of 'character' rather than actor. In a subsequent formulation, the "promissory" is aligned with a strong sense of motivation:

> when an individual appears in the presence of others, there will usually be some reason for him to mobilize his activity so that it will convey an impression to others which it is in his interests to convey.
> (15–16)

In his preamble Goffman had associated, unproblematically, the notion of "theatrical performance" with "principles" that were "dramaturgical", potentially conflating, in one analogy, the functions of actor and dramatic character. In the formulation above a dramaturgical interpretation seems most appropriate, with the "reason" for the behaviour detected as if in a dramatic character. Elsewhere, the analogy seems to envisage the theatrical actor, as in the case where "the performer may not be taken in at all by his own routine" (28). Yet the contrasting case to this seems to fail the analogy completely, by corresponding neither to actor nor to character:

> At one extreme, one finds that the performer can be fully taken in by his own act; he can be sincerely convinced that the impression of reality which he stages is the real reality. (ibid.)

What exactly the "real reality" might be, when "everyday life" is composed of 'presentations', is not a problem that Goffman chooses to examine, although the assertion of its existence creates "inadequacies" that exceed his own anticipations. The difficulty may well lie in some of Goffman's assumptions about the theatre and its drama, the kind of sadly "unreflected aesthetic presuppositions" to which Brewer referred in her brief critique of theatricality as a figure of theory.[42] 'Reality' for Goffman is apparently something to be expected of the "script":

> ...almost anyone can quickly learn a script well enough to give a charitable audience some sense of realness in what is being contrived before them. (78)

Although Goffman uses such terms as "routine" and "mask", the dominant theatrical model would seem to be that of the proscenium arch in a nineteenth-century vision: so "scenery and stage props" form a setting (32), and Goffman later discusses what happens "backstage", or on the other side of the "footlights" (114). Goffman also seems to have some strange assumptions about theatrical practice, and rehearsal in particular:

> We often find a division into back region, where the performance of a routine is prepared, and front region, where the performance is presented.   (231)

Goffman's 'presentations' are inherently 'realistic', those of "everyday life", but the dramaturgy may be even more subtly attuned, if the suggestion of "ideal motives" (54) for some characters combines the 'realism' of the "script" with 'idealism' in the form familiar from the dramas of Ibsen, Chekhov or Shaw.

If difficulty is an inevitable consequence of analogy deployed to such comprehensive ends as it is in *The Presentation of Self in Everyday Life*, then it should hardly be surprising that the discourse employed by Goffman proves fragile to the point of almost total renunciation. Like all calculated retractions, Goffman's is delayed to the last moment:

> And now a final comment. In developing the conceptual framework employed in this report, some language of the stage was used. I spoke of performers and audiences; of routines and parts; of performances coming off or falling flat; of cues; stage settings and backstage; of dramaturgical needs, dramaturgical skills, and dramaturgical strategies. Now it should be admitted that this attempt to press a mere analogy so far was in part a rhetoric and a manoeuvre.   (246)

In this carefree spirit of the final pages the "claim that all the world's a stage" is a "commonplace", and is "not to be taken too seriously" (246), which makes reading Goffman a task of some sophistication. At an earlier stage of the 'presentation', matters in the 'field' of analogy were a little more settled:

> Scripts even in the hands of unpractised players can come to life because life in itself is a dramatically enacted thing. All the world is not, of course, a stage, but the crucial ways in which it isn't are not easy to specify.   (78)

Not, it seems, until the conclusion, when the intellect triumphs over all obstacles:

> An action staged in a theatre is a relatively contrived illusion and an admitted one; unlike ordinary life, nothing real or actual can happen to the performed characters...
>
> A character staged in a theatre is not in some ways real, nor does it have the same kind of real consequences as does the thoroughly contrived character performed by a confidence man... (246–47)

If allusions to the existence of 'performance' in "everyday life" were of considerable importance to the anthropology of performance advocated by Turner and Schechner, then the related use of 'performance' in relation to ritual was of even greater significance. In this respect, Goffman's determination of the concept of "interaction ritual" is of marginal interest in demonstrating the contemporary application of the term 'ritual' to what Goffman calls "social encounters". I shall not provide a detailed analysis of the early essay "On Face Work", which was republished in the volume *Interaction Ritual*; but some comments may be helpful. Goffman's 'rhetorical manoeuvre' in this case is one of the sacralization of the contemporary and 'everyday': "As sacred objects, men are subject to slights and profanation... ."[43] Later in the same essay Goffman writes of "the ritual organization of social encounters" (45). Yet this characterization is juxtaposed to a description that seems to require no reference to 'ritual', but relies instead on conventional terms of the analysis of discourse and communication:

> In any society, whenever the physical possibility of spoken interaction arises, it seems that a system of practices, conventions, and procedural rules comes into play which functions as a means of guiding and organizing the flow of messages. (34)

What remains intriguing is, once again, how we should read Goffman. It might be possible to accept that Goffman is using 'ritual' in a supposedly controlled manner for its value as an illustrative analogy, for 'marking' certain aspects of behaviour distinctively. Alternatively, it may be necessary to construe a more sophisticated rhetorical "manoeuvre", in which the reader is flattered by a comparison of 'his' behaviour to ritual, by that sacralization of it to which I have referred. Goffman's discursive inclinations, which do not sustain themselves with any kind of consistency, and which can only be advanced in the security of an eventual retraction, offer a bizarre referent for the universal aspirations of an anthropology of performance.

I should not be content to conclude any consideration of significance without some reference to power, even though the contextual implications of that term exceed what this book, with its chosen emphasis, is able to supply. In his study of punishment, Foucault drew attention to a transformation from theatricality to observation in the administration and execution of the legal system.[44] Foucault's concern was ultimately with power, and we should note that there are similarities here with the writings of Rousseau. The most conspicuous feature of the *Letter* is its insistence on the replacement of the theatrical *spectacle*, staged for an audience, with the *spectacle* of the public open to the gaze of theorist as legislator. Crucial to this insistence is the contemptuous dismissal of theatrical pity, perceived from the origins of classical theory as a democratic component of the social institution of theatre, and opposed as destabilizing, or commended as therapeutic. Rousseau's objective in the *Letter* is to abolish the audience, and to reconstitute the spectator as object. Understood in this way, the theatre is little more than a figure for the ambitions of theoretical vision, and one might without difficulty accept a parallel in Bentham's obsession with the Panopticon. This 'enlightenment' model of the central observation-tower in the circular prison was interpreted by Foucault, in its largest realization, as pervasive power, as "a faceless gaze that transformed the whole social body into a field of perception", in which each "is seen" but "does not see", and each "is the object of information, but never the subject in communication".[45]

The theorist Foucault maintained his own insistence, which was that his analysis and description were unequivocally of power and state-control, in the pervasive form in which they were instituted toward the close of the *ancien régime*. So Bentham's Panopticon should be interpreted as "the diagram of the mechanism of power reduced to its ideal form", "a figure of political technology", and not merely as a proposal or a design for a "dream building" of imprisonment.[46] The possibility that Foucault does not entertain is that the model of the Panopticon, like the argument of the *Letter*, might function as an advocacy of the universal rights of theoretical vision. This is, in fact, the most precise reading of Foucault's description, since the "ideal form" of the "mechanism of power" is unquestionably written theory, as it was established with little hope of social or political implementation by Plato. That we have lived under the implementation of theory, that "'power of mind over mind'" that Foucault identified, is all too plain. It has been theory, and not the Panopticon, which has remained "a privileged place for experiments on men, and for analysing with complete certainty the transformations that may be obtained from them.".[47] And in our acceptance of the rule of theory, our removal from being the subjects of 'vision' to being its objects, we have resigned ourselves to its impositions:

> He who is subjected to a field of visibility, and who knows it, assumes responsibility for the constraints of power; he makes them play spontaneously upon himself; he inscribes in himself the power relation in which he simultaneously plays both roles; he becomes the principle of his own subjection.[48]

That power, in a diversity of aspirations and illusions, is evident in the discourses discussed in this book should need no particular emphasis from me at this point. To adduce this contextuality has not been a primary objective of these close readings, but I should hope that it is moderately apparent from them. Theory in both Athens and France, in the selections I have made for Part One of this book, is plainly the product of a loss of confidence in a defining institution of a hegemonic culture. Indeed, a more ambitious thesis, in another kind of study, might take as its starting-point the indications that 'classical' theory begins with the decline of the initiatives taken by democracy, and ends with revolution. Power of a different kind is clearly implied in the extraordinary ideological role of 'Stanislavski' across two hegemonic blocs in the twentieth century. One might, without any difficulty, add to this list the ideological profile of Brecht and his collaborators, acknowledging that his overt internationalism is accompanied by a distinct, almost national emphasis on Germany in the final return from exile, and the foundation of the Berliner Ensemble. Confining ourselves to the twentieth century, we could also readily accept that surrealism, as a provocation embraced by Artaud, was provoked by the traumatic defeat of France in the conflict of 1914–18: that the rejection of established forms of composition and expression in favour of automatism was a challenge to a national, 'literary' culture that was seen to have failed. It is also apparent that the temporary relaxation of Soviet hegemony in Poland in the 1950s provided the immediate context for the formulation of Grotowski's asceticism, a form of theatre empowered by theory and a rigorous, physical discipline to resist the politicization of a national cultural tradition. Most recently, the astounding resources of the United States and the American academy, in a period of general recession, have sustained a revision of assumptions about theatrical practice with both national and international implications. These are suitably contained in the cultural ambivalence of the concept of 'performance'.

Intertextuality, contextuality, and the academy; cultural hegemony, crisis, and power; the academy, and the power of theory. I should like to conclude this extensive critique with four morals for reading what is written of the theatre. The first is that the 'theatre' may well be a figure in a discourse, rather than the overt subject that it appears to be. The second is that theoretical discourse may well, despite its monumental appearance, contain the terms which permit its own disruption, or disintegration. The third is that the belief that theory is more 'well-founded' than criticism is itself 'baseless', to answer within the metaphor. The last is, perhaps, self-evident: that is that theory is decisively no less 'literary' than the script.

Notes and References

Preface

1. Poggioli (1968), P. Burger (1984), and Mann (1991). See in addition the definitions offered by Innes (1993).
2. For attempts at a definition of 'discourse', see Benveniste (1971), especially 209, and Todorov (1990). Benveniste assumes that the desire to influence the hearer or reader is a characteristic of discourse, whether spoken or written, while for Todorov "discourse is not a single entity; it is multiple, in its functions as well as its forms" (9–10).

Part One: Before...

1 The Idea of Sight: Plato and Aristotle

1. For overview and general discussion, readers should consult Krant (1992), with ch. 11, E. Asmis, "Plato on Poetic Creativity", 338–64; and Kennedy (1989), with ch. 3, G.R.F. Ferrari, "Plato on Poetry", 92–148. Both works contain contemporary and extensive bibliographies.
2. The most substantial biography is that by Diogenes Laertius in his *Lives of the Philosophers*. But it is surpassed by the collection of *Letters* handed down under Plato's name, at least some of which (notably *Letter* 7) are thought to be genuine, or to be a very close record of Plato's motives and activities. A modern intellectual biography comes from Ryle (1966).

³ *Poetics* ch. 1.
⁴ See, for example, Havelock (1981) and Ong (1982), with the qualifications offered by Harris (1989). Specific historical detail is available in Thomas (1989). In particular, Havelock (1963) advocated an understanding of Plato which located his objectives and achievement at a precise and critical moment in "the transition from the oral to the written and the concrete to the abstract".
⁵ A critical discussion of Plato's *Phaedo* is provided by R. Burger (1984). The page and section references to Plato that follow (e.g. 65a) are drawn from the Greek text, but are conventional in many translations. The translations here are my own.
⁶ The major fragments are published, with translation and commentary, in Kirk, Raven and Schofield (1983), ch. VIII "Parmenides of Elea", 239–62. There is, in addition, a clear and demanding discussion of their meaning in Hussey (1972), 78–106.
⁷ Exclusive of each other, but by no means exhaustive of all possibilities, as is observed by Lloyd in the course of his discussion of early Greek argumentation: Lloyd (1967), 104.
⁸ Cf. Kirk, Raven and Schofield (1983), no. 545, 406–407.
⁹ Ibid., no. 549, 410.
¹⁰ Ibid., no. 552, 411–13.
¹¹ In the invidious task of selecting from scholarship on the *Republic*, I must place an emphasis on post-war studies of a general nature. Taken alongside each other, Havelock (1963) and Ryle (1966) offer a convincing framework in which to understand Plato's intellectual initiative in writing. F.M. Cornford, *The Republic of Plato* (New York, 1945) is a translation with notes by an important interpreter; a further translation by A. Bloom, *The Republic of Plato* (New York: Basic Books, 1968) includes a stimulating introductory essay. Otherwise, I should mention White (1979) and Annas (1981), and the works cited in n. 1 above. There is an interesting collection of essays in Moravscik and Tempo (1982); and Burian has edited a final volume from Else (1986).
¹² Major studies of the this problem have been made by Else (1958) and Kreals (1978). Both Else and Kreals look back to Koller (1954), of whom Else is more critical. I have concentrated here, in a selection from the full range of usage discussed by these writers, on material from theatrical contexts.
¹³ Text and translation in *Hesiod, The Homeric Hymns and Homerica*, trans. H.G. Evelyn-White (Cambridge, Mass.: Harvard University Press, 1914), 336–37, a volume in the Loeb Classical Library.
¹⁴ Pindar *Pythian Odes* 12, 20–1, of Athene making the pipes sound like a human cry.
¹⁵ Text and translation in Aeschylus, *Agamemnon, Libation-bearers, Eumenides*,

Fragments, trans. H.W. Smyth and H. Lloyd-Jones (Cambridge, Mass.: Harvard University Press, 1957), fr. 27 (from the *Edonians*), 398–99, another volume in the Loeb Classical Library.

[16] Thucydides, *The Peloponnesian War*, Bk. 2. 37.

[17] Herodotus Bk. 2. 78 and 86.

[18] In fact, a phantom of Helen had gone to Troy in her place. This is the version of the myth created or exploited by the poet Stesichorus in his *Palinode*, or *Recantation*, and cited by Socrates in *Phaedrus* (243a–b) as his precedent for a recantation in favour of Love, after speeches in favour of the non-lover. In Euripides' *Helen*, Teucer does not remain in Egypt long enough to discover his mistake.

[19] *Women at the Thesmophoria* 154–56.

[20] *The Madness of Heracles* 1294–1300.

[21] *Birds* 1285.

[22] *The Madness of Heracles* 992.

[23] *Women at the Thesmophoria* 849–51.

[24] *Clouds* 1430–31.

[25] It seems important to re-emphasize here, in the light of current interest in metatheatre, that these references are to highly improbable impersonations by comic *characters* (including, in this case, a chorus of 'old Athenians'), and not to the general principle of impersonation by comic *performers*. A contemporary knowledge of mime in Athens would easily lead to this form of condescension: comic performances were sanctioned by the state, and were spectacular, and mime was not. In a final review of his conclusions, Else commented that "*mim-eisthai* in its dramatic signification (= 'miming') still had a flavour of the mime about it in fifth-century Attic Greek. It was not in use as a general term for the acting of roles in drama—tragedy, satyr play, comedy—much less to describe Homer's kind of impersonation. In fact Plato is the author of this extension...": Else (1986), 27.

[26] Most modern proposals (n. 12 above) about the meaning of *mimesis* and its cognates start from the suspicion, or supposition, that Plato is moving the words towards an innovative, conceptual deployment that differs from earlier usage. Kreals (1978), adapting Koller, places an emphasis on "enactment" (22). This view is echoed by G. Nagy, "Early Greek Views of Poets and Poetry", ch. 1 in Kennedy (1989); but Nagy does not distinguish between *mimesis* and the presentation that is Greek drama, as I do here. Havelock (1963), in a long note 22 to an outstanding chapter on "Poetry as Preserved Communication", is insistent on the idea of "sympathetic behaviour" (58), but unwisely dismisses the "pejorative colour" which had been noticed, although not fully explored, by Else. While I have found all of these previous analyses stimulating, that of Else seems the most dispassionate, as least tied to a general thesis.

27 Likely or certain dates for all eight plays of Euripides and Aristophanes mentioned here lie in the period from the later 420s to 388 BC.

28 It is impossible to give an adequate account of the term *thumos*, and its cultural history, in these pages. The relationship between *thumos* and *psyche* in early Greek writing is explored by Adkins (1970), ch. 2 "The Homeric World", 13–48. Rather than anger, *thumos* is impulse, and has a capacity for internal debate, for weighing the issues, which makes it suitable for Plato's co-option of it as an auxiliary to reasoned argument.

29 On the broader background to this kind of analogy, see Lloyd (1967), ch. IV "Metaphor and imagery in Greek cosmological theories", 210–303.

30 This would not, presumably, be necessarily true of the bronze-caster. This consideration is perhaps strong evidence for the pejorative connotations that Plato appropriated and developed in the word *mimesis*, and suggests that *mimesis* should not be taken to apply universally to all representation, to what we should now call art.

31 Havelock's generally sound contention that Plato is alluding to the cultural and educational role played by the "Homeric encyclopedia" should not obscure the fact that Plato does not establish his argument securely. This is particularly true in the case of tragedy, and of drama in general.

32 The expulsion of the practitioners of imitative poetry might appear at a first reading to be conceived as a form of exile (of a fellow citizen). But the use of *prostatai*, "representatives", carries a suggestion of those who represented the *metoikoi*, or resident immigrants at Athens. If this association is implied, it would align the practitioners of imitative poetry with the fifth-century sophists, or itinerant teachers, who were mostly non-Athenian, and who were retrospectively the objects of much of Plato's harshest criticism. But the suggestion of an unwanted intrusion would have to remain subliminal. It could not be argued, because the greatest of the tragic and comic writers at Athens had been Athenian citizens.

33 Barnes (1982) offers a succinct introduction to the philosopher and the range of his interests. Aristotle's understanding of the scope of philosophical enquiry exceeded Plato's, including what we should call the physical and natural sciences; his most decisive contribution probably lay in formal logic. I comment briefly below (1.2.1) on his methodical reformulation of some of the major subjects largely subsumed in Plato's moral philosophy.

34 I shall refer to this work simply as the *Ethics*, although there are two further moral studies attributed to Aristotle (the Eudemian *Ethics*, and the *Magna Moralia*). There is a recent translation by T. Irwin: Aristotle, *Nicomachean Ethics* (Indianapolis: Hakkert, 1985).

35 "The ridiculous has been discussed separately in the *Poetics*", *Rhetoric* I. 11. 29; "It has been stated in the *Poetics* how many forms of jokes there are", *Rhetoric* III. 18. 7. Text and translation in Aristotle, *The "Art" of Rhetoric*,

trans. J.H. Freese (Cambridge, Mass.: Harvard University Press, 1926), a volume in the Loeb Classical Library; there are recent, annotated translations by G.A. Kennedy *Aristotle on Rhetoric* (New York: Oxford University Press, 1991) and by H.C. Lawson-Tancred, published as *Aristotle, The Art of Rhetoric* (Harmondsworth: Penguin Books, 1991). I shall continue to make references to Aristotle's writings by book (Roman numeral), chapter and subsection. Attempts have been made repeatedly to trace in subsequent documents a second, lost book of the *Poetics* on comedy: the most recent of these comes from Janko (1984).

[36] Aristotle also, certainly, wrote a separate treatise on this kind of performance, which has been lost. Other related titles of works now lost were studies of *Homeric Problems*, a dialogue *On Poets*, of which some fragments remain, and an early dialogue debating the merits of rhetoric, *Gryllus*. On the *Politics*, see Lord (1982). Lord has also published a translation, *Aristotle's* Politics (Chicago: Chicago University Press, 1985).

[37] Pleasure and philosophical "contentment" (*eudaimonia*) are two of the concluding subjects of the *Ethics* (X. 1–8).

[38] Aristotle provides some guidance in methodological commentaries in *Metaphysics* I.1 and *Ethics* VI. 3–8 by distinguishing metaphysical speculation from the scientific study of invariable principles and the productive skills of the useful and fine arts: both rhetoric (considered as useful) and poetics would come under the final category.

[39] Earlier works intended for publication (known as 'exoteric') almost certainly included some dialogues in the Platonic mould, such as *Gryllus*: see n. 36 above.

[40] There is no shortage of translations of the *Poetics*, either annotated or with commentaries. The most recent of these are S. Halliwell, *The* Poetics *of Aristotle* (London: Duckworth, 1987) and R. Janko, *Aristotle's* Poetics (Indianapolis: Hakkert, 1987). J. Hutton, *Aristotle's* Poetics (New York: Norton, 1982) offers a translation with an introduction and notes, and Davis (1992) a discursive commentary without translation. Of earlier versions, those by M. Hubbard in D.A. Russell and M. Winterbottom (eds), *Ancient Literary Criticism* (Oxford: Clarendon Press, 1972) and G.F. Else, *Aristotle's* Poetics (Ann Arbor: Michigan University Press, 1970) are extremely valuable; the translation by G.M.A. Grube (originally 1958) has been republished, with an introduction and brief notes by D.J. Conacher, in M. Sidnell (ed.), *The Sources of Dramatic Theory 1: Plato to Congreve* (Cambridge: Cambridge University Press, 1991); and K.A. Telford, *Poetics* (Chicago: Chicago University Press, 1961) and L. Golden and O.B. Hardison, *Aristotle's* Poetics (Eaglewood Cliffs: Prentice-Hall, 1968) are translations with commentaries.

The most impressive recent studies are by Halliwell (1986) and Belfiore (1992); a classic commentary is that of Else (1967). Developments in recent criticism are well represented in the collection edited by Rorty (1992). The relationship between Aristotelian theory and Athenian tragedy of the fifth century BC has been diversely explored by Jones (1962), Vickers (1973) and Nussbaum (1986).

41 I shall not comment further here on the range of meanings attributable to, and the implications of, *mimesis* and *poiesis* (discussed in 1.1.4 and 1.1.5 respectively), but will mostly use the conventional translations "poetry" (occasionally "composition") and "imitation".

42 I do not mean by this statement to obscure the early subordination of drama to epic in the *Republic* (section 1.1.3 above), or the use of arguments from painting to introduce the further critique of drama in the concluding tenth book.

43 In a digression in ch. 3 Aristotle notes that the noun *drama* ('action') comes from an alternative verb for 'to do, to act', *dran*: the more standard verb in use in Athens was *prattein*. Since *dran* was associated with the Dorian dialect, which was predominant in Southern Greece and Sicily, this had led to claims that drama was a Dorian invention.

44 See section 1.1.5 above. Aristotle's ready comparison with painting (ch. 2) also recalls Plato, as does his basic separation of narration from direct speech as a means of classification (ch. 3), although opinions differ on the punctuation and the proper reading for this passage. His use of the images of corpses as an example in ch. 4 curiously recalls the Egyptian images in the passages of Herodotus noted in 1.1.4 above.

45 Some scholars have argued that Plato's short definition is an allusion to Aristotelian theory, and that, accordingly, Aristotle's *Poetics* antedates the tenth book of the *Republic*. It is, however, extremely difficult to read the definition as a summary of the argument in the *Poetics*, or to reconcile this interpretation with the elaborate and provocative challenge in the tenth book. For the debate, and a bibliography, see S. Halliwell's edition of *Republic 10* (Warminster: Aris and Phillips, 1988).

46 Aristotle's assertive tolerance of *mimesis* as a human activity makes him liberal in his interpretation of its appropriate objects. In ch. 25 these objects of *mimesis* (and so of any "image-maker") are listed under three headings: things "either as they were or are, or as they are said or believed to be, or as they must be". But although the term is arguably loosened in its scope to encompass a more convincing range of artistic material, its theoretical validity remains unexamined throughout the treatise.

47 The term for nature (*physis*, literally 'bringing forth', 'becoming') has no single definition, but it was taken generally to include most of the objects of philosophical investigation before the introduction of "being", notably by Parmenides, suggested a possible displacement towards what we should now call metaphysical enquiry or speculation.

[48] Causes are the subject of *Metaphysics* IV. 2; a shorter summary occurs at *Metaphysics* I. 3, where Aristotle refers to his presentation at *Physics* II. 3. 7.

[49] The issue of the 'end' of *mimesis* and of tragedy, which are at times understandably confused in commentaries on the *Poetics*, remains unresolved in critical debate. Commentators are inclined to favour *katharsis*, or the effective construction of the plot or *muthos*, as alternatives to taking pleasure as the end of tragedy: but both these alternatives are weakened by their failure to include a satisfactory place for the unmistakeable emphasis Aristotle gives to pleasure in chs 14 and 26.

[50] Aristotle is insistent at this point that "the incidents and the plot are the end of tragedy", as opposed to (the portrayal of) character, in what is probably an objection to a prevalent view. There is no satisfactory way of making this consistent with his emphases elsewhere on *katharsis* and on the pleasure "proper to tragedy", except to conclude, as I do here, that plot participates closely in the 'end' of tragedy.

[51] The connections of these two parts of tragedy with the related specialized studies are briefly apparent in the summaries in *Poetics* ch. 6: "Character is that which reveals personal choice, and what that is—so that those speeches in which the speaker chooses or avoids absolutely nothing at all do not contain character; whereas thought exists in speeches in which the speakers demonstrate that something is or is not the case, or present some general statement. " In general, the *Poetics* seems to have been the loser by its intertextuality with the other major studies from later in Aristotle's life, which is a further and intriguing comment on its status, and on that of its subject.

[52] A "simple" plot achieves a change of fortune without a reversal (*peripeteia*) or a recognition (*anagnorisis*); a "complex" plot employs either or both. The distinction is first made in ch. 10. The examples Aristotle gives in ch. 11 suggest that, strictly speaking, a *peripeteia* is a reversal of fortune against expectation.

[53] It is, of course, too easily satisfying to fill a lost work with the contents one feels it should have had. An intention to explain *katharsis* is certainly expressed in the *Politics*; but it has to be admitted that it is odd that Aristotle should use the term in *Poetics* I, and delay his explanation to a second book, without referring forwards to that explanation.

[54] On this subject, see the detailed discussion by Lloyd (1979).

[55] *Cratylus* 405b–c. In this passage, "purgations" translates the plural of *katharsis*, and "purifications" translates *katharmoi*.

[56] *Rhetoric* II. 1. 8 to II. 11. 7. Of the collection of essays edited by Rorty (1996), only that by M. Nussbaum, "Aristotle on Emotions and Rational Persuasion", shows much interest—specifically—in pity and fear.

[57] The same term appears in the definition of tragedy at ch. 6.

58 The actions which most arouse fear and pity are determined in ch. 14, where their relationship with *philia* is made explicit: "when the sufferings occur in close relationships, for instance if brother is killed by brother, father by son, son by mother, or mother by son, or if this is planned or something like it done". The word translated by "close relationships" is the plural of *philia*.

59 The principal proponent of the 'objective' interpretation of the *Poetics* in recent times has been Else; this interpretation is reflected in his translation (see n. 40 above).

60 It is clear from the discussion in ch. 9, where Aristotle eventually adds possibility to probability and necessity in his definition of poetic subject-matter, that applicability and conviction are more firmly in his mind than an absolute and unvarying 'universality': poetry is "more philosophical" than history, but that does not unite it exactly with philosophical or logical absolutes.

61 It has to be admitted that unity would, in Aristotelian terms, be a proper quality of an object of methodical enquiry. A similar requirement is apparent in Aristotle's view that tragedy has reached the end of its development, attained "its own nature", in ch. 4.

62 Aristotle's cathartic definition of tragedy in *Poetics* ch. 6 terminates in the phrase "emotions of this kind". Although his rhetorical theory has assigned an exceptional status to fear and pity in the generation of what Plato briefly termed "sympathy", this concluding phrase may be intended to cover any additional emotions which might be shown to participate in the same effect.

63 The mention of shadows alongside puppeteers should probably not be confused with an allusion to shadow puppets: Plato is thinking either of glove puppets (the "screening", as in a booth), or of marionettes. A short summary of the evidence for puppetry in classical antiquity is given by Speaight (1990), ch. 2, who draws on the formative study by Magnin.

64 *Metaphysics* I. 1. As commentators have noted, the structure of this introduction bears some relationship to that of the *Poetics*, as *mimesis* does to the faculty of sight.

65 *On Perception* 437a.

66 An *hedusma* ("pleasant seasoning") was the sauce which accompanied meat; Aristotle here uses a participle from the verb.

67 In the following sentence, Aristotle explains that "pleasantly seasoned" language is language possessing rhythm and harmony, and that the "different sections" contain either verse on its own, or song. From this it seems clear that he is referring to the succession of spoken and sung sections of a tragedy. The successive sections are listed and briefly defined in ch. 12: they include the episodes, which are for the most part in spoken verse, and choral songs.

68 This distinction is already apparent in ch. 4, between the delight in viewing 'images', and the painful experience of looking at the objects themselves.

⁶⁹ *Theaetetus* 184–87.
⁷⁰ *Philebus* 38–40.
⁷¹ Nussbaum and Rorty (1992) contains helpful studies of this particular subject from R. Sorabji, M. Schofield, D. Frede (see n. 72 below), and J. Annas, "Aristotle on Memory and the Self", 297–311, which reviews the shorter treatise *On Memory and Recollection*.
⁷² A constructive interpretation of Aristotle's theories of perception is expressed by Modrak (1987). Modrak argues for an integration of the rational and perceptual capacities; this construction is criticized by D. Frede, "The Cognitive Role of *Phantasia* in Aristotle" in Nussbaum and Rorty (1992), 279–95. Aristotle certainly felt the need to advertise a clear demarcation: "Wisdom is not to be identified with sense perception which, though it is our primary source of knowledge, can never tell us why anything is the case (for example, why fire is hot), only that it is so." (*Metaphysics* I. 1.).

2 Performances of the Mind: Rousseau and Diderot

¹ Critical biographies are Guéhenno (1966), Crocker (1968) and Cranston (1983).
² For a critical introduction to the autobiography, see France (1987). Recent monographs on the *Confessions* come from Williams (1983) and Kelly (1987), and there is an interesting inaugural lecture from the South African novelist J.M. Coetzee (1985).
³ The translations in this chapter, as in the first, are my own. I have provided abbreviated references at the end of each passage to convenient and standard editions of the works concerned: in this case [VO + page number] refers to the pagination in J.-J. Rousseau, *Les Confessions*, ed. J. Voisine (Paris: Garnier, 1964). There is a full translation of the autobiography by J.H. Cohen (Harmondsworth: Penguin, 1953).
⁴ Selection from the immense diversity of Rousseau criticism and scholarship is a slightly preposterous activity, but I would at least direct attention to Broome (1962), Ellrich (1969), Dent (1988), Starobinski (1988) and de Man (1979). The most provocative of all recent studies is that by Derrida (1976), originally of 1967, for whom Rousseau's *Essay on the Origin of Languages* was the principal exemplar in a general thesis on the priority afforded to speech over writing in western thought. Derrida suffered his own critique from de Man, "The Rhetoric of Blindness: Jacques Derrida's Reading of Rousseau", in de Man (1983), 102–41. In view of this extensive and much celebrated treatment of the *Essay*, I shall not discuss it here. Critical studies of Rousseau's *Letter to d'Alembert*, in which he gives express attention to the theatre, will be noted under section 2.1.2 below.

5. There is a translation of the *Project* by B. Rainbow (Kilkenny: Boethius Press, 1982); see also Taylor (1949).
6. Originally intended to be no more than a translation of Chamber's *Cyclopedia* of 1728, the project came to be representative of Parisian intellectual life in the mid-century and beyond: see my comments in section 2.2 below, and the references given there, with Lough (1954) and (1971).
7. The institutional context is examined by Bouchard (1950).
8. My abbreviated references for both *Discourses* are to J.-J. Rousseau, *Oeuvres complètes: vol. III*, ed. B. Gagnebin and M. Raymond (Paris: Gallimard, 1964): here [G/R]. Full translations are available: Rousseau, *The First and Second Discourses*, trans. R.D. and J.R. Masters (New York: St. Martin's Press, 1964), and trans. V. Gourevitch (New York: Harper and Row, 1986).
9. On the play itself, see O'Neal (1985) and Rex (1990).
10. *Préface* to *Narcisse*, in *Oeuvres complètes: vol. II*, ed. B. Gagnebin and M. Raymond (Paris: Gallimard, 1961), 972.
11. Ibid., 973.
12. For this tradition, see the essays collected in Dudley and Novak (1972), especially the essays by White (1972) and Symcox (1972).
13. The further reflections contained in the *Essay on the Origin of Languages* have been the subject of intensive scrutiny by Derrida (1976), Part II: "Nature, Culture, Writing": see n. 4 above.
14. For the function of the state of nature in Hobbes' theory, see Ashcraft (1972).
15. From the *Fable of the Bees* by Bernard de Mandeville, an ironical allegory of the utility of vice which had been translated into French in 1740. There is an edition in two volumes by F. B. Kaye (Oxford: Clarendon Press, 1924). De Mandeville is, grandly, "the most extreme detractor of human virtues" for Rousseau in the previous passage.
16. The examples are taken from Plutarch's *Life of Sulla* and his *Life of Pelopidas*, respectively.
17. Subsequent page references, following quotations from the *Lettre à d'Alembert sur les spectacles*, will be to the editions by M. Launay (Paris: Garnier, 1967) [L] and by M. Fuchs (Geneva: Droz, 1948) [F]. The translation of *spectacles* into English poses an insuperable problem, as is noted by Marshall (1988), who would, trans-literally but rather quaintly, "insist on translating as *The Letter to d'Alembert on Spectacles*" (135). I have adopted "public performances" for the title of the work because I believe it carries some of the ambiguous connotations Rousseau finally intended: Rousseau's exploitation of the ambiguous meanings of the word ("view" or "sight", and "theatrical production") is crucial to his theoretical objectives, and will be examined below. There is a translation of the work by A. Bloom, *Politics and the Arts: Rousseau's Letter to d'Alembert* (Glencoe: Free Press, 1960), with an introduction.

As a general introduction to both Rousseau and Diderot in their capacity as theorists "for and against the theatre", see Niklaus (1963). Recent critical discussions of the *Letter* in English most notably include those by Gearhart (1984), ch. 7, and Marshall (1988), ch. 5. Fralin (1978) and Coleman (1984), like Marshall, understand the *Letter* primarily in the context of Rousseau's political thinking, which was to culminate in *The Social Contract*; Mason (1992) also understands it as a republican document. For Barish (1981) the *Letter* is a rather trite contribution to a continuing tradition of "antitheatrical prejudice", built on "the Platonic foundation", in an interpretation which avoids contention in favour of providing a substantial thematic context. Starobinski (1988) unfortunately has little on the *Letter*.

18 A full text of d'Alembert's article on Geneva is available in Lough (1954), 83–97.

19 On the relationship between Rousseau and d'Alembert, see Grimsley (1963), ch. 6.

20 On the relationship of Rousseau to Plato, see Barish (1981), ch. 9, with the more general commentary by Hall (1982).

21 J.-J. Rousseau, *Oeuvres complètes: tom. 2*, ed. V.D. Musset-Pathay (Paris: Dupont, 1824), 386.

22 Gearhart (1984), 267–69, finds a strong contradiction between the two passages; but the theme of degeneration is plainly present, though subject to different rhetorical emphases, in both citations of the paired examples.

23 On the theme of "sexual politics" in Rousseau, see Schwartz (1984), who cites Lee (1975) for the general context; on "antifeminism" in the *Letter* and in *Émile*, Brooks (1975); and on Rousseau's "politics of visibility", Kamuf de Magnin (1975). Some comments by France (1972) may also provide an important indication of the type of this misogyny: "rhetoric was a mark of social ascension, a key to relatively privileged sorts of employment and thus an integral part of the established order. It was also essentially a masculine subject, at least as far as school rhetoric was concerned..." (5).

24 For this topic, as it relates to France in particular, see the excellent presentation by Barish (1981), chs 7–9.

25 For a short introduction to Diderot's life and work, see France (1983); greater biographical information is available in Furbank (1992). Recent critical studies of Diderot's writings include Crocker (1974), Undank and Josephs (1984), Gearhart (1984), Creech (1986), Caplan (1986) and Marshall (1988). Burwick (1991) looks forward from Diderot to the nineteenth century. A broad rhetorical context for Diderot's work is provided by France (1972). Vexler (1922) is an interesting, early appreciation. Further, specific references are included in the notes below.

26 French texts of *The Natural Son* and *The Father of the Family*, along with those of the *Conversations* and the *Discourse*, are collected in D. Diderot, *Oeuvres*

complètes: tom. X, ed. J. and A.-M. Chouillet (Paris: Hermann, 1980), in the new edition which as yet does not include the *Paradox*. For studies of Diderot's drama, see Whitmore (1973), Waldinger (1981), Connon (1988) and Fowler (1994): Fowler argues interestingly for considering the publication which included both play (*The Natural Son*) and *Conversations* as a "narrative". The Marxist critics Hauser and Lukács, excerpted in Bentley (1968), offer a theory of domestic and bourgeois drama, in which Hauser in particular assigns a significant role to Diderot: Hauser (1968) and Lukács (1968).

[27] Material from the following sections on Diderot was presented, in a different form, in Ley (1995).

[28] As one of Diderot's most favoured modes of composition, dialogue has received repeated critical attention: in particular, the analysis of Sherman (1976) was contested by Adams (1986). See also France (1972), ch. 6, and McDonald (1984), Part 1.

[29] On this particular conjunction, see Szondi (1980).

[30] My abbreviated references for the three works principally under discussion here are to D. Diderot, *Oeuvres esthétiques*, ed. P. Vernière (Paris: Garnier, 1959): here [VE]. A translation of selections from the *Conversations* and from the *Discourse* is available in M. Sidnell (ed.), *Sources of Dramatic Theory Vol. 2: Voltaire to Hugo* (Cambridge: Cambridge University Press, 1994), 35–68.

[31] In an allusion to Voltaire's *The Prodigal Son* of 1736; for the plays of Voltaire, see Wellington (1987).

[32] Rousseau, *Confessions*: [VO 537].

[33] For "reform" in dance, and the writings of Cahusac, Diderot and Noverre see Chazin-Bennahum (1983). Lynham (1972) is a biography of Noverre, whose *Letters on Dancing and Ballets* were translated by C.W. Beaumont (London: Beaumont, 1930); for recent critical discussions, see Goodden (1986), ch. 5, and Haeringer (1990), who devotes a section to "Noverre: premier metteur en scène" at 168–88. The account of Gluck's initiatives in Newman (1964) can be supplemented with the specific attention given to theatre and opera in the mid-eighteenth century by Heartz (1967–8); there is a more recent specialist study of Gluck by Prud'homme (1985).

[34] On the exploitation of the theme "*ut pictura poesis*" from du Bos to Diderot see Saisselin (1961); Marshall (1988) considers the *Reflections* of du Bos in his first chapter. The most important recent discussions are those of Fried (1980) on "theatricality" in painting; Hobson (1982) on "illusion", especially Part Three "Illusion and the Theatre"; Goodden (1984) and (1986); and Caplan (1986), with chs 1 and 2 on the *tableau*. Brief selections from d'Aubignac's *La Pratique du théâtre* are available in a translation by B. Kerslake in M. Sidnell (ed.), *Sources of Dramatic Theory Vol. 1: Plato to Congreve* (Cambridge: Cambridge University Press, 1991).

[35] *Letter to d'Alembert* [L 72; F 24]. This style of interjection is also deployed by Diderot, in various forms, as is the assumption of questions put to the writer by the figure to whom the *Discourse* is nominally addressed, Diderot's friend Melchior Grimm. For further comments on Grimm, in relation to Diderot's *Paradox*, see section 2.2.4 below.

[36] The full title of the work is *Lettre sur les sourds et muets à l'usage de ceux qui entendent et qui parlent*. The *Letter* may be found in Diderot, *Oeuvres complètes: tom. IV*, ed. Y. Belaval, R. Niklaus, J. Chouillet, R. Trousson, J.S. Spink (Paris: Hermann, 1978), 111–91, with this comment coming at 139. A full translation is available in D. Diderot, *Early Philosophical Works*, trans. M. Jourdain (Chicago: Open Court, 1916).

[37] Diderot distinguished between this kind of gesture and "ordinary *pantomime*": the general context for performance is supplied by Goodden (1986), who offers a helpful survey of contemporary "pantomime performances" in her ch. 4.

[38] Diderot, *O. c.: tom. IV* (n. 36 above), 143.

[39] For the full implications of Diderot's theatrical theory in the development of painting in the later eighteenth century see, in particular, Fried (1980), with the related studies by Bryson (1981) and Crow (1985).

[40] The primary study is that by Belaval (1950), Part 3. Marshall (1988) subordinates his consideration of the *Paradox* to an emphasis on the "unseen" or "ignored" spectators of the earlier treatises in his ch. 4. Roach (1985) concentrates on what he identifies as Diderot's "mechanism" in the *Paradox*, registering the "impact of eighteenth-century science on subsequent theories of acting" (13); his thesis is more succinctly presented in Roach (1981). Hobson (1973), Swain (1982), Calzolari (1984) and Gossman and MacArthur (1984) all testify to the provocative quality of Diderot's ironic perversity in this dialogue. Lacoue-Labarthe's essay (1980) is published in an English translation by J. Popp in Lacoue-Labarthe (1989), 248–66.

The complete translation of the *Paradox* by W. H. Pollock of 1883 was promoted by the critic William Archer (1957) in 1888, whose introductory problematic referred to the contention between the actors Coquelin and Irving aroused by Diderot's dialogue. Archer's publication is in itself a substantial document for theatrical history. The translations presented here are, once again, my own.

[41] For this history, see Archer (1957) and Tort (1980), Part I "La généalogie du *Paradoxe*".

[42] On this subject, see Wasserman (1947), and the introduction to Marshall (1988).

[43] The text of the entry is excerpted in *L'Encyclopédie: textes choisis*, ed. A. Soboul (Paris: Messidor, 1984). It is attributed diversely, to Jaucourt by Soboul, and to Fouquet, a doctor, by Lough (1971), 54.

44 The entry is given by Soboul, *L'Encyclopédie* (n. 43 above), 233–4; the irony of the last lines makes an ascription to Diderot highly plausible.
45 On *Rameau's Nephew*, see Josephs (1969) and, more recently, Werner (1987).
46 *Essais sur la peinture* in Diderot, *Oeuvres esthétiques*, ed. P. Vernière [VE 703]. The *Essais*, like the *Salons*, were intended for the *Correspondence littéraire*.
47 The biennial public exhibition of paintings in the *Salon carré* at the Louvre was revived in 1737: for the stimulus it offered to criticism, see Crow (1985).
48 Diderot *Salons*, ed. J. Seznec and J. Adhémar (Oxford: Clarendon Press, 1963), 56. Diderot's critical discourse in his *Salons* is the subject of Brewer (1993), ch. 4.
49 Ibid., 63.
50 For further speculations on what Diderot intends by his concept of the "ideal model", see Creech (1984) and (1986), and Anderson (1990), ch. 5.
51 Consistently with his paternalist views of the emotive qualities of drama, Diderot has compressed a variety of comments made by Philoctetes in the last third of Sophocles' play into a homily on filial duty, and the related subject of fit companions for adolescents.
52 In the legend developed by Horace in *Odes* Bk III. 5, the captured Roman general Regulus is sent by the Carthaginians back to Rome to persuade the Senate to come to terms with Carthage. He rebukes Rome for its lack of military virtue, and returns to Carthage to face torture and death.
53 On the conclusion to the dialogue, see Marshall (1988), and the references given there to Sherman (1976) and Lacoue-Labarthe (1980).

PART TWO: ...AND AFTER

3 BROOK AND THE RHETORIC OF THEORY

1 An earlier version of this section of the argument was published as Ley (1993).
2 All page references to *The Empty Space* are to Brook (1972). The original publication was by McGibbon and Kee in 1968.
3 For this, see Edwards (1965); and, as exemplary texts, Cole (1955) and Easty (1966). An interesting revisionist perspective is offered by Gordon (1987).
4 Williams (1992), 135.
5 Ibid., 266–67. Hunt has repeated this conviction recently in Hunt and Reeves (1995), 2 and 27; but see, for comparison, the commentary in ch. 5 "The

Embracing of Artaud: the Theatre of Cruelty" in the same work, 65–83.
6. Brook interviewed by Trussler in "Private Experiment in Public": Williams (1992), 32.
7. Ibid., 33.
8. Ibid., 32.
9. Ibid., 37, republished from *Drama Review* 11. 2 (1966). The records contained in this account and the interview with Trussler should be compared with Brook's own summary in *The Empty Space*, particularly at 54–8. It is noticeable that in this official version Brook takes care to answer the kind of criticisms made earlier by Trussler: "Anyone who wishes to know what 'Theatre of Cruelty' means should refer directly to Artaud's own writings. We used his striking title to cover our experiments, many of which were directly stimulated by Artaud's thought—although many exercises were very far from what he had proposed." (55).
10. Williams (1992), 35.
11. These 'logs' form a substantial part of Williams (1992), where they are placed alongside a selection of critical review writing as well as evaluative summaries by Williams himself. The typology of Brook's rehearsal methods has recently been analysed by Mitter (1992); it is not, fundamentally, the object of this study.
12. Williams (1992), 30.
13. Ibid., 48.
14. Notably in Williams (1991) and (1992), and in Hunt and Reeves (1995).
15. Smith (1972), and Heilpern (1989), a revised edition (originally 1977) which contains a new introduction and epilogue by the author.
16. Smith (1972), 9.
17. Ibid., 9. Smith's citations are from the original edition of *The Empty Space*, published by McGibbon and Gee in 1968; I have replaced them in my text by page references to the paperback edition in Pelican Books, abbreviating the title (to *E. S.*).
18. Ibid., 15.
19. The selection of Faust contrasts with that of the nuclear physicist Bohr by Grotowski, although neither is exactly free from ill-omen. There can be little doubt that the idea of the 'laboratory' had been confirmed by this stage through analogy with the practice of Grotowski.
20. Ibid., 17–18.
21. Ibid., 19. Smith quotes here from the collection by Braun (1969), itself a further example of the increasing textuality of theory over that decade. Charles Marowitz comments on the influence of Meyerhold on Brook in his review of *A Midsummer Night's Dream*, in Williams (1992), 160.
22. For the language of Orghast, see Hughes (1971) and the critique by Trilling (1972): neither piece is, unfortunately, included in Williams (1992).

Illustrations and excerpts from the language and script occur, sporadically, in Smith's narrative: some helpful indications are given in the short extracts collected in Williams (1992), 172–90.

[23] Smith (1972), 212.
[24] Ibid.
[25] Smith found it difficult to see how Brook reconciled his willingness to make the film "with his insistence that 'an act of theatre exists only as it happens' and that the presence of an audience is essential to 'complete the circle'": Smith (1972), 212.
[26] Ibid., 209.
[27] Ibid., 233.
[28] Ibid., 232.
[29] Smith (1972), 249.
[30] R. Bharucha, "Peter Brook's *Mahabharata*: a View from India", in Williams (1991), 228–52; this commentary occurs at 236. The essay was republished in a revised form in Bharucha (1993). For a discussion of Bharucha, in relation to the concept of 'interculturalism', see section 6.1 below.
[31] Smith (1972), 257.
[32] Ibid., 258.
[33] Ibid., 255.
[34] Williams (1992), 199.
[35] Williams (1992) notes (n. 1, 8) that an incidental reference by Marowitz shows that Brook was using the poem in an illustrative manner as early as the rehearsals of *King Lear* in 1962. A definitive production of *Conference of the Birds* was finally presented at the Avignon Festival in 1979.
[36] These improvisations have a conceptual form very similar to the exercises for the 'Theatre of Cruelty' season mentioned above, based on "objects thrown out on to the stage". The 'shoes' in question (actually boots) were those of a member of the cast; a second object was a loaf of bread, resulting in 'The Bread Show'.
[37] Heilpern (1989), 41–2.
[38] Brook (1988) and (1993) respectively. I was unable to see Brook (1998), an autobiography, before this book went to the press.

4 Theatre Anthropology

[1] A posthumously published volume of essays by Turner, with a preface by Richard Schechner, carries this title: Turner (1987). Turner died in 1983.
[2] Schechner (1985) and (1993).
[3] Barba and Savarese (1991); the Italian title was *Anatomia del teatro*. My brief

quotation is taken from "Theatre Anthropology: First Hypothesis" in Barba (1986), 122. More detailed bibliographical information on Turner, Schechner and Barba is contained in the endnotes to the relevant sections below.

4. Zambia under British rule was known administratively as Northern Rhodesia until the independence of the country in 1964.
5. Turner (1967), 3. A professional biography of Turner is given by F. E. Manning, "Victor Turner's Career and Publications", in Ashley (1990). For a brief intellectual autobiography, see the introduction to Turner (1982), 7–19. A critical assessment of Turner's contribution to ritual theory is provided by Alexander (1992); and a short introduction to Turner's writings, in relation to performance, by Carlson (1996), 19–24.
6. Turner (1967) and (1968).
7. Turner (1968), 1.
8. Ibid., 2.
9. Ibid.
10. Ibid., 7.
11. Ibid., 8.
12. Ibid., 30.
13. Turner (1967), 49–50.
14. Ibid., 50.
15. From Turner's introduction to *Celebration: Studies in Festivity and Ritual* (Washington DC: Smithsonian Institution Press, 1982), 16.
16. Turner (1968), 24.
17. Ibid., 274 and 275.
18. Geertz (1980), in a brief critique of Turner's writing.
19. Turner (1968), 274.
20. Turner (1968), 269.
21. Gluckman (1962).
22. Gluckman (1962), 3. The translation to which I have referred is van Gennep (1960).
23. Turner (1967), 93.
24. Ibid., 100.
25. Ibid., 105.
26. Turner (1969), vii.
27. Turner (1974).
28. Turner (1969), 166–7.
29. Turner (1977) in Moore and Myerhoff (1977), 36–52.
30. Turner provides no reference here; but see Dumazedier (1967) and (1974).
31. Turner refers to the categories of historiography identified by White (1973).
32. Turner refers to the selection of translations from Dilthey in *Selected Writings*, ed. and trans. H.P. Rickman (Cambridge: Cambridge University Press, 1976), a reprint of 1883–1911. Turner's understanding of Dilthey's concept of

Erlebnis is summarized in the later essay "Dewey, Dilthey, and Drama: An Essay in the Anthropology of Experience", in Bruner and Turner (1986), 33–44.

33 Turner (1967), 105.
34 Turner's reference is to Geertz (1975). Yet Geertz is concerned with a critical awareness of the narratives or "thick descriptions" of phenomena offered by the anthropologist: e.g. "In short, anthropological writings are themselves interpretations, and second or third order ones to boot." (15). In *The Anthropology of Performance* Turner ascribes the ideas of "metalanguage and metacommunication" to Bateson, without specific reference; but see Bateson (1972).
35 Turner (1985) and Turner (1987).
36 Singer (1972), 71, quoted by Turner (1987), 23.
37 In *From Ritual to Theatre* Turner had associated the concept of reflection with Myerhoff. He offers no reference in this passage; but see Babcock (1980).
38 This particular concept of 'acting', conceived within an anthropology of cultural performances, correlates with that of Schechner in his essay "Performers and Spectators Transported and Transformed": see section 4.2.3 below.
39 The list covers periods from the Middle Ages forward to the theatre of the absurd in Europe, with additional references to the USA and to Japan and India (27–8).
40 Quoted by Turner from Firth's review of *Dramas, Fields, and Metaphors* in the *Times Literary Supplement*, 13 September 1974, 966.
41 His reference is to Velho (1975).
42 Caillois (1979).
43 Turner (1982), 78.
44 The joint paper to which Turner refers was given at a conference in the University of Wisconsin, Madison in 1980, and later published as Richmond and Richmond (1985). The separate study by F. Richmond to which Turner refers shows the influence of van Gennep on his research: Richmond (1978). For a description of and commentary on *Kutiyattam*, with bibliography, see F. Richmond's entry in Richmond, Swann and Zarrilli (1990), 87–117 (and on the plays from which acts and scenes are taken, 93).
45 The *(Tulane) Drama Review* came from a *Bulletin/Review* originally published at Carleton College, Minnesota, which from 1957 was edited by Robert Corrigan at Tulane University in New Orleans. Schechner himself first was editorial assistant to Corrigan on the *Tulane Drama Review* in 1961 while still a graduate student, and then became editor in 1962.
46 The Performance Group became after his departure the Wooster Group, led by Elizabeth LeCompte.

[47] Schechner (1993), viii.
[48] Schechner (1969) and (1973).
[49] Schechner (1988), originally of 1977.
[50] Schechner (1983) and (1985).
[51] Schechner (1969), 159.
[52] Ibid., 165.
[53] Ibid., 177.
[54] Ibid., 179.
[55] Ibid., 180.
[56] Schechner (1973), vii.
[57] Schechner (1969), 175.
[58] Schechner (1973), 19.
[59] See, for example, the account of the fist-fight between one of Schechner's friends and a newspaper critic in Schechner (1969), n. 16, 167.
[60] Schechner (1973), 19.
[61] An account of Schechner's contention with Shepard is given in Schechner (1973), ch. 7 "Playwright", 227–42.
[62] In his note (n. 3, 104) to the revised version of the essay in the second edition of *Performance Theory*, Schechner questions his original use of the word "script" to refer to an unwritten 'code' (in contrast to a written "text"). This is not an issue I wish to debate here, and so I have avoided reference to his use of the term in the essay.
[63] The two sources cited and quoted by Schechner are La Barre (1954) and Giedion, (1962–4).
[64] Schechner here quotes from Reynolds and Reynolds (1965) in deVore (1965), 408–409, commenting on an earlier report by Garner, which included the suggestion of "carnival".
[65] Schechner refers here as elsewhere to Rappaport (1968).
[66] Schechner's references are specifically to Lorenz (1967) and Freud (1963).
[67] Schechner's reference is to Goodall (1972).
[68] Schechner (1985).
[69] Schechner notes (n. 5, 115) that his quotations from J. Emigh are extracted from "a letter he [Emigh] distributed to a few persons concerning his 1975 work in West Irian".
[70] The frieze forms part of what are termed the 'Elgin marbles', displayed in the British Museum, London.
[71] Bharata-muni (1967), ch. VI. 15–16, 102.
[72] Ibid., VI. 31, 105; and VI. 34–5, 106–107.
[73] "The Decline and Fall of the (American) Avant-Garde", which originally appeared in two parts in *Performing Arts Journal* 14 and 15 (1981), was republished in Schechner (1982).
[74] Schechner (1982), 15–18. Schechner's interest in the category of the

"experimental" largely confined the term to activities in America "cresting in 1970, and then subsiding" into "a formalist deep freeze" (18).

75 Schechner (1988), fig. 1. 1, 3, discussed in section 4.2.2 above.
76 A history of Barba's work with Odin Teatret was recorded in Barba (1979) and updated in Barba (1986). Further biographical details are given by Christoffersen (1993) and Watson (1993); a short sequence of autobiographical images is offered in Barba (1995), ch. 1 "The Genesis of Theatre Anthropology".
77 Watson (1993) devotes his ch. 6 to an account and record of the proceedings of the ISTA: 149–73.
78 See Watson (1993), ch. 1 "Barba: the Early Years", 10–17.
79 Barba (1965a), (1965b), and Barba and Flaszen (1965).
80 Barba (1965b), 153.
81 Barba and Savarese (1991).
82 Barba (1967), 37.
83 Hagested (1969), 55.
84 Ibid., 57.
85 Ibid., 58.
86 Barba (1972), 47–54.
87 Barba (1975), 47–57. This appeared under the title "Letter from the South of Italy" in Barba (1979).
88 Barba (1979), 14.
89 Grotowski (1969), 95, quoted in Barba (1979), 16.
90 Grotowski (1969), 97.
91 Ibid., 97.
92 Bohr, who was, significantly, a Dane by birth, eventually worked on research producing the atomic bomb in the USA, and was instrumental in the foundation of CERN, the Conseil Européen pour la Recherche Nucléaire, in Switzerland.
93 Page references are to the version of the "Letter" in Barba (1975): 54.
94 Ibid., 55.
95 Ibid., 54.
96 Ibid., 55.
97 Ibid.
98 Ibid., 57.
99 Ibid.
100 Dasgupta (1984), 11.
101 Barba and Savarese (1991), 270–1.
102 Watson (1993), 149.
103 Barba does not, in fact, "invert the question" he has posed. A precise 'inversion' would be the intractable 'What kind of society does today's theatre need?'. There may possibly, in Barba's choice of phrase, be a curious echo of

Kennedy's inaugural address of 1962: "ask not what your country can do for you—ask what you can do for your country."
[104] For the most recent theoretical retrospective, in which the Third Theatre is compared to Saturn and its rings, see Barba (1992).
[105] E.g. Barba (1982).
[106] Barba (1986).
[107] Barba (1986), 114.
[108] Ibid.
[109] Barba (1965b).
[110] Hagested (1969).
[111] Barba (1986), 122.
[112] Barba and Savarese (1983) and (1991).
[113] Barba and Savarese (1991), 8.
[114] Barba (1986), 135.
[115] Barba and Savarese (1991), 8.
[116] Ibid.
[117] In the quotation from the "First Hypothesis" which opens the entry on "Opposition" later in the *Dictionary*, the Chinese performer is Barba's leading example. His additional comment, that "this convention is not limited to Chinese theatre, but is a rule which can be found throughout the Orient", is supported by reference to the "sinuous lines" that replace a "straight projectory", in the movements of a Balinese, classical Indian or Thai Khon dancer, or of a Noh or Kabuki actor (176). In this passage, "straight" and "sinuous" are clearly graphic typifications of cultural difference.
[118] Barba (1995). For bibliographies of Barba's essays, see Christoffersen (1993) and Watson (1993).
[119] Zarrilli (1988a), followed by Barba (1988a), and concluded with Zarrilli (1988b). Earlier criticism of this particular ISTA Congress had come from Munk (1986) and Bassnett (1987).
[120] Barba (1988b), 126. The essay is republished in Fischer-Lichte, Riley and Gissenwehrer (1990).
[121] Barba (1988a), 11.
[122] There are, remarkably, no entries for 'audience', 'reception' or 'spectator' in *A Dictionary of Theatre Anthropology*.
[123] De Marinis (1987).
[124] Barba (1990).
[125] De Marinis (1987), 101.
[126] De Marinis (1982) was translated into English as de Marinis (1993); for some brief comments on semiotics as a discourse, see section 6.2 below. De Marinis was influenced in his idea of the "Model Spectator" by Eco (1979).
[127] Barba (1990), 96.

5 Some Observations on Stanislavski and Brecht

[1] The handbooks by Bentley (1968) and, more recently, by Wiles (1980) were exemplary practical attempts to organize widespread assumptions about a 'modern' relevance.

[2] I should refer here to my preliminary comments in section 3.2 above (with the accompanying n. 3 on the reception of Stanislavski); see also the conclusion to Ley (1993).

[3] To take one obvious example, the cult of 'absurd drama', which was intense for a considerable time, granted a favourable attention to provocations that had a considerable history: in other words, the 'absurd' was an ideological formation of the era, rather than a collective noun for a set of contemporary cultural products.

[4] Fuegi (1987), 87.

[5] Fuegi (1994).

[6] See the analyses and reports by Benedetti (1990) and Carnicka (1993). A brief history of the American translations and the Russian editions is provided in the Appendix to Benedetti (1989).

[7] I am not, of course, myself advocating a revisionist history which would fail to register the hegemonic claims of the Austro-Hungarian empire, Germany, Britain or Japan for many catastrophic decades of the century. But the confrontation of the former Soviet Union with capitalism, and latterly with the USA in particular, sustained ideological polarities which were not confined to the nation-state. It is in the context of these polarities that Stanislavski's role appears, at the very least, to be remarkable.

[8] Magarshack (1950), Polyakova (1982) and Benedetti (1988). I am not here passing any comment on the relative merits of the biographies, a matter I am not qualified to judge, nor on the intentions or motives of the writers involved.

[9] Benedetti (1989), 76.

[10] Polyakova (1982), 356 (of *An Actor Prepares*).

[11] Stanislavski (1962), 571–72: my page references are to this edition. The original English-language translation dates from 1924.

[12] Stanislavski confusingly calls this the First Studio, in relation to subsequent foundations, disregarding the claims of the "Studio on Povarskaya" to this title.

[13] It would be smart, but misleading, to complete the allegory with a comparison of the director's supremacy to the realization of revolutionary communism as autocracy, in the rule of successive tyrants. Stanislavski's model is managerial and bourgeois, oligarchic but not totalitarian. For a related conclusion, on the ideological value of the 'system', see Counsell (1996).

[14] Tatlow (1985), 215–20. The quotation comes from 218.

[15] Ibid., 216.

[16] "Die Diderot Gesellschaft", in Brecht (1967), 307. The project dates from 1937.
[17] Wright (1989), 1. Wright's reference is, of course, to Lyotard (1984).
[18] Fuegi (1994).
[19] Wright (1989), 21.
[20] Ibid., 98.
[21] Ibid., 5.
[22] Ibid., 70 and 97.
[23] Ibid., 38 and 113.
[24] Ibid., 134 and 135.
[25] Ibid., 124–45: Wright introduces the contradiction by stating that "Müller's position regarding Brecht has by no means been consistent…" (124). Like Wright and many others, I have adopted the German word in its singular (the type) and plural (the scripts themselves) to indicate the category of plays ('learning-plays') that includes *The Measures Taken*.
[26] Müller (1986), 25. The conversation was first published in the *Theater Heute* Yearbook for 1975, 119–23. For a discussion of Müller's *Mauser* in relation to the Brechtian Lehrstück, specifically *The Measures Taken*, see "Producing Revolution" in Huyssen (1986), 82–93, an essay originally published in 1976.
[27] "Verabschiedung des Lehrstücks", in Müller (1989), 40.
[28] Ibid. This section of Müller's letter, continued until its conclusion, was translated by Case (1983). Case, without giving more precise details, ascribed Müller's statement to "*Die Zeit* 1978".
[29] Wright (1989), 13.
[30] "19 Answers by Heiner Müller", in Müller (1984), 137.
[31] Kleber and Visser (1990), 27 and 48. The volume had its origins in a conference in 1986, and so was composed before the dissolution of the German Democratic Republic.
[32] Ibid., 27.
[33] Brooker (1994), 188.
[34] Wright (1989), 90 and 68. Völker's reference is to Giorgio Strehler's production of *The Good Person of Szechwan* in 1978.
[35] Brecht (1964), 23, with Willett's note on Brecht's reading of Marx (23–4). My references will be to the translations in this volume.
[36] From "A Short Organum for the Theatre".
[37] Kleber and Visser (1990), 27.
[38] Ibid., 66; the quotation is from Brecht (1975), 138.
[39] The quotations are, respectively, from the essay "The Popular and the Realistic" (of 1938) and from the essay "On Experimental Theatre" (of 1939–40).
[40] From the conclusion to the essay "Theatre for Pleasure or Theatre for Instruction" (probably of 1936).
[41] This argument forms the opening to the essay "Theatre for Pleasure or

Theatre for Instruction": ibid., 69–70.
42. From the essay "On Experimental Theatre".
43. Lessing (1962), 176.
44. Achieving a state of amazement in the audience is one of the objectives of the epic theatre. E.g., "It [the theatre] must amaze its public, and this can be achieved by a technique of alienating the familiar.": Brecht (1964), 192.
45. Lessing (1962), 179.
46. Ibid., 218.
47. Brecht (1965), 73.
48. Ibid. The German text is in Brecht (1967), 603–604.
49. Eagleton (1985), 634.
50. Ibid., 636.
51. Ibid., 637.

6   THE SIGNIFICANCE OF THEORY

1. An edited version of the material in this section was given as a paper in the first of two panels on 'Intercultural Issues' at the Annual Conference of the Standing Committee of University Drama Departments in Scarborough, in April 1996. I am grateful to participants at the conference for their comments and encouragement.
2. Bharucha (1993), 13.
3. In the original publication, the essay appeared as "A Collision of Cultures: Some Western Interpretations of the Indian Theatre": Bharucha (1984). It was republished in the book in a "substantially revised version" which, however, was little altered in its critical and polemical emphasis. Schechner's essay "Performers and Spectators Transported and Transformed" was first given as a lecture in 1979, and published in successive versions in journals, notably in *The Kenyon Review* 3. 4 (1981), and then in book form: Schechner (1983) and (1985).
4. Schechner's retrospective compilation, "Intercultural Themes", was included in Marranca and Dasgupta (1991), 308–17.
5. The essay was republished in Schechner (1988), in which this statement occurs at 131.
6. Schechner (1982), and the "Intercultural Performance" issue of *The Drama Review* 26. 2 (1982).
7. "The Decline and Fall of the (American) Avant-Garde" in Schechner (1982), 19.
8. Ibid.
9. Ibid., 43–4.

10. Ibid., 70–1.
11. Ibid., 71.
12. Ibid.
13. Schechner (1982), 120.
14. Ibid., 124.
15. Ibid., 125.
16. Ibid., 126.
17. "Points of Contact Between Theater and Anthropology" in Schechner (1985), 26. This essay was first composed for a conference in 1982, and first published in 1983.
18. For publication details, see n. 3 above.
19. Schechner (1985), 149.
20. Ibid.
21. Bharucha (1984), 2.
22. Ibid., 18.
23. Notably Bharucha (1996) and (1997), despite its title.
24. Pavis (1992). Pavis notes (vi) that the essays in the volume were written between 1983 and 1988. 'Interculturalism' did not appear as an entry a few years earlier in Pavis (1980), his theatrical Dictionary.
25. For Barba's use of 'transculturalism', see sections 4.3.3 and 4.3.4 above.
26. Some "precise definitions" for "culture", drawn from Camilleri, are notably followed by the same classification of '-culturalisms', elevated from a footnote into the main text, in the introduction to Pavis (1996), 5–8, a compilation that explores the contemporary currency of the leading term.
27. Bharucha (1993), 241.
28. Ibid.
29. Pavis (1982), 10.
30. De Marinis (1993), a translation of de Marinis (1982).
31. Readers concerned to take this examination further might care to look at the problems posed by the concepts of "text", "language", and "reading(s)" in the essay "Psychic Polyphony" in Carlson (1990), 95–109; and at the defence of semiotics as a "minority theory" by Pavis, in "On Theory as One of the Fine Arts and Its Limited Influence on Contemporary Drama Whether Majority or Minority", in Pavis (1992), 75–98.
32. Auerbach (1953), 554.
33. Walton (1990).
34. Lacoue-Labarthe (1989), 102–17. Both Freud and Girard (1977) might be referred to the tradition of "virtual theatre" established by Gould (1989).
35. The translation by J. Popp of Lacoue-Labarthe's essay (1980) is available in Lacoue-Labarthe (1989), 248–66: both publications were originally noted in section 2.2.3 above.
36. Lacoue-Labarthe (1989), 255–56.

[37] Ibid., 257.
[38] Turner (1982), 102.
[39] Schechner (1988), 283.
[40] Goffman (1971), 9.
[41] Goffman's essays on this subject were collected in Goffman (1972); I shall discuss some aspects of the concept of "interaction" below. My references here are not to first editions; a complete bibliographical note is probably unnecessary in this context, but the earliest essay on "interaction" dates from 1955, and the first study on "the presentation of self" which I have seen dates from 1956.
[42] Brewer (1985), 14.
[43] Goffman (1972), 31.
[44] Foucault (1991).
[45] Ibid., 214 and 200, respectively.
[46] Ibid., 205.
[47] Ibid., 204.
[48] Ibid., 202–203.

Bibliography

This bibliography is restricted to those articles and books to which an abbreviated reference is made in the endnotes above.

Adams, D.J. (1986) *Diderot, Dialogue and Debate*. Liverpool: Liverpool University Press
Adkins, A.W.H. (1970) *From the Many to the One*. London: Constable
Alexander, B.C. (1992) *Victor Turner Revisited: Ritual as Social Change*. Atlanta: Scholar's Press
Anderson, W. (1990) *Diderot's Dream*. Baltimore: Johns Hopkins University Press
Annas, J. (1981) *An Introduction to Plato's Republic*. Oxford: Clarendon Press
Archer, W. (1957) *Masks or Faces?* New York: Hill and Wang
Ashcraft, R. (1972) "Leviathan Triumphant: Thomas Hobbes and the Politics of Wild Men", in Dudley and Novak (1972), 141–82
Ashley, K.M. (ed.) (1990) *Victor Turner and the Construction of Cultural Criticism*. Bloomington: Indiana University Press
Auerbach, E. (1953) *Mimesis: The Representation of Reality in Western Literature*, trans. W.R. Trask. Princeton: Princeton University Press
Babcock, B. (1980) "Reflexivity: Definitions and Discriminations", in Babcock (ed.) *Signs About Signs: The Semiotics of Self-Reference* (*Semiotica* 30 1/2), 1–14
Barba, E. (1965a) *Alla ricerca del teatro perduto*. Padua: Marsilio
Barba, E. (1965b) "Theatre Laboratory 13 Rzedow", *Drama Review* 9.3, 153–65
Barba, E. (1967) "The Kathakali Theatre", *Drama Review* 11.4, 37–50
Barba, E. (1972) "Words or Presence", *Drama Review* 16.1, 47–54
Barba, E. (1975) "A Letter from Barba in Southern Italy", *Drama Review* 19.4, 47–57

Barba, E. (1979) *The Floating Islands*, ed. F. Taviani. Holstebro: Thomsens Bogtrykerri
Barba, E. (1982) "Theatre Anthropology", *Drama Review* 26.2, 5–32
Barba, E. (1986) *Beyond the Floating Islands*. New York: Performing Arts Journal Publications
Barba, E. (1988a) "Eugenio Barba to Phillip Zarrilli: About the Visible and the Invisible in Theatre and About ISTA in Particular", *Drama Review* 32.3, 7–14
Barba, E. (1988b) "Eurasian Theatre", *Drama Review* 32.3, 126–30
Barba, E. (1990) "Four Spectators", *Drama Review* 34.1, 96–101
Barba, E. (1992) "The Third Theatre: a Legacy from Us to Ourselves", *New Theatre Quarterly* 29, 3–9
Barba, E. (1995) *The Paper Canoe*, trans. R. Fowler. London: Routledge
Barba, E. and Flaszen, L. (1965) "A Theatre of Magic and Sacrilege", *Drama Review* 9.3, 172–89
Barba, E. and Savarese, N. (eds) (1983) *Anatomia del teatro*. Firenze: Casa Usher
Barba, E. and Savarese, N. (eds) (1991) *A Dictionary of Theatre Anthropology: The Secret Art of the Performer*, trans. R. Fowler. London: Routledge
Barish, J. (1981) *The Antitheatrical Prejudice*. Berkeley and Los Angeles: University of California Press
Barnes, J. (1982) *Aristotle*. Oxford: Oxford University Press
Bassnett, S. (1987) "Perceptions of the Female Role: the ISTA Congress", *New Theatre Quarterly* 11, 234–6
Bateson, G. (1972) *Steps to an Ecology of Mind: Collected Essays in Anthropology, Psychiatry, Evolution and Epistemology*. San Francisco: Chandler
Belaval, Y. (1950) *L'Esthétique sans paradoxe de Diderot*. Paris: Gallimard
Belfiore, E. (1992) *Tragic Pleasures: Aristotle on Plot and Emotion*. Princeton: Princeton University Press
Benedetti, J. (1988) *Stanislavski: A Biography*. London: Methuen
Benedetti, J. (1989) *Stanislavski: An Introduction*, second edition. London: Methuen
Benedetti, J. (1990) "A History of Stanislavski in Translation", *New Theatre Quarterly* 23, 266–78
Bentley, E. (ed.) (1968) *The Theory of the Modern Stage*. Harmondsworth: Penguin
Benveniste, E. (1971) *Problems in General Linguistics*, trans. M.E. Meck. Coral Gables: University of Miami Press
Bharata-Muni. (1967) *Natyasastra Vol. 1*, trans. M. Ghosh. Calcutta: Granthalaya
Bharucha, R. (1984) "A Collision of Cultures: Some Western Interpretations of the Indian Theatre", *Asian Theatre Journal* 1.1, 1–20
Bharucha, R. (1993) *Theatre and the World: Performance and the Politics of Culture*. London: Routledge

Bharucha, R. (1996) "Under the Sign of the Onion: Intracultural Negotiations in Theatre", *New Theatre Quarterly* 46, 116–29

Bharucha, R. (1997) "Negotiating the 'River': Intercultural Interactions and Interventions", *Drama Review* 41.3, 31–8

Bouchard, M. (1950) *L'Académie de Dijon et le premier Discours de Rousseau*. Paris: Société Les Belles Lettres

Braun, E. (1969) *Meyerhold on Theatre*. London: Methuen

Brecht, B. (1964) *Brecht on Theatre*, ed. and trans. J. Willett. London: Methuen

Brecht, B. (1965) *The Messingkauf Dialogues*, trans. J. Willett. London: Methuen

Brecht, B. (1967) *Gesammelte Werke VII: Schriften 1*, ed. W. Hecht. Frankfurt am Main: Suhrkamp

Brecht, B. (1975) *Brecht in Gespräch*, ed. W. Hecht. Frankfurt am Main: Suhrkamp

Brewer, D. (1993) *The Discourse of Enlightenment in Eighteenth-Century France*. Cambridge: Cambridge University Press

Brewer, M.M. (1985) "Performing Theory", *Theatre Journal* 37.1, 13–30

Brook, P. (1972) *The Empty Space*. Harmondsworth: Penguin Books

Brook, P. (1988) *The Shifting Point: Forty Years of Theatrical Exploration 1946–1987*. London: Methuen

Brook, P. (1993) *There Are No Secrets: Thoughts on Acting and Theatre*. London: Methuen

Brook, P. (1998) *The Threads of Time*. London: Methuen

Brooker, P. (1994) "Key Words in Brecht's Theory and Practice", in Thomson and Sacks (1994)

Brooks, R.A. (1975) "Rousseau's Antifeminism in the *Lettre à d'Alembert* and *Émile*", in Williams (1975), 209–27

Broome, J.H. (1962) *Rousseau: A Study of His Thought*. London: Edward Arnold

Bruner, E. and Turner, V. (eds) (1986) *The Anthropology of Experience*. Champaign: Illinois University Press

Bryson, N. (1981) *Word and Image: French Painting of the Ancien Régime*. Cambridge: Cambridge University Press

Burger, P. (1984) *Theory of the Avant-Garde*, trans. M. Shaw. Minneapolis: University of Minnesota Press

Burger, R. (1984) *The Phaedo: A Platonic Labyrinth*. New Haven: Yale University Press

Burwick, F. (1991) *Illusion and the Drama: Critical Theory of the Enlightenment and Romantic Era*. University Park: Pennsylvania State University Press

Caillois, R. (1979) *Man, Play, and Games*. New York: Shocken

Calzolari, A. (1984) "Les interprétations du paradoxe et les paradoxes de l'interprétation", in De Fontenay and Proust (1984), 117–29

Caplan, J. (1986) *Framed Narratives: Diderot's Genealogy of the Beholder*. Manchester: Manchester University Press

Carlson, M. (1990) *Theater Semiotics: Signs of Life*. Bloomington: Indiana University Press
Carlson, M. (1996) *Performance: A Critical Introduction*. London: Routledge
Carnicka, S.M. (1993) "Stanislavsky: Uncensored and Unabridged", *Drama Review* 37.1, 22–42
Case, S.-E. (1983) "From Bertolt Brecht to Heiner Müller", *Performing Arts Journal* 19, 94–102
Chazin-Bennahum, J. (1983) "Cahusac, Diderot and Noverre: Three Revolutionary French Writers on the Eighteenth-Century Dance", *Theatre Journal* 35, 169–78
Christoffersen, E.E. (1993) *The Actor's Way*. London: Routledge
Coetzee, J.M. (1985) *Truth in Autobiography*. Cape Town: University of Cape Town Press
Cole, T. (ed.) (1955) *Acting: A Handbook of the Stanislavski Method*. New York: Crown
Coleman, P. (1984) *Rousseau's Political Imagination: Rule and Representation in the "Lettre à d'Alembert"*. Geneva: Droz
Connon, D.F. (1988) "Innovation and Renewal: a Study of the Theatrical Works of Diderot", *Studies on Voltaire and the Eighteenth Century* 258
Counsell, C. (1996) *Signs of Performance: An Introduction to Twentieth-Century Theatre*. London: Routledge
Cranston, M. (1983) *Jean-Jacques: The Early Life and Work of Jean-Jacques Rousseau 1712–54*. London: Allen Lane
Creech, J. (1984) "Diderot's 'Ideal Model'", in Undank and Josephs (1984), 85–97
Creech, J. (1986) *Diderot: Thresholds of Representation*. Columbus: Ohio State University Press
Crocker, L.G. (1968) *Jean-Jacques Rousseau: The Quest*. New York: Macmillan
Crocker, L.G. (1974) *Diderot's Chaotic Order*. Princeton: Princeton University Press
Crow, T.E. (1985) *Painters and Public Life in Eighteenth-Century Paris*. New Haven: Yale University Press
Dasgupta, G. (1984) "Eugenio Barba Interviewed by Gautam Dasgupta", *Performing Arts Journal* VIII.3, 8–18
Davis, M. (1992) *Aristotle's Poetics: The Poetry of Philosophy*. Lanham: Rowman and Littlefield
De Fontenay, E. and Proust, J. (eds) (1984) *Interpréter Diderot aujourd'hui*. Paris: Le Sycomore
De Man, P. (1979) *Allegories of Reading: Figural Language in Rousseau, Nietzsche, Rilke and Proust*. New Haven: Yale University Press.
De Man, P. (1983) *Blindness and Insight: Essays in the Rhetoric of Contemporary Criticism*, second edition. London: Methuen

De Marinis, M. (1982) *Semiotica del teatro*. Milan: Bompiani
De Marinis, M. (1987) "Dramaturgy of the Spectator", *Drama Review* 31.2, 100–13
De Marinis, M. (1993) *The Semiotics of Performance*, trans. A. O'Healy. Bloomington: Indiana University Press
Dent, N.J.H. (1988) *Rousseau: An Introduction to his Psychological, Social, and Political Theory*. Oxford: Blackwell
Derrida, J. (1976) *Of Grammatology*, trans. G.C. Spivak. Baltimore: Johns Hopkins University Press
DeVore, I. (ed.) (1965) *Primate Behavior: Field Studies of Monkeys and Apes*. New York: Holt, Rinehart and Winston
Dudley, E. and Novak, M. (eds) (1972) *The Wild Man Within: An Image in Western Thought from the Renaissance to Romanticism*. Pittsburgh: Uiversity of Pittsburgh Press
Dumazedier, J. (1967) *Toward a Society of Leisure*, trans. S.E. McClure. New York: Free Press
Dumazedier, J. (1974) *Sociology of Leisure*, trans. M.A. McKenzie. Amsterdam: Elsevier
Eagleton, T. (1985) "Brecht and Rhetoric", *New Literary History* 16, 633–8
Easty, E.D. (1966) *On Method Acting*. New York: Allograph Press
Eco, E. (1979) *The Role of the Reader*. Bloomington: Indiana University Press
Edwards, C. (1965) *The Stanislavski Heritage*. New York: New York University Press
Ellrich, R.J. (1969) *Rousseau and His Readers: The Rhetorical Situation of the Major Works*. Chapel Hill: University of North Carolina Press
Else, G.F. (1958) "Imitation in the Fifth Century", *Classical Philology* 53, 73–90
Else, G.F. (1967) *Aristotle's* Poetics: *The Argument*. Cambridge Mass.: Harvard University Press
Else, G.F. (1986) *Plato and Aristotle on Poetry*, ed. P. Burian. Chapel Hill: University of North Carolina Press
Fischer-Lichte, E., Riley, J. and Gissenwehrer, M. (eds) (1990) *The Dramatic Touch of Difference: Theatre, Own and Foreign*. Tübingen: Gunter Narr
Foucault, M. (1991) *Discipline and Punish: The Birth of the Clinic*, trans. A. Sheridan. Harmondsworth: Penguin
Fowler, J.E. (1994) "Reading *Le Fils naturel* as a Narrative", *Studies on Voltaire and the Eighteenth Century* 323, 167–92
Fralin, R. (1978) *Rousseau and Representation*. New York: Columbia University Press
France, P. (1972) *Rhetoric and Truth in France: Descartes to Diderot*. Oxford: Clarendon Press
France, P. (1983) *Diderot*. Oxford: Oxford University Press
France, P. (1987) *Rousseau: Confessions*. Cambridge: Cambridge University Press

Freud, S. (1963) *Jokes and Their Relation to the Unconscious.* New York: Norton
Fried, M. (1980) *Absorption and Theatricality: Painting and the Beholder in the Age of Diderot.* Berkeley and Los Angeles: University of California Press
Fuegi, J. (1987) *Bertolt Brecht: Chaos, According to Plan.* Cambridge: Cambridge University Press
Fuegi, J. (1994) *The Life and Lies of Bertolt Brecht.* London: Harper Collins
Furbank, P.N. (1992) *Diderot: A Critical Biography.* London: Secker and Warburg
Gearhart, S. (1984) *The Open Boundary of History and Fiction: A Critical Approach to the French Enlightenment.* Princeton: Princeton University Press
Geertz, C. (1975) *The Interpretation of Cultures.* London: Hutchinson
Geertz, C. (1980) "Blurred Genres: the Refiguration of Social Thought", *The American Scholar* 49, 165–79
Giedion, S. (1962–64) *The Eternal Present.* New York: Bollingen Foundation
Girard, R. (1977) *Violence and the Sacred,* trans. P. Gregory. Baltimore: Johns Hopkins University Press
Gluckman, M. (ed.) (1962) *Essays on the Ritual of Social Relations.* Manchester: Manchester University Press
Goffman, E. (1971) *The Presentation of Self in Everyday Life.* Harmondsworth: Penguin
Goffman, E. (1972) *Interaction Ritual: Essays on Face-to-Face Behaviour.* Harmondsworth: Penguin
Goffman, E. (1974) *Frame Analysis.* New York: Harper and Row
Goodall, J. van L. (1972) *In the Shadow of Man.* New York: Dell
Goodden, A. (1984) "'Une peinture parlante': the *tableau* and the *drame*", *French Studies* 38, 397–413
Goodden, A. (1986) *"Actio" and Persuasion: Dramatic Performance in Eighteenth-Century France.* Oxford: Clarendon Press
Gordon, M. (1987) *The Stanislavsky Technique: Russia.* New York: Applause Books
Gossman, L. and MacArthur, E. (1984) "Diderot's Displaced *Paradoxe*", in Undank and Josephs (1984), 106–20
Gould, E. (1989) *Virtual Theatre: From Diderot to Mallarmé.* Baltimore: Johns Hopkins University Press
Grimsley, R. (1963) *Jean d'Alembert (1717–83).* Oxford: Clarendon Press
Griswold, C.L. (1986) *Self-Knowledge in Plato's* Phaedrus. New Haven: Yale University Press
Grotowski, J. (1969) *Towards a Poor Theatre,* ed. E. Barba. London: Methuen
Guéhenno, J. (1966) *Jean-Jacques Rousseau,* trans. J. and D. Weightman. London: Routledge and Kegan Paul
Haeringer, E. (1990) "L'Esthétique de l'opéra en France au temps de Jean-Philippe Rameau", *Studies on Voltaire and the Eighteenth Century* 279
Hagested, B. (1969) "A Sectarian Theatre: an Interview with Eugenio Barba", *Drama Review* 14.1, 55–9
Hall, R.W. (1982) "Plato and Rousseau", *Apeiron* 16.1, 12–20

Halliwell, S. (1986) *Aristotle's* Poetics. Chapel Hill: University of North Carolina Press
Harris, W.V. (1989) *Ancient Literacy*. Cambridge Mass.: Harvard University Press
Hauser, A. (1968) "The Origins of Domestic Drama", trans. S. Godman, in Bentley (1968), 403–19
Havelock, E.A. (1963) *Preface to Plato*. Cambridge Mass.: Harvard University Press
Havelock, E.A. (1981) *The Literate Revolution and Its Consequences*. Princeton: Princeton University Press
Heartz, D. (1967–68) "From Garrick to Gluck: the Reform of Theatre and Opera in the Mid-Eighteenth Century", *Proceedings of the Royal Musical Association* 94, 111–27
Heilpern, J. (1989) *Conference of the Birds: The Story of Peter Brook in Africa*, revised edition. London: Methuen
Hobson, M. (1973) "Le 'Paradoxe sur le comédien' est un paradoxe", *Poétique* 15, 320–39
Hobson, M. (1982) *The Object of Art: The Theory of Illusion in Eighteenth-Century France*. Cambridge: Cambridge University Press
Hobson, M., Leigh, J.T.A. and Wokler, R. (eds) (1992) *Rousseau and the Eighteenth Century: Essays in Memory of R.A. Leigh*. Oxford: Voltaire Foundation
Hoffman, A. (1968) *Revolution for the Hell of It*. New York: Dial Books
Hughes, Ted (1971) "Orghast: talking without words", *Vogue* December, 96–7
Hunt, A. and Reeves, G. (1995) *Peter Brook*. Cambridge: Cambridge University Press
Hussey, E. (1972) *The Presocratics*. London: Duckworth
Huyssen, A. (1986) *After the Great Divide: Modernism, Mass Culture, Postmodernism*. Bloomington: Indiana University Press
Innes, C. (1993) *Avant-Garde Theatre 1892–1992*. London: Routledge
Janko, R. (1984) *Aristotle on Comedy: Towards a Reconstruction of Poetics II*. Berkeley and Los Angeles: University of California Press
Jones, J. (1962) *On Aristotle and Greek Tragedy*. London: Chatto and Windus
Josephs, H. (1969) *Diderot's Dialogue of Language and Gesture:* Le Neveu de Rameau. Columbus: Ohio State University Press
Kamuf de Magnin, P. (1975) "Rousseau's Politics of Visibility", *Diacritics* 5.4, 51–6
Kelly, C. (1987) *Rousseau's Exemplary Life:* The Confessions *as Political Philosophy*. Ithaca: Cornell University Press
Kennedy, G.A. (ed.) (1989) *The Cambridge History of Literary Criticism Vol.I: Classical Criticism*. Cambridge: Cambridge University Press
Kirk, G.S., Raven, J.E. and Schofield, M. (eds) (1983) *The Presocratic Philosophers*, second edition. Cambridge: Cambridge University Press
Kleber, P. and Visser, C. (eds) (1990) *Re-Interpreting Brecht*. Cambridge: Cambridge University Press

Koller, H. (1954) *Die Mimesis in der Antike*. Bern: Francke.
Krant, R. (ed.) (1992) *Companion to Plato*. Cambridge: Cambridge University Press
Kreals, E.C. (1978) *Plato and Greek Painting*. Leiden: Brill
La Barre, W. (1954) *The Human Animal*. Chicago: Chicago University Press
Lacoue-Labarthe, P. (1980) "Diderot, le paradoxe et la mimésis", *Poétique* 11.43, 267–81
Lacoue-Labarthe, P. (1989) *Typography: Mimesis, Philosophy, Politics*, ed. C. Fynsk. Cambridge, Mass.: Harvard University Press
Lee, V. (1975) *The Reign of Women in Eighteenth-Century France*. Cambridge, Mass.: Schenkman
Lessing, G.E. (1962) *Hamburg Dramaturgy*, trans. H. Zimmern. New York: Dover
Ley, G. (1993) "The Rhetoric of Theory: the Role of Metaphor in Brook's *The Empty Space*", *New Theatre Quarterly* 35, 246–54
Ley, G. (1995) "The Significance of Diderot", *New Theatre Quarterly* 44, 342–54
Lloyd, G.E.R. (1967) *Polarity and Analogy: Two Types of Argumentation in Early Greek Thought*. Cambridge: Cambridge University Press
Lloyd, G.E.R. (1979) *Magic, Reason, and Experience*. Cambridge: Cambridge University Press
Lord, C. (1982) *Education and Culture in the Political Thought of Aristotle*. Ithaca: Cornell University Press
Lorenz, K. (1967) *On Aggression*, trans. M. Latzke. New York: Bantam Books
Lough, J. (ed.) (1954) *The* Encyclopédie *of Diderot and d'Alembert: Selected Articles*. Cambridge: Cambridge University Press
Lough, J. (ed.) (1971) *The* Encyclopédie. London: Longman
Lukács, G. (1968) "The Sociology of Modern Drama", trans. L. Baxandall, in Bentley (1968), 425–50
Lynham, D. (1972) *The Chevalier Noverre: Father of Modern Ballet*. London: Dance Books
Lyotard, J.-F. (1984) *The Postmodern Condition: A Report on Knowledge*, trans. G. Bennington and B. Massumi. Minneapolis: University of Minnesota Press
McDonald, C.V. (1984) *The Dialogue of Writing: Essays in Eighteenth-Century French Literature*. Waterloo, Ont.: Wilfrid Laurier University Press
Magarshack, D. (1950) *Stanislavsky: A Life*. London: McGibbon and Gee
Mann, P. (1991) *The Theory-Death of the Avant-Garde*. Bloomington: Indiana University Press
Marranca, B. and Dasgupta, G. (eds) (1991) *Interculturalism and Performance: Writings from Performing Arts Journal*. New York: Performing Arts Journal Publications
Marshall, D. (1988) *The Surprising Effects of Sympathy: Marivaux, Diderot, Rousseau, and Mary Shelley*. Chicago: Chicago University Press
Maskell, D. (1991) *Racine: A Theatrical Reading*. Oxford: Clarendon Press

Mason, J.H. (1992) "The *Lettre à d'Alembert* and Its Place in Rousseau's Thought", in Hobson, Leigh and Wokler (1992), 251–69
Mitter, S. (1992) *Systems of Rehearsal*. London: Routledge
Modrak, D. (1987) *Aristotle: The Power of Perception*. Chicago: Chicago University Press
Moore, S.F. and Myerhoff, B.G. (eds) (1977) *Secular Ritual*. Amsterdam: Van Gorcum
Moravscik, J. and Tempo, P. (eds) (1982) *Plato on Beauty, Wisdom, and the Arts*. Totowa, NJ: Rowman and Littlefield
Müller, H. (1984) *Hamletmachine and Other Texts for the Stage*, trans. C. Weber. New York: Performing Arts Journal Publications
Müller, H. (1986) *Gesammelte Irrtümer: Interviews und Gespräche*. Frankfurt am Main: Verlag der Autoren
Müller, H. (1989) *Heiner Müller Material*, ed. F. Hornigk. Leipzig: Reclam
Munk, E. (1986) "The Rites of Women", *Performing Arts Journal* X.2, 35–42
Newman, E. (1964) *Gluck and the Opera*. London: Gollancz
Niklaus, R. (1963) "Diderot et Rousseau pour et contre le théâtre", *Diderot Studies* 4, 153–89
Nussbaum, M.C. (1986) *The Fragility of Goodness: Luck and Ethics in Greek Tragedy and Philosophy*. Cambridge: Cambridge University Press
Nussbaum, M.C. and Rorty, A.O. (eds) (1992) *Essays on Aristotle's de Anima*. Oxford: Clarendon Press
O'Neal, J.C. (1985) "Myth, Language and Perception in Rousseau's *Narcisse*", *Theatre Journal* 37.2, 192–202
Ong, W.J. (1982) *Orality and Literacy*. London: Methuen
Paulson, W.R. (1987) *Enlightenment, Romanticism, and the Blind in France*. Princeton: Princeton University Press
Pavis, P. (1980) *Dictionnaire du Théâtre*. Paris: Éditions sociales
Pavis, P. (1982) *Languages of the Stage: Essays in the Semiology of Theatre*, trans. S. Melrose and others. New York: Performing Arts Journal Publications
Pavis, P. (1992) *Theatre at the Crossroads of Culture*, trans. L. Kruger. London: Routledge
Pavis, P. (1996) *The Intercultural Performance Reader*. London: Routledge
Poggioli, R. (1968) *The Theory of the Avant-Garde*, trans. G. Fitzgerald. Cambridge, Mass.: Harvard University Press
Polyakova, E. (1982) *Stanislavsky*, trans. L. Tudge. Moscow: Progress Publishers
Prud'homme, J.-G. (1985) *Christophe-Willibald Gluck*. Paris: Fuyard
Rappaport, R.A. (1968) *Pigs for the Ancestors*. New Haven: Yale University Press
Rex, W.E. (1990) "Sexual Metamorphoses on the Stage in the Mid-Eighteenth Century: the Theatrical Background of Rousseau's *Narcisse*", *Studies on Voltaire and the Eighteenth Century* 278, 265–76
Reynolds, F. and Reynolds, V. (1965) " Chimpanzees of the Bundongo Forest", in DeVore (1965), 368–424

Richmond, F. (1978) "The Rites of Passage and *Kutiyattam*", *Sangeet Natak* 50, 27–36

Richmond, F. and Richmond Y. (1985) "The Multiple Dimensions of Time and Space in *Kutiyattam*, the Sanskrit Theatre of Kerala", *Asian Theatre Journal* 2.1, 50–60

Richmond, F., Swann, D.L. and Zarrilli, P. (eds) (1990) *Indian Theatre: Traditions of Performance*. Honolulu: University of Hawaii Press

Roach, J.R. (1981) "Diderot and the Actor's Machine", *Theatre Survey* 22, 51–68

Roach, J.R. (1985) *The Player's Passion: Studies in the Science of Acting*. Newark: University of Delaware Press

Rorty, A.O. (ed.) (1992) *Essays on Aristotle's* Poetics. Princeton: Princeton University Press

Rorty, A.O. (ed.) (1996) *Essays on Aristotle's* Rhetoric. Berkeley: University of California Press

Ryle, G. (1966) *Plato's Progress*. Cambridge: Cambridge University Press

Saisselin, R.G. (1961) "'Ut Pictura Poesis': Dubos to Diderot", *Journal of Aesthetics and Art Criticism* 20, 145–56

Schechner, R. (1969) *Public Domain*. Indianapolis: Bobbs-Merrill

Schechner, R. (1973) *Environmental Theater*. New York: Hawthorn

Schechner, R. (1977) *Essays on Performance Theory*. New York: Drama Book Specialists

Schechner, R. (1982) *The End of Humanism*. New York: Performing Arts Journal Publications

Schechner, R. (1983) *Performative Circumstances: From the Avant-Garde to Ramlila*. Calcutta: Seagull Books

Schechner, R. (1985) *Between Theater and Anthropology*. Philadelphia: University of Pennsylvania Press

Schechner, R. (1988) *Performance Theory*. London: Routledge

Schechner, R. (1991) "Intercultural Themes", in Marranca and Dasgupta (1991), 308–17

Schechner, R. (1993) *The Future of Ritual: Writings on Culture and Performance*. London: Routledge

Schwartz, J. (1984) *The Sexual Politics of Jean-Jacques Rousseau*. Chicago: Chicago University Press

Sherman, C. (1976) *Diderot and the Art of Dialogue*. Geneva: Droz

Sidnell, M. (ed.) (1994) *Sources of Dramatic Theory Vol.2: Voltaire to Hugo*. Cambridge: Cambridge University Press

Singer, M. (1972) *When a Great Tradition Modernizes*. New York: Praeger

Smith, A.C. (1972) *Orghast at Persepolis*. London: Methuen

Speaight, G. (1990) *The History of the English Puppet Theatre*, second edition. London: Hale

Stanislavski, C. (1962) *My Life in Art*, trans. J.J. Robbins. London: Bles
Starobinski, J. (1988) *Jean-Jacques Rousseau: Transparency and Obstruction*, trans. A.Goldhammer. Chicago: Chicago University Press
Swain, V.E. (1982) "Diderot's *Paradoxe sur le comédien*: the Paradox of Reading", *Studies in Voltaire and the Eighteenth Century* 208, 1–71
Symcox, G. (1972) "The Wild Man's Return: The Enclosed Vision of Rousseau's Discourses", in Dudley and Novak (1972), 223–47
Szondi, P. (1980) "*Tableau* and *Coup de Théâtre*: on the Social Psychology of Diderot's Bourgeois Drama", *New Literary History* 11, 323–43
Tatlow, A. (1985) "The Way Ahead II: Brecht and Postmodernism", in *The Brecht Yearbook Vol. 12: 1983*. Detroit: Wayne University Press
Taylor, R. (1949) "Rousseau's Conception of Music", *Music and Letters* 30, 231–42
Thomas, R. (1989) *Oral Tradition and Written Record In Classical Athens*. Cambridge: Cambridge University Press
Thomson, P. and Sacks, G. (eds) (1994) *The Cambridge Companion to Brecht*. Cambridge: Cambridge University Press
Todorov, T. (1990) *Genres in Discourse*, trans. C. Porter. Cambridge: Cambridge University Press
Tort, P. (1980) *L'Origine du Paradoxe sur le comédien: la partition intérieure*, second edition. Paris: Vrin
Trilling, O. (1972) "Playing with words at Persepolis", *Theatre Quarterly* 5, 33–40
Turner, V. (1967) *The Forest of Symbols*. Ithaca: Cornell University Press
Turner, V. (1968) *The Drums of Affliction: A Study of Religious Processes Among the Ndembu of Zambia*. Oxford: Clarendon Press
Turner, V. (1969) *The Ritual Process: Structure and Anti-Structure*. London: Routledge and Kegan Paul
Turner, V. (1974) *Dramas, Fields, and Metaphors: Symbolic Action in Human Society*. Ithaca: Cornell University Press
Turner, V. (1977) "Variations on a Theme of Liminality", in Moore and Myerhoff (1977), 36–52
Turner, V. (1982) *From Ritual to Theatre: The Human Seriousness of Play*. New York: Performing Arts Journal Publications
Turner, V. (1985) *On the Edge of the Bush*. Tucson: University of Arizona Press
Turner, V. (1987) *The Anthropology of Performance*. New York: Performing Arts Journal Publications
Undank, J. and Josephs, H. (eds) (1984) *Diderot: Digression and Dispersion: A Bicentennial Tribute*. Lexington: French Forum
Van Gennep, A. (1960) *The Rites of Passage*, trans. M.B. Vizedom and G.L. Caffee. Chicago: Chicago University Press
Velho, Y.M.A. (1975) *Guerra de Orixa: Un Estudo de Ritual e Conflito*. Rio de Janeiro: Zahar

Vexler, F. (1922) *Studies in Diderot's Esthetic Naturalism*. New York: Columbia University Press
Vickers, B. (1973) *Towards Greek Tragedy*. London: Longman
Waldinger, R. (1981) "Diderot as Dramatist: Dramatic Prose? Prosaic Drama?", *Diderot Studies* 20, 287–97
Walton, K.L. (1990) *Mimesis as Make-Believe: On the Foundation of the Representational Arts*. Cambridge, Mass.: Harvard University Press
Wasserman, E.R. (1947) "The Sympathetic Imagination in Eighteenth-Century Theories of Acting", *Journal of English and Germanic Philology* 46, 264–72
Watson, I. (1993) *Towards a Third Theatre: Eugenio Barba and the Odin Teatret*. London: Routledge
Wellington, M. (1987) *The Art of Voltaire's Theatre: An Exploration of Possibility*. New York: Lang
Werner, S. (1987) *Socratic Satire: An Essay on Diderot and* Le Neveu de Rameau. Birmingham, Al: Summa Publications
White, H. (1972) "The Forms of Wildness: Archaeology of an Idea", in Dudley and Novak (1972), 3–38
White, H. (1973) *Metahistory: The Historical Imagination in Nineteenth-Century Europe*. Baltimore: Johns Hopkins University Press
White, N.P. (1979) *A Companion to Plato's* Republic. Indianapolis: Hackett
Whitmore, R.P. (1973) "Two Essays on *Le Père de famille*", *Studies on Voltaire and the Eighteenth Century* 116, 137–209
Wiles, T. (1980) *The Theater Event: Modern Theories of Performance*. Chicago: Chicago University Press
Williams, C.G.S. (ed.) (1975) *Literature and History in the Age of Ideas: Essays on the French Enlightenment Presented to George R. Havens*. Columbus: Ohio State University Press
Williams, D. (ed.) (1991) *Peter Brook and the Mahabharata: Critical Perspectives*. London: Routledge
Williams, D. (ed.) (1992) *Peter Brook: A Theatrical Casebook*, revised edition. London: Methuen
Williams, H. (1983) *Rousseau and Romantic Autobiography*. Oxford: Oxford University Press
Wright, E. (1989) *Postmodern Brecht: A Representation*. London: Routledge
Zarrilli, P. (1988a) "For Whom Is the 'Invisible' Not Visible? Reflections on Representation in the Work of Eugenio Barba", *Drama Review* 32.1, 95–106
Zarrilli, P. (1988b) "Zarrilli Responds", *Drama Review* 32.3, 15–16

Index

Aboriginal culture 193
Académie Française 68
Academy of Dijon 55, 58
Academy of Sciences 54
Adeimantus 12, 13, 22
Aeschylus 130; *Eumenides* 78; *Oresteia* 18, 78, 187, 188; *Persians* 128
aesthetic(s) 13, 168, 177–8, 183, 198, 203, 209–10, 261, 263, 267, 272, 276
agon 203
Alexander of Pheros 61, 67
allegory (allegorical) 6, 45–6, 131, 254–5, 258, 261
amour 62, 68, 69
amour de soi 62
amour-propre 62, 63, 74, 86
anagnorisis (*anagnoriseis*, pl.) 34, 40
analogy (analogies, analogous) 22, 25, 34, 45–6, 98, 146, 149, 152, 160, 167–8, 195, 196, 234, 253, 291, 295–9
anamnesis 6, 11, 16, 17, 20
Andrews, Raymond 199
antistructure 165, 171–2
antithesis (antithetical) 87, 121, 136, 149
Apollodorus 4
apologia 76, 160, 169, 189, 288, 289
Appia 213
Arden, John: *Serjeant Musgrave's Dance* 119
Aristodemus 4
Aristophanes 85; *Birds* 20; *Clouds* 20; *Frogs* 19, 204; *Wealth* 20; *Women at the Thesmophoria* 19, 20
Aristotle 9, 27, 48–9, 85, 267, 270, 292; *Ethics* 27–8, 30, 31, 34; *Metaphysics* 33, 46; *On Memory and Recollection* 50; *On Music* 34; *On Perception* 46, 50; *On the Soul* 50; *Physics* 33, 294, 295; *Poetics* 3, 27–8, 28–35, 35–44, 46, 86, 89, 162, 295; *Politics* 36, 37, 39, 43, 44; *Rhetoric* 27–8, 30, 31, 32, 33, 34, 40, 42, 43, 44, 50
Artaud 117, 119, 120, 123, 124, 128, 168–9, 180, 191, 213, 215, 251, 285, 290, 301; *Theatre and Its Double, The* 123
Arte Nuevo 218
Asian Theatre Journal 276, 284
Auden, W.H. 151, 262
audience 43, 48, 49, 69, 79, 105, 107, 112, 127, 176, 185, 203, 296, 300
Auerbach, E. 292–3
avant-garde 161, 176, 184, 189–20, 191, 207, 222, 244–5, 277–80, 282
Aztecs 227

Babcock, B. 167
Balinese theatre 236
ballet d'action 83
Barba, Eugenio 141, 178, 207, 210, 279, 282, 283, 285, 286; *Beyond the Floating Islands* 229; 'Eurasian Theatre' 240–3; *Floating Islands, The* 215, 216, 218, 221, 229; 'Four Spectators' 244–8; 'Kathakali Theatre, The' 212–14; 'Letter from Barba in Southern Italy, A' ('Letter from the South of Italy') 215, 218; 'Letter to Actor D' 217; *Paper Canoe, The* 240; 'Questions on Training' 218, 224–5; 'Theatre Anthropology: First Hypothesis' 229–31, 234, 236, 237; 'Theatre–Culture' 225; 'Theatre Laboratory 13 Rzedow' 211, 215; 'Waiting for the Revolution' 216
Barba, Eugenio and Savarese, Nicola: *Dictionary of Theatre Anthropology, A* 141, 212, 220–1, 231, 232, 234

barter 218–20, 225
Bausch 264
Beckett, Samuel 119, 120, 152, 156, 163, 119; *Waiting for Godot* 187, 188
behaviour 143, 155, 195–6, 201, 209, 232, 247
Benedetti, J. 253
Bentham, Jeremy 300
Bergson 116
Berliner Ensemble 198, 265, 266, 267, 301
Bharucha, R. 275–6, 279–86; 'Collision of Cultures' 276, 279–80, 283–4; *Theatre and the World* 275–6, 279–84
bhavas 205
bios 243
Bohr Institute 216
Boileau 85
Brecht 119, 123, 124, 199, 205, 251, 252, 261–74, 301; *Baal* 263; *In the Jungle of the Cities* 263; *Messingkauf Dialogues, The* 263, 271; 'Short Description of a New Technique of Acting, A' 269; *Short Organum for the Theatre, A* 267, 270, 272; 'Street Scene, The' 272–4
Brewer, M. 297
Brook, Peter 176–8, 196, 279, 282, 283, 285, 286; *Empty Space, The* 111–22, 125–30, 136, 137, 140, 176; *Ik, The* 123–4; *Orghast* 124, 125, 134, 285; *Shifting Point, The* 137; 'Slyness of Boredom, The' 137–9; 'Theatre of Cruelty' season 122–5, 126, 128, 132 ; *There Are No Secrets* 137; *US* 122, 123, 124, 127
Brooker, P. 266, 267
burlesque 80

Cage, John 175–6
Caillois, R. 171, 184
Calderon: *Life Is a Dream* 128
Cannan, Denis 124
Carnaval 171-2
Carrière, Jean-Claude 124
catharsis 117, 267, 269 [see also *katharsis*]
Cenci, The 128
censorship 24–5
Chaikin, Joseph 196; *Presence of the Actor, The* 123

Chekhov, Anton 114, 195, 199, 257, 298; *Three Sisters* 187, 188
chiasmus 121
CIRT (International Centre for Theatre Research) 125, 126, 130, 131
Clairon, Mlle 96–7, 103, 104
classical 61, 96, 100, 102, 164, 293, 300–1
Comédie Française 57
comedy (comic) 15, 19, 26, 27, 29, 44, 57, 68, 80, 81, 82
commedia dell'arte 236
communitas 148–53, 162
comparison 10, 11, 12, 63, 64, 146, 160, 168, 174, 201, 266
composition 13, 15, 17, 21, 23, 24, 26, 27, 29, 30, 31, 34, 47, 49, 83, 84, 85, 111, 245
contradiction 63, 96
contrast 97, 159, 161
Copeau 215
Corneille 68, 100; *Le Cid* 68
Cornford, Francis 182
Cortez 130
coup de théâtre 76, 81, 83
Craig, E. Gordon 119, 213, 275, 280, 282
Crébillon; *Atrée* 68; *Thyeste* 68
cultural theory 162–3, 166–74
Cunningham 119, 120

d'Alembert 74; *Encyclopédie* 55, 65, 75, 84, 90
d'Aubignac: *Pratique du théâtre, La* 84
dance (dancing, *danse*) 64, 73, 74, 83, 189–90, 192–4, 199, 200, 235–8, 242
Darwin, Charles 196
de Marinis, M. 244; 'Dramaturgy of the Spectator' 244–5; *Semiotics of Performance, The* 287, 290–2
Decroux 238
definition 20, 39, 121, 147, 175, 211, 222–3, 226, 230, 232–3, 285
Democritus 9–10
Derrida, Jacques 294
diagram 184–5, 206, 208–9
dialogue (dialectic) 3–4, 7–8, 13, 15, 18, 46, 75, 76, 84, 92, 97, 99, 104, 106, 187, 285, 300

dianoia 10, 34
Diderot, Denis 52, 55, 65, 66, 74–5, 270, 271; *Conversations on The Natural Son* 75–9, 79–84, 85, 90, 92, 100; *Discourse on Dramatic Poetry* 75, 84–91, 92–3, 100, 101, 103; *Encyclopédie* 75, 84, 90, 94; *Essays on Painting* 101; *Father of the Family, The* 75, 84; *Letter on the Deaf and Dumb* 90; *Natural Son, The* 75, 79, 81; *Paradoxe sur le comédien (Paradox on the Actor)* 75, 91–107; *Rameau's Nephew* 99–100, 102
Diderot Society 262
diegesis 13, 14, 17
Dilthey, Wilhelm 164
discourse (discursive) 84–91, 93, 112, 117, 133, 137, 143, 166, 168, 174, 179, 181–91, 198, 201, 208, 220, 226, 227–8, 229–40, 251 252–3, 257, 261, 274, 275, 281, 283, 287–92, 297–8, 302
dismissal 111–22, 176–7, 209, 211, 220
distinction 159, 161
division 23, 63
Dort 266
Drama Review 175, 181, 211, 218, 240, 276, 278
du Bos: *Critical Reflections on Poetry and Painting* 84
Dumazedier, J. 156
Dumesnil, Mlle 97
Durkheim, E. 154, 212

Eagleton, T. 272
eidos 10
Eisenstein 262
ekmimeisthai 20
Elephant Man, The 203
emic models 162
Emigh, John 200
Enlightenment 75, 94
environment(al) 176–81, 276
epic 14, 16, 21, 29, 30, 33, 83
epic theatre 273
Erlebnis 164
Esslin 262
etic models 162
étranger 74
etymology 144, 155, 173, 234

eudaimonia 31
Eurasian theatre 242, 246
Euripides: *Bacchae* 158; *Electra* 18; *Helen* 19; *Iphigenia in Tauris* 36; *Madness of Heracles, The* 19
Euro-American 282
Evanchuk, Robin 199
everyday 295–9
exchange(s) 130, 176, 241, 276, 282–3, 285, 296
experiment(al) 124–5, 126, 130, 132, 134, 137, 155, 156, 179, 191, 199, 207, 276

fable 255
fantome 97
Farîd al-Dîn 'Attâr of Nîshâpûr 131
fear 33, 35–7, 39–44, 49, 50, 270
Fergusson, Francis 181
figure (figurative) 6, 56, 115, 184–8, 191, 197–8, 199, 206, 208, 210, 226, 227, 239, 274, 286, 297, 300, 302
Firth 169
Flaszen 211
Forms, doctrine of 7–8, 23
Foucault, M. 300
Frazer, James: *Golden Bough, The* 182
Freud, Sigmund 196, 293
Fuegi, John 252, 262

Gahuku 202, 203
games 156, 182–8, 201
Garrick, David 75, 92, 103, 104, 105
Geertz, C. 145, 165, 200
Genet, Jean 119; *Maids, The* 188
Geneva 52–4, 58, 65–6, 69, 72–4
genre sérieux, le 75, 80–1
gest 272
gesture 49, 60, 77, 90, 258
Gielgud, Sir John 120
Girard, R. 293
Glaucon 10, 27, 44, 45–6
Gluck 83–4; *Don Juan* 84; *Orfeo* 84
Gluckman, Max 141–2, 146, 147
Godard 115
Goffman, E. 295–9; *Interaction Ritual* 299; 'On Face Work' 296, 299; *Presentation of Self in Everyday Life, The* 295–6, 298

Goodall, J. van L. 196
Gray, Spalding 199
Grimm, Melchior 85, 88, 101; *Correspondence littéraire* 92, 102
Grotowski, Jerzy 119, 120, 136, 178, 179, 191, 196, 207, 210–16, 251, 275, 279, 280, 282, 301; *Towards a Poor Theatre* 123, 210, 215–16

Hall, Peter 119, 125
hamartia 30, 43–4
hana 205
Harrison, Jane 182
Havelock, E.A. 3
Heilpern, J. 126; *Conference of the Birds* 124, 125, 130–4
Herodotus 19, 59
Hidalgo 163
Hobbes, Thomas 59; *Leviathan, The* 60
Homer 13, 16, 24, 29, 252; *Iliad* 14; *Odyssey* 14
homoios 40–1, 42, 44
Horace 85, 107
Hughes, Ted 122, 124, 127; *Oedipus* 127
Huizinga 184
humanité 94
Humphrey, Doris: *Shakers, The* 199
Hunt, Albert 123
Hymn to Delian Apollo 18

Ibsen, Henrik 195, 298
ideai 10
ideal model 103
idein 10
image(s) (imagery) 9, 19, 20, 22, 24, 45, 50, 56, 76, 79, 84, 90, 96, 97, 103, 113, 126, 166, 194, 204, 217, 221–2, 227–9, 286
imitation (imitative) 13–14, 15–17, 18, 21, 24–6, 29, 30, 47, 83, 98, 102–3
imitator(s) 17, 23, 24, 70, 95
Indian theatre 204, 205, 282
interculturalism 130, 207, 275–87
International Brecht Society 262
International Centre for Theatre Research 124, 125 [see also CIRT]
International School for Theatre Anthropology (ISTA) 210, 220, 221, 229, 230, 231, 234, 239, 240, 242, 243
intertextual(ity) 125–30, 280, 282, 301
invisible (the) 9, 121, 129, 135, 136, 137, 138–40, 147, 151
intracultural 283
Ionesco 195; *Lesson, The* 187

Japanese Buyo 238
Jonson, Ben 114
Joyce, James 156

Kabuki theatre 236
Kathakali theatre 130, 212–14, 236, 277
katharsis 36–8, 39, 43, 44, 67, 204, 205, 292–3 [see also *catharsis*]
Kerensky 255
kosmos 48
Kutiyattam 172–4

La Barre, W. 189
laboratory 125, 127, 128, 191, 210–16, 230, 234, 243
Laboratory Theatre 212–13, 230
Lacan 293
Lacoue-Labarthe, P. 293–5; 'Diderot's Paradox and Mimesis' 293–4
laughter 26, 27, 116
Lawrence, D.H. 127
leisure 156–7
Lenin 255
LePage 207
Lessing, G.E. 270, 271; *Hamburg Dramaturgy* 270
Leucippus 9
lexis 34
Lillo: *London Merchant, The* 78
liminal contemporary theatre 194
liminal *personae* 148, 149
liminal phenomena 159
liminal zone 161
liminality 146–53
liminoid genres 153–66
logos 21, 33, 50, 51, 243
lokadharmi 235
Lorenz, Konrad 196
Lyotard, Jean-François 262

lyric theatre 83

macrocosm 25, 38
Magarshack, D. 253
Mahabharata, The 124, 207
Marlowe, Christopher: *Doctor Faustus* 126
Marowitz, Charles 123, 124, 125, 126
Marx, Karl 164
Mayhew 296
melopoia 34
merveilleux, le 80
metaphor(ic) (-ical) 6, 10, 34, 37–8, 43, 44, 46, 55, 97, 112–22, 132, 136,137–8, 151, 153, 159, 164, 167, 169, 177–8, 204–5, 220, 227, 234, 290, 302
metascience 291
Meyerhold 127, 213, 215
microcosm 25, 38
mime 20, 77, 145, 238
mimeisthai 20
mimema (*ta*, pl.) 15, 17, 19, 20, 31
mimesis 13, 14, 16, 17–21, 29, 30–1, 32–5, 51, 268, 292–3, 294–5
mimetai 11, 13, 17
mimicry 15–16, 18, 19, 20, 99
mimoi 18
mirror(s) 164–5, 167
mise en scène 284–7
Mnouchkine 285, 286
modern(ism) (-ist) (-ity) 172, 251, 267, 269
Molière 85, 90, 104; *Dépit amoureux, Le* 104; *Misanthrope, The* 68; *Miser, The* 90
Montaigne 59
Moore: *Gamester, The* 78
Moscow Art Theatre 198, 259
mousike 27, 31
Müller, H. 264–5
Murray, Gilbert 182
music 27, 31, 34–5, 37, 52, 54–5, 57, 134–5, 182–3, 194
muthos 34, 40, 43, 49, 50
myth(s) 130, 157, 180, 258, 290

narration (narrative) 4, 13–14, 21, 53, 131, 169–71, 254–9, 262
nature (natural) 31, 33, 58, 89, 91, 95, 102, 107, 214, 273–4
natyadharmi 235
Natyasastra 203, 204, 205, 206
Ndembu 142–8, 151, 158, 162–3, 165, 169
Nemirovich-Danchenko 254, 259
New Orleans Group 178, 179
New Theatre Quarterly 240
Noh drama 203, 205, 236
Nordisk Teaterlaboratorium for Skuespillerkunst 210
Noverre 83–4; *Lettres sur la danse* 83

Occidental theatre 236–7, 241
Odin Teatret 210, 214, 215, 218–20, 222–4, 230, 232, 240, 243, 246
Odissi 236, 237
Oedipus 36, 42
Ong, W.J. 3
opera buffa 57
opposition, principle of 237, 238
opsis 34, 35, 45, 46–8, 49, 50
Orient/Orient(al) (-ism) 174, 213, 215, 223–4, 227, 235, 238–9, 241

paidia 16
Panigrahi, Sanjukta 235, 238, 239
Panopticon 300
pantomime 77, 78, 81, 82, 83, 86, 89–91, 99
paradeigma 10, 18
paradigm(atic) 10, 11, 17, 21, 22, 24, 28, 124, 152, 163, 196
paradox(ical) 32, 55, 71, 93, 97, 98–9, 104–5, 107, 129, 135, 140, 153, 209, 219, 256, 264, 293–4
Parmenides 9
parody(ing) (parodied) 20, 81
Pavis, P. 275–87, 291; 'Discussion on the Semiology of Theatre' 289; 'Interculturalism in the Contemporary *Mise en Scène* ...' 286–7; *Languages of the Stage* 287, 289; 'Possible Definition of Theatre Semiology, A' 288; 'Reflections on the Notation of the Theatrical Performance' 290; *Theatre at the Crossroads of Culture* 284, 287; 'Towards a Theory of Culture and *Mise en Scène*'

284–5
Peking Opera 238
perfectibilité 63
Performance Garage 178, 191
Performance Group, The 175, 178, 179, 189, 190, 196
Performing Arts Journal 162
peripeteia 34, 40
persuasion 9, 112, 161, 185
Peulh, the 134–5
phantasia 50
phantasma 103
phobos 270
pilgrim(age) 55, 132, 152, 154
Piscator 213, 262
pitié 61–2
pity 33, 35–7, 39–44, 49, 50, 61–2, 67, 80
Plato 3, 10, 28, 66, 72, 102, 289, 300; *Charmides* 38; *Cratylus* 38; *Gorgias* 30; *Laws* 73; *Phaedo* 4–10, 11, 38, 44, 45; *Phaedrus* 6, 9, 11, 22, 30; *Philebus* 31, 44, 50; *Republic* 10–17, 21–7, 30, 32, 39, 42, 44–5, 67, 103; *Symposium* 4; *Theaetetus* 50
play 155, 156, 157–8, 171, 182–8
pleasure 22, 31–2, 33, 39, 44, 51, 66, 112, 186, 265–72
Plutarch 61, 67
Poel, William 119
poiesis 23, 24
polarity (poles) 129, 180, 237, 240, 243, 246–7
Polyakova 253
Polyclitus 102
postmodern(ism) (-ist) (-ity) 261–5, 206
prasad 204
praxis 34, 191, 269
Primal Ritual 184–5, 209
productivism (productivity) 184, 261, 266, 268, 269
proscenium theatre 194–5
psyche 6

Rabelais 156
Racine 100
Rappaport 193
rasa 203, 204–5
Rasmussen, Iben Nagl 239
recall 4, 17, 28
reception 35, 43, 74, 204–5, 244–5, 251, 262, 284, 291
Reeves, Geoffrey 129
religion (religious) 37, 38, 126–7, 142, 153, 154, 159, 174, 204, 209, 268
Renoir, Jean 262
restored behavior 197–201
revelation 111, 122, 137, 277, 287
rhapsodes 15, 17
rhetoric(al) 42, 56, 57, 71, 73, 95, 96, 111–40, 158, 173, 177, 188, 220–1, 228, 239, 272, 277, 289
Richmond, F. 172, 173, 174
Richmond, Y. 172, 173, 174
rites de passage 146, 147, 152
rites (ritual) 142–6, 148, 149, 150, 153, 155, 157, 169, 172, 173–4, 182–8, 191, 201, 202–3, 206, 208–9, 213, 296, 299
ritualization 194, 208–9, 243
Rossi, Ernesto 256
Rousseau, Jean-Jacques 52–4, 84–5, 86, 87–8, 105, 155, 172, 300; *Confessions* 52, 53, 54, 55; *Devin du village* 57; *Discourse on the Origin of Inequality* 58–64, 106; *Discourse on the Sciences and the Arts* 55–7; *Emile* 52; *Encyclopédie* 55, 65; *Letter to d'Alembert on Public Performances* 54, 65–74, 79, 84, 106, 172, 300; *Narcisse* 57–8; *On the Social Contract* 52; *On Theatrical Imitation: An Essay Drawn from the Dialogues of Plato* 67; *Project Concerning New Symbols for Music* 55
Royal Shakespeare Company (RSC) 118, 123, 125
Rudkin, David: *Afore Night Come* 119
Ruffini, Franco 218, 224, 225, 230
Russian Musical Society 256

Salons 92, 100, 102, 103
Sanskrit theatre 203, 204, 206
satire (satirical, satirist) 60, 99, 100
Schechner, Richard 141, 175, 275–87, 295, 296, 299; 'Approaches to Theory/Criticism' 181–91, 194; *Between Theater and Anthropology* 175, 197, 279, 282;

'Crash of Performative Circumstances, The' 278; 'Decline and Fall of the (American) Avant-Garde' 207, 276, 278, 279, 280; *Dionysus in 69* 179, 180, 203, 204; 'Drama, Script, Theater, and Performance' 189; *End of Humanism, The* 276, 278; *Environmental Theater* 175–81, 189; 'Ethology and Theater' 195; 'From Ritual to Theater and Back' 276; *Future of Ritual, The* 175; 'Intercultural Themes' 276; *Makbeth* 179; *Performance Theory* 175, 195–6; *Performative Circumstances* 175, 282; 'Performer Training Interculturally' 279; 'Performers and Spectators Transported and Transformed' 175, 197, 201–2, 276, 279; *Public Domain* 175–81; 'Restoration of Behavior' 175, 197–8; 'Six Axioms for Environmental Theatre' 175–6, 177, 179, 180, 181; 'Towards a Poetics of Performance' 192–7

Schrecken 270

science (scientific, scientist) 27, 33, 94, 98, 127, 128, 136–7, 146, 178, 181, 193, 214, 216, 230, 233, 267–8, 289, 291, 295

Scofield, Paul 120

sculptor (sculpture) 23, 102

semiology 287–92

semiotics 244, 287–92

Seneca 128; *Oedipus* 122

sensibilité 93–4, 95, 105

sensibility 92, 93–4

Shakespeare, William 113–14, 115, 119, 121, 122, 124, 136, 139, 195; *Coriolanus* 119–20; *Hamlet* 187, 188; *King Lear* 123; *Measure for Measure* 117; *Richard III* 270; *Romeo and Juliet* 118; *Tempest, The* 117, 140; *Titus Andronicus* 114, 117, 119; *Winter's Tale, The* 114

Shaw, George Bernard 298

Shepard, Sam 190; *Tooth of Crime, The* 179, 189

simile 6, 137

Singer, M. 166

Smith, A.C.: *Orghast at Persepolis* 124, 125–30

social drama 145, 151–3, 195

sociality 224, 226, 228–9, 243

Socrates 3, 4–6, 10–11, 12, 13, 14, 23, 27, 44–6, 289

Sophocles 85, 106

Sophron 3

sophrosyne 16

sparagmos 158, 159, 191

spectacle 61, 65, 66, 70–1, 72–3, 74

spectator(s) 66, 127, 245–8

spoudaioi 42

Stanislavski, C. 215, 251–61; *Actor Prepares, An* 252; *My Life in Art* 253–61

Ste Albine, Rémond de: *Actor, The* 91

Steinweg 252

Sticotti, Antonio 92, 93, 106

Strehler 266

Sulla 61, 67

Swados 136

symbol(ic) (-ism) (-ogy) 130, 142–6, 148, 183, 185–6

Ta'azieh 139

tableau 53, 60, 61, 76–7, 78, 81, 83, 86, 90–1, 107

Tacitus 59

Tatlow, A. 266; 'Way Ahead: Brecht and Postmodernism, The' 261

Taviani 215, 216, 221

Tenschert 265, 267

Terence 85, 89; *Mother-in-Law, The* 80

terror 80, 270–1

theatai 48

Theatre of Roots 207

Theatre of Sources 207

theoria 73

Third Theatre 210, 218, 221–4, 225, 226–7, 229–30, 244, 245

thumos 21

tragedy (tragic) 15, 23, 27–9, 33–6, 42, 47, 68, 79–82, 127

training 212, 213–14, 218, 224–5

transcultural(ism) 233, 241, 285

transformation 159, 192–210, 270–1, 273, 300

Trussler, Simon 123, 126

Tuc d'Audoubert, cave of 189, 190

Turner, Victor 141–2, 195, 295, 296, 299;

Anthropology of Performance, The 166; 'Carnaval in Rio: Dionysian Drama in an Industrializing Society' 171–2; *Dramas, Fields, and Metaphors* 151–3, 156–8, 163; *Drums of Affliction* 143; *Forest of Symbols, The* 143, 147, 148–9, 150, 165; *From Ritual to Theatre* 162, 163, 164, 165; 'Images and Reflections: Ritual, Drama, Carnival, Film, and Spectacle in Cultural Performance' 166–9; *Ritual Process, The* 148; 'Social Dramas in Brazilian Umbanda: The Dialectics of Meaning' 169–71; 'Variations on a Theme of Liminality' 153–62

Umbanda 170–1
UNESCO 224
universal(ity) 77, 80, 81, 134, 137, 140, 152–3, 163, 183, 191, 193, 201, 206, 233, 237, 272, 288, 299, 300

Vakhtangov 213, 215
van Gennep, Arnold 146–7, 152, 153, 164; *Rites of Passage* 146
Velho, Y.M.A. 170
Verfremdung 205

visible (the) 46, 121, 129, 136, 140, 301
vision 19, 22, 24, 31, 50, 51, 70, 73–4, 78, 88, 104, 146, 180, 300–1
visual effect 48–9
Völker 266, 267
Voltaire 65, 66, 85, 119; *Mahomet* 68

Walton, K.L.: *Mimesis as Make-Believe* 293
Watson, I. 210, 221
Weiss 119; *Marat/Sade* 127
Wekwerth 265, 267
White, H. 163–4
Wiles, T. 293
Willett, John: *Brecht on Theatre* 122
Williams, David 123, 130
Wilson, Robert 199, 264, 265
Witkacy 213
Wooster Group 207
Wright, E.: *Postmodern Brecht: A Representation* 262–5

Xenophon: *Symposium* 20

Zarrilli, P. 240, 242
Zeno 9

www.ingramcontent.com/pod-product-compliance
Lightning Source LLC
Chambersburg PA
CBHW021134230426
43667CB00005B/114